ESSENTIALS
of Early Childhood Education

Fifth Canadian Edition

ESSENTIALS
of Early Childhood Education

Jane Bertrand
School of Early Childhood, George Brown College

Carol Gestwicki
Central Piedmont Community College

NELSON
EDUCATION

Essentials of Early Childhood Education, Fifth Canadian Edition

by Jane Bertrand and Carol Gestwicki

Vice President, Editorial Higher Education:
Anne Williams

Publisher:
Lenore Taylor-Atkins

Marketing Manager:
Terry Fedorkiw

Developmental Editor:
Joanne Woods

Photo Researcher:
Debbie Davies-Wright

Permissions Coordinator:
Debbie Davies-Wright

Production Service:
Cenveo Publisher Services

Copy Editor:
Elspeth McFadden

Proofreader:
Manikandan

Indexer:
BIM Indexing Services

Design Director:
Ken Phipps

Managing Designer:
Franca Amore

Interior Design:
Cathy Mayer

Cover Design:
Cathy Mayer

Cover Image:
Gandee Vasan/Getty Images

Compositor:
Cenveo Publisher Services

Library and Archives Canada Cataloguing in Publication Data

Bertrand, Jane, 1951-, author
Essentials of early childhood education / Jane Bertrand, School of Early Childhood, George Brown College; Carol Gestwicki, Central Piedmont Community College. — Fifth Canadian edition.

First Canadian edition: The essentials of early education / Carol Gestwicki, Jane Bertrand.

Includes bibliographical references and index.
ISBN 978-0-17-653175-1 (pbk.)

1. Early childhood education—Canada—Textbooks. 2. Early childhood teachers—Canada. 3. Teaching—Vocational guidance—Canada. I. Gestwicki, Carol, 1940-, author II. Title.

LB1775.6.G47 2015
372.210971   C2015-900194-3

ISBN-13: 978-0-17-653175-1
ISBN-10: 0-17-653175-0

Contents

SECTION 2
THE EARLY CHILDHOOD WORKFORCE ... 118

CHAPTER 6
THE WORK ENVIRONMENT ... 166

SECTION 3
THE EARLY CHILDHOOD WORKFORCE COMES OF AGE ... 189

CHAPTER 7
THE ROOTS OF EARLY CHILDHOOD EDUCATION IN CANADA ... 194

CHAPTER 8
THE MODERN PROFESSION ... 231

CHAPTER 9
ADVOCACY ... 257

Preface

The profession and practice of early childhood education is coming of age in Canada. Early childhood educators are gaining respect and recognition, and remuneration is increasing. The public is looking to early childhood educators to support young children's early learning and development in a variety of settings. The many decades of ambiguity about what to call ourselves—teachers, early childhood teachers, caregivers, early childhood workers, child care workers—are over. We are early childhood educators, and ours is a profession that is understood and valued by families and other professionals.

Early childhood educators are gaining unprecedented opportunities to work with young children in quality environments. With the expanded opportunities and recognition come new expectations and responsibilities. Our understanding of childhood, curriculum, and pedagogy is expected to encompass knowledge and expertise from biological sciences, education, psychology, sociology, and anthropology. We must stay current and engaged with ongoing new information about early human development and early learning. A commitment to lifelong learning is essential for early childhood educators.

WHY WAS THIS BOOK WRITTEN?

This book was written from the authors' strong conviction that the care and education of children in their earliest years must go beyond rhetoric, to provide optimum experiences and environments for real children in our very real world. Those who enter the early childhood workforce find both enormous challenges and immense gratification as they nurture the healthy development of children and families. Child development research continues to reinforce the importance of the experiences, interactions, and environments that support children in the first years of their lives. The adults responsible for children's learning and care must be prepared to provide the best opportunities for children. As the need and demand for early childhood programs for children from birth through the elementary school years continues to expand in unprecedented dimensions, so too does the need for educated early childhood professionals.

This demand is related to a second strong conviction from which this book grows: that not just anyone can, or should, work with young children, and moreover, that young children do not need "just anyone." They need particular people, with specific characteristics, knowledge, skills, and attitudes, who have thoughtfully and deliberately prepared to enter into caring relationships with young children and their families. They need people who have committed themselves to following career paths in early childhood education, and who understand and accept the realities of the profession as it has evolved to this point. They need people who have decided to touch young lives and are willing to stay the course.

TWO MAIN THEMES

These are the two main themes of this book: (1) that early childhood educators do important, meaningful, valuable work, supporting children and families during the most critical period of development; and (2) that only individuals who are willing to accept the need for thoughtful and careful professional preparation will be able to help children reach their full potential. This book, then, proposes to examine the world of early childhood education and to assist the process of professional growth for those who are considering it as their future, a future that impacts generations to come.

Students will most likely use this text in a course that introduces them to concepts of early childhood education, near the beginning of their professional education, whether in a two- or a four-year program. Because the text is designed for students who will continue with other courses in an ECE college program, the specifics of theoretical perspectives, curriculum ideas and activities, and program management are left for those later courses.

Since the intention of the text is to help students begin active construction of themselves as early childhood educators, the style is both informative, so that students may truly understand the current field, and introspective, so that students may actively juxtapose their personal knowledge, goals, and experiences as they consider the professional roles and possibilities of working with young children. So, however you as a student came to study the essentials of early childhood education, you are invited to reflect on the profession.

COVERAGE

The Introduction to this book outlines the social and political context for early child development programs in Canada.

Section One, *Early Childhood Programs Today*, introduces you to the field in Canada.

- **Chapter 1,** *Early Childhood Programs*, defines the parameters of the field and explores the diversity of program structures, age groups that early childhood educators work with, special population groups, and program sponsors.
- **Chapter 2,** *Early Childhood Education Curriculum*, discusses different approaches to organizing early childhood environments for young children.
- **Chapter 3,** *Quality in Early Childhood Education Programs*, describes the central elements of quality in early childhood settings.

Section Two, *The Early Childhood Workforce*, introduces the roles and responsibilities of early childhood educators.

- **Chapter 4,** *Early Childhood Educators*, explores the various roles of early childhood educators who work with children and families in a wide spectrum of settings.
- **Chapter 5,** *Becoming an Early Childhood Educator*, demonstrates that good early childhood educators are not born but grow actively, with much personal effort and thought. This chapter considers the skills, knowledge, and experiences that are important in developing yourself as an early childhood educator.

- Chapter 6, *The Work Environment*, discusses the career opportunities now open to early childhood educators. It also examines some of the current challenges you will face as you enter the early childhood workforce.

Section Three, *The Early Childhood Workforce Comes of Age*, looks at how far we have come and what lies ahead. As we enter the 21st century, the combination of a seemingly unending need for early childhood educators, clear knowledge about what contributes to quality programs, and demands for professional standards and acceptance offers us positive directions for the future.

- Chapter 7, *The Roots of Early Childhood Education in Canada*, describes the history of early childhood programs. In this chapter, you will see the multiple traditions and various philosophies and historic/social influences that have shaped the modern world of early childhood education. Many of the names and events you will read on the historical timeline will appear in this chapter to describe our historical roots.
- Chapter 8, *The Modern Profession*, considers the current emphasis on professionalism, which will shape your introduction to joining the early childhood workforce.
- Chapter 9, *Advocacy*, discusses the role of advocacy for early childhood educators, both within early childhood settings and in the world at large. The chapter summarizes the arguments for public investment in early childhood programs. It leaves you with the challenge to become an early childhood educator and advocate for young children and their families, early childhood programs, and the early childhood workforce.

CHANGES IN THIS EDITION

The fifth Canadian edition of *Essentials of Early Childhood Education* is now in full colour, with a new interior design and updated photos throughout the text.

Public education continues to reach down into the early years, expanding the numbers and types of opportunities open to early childhood education graduates. *Early Years Study 3* (Akbari & McCuaig, 2014) introduced the Early Childhood Education Report, which compares how provinces are developing early childhood education as an extension of public education. The benchmarks are organized into five categories—governance, access, funding, quality, and monitoring. The second Early Childhood Education Report was launched in November 2014. Throughout this text, findings from the Early Childhood Education Report are used to update statistics. Other recent research and policy reports make it possible to provide a more complete picture of the Canadian situation. This edition also updates Canadian and international findings related to early learning and development and early childhood education.

Early childhood educators are practising their profession in many different settings, including child care centres, family resource programs, prekindergartens, and kindergartens. Some of these settings require early childhood educators (e.g., regulated child care centres, full-day kindergarten in Ontario and Strong Start centres in British Columbia). Chapter 1 includes a summary of recent Canadian research that is tracking the impact of full-day kindergarten programs. Chapter 2 offers an expanded section on play and play-based learning. Chapter 3 updates what we know from research about quality in early childhood settings. Section Two considers the opportunities now to early childhood education graduates and to the work environment evolving across Canada. Chapter 7 has an expanded discussion about the roots of early childhood education curriculum and pedagogy. Chapter 8 updates the growing professional requirements and obligations for early childhood educators in Canada. Chapter 9 uses the policy framework found in the Early Childhood Education Report and recent Canadian economic studies to make the case for more public investment in early childhood education programs.

FEATURES

Each chapter features objectives, review questions, study activities, and suggested readings. The key terms are bolded and defined at the end of each chapter.

To help spark discussion and thought, **timelines** outlining early childhood education facts appear throughout the book.

Watch for the **Research into Practice** feature, which highlights examples of evidence-based practice and practice-based evidence that guide early child development policies and practices. The **Making It Happen** boxes feature early childhood programs from across the country.

We welcome you to consider studies in early childhood education. We hope that you and your fellow students will discuss the topics and issues in depth and work through some of the additional readings and assignments at the end of each chapter.

We need and want you to stay. Early childhood educators, families, and communities can join together to nurture, stimulate, and educate young children. At no time in the history of Canada have children and families needed more the support, care, and expertise that early childhood education has to offer. Together we can prepare today's youngest Canadians for a rapidly changing and diverse world. The future might be uncertain and world tensions overwhelming, but we can be certain that a strong start is the best foundation for life.

ABOUT THE NELSON EDUCATION TEACHING ADVANTAGE (NETA)

The Nelson Education Teaching Advantage (NETA) program delivers research-based instructor resources that promote student engagement and higher-order thinking to enable the success of Canadian students and educators. Be sure to visit Nelson Education's Inspired Instruction website at www.nelson.com/inspired to find out more about NETA. Don't miss the testimonials of instructors who have used NETA supplements and seen student engagement increase!

INSTRUCTOR RESOURCES

All NETA and other instructor ancillaries can be downloaded directly from the book's companion site at www.nelson.com/essentialsofece5Ce.

NETA Test Bank

This resource was written by the author, Professor Jane Bertrand. It includes multiple-choice questions written according to NETA guidelines for effective construction and development of higher-order questions. Also included are short answer and essay questions.

Instructor's Manual

The Instructor's Manual to accompany *Essentials of Early Childhood Education* has been prepared by Professor Jane Bertrand. It is organized according to the textbook chapters and contains suggested classroom activities and additional resources.

Acknowledgements

Over the years we have heard the stories of many students, early childhood educators, and colleagues who have made their own discoveries of the essential truths and pleasures of working with young children. This book is dedicated to them, with thanks for their friendship along the way.

This Canadian edition is indebted to the generous permissions I received to reprint materials. Thanks to the Atkinson Centre, Canadian Child Care Federation, Early Childhood Educators of British Columbia, Childcare Resource and Research Unit, the journal *IDEAS*, SpeciaLink, and the Early Childhood Education program at Red River College.

Since I completed the first Canadian edition of this book, I have had the privilege of continuing to work with J. Fraser Mustard and the Hon. Margaret Norrie McCain to move the early years' agenda forward in Canada and internationally.

In addition, I appreciate the efforts and responses of the editorial and production staff at Nelson Education.

Jane Bertrand
George Brown College

Introduction

Early childhood education is a field of study that prepares individuals to work with young children and their families. Commitment to early childhood education is a commitment to children. It is also a commitment to family, evidence, and Canada.

FAMILIES

Families come in all sizes and shapes. None are perfect; but in all their varied and wonderful configurations, they are here to stay. Families are the anchor for the human species. Families nurture the next generation. Mothers, fathers, grandparents, aunts, uncles, brothers, sisters, cousins, and even family friends can make a big difference in the lives of our youngest citizens. Families and work life should be compatible. Work–life conflict should not require people to stand down from advancing their careers or deny them the opportunity to be parents. As you pursue your chosen career in early childhood education, you will have opportunities to support families.

Modern families need a modern support system of learning and caring, one that places the healthy development of children at the centre but also recognizes that children do not exist in isolation from their families. Early childhood education can be designed to accommodate people who are earning a living and at the same time raising a child. *Early Years Study 3* (McCain, Mustard, & McCuaig, 2011) introduced a new tool, the Early Childhood Education Report, to monitor the growth and development of early childhood education across Canada. In November 2014, the second edition of the Early Childhood Education Report (Akbari & McCuaig, 2014) demonstrated that Canada is making progress and that many provinces are well on their way towards an early childhood education system that can be an extended family for the 21st century. But we need to move faster. Greater public investment in early childhood education is needed to meet the needs of families, or young parents will face the same dilemmas earning a living and raising children as their parents and grandparents did.

EVIDENCE

A new picture of childhood and human nature is emerging from the research of the past two decades, and this new understanding can guide our thinking about education. Babies and young children are exquisitely designed to explore and innovate, to investigate and test hypotheses, to change and create, and to learn. Our most valuable human accomplishments are possible because we were once helpless children who actively engaged in the world around us. When we organize caregiving and education to value these capacities in the early years and beyond, learning soars.

Think about 20-month-old Ashraf. He attends a community early childhood program while his parents work. He is intently dropping a beach ball into a box placed in the middle of the playroom floor. At first, he stands directly over the box, carefully letting go of the ball and watching it land in the box. He reaches down and picks the ball up, stands up, and repeats the same action. The sequence happens over and over. After the 10th cycle, Ashraf pauses and stares at his feet. He deliberately steps backward two steps and tosses the ball towards the box. It falls outside the box. Ashraf scrambles to pick it up. He moves up to the box again and deliberately steps back one step and tosses the ball. It lands in the box. Ashraf squeals with delight and turns with a big smile directed to an educator who is sitting on the floor nearby. She claps her hands, says "Yea," and smiles back. Ashraf repeats the action a few more times and then steps to the corner and a different angle. And the game continues for 20 minutes.

A simple moment is often dismissed as children's play that does not have much to do with learning. But what Ashraf is doing is complicated: he is predicting, adapting, attending, planning, testing hypotheses, and learning from his actions. Ashraf is learning and learning how to learn.

Rigorous evidence holds our thoughts up to scrutiny and demands that we search out the best information. The past two decades have been remarkable: the science of early child development has exploded, and the findings are abundantly clear. The early years of life have a long reach forward. The dynamic interaction between our genetic inheritance and our early experiences defines the architecture of our brains and influences learning, behaviour, and health throughout our lives.

The brain of a newborn is exquisitely sensitive to early life, which is a time of enormous opportunity and risk. In nurturing environments, babies and young children are launched on trajectories to well-being. Adverse environments have an equally powerful negative effect.

If we want to put families at the centre of our society, if we want every child to be the best he or she can possibly be, if we want to reverse declining birthrates, we need to use the evidence to design early childhood education programs that promote optimal early learning and well-being in addition to accommodating labour force participation.

CANADA

We live in a truly magnificent country; we Canadians often forget how blessed we are. There have been intolerable injustices—none greater than the history of colonialism and the toll it extracted from Aboriginal peoples. The past decade has seen a worrisome increase in inequality between haves and have-nots. Given the wealth across Canada, our children's well-being is not what it should be. Still, we are a democratic, pluralistic, and prosperous society. We believe that there is room at the table for everyone and we remain committed to public education and health care. Our public infrastructure works. Crime and violence are relatively low.

Our future in Canada depends on how we prepare the next generation. We cannot afford to leave a single child behind. The babies born today need childhoods that prepare them for Canada 20 or 30 years from now. Schools must prepare students now for jobs that don't yet exist. You are entering careers that will be transformed several times during your working years. A few decades from now, the quality of your lives will depend on those babies born today. They will determine whether Canada remains a good place to live and to grow old. It is in our enlightened self-interest to ensure that today's babies get the experiences and support they need to take on the challenges ahead.

A strong and vibrant Canada is a Canada where every child has the chance to thrive. Family is what matters most and the science of early child development must inform how we design early childhood education to accommodate what families need. Early childhood educators can move the agenda forward and make Canada the best place it can be.

IMPLICATIONS FOR EARLY CHILDHOOD EDUCATORS

In Canada, early childhood education programs continue to evolve from earlier child care arrangements, kindergarten, and family support programs.

Early childhood education includes a broad range of interconnected programs and services that support children's optimal development and families' childrearing skills. Educators who make up the early childhood workforce are equipped to work with young children in all of these settings.

Early childhood education continues to expand across Canada. There is growing awareness that early learning opportunities must be provided for young children living in an increasingly pluralistic society. Effective early childhood education that supports learning focuses on children's overall coping and competence. Increasingly, early childhood education is viewed as a downward extension of the public education system. Growing numbers of young children are taking part in early childhood education and the opportunities for early childhood educators will continue to expand.

SUGGESTED READINGS

Akbari, E., & McCuaig, K. (2014). *Early childhood education report, 2014.* Toronto: Atkinson Centre, University of Toronto.

McCain, M., & Mustard, J. F. (1999). *Early years study.* Toronto: Ontario Children's Secretariat.

McCain, M., Mustard, J. F., & McCuaig, K. (2011). *Early years study 3.* Toronto: Margaret and Wallace McCain Family Foundation.

McCain, M., Mustard, J. F., & Shanker, S. (2007). *Early years study 2: Putting science into action.* Toronto: Council for Early Child Development.

EARLY CHILDHOOD PROGRAMS TODAY

In this section, you are introduced to the field of early childhood education in Canada. Chapter 1 defines early childhood programs in Canada, and Chapter 2 considers how early childhood settings are organized to provide learning and caring to young children. Chapter 3 explores the issue of quality from the perspective of children, parents, early childhood educators, and society, and it discusses specific components of quality in early childhood programs.

A PROFESSIONAL AND LIFE CHOICE

Loris Malaguzzi was the founder of the Reggio Emilia approach to early childhood education after World War II. The Reggio Emilia approach continues to be an inspiration for early childhood educators around the world. In the following excerpt, Malaguzzi explains how he came to early childhood education.

GANDINI ▶ It seems that you made a choice to dedicate your life to the education and care of young children. When did you make this life choice?

MALAGUZZI ▶ I could just avoid answering, as others have done before, by saying that when you don't ask me I know, but when you ask me, I do not know the answer anymore. There are some choices that you know are coming upon you only when they are just about to explode. But there are other choices that insinuate themselves into you and become apparent with a kind of obstinate lightness, that seem to have slowly grown within you during the happenings of your life because of a mixing of molecules and thoughts. It must have happened this latter way. But also World War II, or any war, in its tragic absurdity might have been the kind of experience that pushes a person toward the job of educating, as a way to start anew and live and work for the future. This desire strikes a person, as the war finally ends and the symbols of life reappear with a violence equal to that of the time of destruction.

I do not know for sure. But I think that is where to look for a beginning. Right after the war I felt a pact, an alliance, with children, adults, veterans from prison camps, partisans of the Resistance, and the sufferers of a devastated world. Yet all that suffering was pushed away by a day in spring, when ideas and feelings turned toward the future, seemed so much stronger than those that called one to halt and focus upon the present. It seemed that difficulties did not exist, and that obstacles were no longer insurmountable.

It was a powerful experience emerging out of a thick web of emotions and from a complex matrix of knowledge and values, promising new creativity of which I was only becoming aware. Since those days I have often reassessed my position, and yet I have always remained in my niche. I have never regretted my choices or what I gave up for them.

Source: Edwards, Gandini, & Forman (Eds.). *The hundred languages of children.* Ablex Publishing Corp. Copyright © 1998 by Ablex Publishing Corp. Reprinted with permission of ABC-CLIO, LLC.

EARLY CHILDHOOD PROGRAMS

OBJECTIVES

After studying this chapter, students will be able to

- define early childhood programs
- identify different types of settings that provide early childhood programs
- describe how learning and caring are becoming more integrated in Canada
- discuss the availability of early childhood programs found in different regions across Canada

Every day almost two million Canadian children, from **infants** to **school-age children**, are cared for and educated by people other than their families, outside the regular school system. As they climb onto buses, streetcars, and trains, are strapped into car seats and strollers, or wave goodbye as their parents leave home, these children will be cared for and educated by adults who are designated as "teachers" or "caregivers." Some children will go to **child care centres** or after-school programs, which might be located in school buildings, work sites, community centres, or churches. Other children will be cared for and educated in home settings, either the child's own home or the caregiver's home. Some children will spend only a few hours a week in early childhood settings, whereas others will be there for most of their waking hours.

Additional programs help parents and other family members to participate fully in their young children's early learning and development. Young children and their mothers, fathers, grandparents, uncles, aunts, or older brothers and sisters may attend playgroups or drop-in centres together. Child care centres offer parents opportunities to learn about their children's new interests and achievements, as well as to access community resources and information about child development.

More and more children will take part in early childhood programs aligned with the education system. In addition to kindergarten for five-year-olds and often junior kindergarten or prekindergarten for four-year-olds, many schools offer programming for younger children and their families.

All of these children and their families participate in situations that fall into our definition of **early childhood education programs**. **Early childhood educators**, individuals with specific qualifications in early childhood education, can choose to work in a variety of settings and with children in several different developmental phases. ECEs also work with parents and other family caregivers to better understand each family's values and strengths and to offer support. In this chapter, we shall examine the many facets and faces of early childhood education programs.

A Note on the Timeline

As you read this text, you will be able to follow a timeline that documents events, sociological trends, and contributions that people have made to early childhood education through the years. The timeline demonstrates that our current concerns and immediate issues play out against the backdrop of ideas and events from earlier times. Real events in history and past sociological trends have contributed to the shaping of the profession of early childhood education and care, and its practitioners. Changes in the profession take place in response to particular events and needs in society.

The timeline will show, for example, that there have been various types of early childhood education programs in Canada over the past two centuries. Early public expenditures on children included funds for schools to teach primary academic skills. Public schools then expanded to include kindergartens, which began as products of a particular philosophy of early childhood. With their inclusion in the public schools, kindergartens have undergone changes in both philosophy and format, and the debate about these changes is ongoing. The first child care centres sprang up at the end of the 19th century to provide care and protection for poor mothers seeking employment. The nursery schools that middle-class Canadian children began attending in the 1920s reflected both the societal value of early education and the cultural acceptance of the importance of childhood.

So, as you follow the timeline, you will see the names and accomplishments of some of the major contributors to the development of early childhood education philosophy and practice. You will note changes in family structure and the resulting needs of the family, as well as events that have focused national attention on children's early education. You will watch the profession of early childhood education and care as it comes of age.

EARLY CHILDHOOD EDUCATION DEFINED

In *Early Years Study 3* (2011), McCain, Mustard, and McCuaig, defined **early childhood education**:

> Early childhood education refers to programs for young children based on an explicit curriculum delivered by qualified staff and designed to support children's development and learning. Settings may include child care centres, nursery schools, preschools, pre- or junior kindergarten and kindergarten. Attendance is regular and children may participate on their own or with a parent or caregiver. (p. xi)

Early childhood education programs are programs specifically designed and organized for young children and their families. Their primary goal is to provide an intentional educational program to young children. Early childhood education programs care for and educate young children, while supporting parenting, families, and communities. Early childhood programs include

- child care centres
- nursery schools and preschools
- early childhood intervention

1628

John Comenius, a Czech educator, writes *The School of Infancy*, referring to the "school of the mother's lap," in which a child from birth through age six would achieve the rudiments of all learning.

| 1650 | 1700 | 1750 | 1800 |

- kindergarten and prekindergarten
- family literacy
- Aboriginal Head Start
- integrated child and family centres

Early childhood education programs are sometimes called **early childhood education and care (ECEC)** or **early learning and child care (ELCC)**.

Early Childhood Education

- Simon lives in Calgary. He is three years old and goes to a nursery school three mornings a week. His father works a night shift and his mother works at the shopping mall on Friday nights and all day Saturdays. One parent is at home with Simon all of the time except for Friday nights when he stays with his Grandma.
- Carla is twelve months old and goes to a child care centre at the university in Vancouver where her dad works. She is often there by 8:00 a.m. and goes home with her dad around 5:00 p.m.
- Elisheva is a four-year-old who is severely brain-damaged. She can sit only with support, cannot speak, and needs to be fed. For a year, she has been in a municipally operated child care centre in a small Ontario town where a specially trained resource teacher provides the extra help that allows her to be part of her group. Her mother and father are in the labour force.
- Ian's parents are both professionals working full time. Almost every day, Ian goes to a community-based child care centre run by a parent board in Winnipeg. His special group of friends includes Tyson, whose mom is struggling to move from welfare to work; Katie, whose parents are both factory workers; and Liam, a psychiatrist's son.
- Jessica, who is two and a half, goes with her mother and younger brother to a Strong Start program located in the neighbourhood public school two or three mornings a week in Victoria. Sometimes Jessica's mother stays and sometimes she will leave for a couple of hours and then come back for Jessica and her brother.
- Etan is four years old and lives in a small town in New Brunswick. He and his grandmother attend an integrated child and family centre located at the local school three mornings a week. On Tuesdays and Thursdays, Etan attends the program all day from 8:00 a.m., when his dad drops him off on the way to work. Next year Etan will attend everyday from 8:00 a.m. until around 4:00 p.m. The centre is an extension of the school.

Ayesha, Carmen, Simon, Carla, Elisheva, Ian, and Etan are all in early childhood education programs. Although the funding, management, and administration of the programs differ, their daily activities are similar. If the settings are of high quality, the children are exploring rich social and physical environments that support their healthy development.

In each of the early childhood programs, the physical environment is set up for children. Carla's infant room has a large, open play area with lots of soft cushions and pillows. The wall is lined with a cruising rail for beginning walkers, and there are low shelves with several bright toys for shaking, poking, pushing, and pulling. Jessica's favourite time at Strong Start is circle time when one of the staff or a parent reads stories from picture books, and all the children and parents join in songs and child-centred activities. Ayesha's kindergarten, Simon's nursery school, Ian's and Elisheva's child care, and Carla's infant room all have a circle or group time. Simon often plays in the dramatic play centre at his nursery school; there are dress-up clothes and lots of dishes and pots and pans. Simon likes to pretend he is a busy chef at a big restaurant.

1850   1900   1950   2000

Ayesha's kindergarten looks a lot like Simon's nursery school. Her favourite place is the art easel with its fresh pots of paint each day. Etan plays with the same group of children in the same setting whether he comes with his grandma for mornings or attends full days on his own.

In each of these settings, adults educate and care for each child as they build relationships that are both responsive to and respectful of children's growing competence and abilities to cope. They make sure their needs for food, physical safety, sleep, and toileting are met. These adults know that children are not isolated individuals but are part of families, and that support to those families is critically important. They are intentional in choosing strategies that best support children's learning. There are also other children to play with in each of these settings as well as adults who play a role in setting the stage and encouraging the play among the children.

Children do not come to an early childhood education setting merely to do their "learning." Rather, they "live" in these settings for several hours every week. Just as they are learning at home when they discover how the flusher on the toilet works, or how to use simple tools to fix things, or how soothing it is to hear dad's voice sing them to sleep, every hour in an early childhood setting is filled with new information and experiences.

Sources: Beach & Bertrand, 2000; Bertrand, 2008; Pascal, 2009a.

The children described in the box "Early Childhood Education Programs" are guided by early childhood educators (ECEs)—adults who have studied early childhood education or have a combination of equivalent education and experience. In quality settings, children are offered rich social and physical environments that support their healthy development.

Early childhood programs support children's early development, learning, care, and families' capacity to participate fully in their children's early development. Early childhood programs include all forms of non-parental care and early education programs (with the exception of the formal education system that starts at Grade 1 in Canada) for children from infancy through middle childhood. High-quality early childhood programs ensure that the programs are geared toward young children, families, and communities, and involve the participation of ECEs. Quality programs must be responsive to each child's individual development, each family's values and childrearing practices, and each community's cultural context.

The definition gives us a sense of the variety of settings that early childhood education programs encompass. It conveys the concept that early childhood education programs include various structures that meet individual needs for different families. Learning and caring are central in this definition. Early childhood education programs encourage families' active participation in their children's early development and promote communities' capacity to support families.

Across Canada, regulated family child care and informal care arrangements in a caregiver's own home are not required to offer early childhood education. Their primary purpose is to provide care for children. On the other hand, family resource programs, parenting programs, home visiting, and

[Handwritten margin notes: Quality of programs — each family's value — childrearing practice — each community's cultural context; early childhood education programs encompass. 各种 [方式]]

1693

John Locke, in England, writes *Some Thoughts Concerning Education* and proposes the mind of a child as *tabula rasa* (a "blank slate").

1650   1700   1750   1800

prenatal and postnatal programs are closely related and sometimes interconnected with early childhood education. They are directed toward parents and other caregivers and share the common goal of supporting young children's health and well-being. Recreation and leisure programs and public libraries are environments that complement early childhood programs and support family life.

Early childhood education programs provide educational activities to encourage children's competence and provide care to support children's development of coping skills and their overall well-being. Good programs for children present opportunities for learning; assistance with personal routines in safe, healthy, and nurturing environments; and, most importantly, positive relationships with adults and other children. Therefore, the joint functions of learning and caring are essential to early childhood education. Early childhood education programs recognize that families have the most powerful influence on early learning and development. We can support families only when we begin with full respect for individual childrearing values and practices and the strengths of each family.

In this chapter, we will explore different types of early childhood education and related programs. In later chapters, we will uncover their historical roots in education, social welfare, recreation, and health concerns that defined a need for young children to receive care and education outside their families.

▲ Children have opportunities to play together at early childhood programs.

EARLY CHILDHOOD EDUCATION PROGRAMS

There are almost five million children from newborn to twelve years of age in Canada (Statistics Canada, 2014). Nearly 1.5 million children under twelve years of age are enrolled in some form of early childhood education or school-age child care program outside of Grade 1 to 6 elementary school programs (Beach et al., 2009; McCain, Mustard, & McCuaig, 2011; Ferns & Friendly, 2014; McCuaig & Akbari, 2014). About one million are in regulated child care programs. Over 500 000 children attend school kindergarten and prekindergarten programs. There are also more than 50 000 children who participate in early intervention and other early childhood education programs that are operated apart from regulated child care or kindergarten programs (McCain, Mustard, & Shanker, 2007).

The need for non-parental care arrangements while parents are working or attending school often determines the type of early childhood education programs families choose. Child care centres are designed to accommodate the needs of working parents and promote children's early development and learning. More than 3 million children from 0 to 12 years have working parents. As mentioned above, about one million children from 0 to 12 years are in regulated child care programs. Another 1.5 million children are in non-parental care arrangements outside of organized early childhood programs. In two-parent families, parents may be able to work their schedules so that one parent is at home with young children. Many are cared for by other family members. Sometimes school-age children are left on their own or with an older sibling before and after school and on school holidays.

Many children take part in an early childhood education program while they are cared for in private arrangements. For instance, many take part in kindergarten or preschool programs for half a day and are cared for by a private caregiver or other family member for the remaining hours while parents are at work. An informal caregiver may attend a family resource centre with the children in her care. Also, approximately 300 000 children who have a parent at home full time take part in early childhood education and care programs and about one-third of all children are in more than one ECEC program and/or private non-parental care arrangement (Johnson, Lero, & Rooney, 2001).

Because there are so many different types of early childhood education programs and no organized system for early childhood, it is difficult to determine exactly how many children and families are participating in what programs. Table 1.1 offers a broad overview of how many children participate in various early childhood education programs.

As early childhood educators entering the field, you can gain a better understanding of potential career opportunities by becoming familiar with early childhood education and care programs available across Canada. Table 1.2 gives an overview of five different categories of early childhood education programs. Some programs might be included in more than one category, or they might

TABLE 1.1 Early Childhood Education Programs for Newborns to Twelve-Year-Olds in Canada

Early Childhood Education Program	Children 0–12 Attending
Centre-based program*	860 000
Kindergarten/prekindergarten (public education)	500 000
Regulated family child care	140 000
Aboriginal Head Start	12 000
Early intervention programs	50 000
TOTAL	1 562 000

* Includes regular full-time or part-time participation in nursery schools, child care centres, preschool centres, and after-school programs.

Sources: Adapted from Cleveland, Forer, Hyatt, Japel, & Krashinsky, 2008; Eggleton & Keon, 2009; Fern & Friendly, 2014; McCuaig & Akbari, 2014; McCain, Mustard, & McCuaig, 2011.

1762

Jean-Jacques Rousseau publishes *Emile*, a story that illustrates his view that children are born naturally good and that development unfolds accordingly if adults do not interfere.

| 1650 | 1700 | 1750 | 1800 |

◀ Parents who work often require full-day, full-year non-parental care for their children.

TABLE 1.2   Early Childhood Education Programs

Child Care Centres *full or part-day*	Full-day or part-day programs for groups of children under school age or for school-age children during out-of-school hours. Organized to provide programs that are stimulating and nurturing for children and that accommodate parents' work schedules.
Preschool/Nursery School *4hrs<i'*	Part-day, often part-week, programs for children between the ages of approximately 2 1/2 and 5 years. Usually less than four hours per day.
Early Childhood Intervention	Organized programs and activities available to young children and families who have developmental challenges or who are at risk of developmental delays.
Kindergarten/ Prekindergarten *4 - 5+*	Early education program available to all five-year-old children through the education system. In some parts of Canada, prekindergarten programs delivered through the education system are available to three- and four-year-old children.

overlap with related programs. We need to understand the terms and concepts used to describe each type of program and each program's potential to meet the needs of young children and their families.

Child Care Centres *fullday program 5days*

Child care centres include group or centre-based programs outside regular schooling for children from as young as three months to those up to twelve *3甲~12才才亡* years of age. Most offer **full-day programs** five days a week and programs before and after school and during school holidays for school-age children. The majority of child care centres in Canada offer service for preschool children two to five years of age. Nursery schools and preschools are **part-day programs**; they may be part of a child care centre or operate as an individual program.

1850	1900	1950	2000

Child care centres are organized to serve the needs of parents working outside the home or pursuing further education or training and who therefore need supplemental care for their children for eight or more hours a day. Many full-day programs operate from early morning (for example, from 7:00 or 7:30 a.m.) until 6:00 p.m. or later, to allow parents time to drop off their children, put in a full work or study day, and return to pick up the children. Child care centre staff usually work at staggered times, to provide adequate coverage over the full period.

Some child care centres that serve particular corporations, health care institutions, or businesses offer several shifts of child care to accommodate the needs of parents who work during the evening or night. However, most programs offer regular daytime care only. Child care centres may accept children on a part-time basis, but seasonal or emergency care or services for parents who work shifts and irregular hours are scarce across the country.

Child care centres are regulated by provincial and territorial governments' child care legislation. Each province has established its own approach to organizing and licensing child care and preschool or nursery school programs, and it is difficult to make direct comparisons across jurisdictions. However, Table 1.3 provides an overview of what types of services are regulated, how many children attend, and what the different services are called. Regulated child care programs are the anchor of Canada's early childhood education, although less than 20 percent of all Canadian children are enrolled in these programs.

Specific requirements may concern staff qualifications, maximum number of children, adult–child ratios (the maximum number of children allowed for every staff member), physical space regulations, including the minimum amount of space necessary for each child, daily care routines, and program activities. We will examine these requirements in more detail in Chapter 3.

In Canada, regulated child care programs may be operated by non-profit organizations or commercial or by independent operators, or they may be publicly operated by governments such as local municipalities or school boards.

Most child care centres in Canada are non-profit and are operated for the primary purpose of supporting child and family needs and well-being. A non-profit centre might be a stand-alone organization with a volunteer board of directors, including parents, community members, and individuals with child care expertise; or it might be operated by a larger agency or institution. The YMCA in Canada, for instance, operates over 600 centres. Many community colleges and a few universities directly operate child care centres, which also provide model sites for ECE students.

Commercial child care centres, also called proprietary or for-profit centres, are privately owned businesses. About 25 percent of Canada's child care centres operate as commercial businesses, ranging from small, owner-operated programs to large chains. In Newfoundland, Alberta, Prince Edward Island, and

1815

The first Maternal Association is established by a group of ministers' wives in Portland, Maine, to encourage the moral and religious training of children.

1650 1700 1750 1800

TABLE 1.3   Regulated Child Care Centres

Province/Territory	Child Care Centres
Newfoundland and Labrador	Child care centres (full-time and part-time) School-age child care
Prince Edward Island	Early childhood centres (full-time and part-time, including nursery school and child care centre) School-age child care centres
Nova Scotia	Child care centres (full-time and part-time, including nursery schools, preschools, child development centres and school-age)
New Brunswick	Child care centres and school-age programs (full-time and part-time)
Quebec	*Centres de la petite enfance* (full-time and part-time educational child care) *Services de garde en milieu familial* (family child care) *Garderies privé*es (private centres) *Services de garde pour les enfants d'âge scolaire* (school-age child care)
Ontario	Child care centres (full-time and part-time, including nursery schools) School-age child care
Manitoba	Daycare centres (full-time and part-time, including nursery schools) School-age child care centres
Saskatchewan	Child daycare agencies (full-time) School-age child care centres Family child care homes *(Nursery schools/preschools are not licensed)*
Alberta	Daycare centres (full-time and part-time, including nursery schools, parent co-ops, kindergartens in regulated centres and drop-in centres) School-age child care centres
British Columbia	Child care centres (full-time and part-time, including preschools) Out-of-school care
Northwest Territories	Child care centres (full-time and part-time, including nursery schools) After-school care
Nunavut	Daycare centres School-age child care
Yukon	Child care centres (full-time and part-time) School-age child care

Note: Regulated child care centres may have different names and age categories in various parts of the country, but they have commonalities in the care and education they provide.

Sources: Beach et al., 2009; Bertrand, 2008; McCain, Mustard, & Shanker, 2007, McCuaig & Akbari, 2014.

New Brunswick, most child care centres are commercial operations, whereas some other provinces or territories, such as Manitoba, have no commercial child care centres.

Public child care centres, which are directly operated by a government, are less common in Canada. Twenty-seven Ontario municipalities do operate close to 100 child care centres, as do three municipalities in Alberta and four

| 1850 | 1900 | 1950 | 2000 |

in Saskatchewan. Some Alberta municipalities operate school-age child care programs. In Quebec, the provincial department of education administers school-age child care centres, which are located in elementary schools.

Parents' fees, which may be eligible for government subsidies, pay for the majority of the costs of child care centres. In some jurisdictions, provincial or territorial governments provide grants directly to child care centres. These funds may include operating, startup, and capital funding, funding for children with **special needs**, and funds to enhance wages. Chapter 3 examines the funding of regulated child care centres in more detail.

Nursery Schools and Preschools

Nursery schools and preschools offer two- to three-hour care for preschool children (two to six years old) during the school year (September to June). These programs may not function during a full week (for example, a group of three-year-olds might attend classes from nine until noon, on Monday, Wednesday, and Friday mornings). The usual purpose of these programs is to offer stimulation, activities, and group experiences to help the children develop optimally. Many of these programs have their roots in early nursery school or kindergarten education (see Chapter 7).

MAKING IT HAPPEN

Innovation in Alberta: The Drayton Valley Early Child Development Centre

The centre's vision calls for

- a community gathering place, where all parents feel comfortable and supported;
- a child development centre with a full range of child care options, family support, satellite family day homes, and out-of-school-care programs;
- a hub for other services with coordinated information for families with young children;
- an integrated service delivery facility in which the whole community is working together to ensure the health and well-being of the children.

The Drayton Valley Early Child Development Centre is a regulated child care program publicly operated by the Town of Drayton Valley. It includes a child care centre licensed for 83 spaces for children from 12 months to 12 years as well as a regulated family day home agency. The Centre is fully inclusive of children with special needs. It co-operates with other children's services and family support programs in the community.

The Town of Drayton Valley provided $1.2 million for the facility. The province provided another $84 000 from the Alberta Space Creation Fund.

Sources: CUPE (2009); McCain, Mustard, & McCuaig (2011); Friendly, 2010. www.draytonvalley.ca/living-here/ecdc

---

In most provincial/territorial jurisdictions, nursery schools and preschools are regulated through the same legislation as child care centres and must meet similar structural, funding, and organizational requirements. However, nursery schools in Saskatchewan, the Yukon, and Quebec are not covered by child care legislation. Nursery schools and preschool programs may be non-profit or commercial operations, or they may be publicly run.

◀ Early childhood programs are spaces and places designed for children.

Claudia Paulussen/Shutterstock

There are no statistics available on how many children attend nursery school programs or how many programs exist. Some provinces and territories include nursery schools in their report of regulated child care centre spaces, whereas others exclude them. Sometimes nursery schools are considered part-time child care centre programs and are combined with school-age child care programs.

At least half of the 300 000 children whose mothers are not in the paid labour force but who attend ECEC programs attend nursery school or preschool programs. Some of the children whose parents participate in the paid labour force or in training and education programs also attend nursery school programs. Families might use nursery school services in combination with other non-parental child care arrangements, or they might juggle their work and study responsibilities around the nursery school hours.

Regulated Family Child Care 一家や先生の家でデイケア

Regulated family child care refers to the small groups of children that a child care provider cares for in a private residence. The residence is usually the home of the provider. These programs are regulated through provincial/territorial legislation and require safe and healthy environment that promotes children's optimal development and well-being. Government regulations, policies, and funding shape the organization of regulated family child care services in each province or territory. Each jurisdiction sets out the maximum number of children who may be cared for by an individual in a regulated or unregulated home setting. If there are additional children, the program must meet the province or territory's requirements for regulated child care centres.

特に数字把握していない
どれだけの子どもが プログラムに参加しているか

30万の子どものうち半分は
ECECのプログラムに参加している
だろう

TABLE 1.4 Regulated Family Child Care in Canada

Province/Territory	Regulated Family Child Care
Newfoundland	Regulated family child care homes may be directly licensed or supervised by a licensed agency. Up to four children (including the caregiver's own children under seven years) are permitted.
Prince Edward Island	Regulated family child care homes are licensed and monitored by the provincial government. Up to seven children (including the caregiver's own, under ten years of age), with a maximum of three children under two years of age in regulated homes.
Nova Scotia	Regulated family child care homes are supervised by licensed agencies. Six children, including the caregiver's own preschool children, are permitted. If all the children, including the caregiver's own, are school-age, eight children are allowed.
New Brunswick	Regulated community child care homes are regulated by the provincial government. Care for one of the following groups of children: a maximum of three infants, five children between two and five years of age, nine school-age children, or a mixed-age group of six children, including the caregiver's own children under twelve years.
Quebec	Regulated family child care settings are supervised by Child Care Coordinating Offices, which may be party of early childhood agencies (centres de la petite enfance) that also offer licensed centre-based programs. Up to six children, including the caregiver's own children under twelve years. Up to a maximum of nine children if more than one caregiver.
Ontario	Province licenses private home daycare agencies (which may also offer centre-based programs) to supervise family child care homes. Up to a maximum of five children up to twelve years of age. No more than two of the children may be under two years, and no more than three of the children may be under three years, including the caregiver's own children under six years.
Manitoba	Regulated family child care homes are directly licensed by the province. Up to eight children under twelve years, including caregiver's own children under twelve years. No more than five children may be under six years, and no more than three children may be under two years.
Saskatchewan	Regulated programs are licensed and monitored by the provincial government. Up to eight children between six weeks and twelve years, including her own children under thirteen years. Only five of the children may be younger than six years, and only two may be younger than thirty months.
Alberta	The provincial government does not license family child care homes or agencies, but does enter into contracts with agencies to approve and monitor caregivers according to provincial standards. Up to six children under eleven years, including the caregiver's own children under eleven years. A maximum of three children may be under three years, and no more than two children may be under two years.
British Columbia	Family child care homes are individually licensed by the provincial government. Up to seven children under two years, including the children living in the home. Of the seven children, there may be no more than five **preschoolers** and two school-age children, no more than three children under three years of age, and no more than one child under twelve months.
Northwest Territories	Regulated family day homes are individually licensed by the territorial government. Up to a maximum of eight children under twelve years, including the caregiver's own children. No more than six of the eight children may be five years or under, no more than three children may be under three years, and no more than two children may be under two years.

Province/Territory	Regulated Family Child Care
Nunavut	Regulated family day homes are individually licensed by the territorial government. Up to a maximum of eight children under age twelve, including the caregiver's own children. No more than six children may be age five or younger and no more than two children may be under two years.
Yukon Territory	Regulated homes are individually licensed by the territorial government. Up to eight children, including the caregiver's own children under six years. No more than three infants are permitted if there are also three preschool or school-age children. If there are two caregivers, an additional four school-age children are permitted.

Sources: Beach et al., 2009; Eggleton & Keon, 2009; Friendly, Halfon, Beach, & Forer, 2013.

The structure and organization of family child care varies across provinces and territories (Beach et al., 2009; Flanagan & Beach, 2010). The provincial and territorial governments either license and regulate caregivers or license a family child care agency that supervises individual programs.

Training requirements also vary across the country. Nine provinces and territories (Newfoundland, Prince Edward Island, Nova Scotia, Quebec, Manitoba, Saskatchewan, Alberta, British Columbia, and Yukon) require family caregivers to have some training, beyond first aid. In Manitoba, family child care givers in regulated programs are required to complete an approved 40-hour course from a community college in family child care or early childhood education by the end of their first year of operation (Beach et al., 2009). In Newfoundland, caregivers in regulated family child care are required to have a 30-to-60-hour course in family child care. They must also complete a minimum of 30 hours of professional development every three years. Although Ontario does not require caregivers in regulated family child care to complete specific training, most agencies do provide training. Home visitors, who are agency staff, support caregivers. These home visitors must have completed post-secondary education in child development or family studies and have at least two years' work experience with young children (Beach et al., 2009).

Regulated family child care programs can often be adapted to meet the needs of working parents and diverse families in both isolated settings and urban settings. Also, these programs can accommodate an individual child or a small mixed-age grouping from infancy to early adolescence.

Early Childhood Intervention

Specific public policies, programs, and activities have been designed to meet the needs of young children and their families with specialized needs in order to promote healthy development during early childhood (Shonkoff & Meisels, 2000). These initiatives are included under the broad term "early intervention." Early childhood intervention draws on the knowledge and expertise of early childhood education, child and family development, education, health, and **social services**. Early childhood intervention services include a wide range of programs and approaches offered to families with children who have developmental challenges or who are **at risk** of developmental delays owing to disability or negative environmental conditions.

An early childhood intervention service refers to "any non-medical, non-protection service, primarily developmental, that is used to assist a young child and his or her family. Thus attendance in an appropriate nursery school or daycare program can be seen as an early intervention" (Irwin, 1995, p. vii).

In Canada, early childhood intervention services include the following:

- **Inclusive early childhood programs** are "programs that include children with disabilities in the same programs they would attend if they did not have disabilities" (Irwin, 1995, p. vii). Inclusive programs encourage and facilitate the full participation of children with disabilities or special needs, not only their physical presence (Irwin, 1995). Early childhood education and care programs that include all children require financial support to accommodate the requirements of children with special needs. Most provinces and territories provide additional funding to accommodate children with special needs in regulated child care programs (Eggleton & Keon, 2009). For example, the Child Care Inclusion Program in Saskatchewan provides specific grants to centres to include children with special needs. The program is based on the principle that every child has the right to be included in a program that is developmentally appropriate.
- **Compensatory programs** are designed for children up to six years old who have developmental delays, or who are at risk of developmental delays, because of environmental conditions, including disadvantaged communities.
- **Early intervention (EI)** programs support families whose children up to three or six years have special needs or are at risk of developmental delays owing to disability or psychological or social factors (Irwin, 1995).

Early intervention programs may be discrete services or integrated into another health, social service, or education program. These other early childhood education and care programs include centre-based programs, family child care services, nursery schools, and family support programs.

As you can see, the delivery of early intervention programs varies. But the provision of early intervention programs does follow two basic principles: (1) They are interdisciplinary, meaning that they include services and strategies from more than one field. (2) They are family-centred, which means that the family is the primary focus of the services, rather than an individual child out of the context of her or his family (Meisels & Shonkoff, 1990).

Compensatory programs. These programs are designed to support families whose children's development is delayed or at risk because of environmental conditions, particularly conditions related to economic disadvantage and poverty. The term "at risk" refers to concerns about developmental delays, learning abilities, or challenging behaviours. Compensatory programs provide specific interventions to families to reduce the child's vulnerabilities and to

1816

Robert Owen establishes an infant school providing care for children of mill workers in Lancaster, England.

1650   1700   1750   1800

increase the likelihood of success in formal schooling. While this intervention may include a high-quality early childhood education and care program that stimulates and supports preschool children's development, it also offers specific supports and services to other family members.

Canada has a number of early childhood intervention services that are compensatory programs. In some instances, they provide an early child development program for preschool children that also involves their parents and a number of other health and social services. These programs may be identified as Head Start programs. (Head Start programs originated in the United States during the 1960s; we will learn more about them in Chapter 7.) Compensatory programs focus on improving parents' and other family members' abilities to nurture and stimulate their children.

Early intervention (EI) programs. These programs deliver services to children (from birth to age three or from birth to age six, depending on the province or territory) who have developmental challenges or who are at risk because of a disability or psychological/social factors. EI programs usually include a home-based component, early identification assessment, program planning (family service plans and individual program plans), and specialized equipment. The programs may also offer family support and early childhood services such as family resource programs, parent/caregiver support groups, nursery schools, and toy-lending libraries.

EI programs, like regulated child care programs, lie within provincial/ territorial jurisdiction. Each province and territory organizes the structure of the EI services and determines how they are funded. Some provinces refer to these services as Infant Development Programs or Direct Home Services (Irwin, 1995). Most provinces offer preschool speech and language services to support children with language delays. There are over 170 specific EI programs across Canada, although, in some instances, a single EI program is province-wide with several separate delivery sites (Eggleton & Keon, 2009).

Aboriginal Head Start (AHS) is Canada's largest early intervention program and is intended to prepare Aboriginal children for their school years. The federal government developed AHS to provide comprehensive experiences for Indian, Métis, and Inuit children and their families, based on caring, creativity, and pride flowing from the knowledge of their traditional beliefs within a holistic and safe environment (Bertrand, 2005). AHS began in 1994 with a focus on Aboriginal families living off-reserve in cities and large northern communities. In 1998, AHS was extended to First Nations communities. The AHS program is intended to prepare children for their school years and to establish early child development programs created and controlled by First Nations (on-reserve) communities. There are now 350 AHS On-Reserve programs serving First Nations communities and 130 Aboriginal Head Start programs in urban and northern communities.

jarenwicklund/iStock/Thinkstock

▲ Early intervention programs support children with developmental challenges.

1850   1900   1950   2000

In 2005, 160 Aboriginal and non-Aboriginal leaders and 11 national organizations came together to help define child health, acknowledge barriers and strengths in current systems, and articulate how to better support the health and well-being of all Aboriginal children and youth. They identified the need for healthy communities, including the need for appropriate and accessible services for young children (Blackstock, Bruyere, & Moreau, 2006). The collaborative process identified seven principles for child health that are applicable to Aboriginal early childhood programs:

1. Aboriginal peoples are in the best position to make decisions that affect their children, youth, families, and communities.
2. The ability of families to define their own cultural identities must be respected and not imposed on them by others.
3. There is a need to acknowledge discrimination and to articulate the tangible expressions of racism in the system.
4. The health and development of Aboriginal children is a balance between the physical, spiritual, emotional, and cognitive senses of self and how these interrelate with family, community, the world and the environment, in the past, present, and future.
5. Because culture and language are ways of seeing and understanding the world, the program will be most effective when it can relate to Aboriginal children and their families in that context.
6. Aboriginal children need the best that Aboriginal and non-Aboriginal systems have to offer. For that to happen, the mainstream system needs to make space for Aboriginal concepts.
7. Aboriginal people should take a lead role in addressing issues and establishing relationships with non-Aboriginal providers and organizations. These relationships should be characterized by reciprocity, respect, and a balance of power.

Aboriginal children, families, and communities benefit from effective early childhood programs (Ball, 2008). In 2006, 20 percent of Aboriginal children under six years old living off-reserve were in an early childhood education program outside of school kindergarten programs (Statistics Canada, 2008). This is in contrast to 51 percent of all Canadian children (excluding those living on-reserve and those living in the territories). About 24 percent were in child care arrangements that promoted First Nations, Métis, or Inuit traditional and cultural values and customs, and 15 percent were in child care arrangements in which Aboriginal languages were used as against only 4 percent in the early 1990s (Statistics Canada, 2001). This increase is largely a result of Aboriginal Head Start programs

1822

Robert Owen moves to New Harmony, Indiana, and establishes an infant school and daycare centre as part of the community.

1819

Johann Pesalozzi, a Swiss educator, becomes the first recognized early childhood teacher in Yverdon, Switzerland.

| 1650 | 1700 | 1750 | 1800 |

and Aboriginal Community Action Plan for Children (CAPC) programs (Ball, 2008; McCain & Mustard, 1999).

National evaluations of Aboriginal Head Start programs to date suggest parental satisfaction, increased use of Aboriginal languages and cultural practices, moderate improvements in literacy, and increased health and physical development (Public Health Agency of Canada, 2007). An evaluation study of Aboriginal Head Start programs in the Northwest Territories reports that children had widely varying skill levels when they began the program and these differences persisted into Grade 11 (Western Arctic Aboriginal Head Start Council, 2006). The study also reported that the percentage of children assessed with above-readiness skills after one term of programming increased from 29 percent in 2001 to 47 percent in 2004.

Significant barriers limit access to and utilization of Aboriginal early childhood programs. Access to Aboriginal early childhood programs is challenged by the multiple jurisdictions involved in program delivery and funding (Ball, 2008). On-reserve children's services are mainly dependent on the federal government for funding (Friendly, Beach, Fearns, & Turiano, 2007). As provinces developed their child care services and mechanisms, most did not extend these services to Aboriginal communities (Friendly, Beach, Fearns, & Turiano, 2007). Further complicating the overlap is the relative mobility of Aboriginal families, who often move back and forth between their reserve and off-reserve communities.

Kindergarten and Prekindergarten

Provincial and territorial public education systems offer **kindergarten** across Canada. Many are reaching down and offering early childhood education to younger children.

Most **kindergarten** programs across the country are offered through the public school system and are operated under provincial/territorial education legislation. A few kindergarten programs operate outside the public school system on a fee-for-service basis, either as private schools or as part of licensed child care programs. Provincial/territorial education legislation sets out requirements for a child's minimum age, the number of instructional days and hours, and teacher qualifications. There may also be specific adult–child ratio and maximum group size requirements. At this time in Canada, most five-year-old children attend a full-day kindergarten program. In September 2010, British Columbia, Prince Edward Island, and Ontario joined New Brunswick, Quebec, and Nova Scotia in offering full-day kindergarten. In other jurisdictions, most kindergarten is offered on a part-time basis, either half-days (morning or afternoon) or two to three full days (school days) per week. But even in these jurisdictions, many individual schools offer full-day programs, often targeted toward disadvantaged communities. Half-day programs are usually two to three hours in length, and full-day programs are four to five hours long (excluding lunch programs). In all jurisdictions except New Brunswick, attendance is voluntary. Families are not required to pay fees for their children's participation in publicly funded kindergarten.

Ontario has **junior kindergarten** programs for all four-year-old children and **senior kindergarten** programs for five-year-old children; and in September 2010, the province began to phase in Full Day Early Learning programs that will include extended-day options for children from early morning until 5:30 or 6:00 p.m. Kindergarten programs in other jurisdictions are generally available only to five-year-old children, although there are growing numbers of **prekindergarten** programs for four-year-old children in Quebec, Winnipeg, Saskatchewan, Alberta, and British Columbia. There are approximately 350 000 children attending public education kindergarten or senior kindergarten programs and 150 000 children attending junior kindergarten or prekindergarten programs in Canada (McCain, Mustard & McCuaig, 2011).

Age limits for attending kindergarten programs vary slightly across provincial/territorial jurisdictions, but most require children to be at least four years and eight months old in September (five years by December 31) to attend kindergarten or senior kindergarten programs, and at least three years and eight months old in September (four years by December 31) to attend junior kindergarten programs.

Kindergarten programs often intersect with child care services. Children who attend public kindergarten programs also attend other early childhood education and care programs. Licensed child care programs are often located in public school buildings. Ontario is moving toward a seamless Full Day Early Learning Kindergarten Program that combines learning and caring for four- and five-year-old children. Kindergarten programs are intended to provide educational and social experiences for young children in preparation for formal schooling. At the same time, many Canadian families use kindergarten programs as part of a child care package (Cleveland et al., 2008). Kindergarten programs and early childhood education and care programs for young children often share many of the values and assumptions that underlie curriculum approaches. There are a number of initiatives that have attempted to coordinate child care and kindergarten programs, including school board policies and practices to encourage increased collaboration, shared physical space, and common curriculum planning and professional development opportunities (Corter et al., 2006; McCain, Mustard, & McCuaig, 2011, in press).

Kindergarten programs may also intersect with early intervention services and family support programs, particularly as provincial and territorial governments explore options for integrated child and family centres, which are discussed later in this chapter.

Full-day kindergarten programs promote children's early learning and development. Several quasi-experimental and descriptive studies have compared the benefits of full-day versus half-day kindergarten programs, and the evidence suggests that increased access to full-day kindergarten can result in an initial and relatively immediate payoff in greater academic achievement and social success (Ackerman, Barnett, & Robin, 2005; Baskett, Bryant, White, & Rhoads, 2005; da Costa & Bell, 2003; deCesare, 2004; Herry, Maltais, & Thompson, 2007; Plucker et al., 2004; Robin, Frede, & Barnett, 2006).

1830s

Infant schools are introduced in Halifax by factory owners.

1826

Friedrich Froebel writes *Education of Man*, describing the kindergarten (children's garden) system.

| 1650 | 1700 | 1750 | 1800 |

Full-day kindergarten for four- and five-year-old children is now implemented across the province of Ontario. Early findings report positive outcomes for young children, including increased vocabulary and self-regulation skills in grades 1 and 2 when children who attended full-day kindergarten are compared to those who attended half-day kindergarten (Pelletier, 2014).

The rapid expansion of full-day kindergarten programs in the United States has encouraged many U.S. studies. In 1969, in the U.S., kindergartners usually attended short half-day programs. Only 11 percent were in full-day programs (more than four hours, but usually closer to six). By 2010, the percentage enrolled in full-day programs had grown to 60 percent (Barnett, Epstein, Friedman, Sansanelli, & Hustedt, 2010).

A number of studies examining the impact of full-day kindergarten in the United States draw on data from the Early Childhood Longitudinal Study, Kindergarten Class. This study suggested that full-day kindergarten does not make have a lasting impact on learning outcomes over time (Le, Kirby, Barney, Setodji, & Gershwin, 2006; Magnuson, Meyers, Ruhm, & Waldfolgel, 2006; National Center for Education Statistics, 2004; West, Denton, & Germino-Hausken, 2000). Other American studies point out that children in public school full-day kindergarten programs do better than children in public half-day kindergarten programs; however, when children attend private (non-profit and commercial) half-day and full-day programs, the full-day/half-day differences disappear (National Center for Education Statistics, 2004).

Collectively, American and Canadian studies indicate that full-day kindergarten offers continuity for children accustomed to full-day experiences outside of the home, continuity with schedules in first grade and beyond, and reductions in the number of disruptions and transitions children experience in a typical day. Full-day kindergarten also allows more time for both formal and informal instruction that provides meaningful learning opportunities. Full-day kindergarten provides an opportunity to align the policies and practices of the grades that follow kindergarten with those of the early learning programs that typically come before.

Full-day programs seem to provide a relaxed, unhurried school day with more time for a variety of experiences, for assessment opportunities, and for quality interaction between adults and children. Parents pointed out a number of advantages as well: no more shuttling children from school to an afternoon babysitter or worrying about whether their child had been safely picked up. Full-day kindergarten allows children and teachers time to explore topics in depth, reduces the ratio of transition time to class time, provides for greater continuity of day-to-day activities, and provides an environment that favours a child-centred, developmentally appropriate approach.

▲ Parents participate in their children's early learning during daily routines.

Massachusetts passes the first child labour law in the United States, prohibiting children under fifteen from working in factory mills unless they had three months of schooling in the previous year. (The law is seldom enforced.)

1836

1850   1900   1950   2000

Family Literacy Programs

[handwritten: support children's literacy — storytelling — music circles]

Family literacy initiatives "recognize the influence of the family on the literacy development of family members and try to support families in literacy activity and in accessing literacy resources" (Thomas, 1998, p. 6). Family literacy is about the ways families use literacy and language in their daily lives to do everyday tasks. Family literacy programs help children develop literacy. Specific family literacy programs and activities include storytelling and music circles for young children and parents or caregivers, adult education using family experiences, book bags for infants and young children and their parents, and the creation and use of play materials that encourage the acquisition of skills necessary to support literacy. Two excellent family literacy initiatives are the StrongStart BC program and the Peel District School Board initiative described in the Making It Happen boxes.

MAKING IT HAPPEN

StrongStart BC *[handwritten: = preschool]*

StrongStart BC provides school-based drop-in centres for families or caregivers and their preschool children, at no cost to families. The centres are designed to fill a community need and are located near other services for families of young children. StrongStart BC centres are intended to fill an early learning niche for preschool children who are not in full-day childcare, but may be at home with their parents or other caregivers such as grandparents, other relatives, or nannies.

In the 2006–07 school year, the British Columbia Ministry of Education funded 12 school districts to pilot 12 StrongStart BC centres for families and caregivers and preschool-aged children (Ministry of Education, 2006). StrongStart BC expanded to 85 sites in 2007–08 and to almost 400 sites in 2008–09. StrongStart BC centres are located in schools and may be co-located with other early childhood programs such as child care or parent resource centres, as part of emerging school-based hubs. They are intended to support early learning, that is, the knowledge and skills that young children acquire through physical means, language, and communication, and in social and emotional domains. StrongStart BC centres help (1) parents to participate in their children's early learning and development, (2) children to establish school–family relationships before they enter kindergarten, and (3) families to enhance the home environment.

StrongStart BC centres are defined by four characteristics:

1. location in school settings and operation by school districts;
2. participation of primary caregivers (usually parents) in activities that encourage children's early learning and development;
3. participation of young children (0- to 5-years-old); and
4. a program designed to support children's early learning, emergent literacy, readiness for school settings, and parents' active participation in their children's early development.

Both children and caregivers benefit from the StrongStart BC centre by engaging in program offerings that include literacy as well as physical and social experiences, all modelled by a qualified early childhood educator (ECE). The program's intentions are to supplement activities that can be offered in the home and to offer parents and caregivers new ideas and skills they can transfer to the home environment.

Sources: Bertrand, 2008; Mort, 2008; Eggleton & Keon, 2009.

INTEGRATED CHILD AND FAMILY CENTRES

Across Canada there are signs of a more integrated approach to the delivery of early childhood education programs, applying the recommendations coming from the Organization for Economic and Co-operative Development (OECD) and other policy research (McCain & Mustard, 1999). The Canadian review completed in 2004 by the Organization for Economic Co-operation and Development (OECD) focused attention on the problems created by the two solitudes: education and child care. The OECD review team stressed the need to heal the rift between kindergarten programs and child care and emphasized the need to create "bridges between child care and kindergarten education, with the aim of integrating ECEC both at ground level and at policy and management levels" (OECD, 2004, p. 7).

Toronto First Duty (TFD) expanded the concept to include the transformation of kindergarten, child care and family support programs, and funding into a new delivery model. TFD is an early learning and care initiative for *every child* and it supports healthy development from conception to entry to Grade 1 *at the same time* as it supports parents to work or study, and in their parenting roles. It is a single, accessible program delivery platform located in primary schools and coordinated with early intervention and family health services. TFD's starting point is the integration of child care and kindergarten programs for four- and five-year-old children.

The joining up of early childhood programs can be monitored on a continuum from co-location to integration. The *Early Years Study 2* (McCain, Mustard, & Shanker, 2007) reinforced the importance of setting a goal to consolidate the array of early childhood programs into a comprehensive program. Toronto First Duty created a tool to measure service integration, called "Indicators of Change," which assesses progress on a continuum from co-existence to integration for items in five categories: governance, access, parent participation, early learning environment, and staff team (Corter et al., 2006; Corter et al., 2012).

Toronto First Duty

Toronto First Duty (TFD) was established in 2001 to combine three service silos—regulated child care, kindergarten, and parenting resources—into an integrated early childhood education program located in a neighbourhood public school. TFD implemented the central recommendation of the Early Years Study for a "first tier program for early child development, as important as the elementary and secondary school system.... The system should consist of community-based centres operating at the local level within a provincial framework" (McCain & Mustard, 1999, p. 23).

Toronto First Duty allowed local and provincial governments and communities to test-drive the transformation of the existing patchwork of programs into a single, integrated, and comprehensive early childhood program. A professional team of kindergarten teachers, early childhood educators, family support staff, and teaching assistants plan and deliver the program. The school principal is the administrative and pedagogical leader. Space and resources are combined. There is a single intake procedure and flexible enrollment options. Children and families are linked to specialized resources as required.

Major Findings of TFD Research

TFD set out to redefine the delivery of programs for young children. The research (Corter et al., 2006; Corter et al., 2008) found benefits for children, parents, staff, and communities, and identified specific practices of integration and informed policy recommendations:

- *Communications.* Ongoing, consistent communications began with staff and parents. A new name for the program helped to define it as something new. The term "First Duty" was selected to identify a new service delivery model that offered a seamless service for young children and their families.
- *Practices of integration.* Integrated early childhood programming that paid attention to involving parents increased parents' engagement with schools, early childhood programs, and their own children's development. Integration can be accomplished within current staff, but it requires a realignment of job responsibilities, time for program planning, and shared professional development. Leadership, particularly from the school principal, in a school-based program is essential, as are his or her support and direct involvement. Regular common assessment and evaluation provide accountability. When shared with early childhood educators and other staff, evaluation information supports program quality and contributes to improved child outcomes. The evaluation revealed that increased practices of integration were related to increases in quality measures.
- *Program delivery.* Universal access to an integrated program delivery platform did not push out more disadvantaged families. Child care is essential, but it remains the program component most difficult to incorporate and expand in an integrated model. It is the only program that relies on parents and is the most highly regulated component. Integrated early childhood programs benefit children, parents, early childhood educators, and other staff members and communities.
- *System change.* Sustainable change requires an overhaul of legislative requirements, professional education, funding mechanisms, and governance structures from the ministry through to the program management. New investments should complement and extend existing services rather than adding new program layers. Integrated programming serves more children for the same costs as traditional program delivery. An effective demonstration prototype that test-drives new approaches can influence broader public policy.

Sources: Corter, C., et al. (2006) *Toronto First Duty Phase 1 Summary: Evidence-based Understanding of Integrated Foundations for Early Childhood.* Toronto: Atkinson Centre at OISE/UT; Corter et al, 2008; Centre for Child and Community Health, 2009.

TFD has inspired similar experimentation in New Brunswick, Prince Edward Island, Nova Scotia, and two British Columbia communities, Coquitlam and Mission (McCain, Mustard, & McCuaig, 2011).

PROGRAMS AND SERVICES RELATED TO EARLY CHILDHOOD EDUCATION

Other programs that are related to early childhood education services deliver programs to families. While they may include young children and offer play opportunities, their primary purpose is to resource, support, and strengthen families. Typically, they do not offer a consistent, intentional early learning program to a group of young children.

Family Resource Centres

A **family resource program** benefits families and young children and can be accessed in most neighbourhoods and communities across Canada. Family support programs complement and aim to enrich a family's existing strengths and resources. These programs may address existing problems or aim to prevent potential problems. Family resource programs may be offered as separate programs or in combination with each other or with other early childhood programs. They may provide regular learning and caring opportunities for young children while parents and other caregivers participate. The category is a broad one that includes a variety of services, strategies, and activities.

Family resource programs are family-focused; that is, they offer activities directed to young children and to parents or other caregivers. There are approximately 2500 such programs across Canada, with representation in each province and territory (Malcomson, 2002). They offer a range of services in diverse physical settings and with different types of funding and sponsorship. Nevertheless, family resource programs can be identified by common principles, functions, and types of activities.

Family resource programs share the following set of principles:

- an ecological approach to services for children, families, and communities;
- an emphasis on prevention and wellness of families;
- a recognition of the need for social networks to support families;
- an emphasis on interdependence in families' needs and abilities to give and receive support;
- a view of parenthood as an important stage of adulthood;
- an acceptance of cultural diversity in approaches to childrearing; and
- a recognition that play is essential to optimum child development (Kellerman, 1995).

On the basis of these principles, family resource programs provide services that have voluntary attendance and involve the entire family, including non-family caregivers (McCain, Mustard, & Shanker, 2007). Parents and program staff work together to determine which services will be offered. Family resource programs encourage peer support groups among mothers, fathers, other family members, and caregivers. Family resource programs are multidisciplinary; they cut across health, social services, education, recreation, and child care service categories. Program staff bring experience and credentials from different disciplines, and programs establish working links with other community services. Family resource programs may direct specific services toward problems, but the overall approach is to provide support with the realization that all families experience difficulties from time to time and that their strengths can be used to work through the difficulties. Toy-lending libraries promote optimal child development, provide material support, draw parents together to encourage informal social networks, and provide adaptive play materials and activities for children with disabilities and their families.

Family and in-home child care providers are the main users of over half of the family resource programs in Canada. Support to this group of users may include in-service training such as workshops, drop-in programs, child care information and referral services, and toy-lending libraries.

In Canada, the most common family resource program activities are

- playgroups and drop-in programs;
- parent support groups;
- parenting, caregiver, and early educator courses and workshops;
- toy-lending libraries;
- special events for children and families;
- child care information and referral services;
- respite care for parents and caregivers, and child care while parents/caregivers participate in other family resource program activities;
- "warm-lines" (non-crisis telephone support or electronic discussion groups);
- crisis intervention and counselling (including informal and peer counselling);
- early childhood intervention services for families and their children with developmental challenges or at risk of developmental delays;
- services and support programs to meet specific needs, such as prenatal and postnatal support for teen mothers and fathers, support groups for survivors of violence, ESL classes, life-skills courses, and literacy programs; and
- community development initiatives, including planning and advocacy for children's and family services (Kellerman, 1995).

Family resource programs offer program activities that best serve their own mandate, primary functions, and community. Think about how a family resource program could best support families with young children in your community. What would be the program's primary function? What types of activities should be included? Can you identify a role for an ECE as part of the program staff?

Program activities vary from one family resource program to another; they are also found in a variety of settings and under different sponsorship and funding across Canada. Almost two-thirds of the programs are offered by not-for-profit organizations, governed by boards of directors (Malcomson, 2002). Almost a quarter of the programs are part of other community, recreation, health, or social service organizations, such as community centres, YMCAs or YWCAs, public libraries, and community health centres. About eight percent are offered in conjunction with other types of early childhood education programs, including child care centres and/or regulated family child care; and another seven percent are operated by social service agencies, such as child welfare or children's aid associations.

[handwritten margin notes: 2/3 程序 by 54 NON-profit / 1/4 community / 8% mix 可 other type or daycare childcare + regulate family childcare / 7% by social agencies]

The broad definition of family resource programs we have used in this book is typical of the direction of the family resource program network across Canada. In Alberta, 46 Parent Link Centres are custom-designed to meet the needs of local communities; however, all offer four core services: parent education, early learning opportunities for young children, family support, and information and referrals (Eggleton & Keon, 2009).

In Ontario, Ontario Early Years Centres are provincially funded family resource programs delivered in local communities. Early learning and family support programming are offered to parents and other caregivers of young children. In Newfoundland, family resource programs are funded to support both regulated and unregulated family child care.

In British Columbia, a separate system of family resource programs, called child care support programs, is funded by the provincial government to support caregivers by offering services such as child care registries and family child care training courses. The government of British Columbia also funds another group of family resource programs, known as Family Places, which focus on services to families with young children. A Family Place typically offers drop-in and playgroups services, which are not offered by the child care support programs. Although the programs are intended for parents, other caregivers often participate (Kellerman, 1995).

[handwritten margin note: KFP]

The federal Community Action Program for Children (CAP-C) provides funding support to high-risk families with young children. Many family resource programs across Canada are part of CAP-C projects. The initiative involves community coalitions, which deliver health and community services, including early education, to children up to six years of age living in conditions

1837

First public normal school is established in Lexington, Massachusetts.
Friedrich Froebel establishes the first kindergarten for children ages three to six years in Blankenburg, Germany.

| 1850 | 1900 | 1950 | 2000 |

of risk. Project initiatives include home visits, Head Start programs, parent training, nutrition education, counselling, collective kitchens, and traditional Aboriginal healing programs. There are approximately 500 CAP-C initiatives in over 300 communities across Canada. Over 100 000 children, parents, and other caregivers visited CAP-C projects in 2008 (Eggleton & Keon, 2009) and as many as 28 000 of them visit every week.

Informal Child Care Arrangements

Over 1 million children are cared for in their own home or in a caregiver's home in a private or informal care arrangement (McCain, Mustard, & McCuaig, 2011).

Informal or unregulated child care is the most common child care arrangement in Canada. It is also the least visible and most variable form of child care. It can be an ECE who has access to resources and support in her community and is providing nurturing care and stimulating education to children in a home setting. It also includes custodial arrangements in which children are left in the care of another adult who "keeps an eye on the kids" while carrying out other housekeeping tasks.

Informal child care includes care in the caregiver's home or care in the child's own home (in-home child care). The number of children allowed in the caregiver's home is determined by provincial/territorial regulations, which are outlined earlier in this chapter.

MAKING IT HAPPEN

In-Home Child Care

In-home child care arrangements include caregivers who provide care and education in the child's own home. The caregivers may live in the child's home, or they may live elsewhere and come for designated work periods. Live-in caregivers are typically called "nannies" in Canada. Many families specifically seek out early childhood educators to provide in-home child care, hoping to ensure nurturing and safe care and stimulating experiences for their children.

In-home child care can provide greater flexibility for parents who commute long distances or work long hours. Children remain in their own home and have the constant care of one individual in their parents' absence. In many instances, children will also participate in other early child development programs, including nursery schools, family resource programs, and kindergarten.

Parents often find someone to provide in-home child care in their local communities through family resource programs, community information services, or post-secondary services. Alternatively, parents might purchase the services of an agency that selects candidates to provide in-home child care. In Canada, there are no governmental regulations or requirements for such agencies, although in British Columbia, Ontario, and Quebec, the agencies must obtain a licence to operate.

Many live-in nannies are from other countries and are able to move to Canada through the federal Live-In Caregiver Program, which allows future employers to sponsor immigrants who wish to enter Canada to provide in-home child care. The nanny has to live in the family's home for a two-year period; at the end of that period, she may apply for landed immigrant status. These arrangements are usually conducted through an agency.

| 1650 | 1700 | 1750 | 1800 |

Prenatal and Postnatal Programs 生後の 生悔すぐのディイア

Federal, provincial, and local governments in Canada invest in a range of programs, services, and information campaigns to promote healthy pregnancy, birth, and infancy. Some programs are directed at reducing risks that are associated with exposure to alcohol and tobacco. Others provide information and support to promote healthy births and infancy.

ECEs work with families. Prenatal, postnatal, and early infancy programs may be delivered in conjunction with other types of early childhood programs. Knowing about the prenatal, postnatal, and early infancy programs that exist in communities expands your ability to support young children and families.

Home Visiting 家庭訪問

Home visiting is a family support program that brings professionals with expertise and resources to the homes of families with young children. Many home visiting programs are offered as early childhood intervention strategies and are part of early intervention programs for children with developmental difficulties or compensatory programs. Home visiting has a long tradition in early childhood programming; it includes single visits by public health nurses to smooth the transition to parenting and single visits by kindergarten teachers to smooth transition to school. Over the past 25 years, home visiting has been included in a number of more intensive and focused prevention programs, and has also been used as an adjunct to other forms of programming, including Early Head Start (Love et al., 2002) and Parent Child Centres (Johnson & Walker, 1991).

A small-scale, rigorous home visiting research study in Elmira, New York (Olds, Henderson, Chamberlin, & Tatelbaum, 1986) sparked an early rush of enthusiasm for home visiting approaches based on good evidence of success. The Elmira project focused on nurse family practitioners supporting the mother–child relationship and prevention of abuse in high-needs families with very intensive visiting over the early years. Other home visiting programs span a variety of aims. For example, the Home Instruction for Parents of Preschool Youngsters (HIPPY) program aims at literacy and other child development goals and early successes were reported for this program (Hebrew University of Jerusalem, 1993).

Home visiting combined with centre-based programs appears to work better than both home visiting alone and centre-based programs alone. For example, in the evaluation of Early Head Start (Love et al., 2002), "mixed programs" combining home visits and centre-based programs had broader impact on children than either approach alone. Researchers suggest that the

1846

Common School Act is passed in Canada West (later Ontario) and brings about curriculum standardization. At this time, attendance was not compulsory, but schools were offered and children attended voluntarily.

1847

Egerton Ryerson publishes his *Report on a System of Elementary Public Instruction for Upper Canada.*

| 1850 | 1900 | 1950 | 2000 |

Home Visiting

Home visiting programs vary dramatically in their underlying theoretical models; the characteristics of target families; the number and intensity of visits prescribed; the duration of the program; the curriculum and approaches, and the degree to which they are specifically described in a manual; the fidelity of program implementation; and the background and training of visitors.

With so many variables involved, it is no surprise that the effects of home visiting programs have also been variable. Several reviews have concluded that home visiting can be an effective strategy to promote health and development outcomes of children from socially disadvantaged families, while other studies have reported no impact. Even when parent behaviour is altered, improvements in child outcomes are not always seen.

According to available research, better outcomes are achieved when home visiting programs are based on theories of development and behaviour change, target empirically derived risk factors, employ more highly trained visitors (such as nurses), and follow a well-constructed curriculum across the series of visits.

For even greater effects, more intensive intervention directly with the child may be required.

For more information, see: Home visiting programs. How important is it? In Tremblay, R. E., Barr, R. G., Peters, R. De V., & Boivin, M. (Eds.). (2009). *Encyclopedia on early childhood development.* Montreal: Centre of Excellence for Early Childhood Development. Available http://www.child-encyclopedia.com/en-ca/home-visiting-programs-prenatal-postnatal/how-important-is-it.html, accessed September 9, 2014.

combination offered more flexible options for engaging a variety of families, a reminder that it is only rarely true that "one size fits all."

In Canada, several provinces have initiated home visiting programs. Most are delivered through public health departments and build on universal visits or telephone calls to all families with newborns (McCain, Mustard, & Shanker, 2007). In Ontario, the Healthy Babies, Healthy Children program is delivered by the province's 37 public health units. The program offers all families with new babies information on parent and child development, and it delivers extra help and support to families experiencing difficulties. Healthy Babies, Healthy Children screens families for any risks to healthy child development during the mother's pregnancy, at birth, and anytime up to age six. All new parents who consent receive a phone call after the birth of a baby and are offered a home visit from the local public health nurse. Home visits from peer or family home visitors (experienced mothers who live in the community) as well as from public health nurses are offered to young children at risk for developmental problems.

Parenting Programs

Parenting programs are designed to build family knowledge to foster better outcomes for children. They target parents and caregivers and attempt to build their skills in guiding their children's behaviour, supporting early learning, and responding to challenges that are part of childrearing. While all early childhood programs aim to support parents and caregivers, the primary purpose and focus of these programs is parenting capacity. They can be delivered in group sessions, individual sessions, during home visits, or online, typically using an adult education model. For example, Manitoba introduced the

Triple P—Positive Parenting Program across the province. Its target is all parents and primary caregivers. It includes a general, universal public promotion of positive parenting through to intense case management for children and families with complex needs (Eggleton & Keon, 2009).

Recreation and Leisure Programs

Recreation and leisure programs include many activities that support early development.

You are probably familiar with recreation and leisure programs in your community—from swimming classes at the community centres to preschool storytime at the local library to T-Ball leagues at the local park. Most Canadian neighbourhoods offer physical and creative activities to young children and their families. Public libraries, children's museums, and out-of-school recreation programs are three examples of recreation and leisure programs:

- *Public libraries* encourage children to enjoy books and learning to read from an early age. Collections include a designated children's section that features children's picture books, easy-to-read books, first novels, video and audiotapes, CDs, and computer activities. Many offer regular parent/ caregiver and child storytimes.
- *Children's museums* are interactive displays designed to engage children in learning about a particular topic or concept. They may be part of larger museums or may be established as separate museums for children.
- *Out-of-school recreation programs* offer a variety of regular physical activities to school-age children. They may be organized to accommodate parents' work and provide regular non-parental care arrangements.

Summary

- Early childhood education programs are designed and organized to care for and educate young children, while supporting parenting, families, and communities. Early childhood education programs include child care centres, nursery schools, preschools, playgroups, early intervention programs, kindergarten, prekindergarten, family support programs for children and adults, and integrated child and family programs.
- Early childhood education programs take place in schools, workplaces, community centres, purpose-built buildings, apartment buildings, private homes, and other rural and urban settings. Some are publicly operated; others are operated by non-profit organizations or are commercial operations.
- Early learning and child care are joining together in many parts of Canada to offer integrated programs for families.
- The availability of early childhood education programs in Canada varies. All children are entitled to kindergarten in the school system. Only 20 percent of young children have access to a regulated child care program.

REVIEW QUESTIONS

1. Define early childhood education in your own words.
2. Describe what is meant by each of the following terms: full-day care, part-day care, commercial centres, non-profit centres, family child care, special needs, early childhood intervention, and Head Start.
3. Compare and contrast the early childhood education and care programs offered in the provinces and territories.

STUDY ACTIVITIES

1. Read one of the following books for insight into working with a particular age group or in a particular setting. See the references at the end of this book for bibliographic information.
   a. Ashton-Warner, Sylvia. *Teacher* (preschoolers in New Zealand).
   b. Ayers, William. *The Good Preschool Teacher* (includes profiles of infant and toddler caregivers, family child care providers, kindergarten teachers, and a teacher of homeless children).
   c. Hillman, Carol. *Teaching Four-Year-Olds: A Personal Journey.*
   d. Kidder, Tracy. *Among Schoolchildren* (elementary school).
   e. Roemer, Joan. *Two to Four from Nine to Five* (family child care).
   f. Wollman, Patti G. *Behind the Playdough Curtain: A Year in My Life as a Preschool Teacher.*
2. Talk with a variety of ECEs from various early child development settings. Your instructor may invite some to class. Summarize their responses to the following questions: What contributes to their job satisfaction? Job dissatisfaction? What specialized training do they have? What are three or four typical events during their day with the children?
3. Spend some time in the early childhood setting of at least one of the following: infant care, toddler care, a preschool setting, a kindergarten classroom, a classroom of one of the early grades, a family child care home, or a Head Start program. Be prepared to share your observations with your classmates and discuss the reports of others about their visits.
4. Search online to see what child care programs and preschools are located in your community. What types of program do you suppose they are, judging from their advertisements?
5. Find out what prenatal programs are available for pregnant women in your community. Who is eligible to attend? Are there any fees?
6. Find out what early childhood programming is taking place in local schools? Does your local school board or school district offer programs for children before kindergarten?
7. Review the Toronto First Duty website. Discuss the working relationships of teachers and ECEs.
8. What kinds of leisure and recreation programs are available in your community, and how do they complement other early childhood education programs?

KEY TERMS

Aboriginal Head Start: An educational program first established in 1965 for preschoolers in families below the poverty level. Comprehensive services now include education; family support through social services and parent education; and medical, dental, and nutritional services for children.

adult–child ratios: The number of children of a particular age who may legally (by regulation) or optimally (by accreditation standards) be cared for by one adult.

at risk: Term used when concerns exist about developmental delay owing to negative environmental or physical conditions.

child care centre: Programs that provide non-parental care and early education to groups of children in a setting outside the children's home.

commercial: Also called proprietary and for-profit. Early childhood programs established to earn profit for their owners.

compensatory programs: Preschool programs designed to ameliorate the impact of social or economic disadvantage through an enriched environment.

early childhood education and care (ECEC): Early childhood education programs organized to provide care and learning opportunities for children from infancy through middle childhood.

early childhood education programs: Programs specifically designed for young children, their families, and communities to promote children's well-being and early learning, and to provide non-parental care.

early childhood educator (ECE): Educators who work directly with children in early childhood education programs, have early childhood post-secondary education credentials and are recognized by provincial/territorial legislation as qualified staff in licensed child care, nursery schools, preschools, or primary school programs.

early intervention (EI): Programs that work with children whose development is delayed or at risk, often offering comprehensive services.

early learning and child care (ELCC): Another term for early childhood education and care programs.

family literacy: Literacy programs for young children and their parents and caregivers.

family resource program: Family-focused program that offers activities and services to young children and their families and caregivers.

full-day programs: Programs that provide care for children throughout the day, including meal and sleep arrangements.

home visiting: Brings services and expertise to children's homes. May be directed to children, adults, or both.

inclusive early childhood programs: Early childhood development programs that facilitate children's full participation, regardless of abilities/disabilities.

infants: Children from birth through the first year to eighteen months of life.

in-home child care: Non-parental child care provided in the child's own home.

junior kindergarten: Half-day program for four-year-old children operated in Ontario's school system and in some Quebec at-risk communities.

kindergarten: Program for five-year-olds, now generally operated in every school system.

non-profit: Early childhood programs subsidized by government or agency funds, in which any surplus funds are used for program improvement.

part-day programs: Programs for children that operate for only less than a full day.

preschool: Early childhood programs for children who don't yet attend school, generally aged three to five.

regulated family child care: Arrangements for child care in small groups (often less than six children), usually in the care provider's home.

school-age children: Children in Grades 1 through 6.

senior kindergarten: Half- or full-day programs for five-year-old children operated in Ontario.

social services: The branch of professional services that helps provide for basic needs for families and individuals.

special needs: Needs of individuals whose development and learning do not follow typical patterns, requiring intervention through modifications in the environment or teaching techniques to help them develop optimally.

Suggested Readings

Assembly of First Nations. (1995). *National overview of First Nations child care in Canada*. Ottawa: Assembly of First Nations.

Beach, J. (2010). *Environmental scan for the Coalition of Child Care Advocates of British Columbia and Early Childhood Educators of British Columbia Integrated System of Early Care and Learning Project*. Vancouver: CCCABC.

Beach, J., Friendly, M., Ferns, C., Prabhu, N., & Forer, B. (2009). *Early childhood education and care in Canada 2008*. Toronto: Childcare Resource & Research Unit.

Canadian Council on Social Development. (2006). *Growing up in North America*. Ottawa: CCSD.

Corter, C., Bertrand, J., Pelletier, J., Griffen, T., McKay, D., Patel, S., & Ioannone, P. (2006). *Toronto First Duty phase 1 summary: Evidence-based understanding of integrated foundations for early childhood*. Toronto: Atkinson Centre at OISE/UT.

Corter, C., Pelletier, J., Jahnmohomed, Z., et al. (2008). *Toronto First Duty Phase 2 report*. Toronto: Atkinson Centre at OISE/UT.

Health Canada, Human Resources Development Canada, and Indian & Northern Affairs Canada. (2005). *Federal/provincial/territorial early childhood development agreement: Report on government of Canada activities and expenditures 2005–2006*. Ottawa: Minister of Public Works and Government Services Canada. http:// www.socialunion.gc.ca/ecd_e.html

EARLY CHILDHOOD EDUCATION CURRICULUM

OBJECTIVES

After studying this chapter, students will be able to

- connect theories and knowledge about early childhood to ideas about how best to structure daily experiences for young children in early childhood education programs
- discuss image of the child
- identify different curriculum and pedagogical approaches used in early childhood education programs
- discuss common concerns regarding transition to school

- identify what is meant by inclusion and discuss the benefits for all children and adults involved
- discuss the concepts that lie behind antibias curriculum
- describe some of the benefits of mixed-age groupings in early childhood education settings
- discuss some ideas regarding the use of technology in early childhood education

Looking back at our definition of early childhood education, we can see that it takes into account what children actually *do* while taking part in a program. A program's organization, or its **curriculum** and **pedagogy**, in early childhood programs includes all that a child experiences. Curriculum is *what* we include in the environment and embed in children's learning and daily care experiences. Pedagogy, on the other hand, refers to *how* we deliberately cultivate children's development and learning (National Research Council, 2001). Curriculum and pedagogy are education in its broadest sense (Moss, 2004).

This chapter considers different curriculum and related pedagogical approaches, and how you can begin to identify which approaches best suit your image of the child and your understanding about how children develop and learn. You will examine a few specific early childhood education curriculum models to give you an idea of the many different ways that early childhood educators can provide care and education to young children and their families. You will be introduced to some of the current issues facing early childhood educators in their day-to-day implementation of curriculum in family child care settings, child care centres, nursery schools, family support programs, early childhood intervention initiatives, and kindergartens.

Early childhood education pedagogy and curriculum begin with your image of the child—your concept about children's abilities and potential and your assumptions about childhood. Do you see young children as dependent and needing you to direct their learning? Or do you see children as competent with the potential to be active participants in their learning? Your understanding about how children learn is based on your image of the child and your knowledge about child development, and on beliefs and goals geared to the optimal development of the whole child. This approach is in contrast to a **philosophy** that concentrates only on intellectual development for academic achievement.

Curriculum in early childhood education programs includes both the care and the learning that occur when the child participates in an early childhood education setting. It is everything that is part of the hours a child spends in an early childhood education program. Curriculum and pedagogy include daily schedules and routines, the physical environment, play materials, learning experiences, and, most importantly, the people who are part of the early child development setting.

UNDERSTANDING OF CHILDHOOD

Just as there are many forms or models of early childhood education programs, there are a number of curriculum and pedagogical approaches that can be adapted to different types of settings for children of varying ages. Curriculum and pedagogical approaches begin with our values and beliefs about children and our image of children and childhood. Cultural values and beliefs shape our understanding of what is worth knowing. Theories about childhood build on values and beliefs and shape a program's philosophy, pedagogy, and curriculum.

The past three decades have radically changed what we know about babies and young children. Not only does science confirm that early experiences are the foundation for lifelong learning, behaviour, and health; science also reveals that young children learn more, innovate more, care more, and feel more than we thought possible (Gopnik, 2009). Children are natural and active learners. They are born curious about the world around them and have remarkable abilities to learn.

You will learn more about the history of educational and psychological theories (or theories of human development) in your other early child development studies. Chapter 7 offers you a brief history about several child development theories. Before we consider the theories and research of others, examine what you know about childhood.

The following sections present an image of children as competent, curious, and capable (Bertrand & Riehl, 2009). They are active participants in their own learning.

Children have a sense of self.   Children learn to understand and express emotions. They develop the capacity to "wait a moment" and sometimes delay gratification. As children develop a positive sense of themselves, they become confident and more receptive to relating to others and take pleasure in new learning. They demonstrate autonomy in selecting materials, making choices, and setting goals for themselves.

As you know by looking around your class or your family, individuals vary in their ability to regulate their own emotions. Culture also contributes to emotion regulation. Children learn from their families how and when to express emotions to others. When early childhood educators understand the intersection of culture and individual differences, they contribute to the child's development of a sense of self.

Children's growing sense of self finds expression in movement, drawing, painting, music, and socio-dramatic play. Opportunities for expression develop decision-making skills, stimulate memory, facilitate understanding, encourage symbolic communication, promote sensory development, and encourage creative thinking. Expression encourages children's imaginations, helps to develop empathy, promotes relationships, and builds self-esteem. Children experience a sense of accomplishment.

Children want to relate with others and the world around them. Children need to interact with others in many different places and for many purposes. As children learn about themselves and the world around them, they also begin to understand that all people have similar needs, feelings, and aspirations. They start to build concepts of equality, fairness, and tolerance in relation to how people are treated—including members of visible minorities, English language learners, individuals of both genders, people with special needs, and those with diverse family structures. In early childhood programs, children should take part in activities that increase their awareness of others and foster respect for individual differences.

Children's experiences in nurturing environments encourage the knowledge and skills they will require to be constructive citizens. Children must be affirmed as individuals and as members of a diverse community of learners. Understanding the influence of social and cultural contexts on learning enables early childhood educators to recognize and support the children's social competence and to find a variety of ways in which the children can express their achievements.

Social competence is developed through interactions with others and is interconnected with other areas of development. For example, children take on the perspective of others when they role-play at the dramatic play centre, experimenting with a variety of social roles (e.g., firefighter, parent, or restaurant cook). They learn to persevere and to work independently as they solve puzzles, create sculptures, and construct models. Toddlers learn to wait for others during bathroom and meal times.

Children are involved and confident learners. Young children take their prior knowledge and experience into new situations to build an understanding of the world around them. Children construct knowledge by defining, sorting, classifying, comparing, making connections and predictions, testing theories, and using their imaginations. Children's emotional maturity influences their capacity to engage in intellectual challenges.

1848
Interest in kindergartens is growing in Germany. Forty-four kindergartens are opened this year.

1850
Roman Catholic nuns open Canada's first crèche (daycare centre) in Montreal.

0   1900   1950   2000

By three years of age, children are able to build bridges between ideas, an ability which supports problem-solving and planning abilities (Greenspan & Shanker, 2004). As early childhood educators, you are able to guide experiences that are within the range of things children can do with and without guidance. You can support children through the problem-solving process and encourage them to try new things, to persist, and to find alternative solutions. You can challenge children to use their observations to predict and draw conclusions, to think about how things work, to think about why something happened. This process encourages them to reflect on what they could do differently or change the next time.

Children's ability to regulate attention, behaviour, and emotion shapes their learning style, including how they are able to focus and shift attention, inhibit distractions, resolve competing demands for attention, delay gratification, and tolerate frustration.

Children communicate and use symbols.   Children begin to communicate at birth using sounds and then gestures. Oral language expands their communication. They start to express their needs, exchange ideas, express feelings, and make connections with others. Oral language increases young children's ability to regulate their emotions and behaviour and get along with others.

Literacy and numeracy are part of communication and critical to successful learning in the early grades and beyond. Literacy is the ability to use language in many forms—including listening, talking, reading, writing, music, dance, storytelling, visual arts, drama, and digital media. Numeracy is the language of numbers and the ability to use mathematics in daily life. Early childhood programs build on the language, literacy, and numeracy experiences children bring from home, from their communities, and from prior participation in early childhood programs.

Language, representation, and thought are interdependent. Language is a tool for making meaning and is central to cognitive development. Children need time to explore, to reflect, and to make connections between what they already know and new learning.

PLAY: THE CORNERSTONE OF EARLY CHILDHOOD EDUCATION

Play is the predominant activity of early childhood education—from programs for infants to programs for school-age children. Increasingly, educators in public school, particularly the primary grades, are recognizing the role of play in supporting academic learning. Play is the predominant activity of early childhood development programs. An understanding of play and its role as an essential part of curriculum will be a central component of your studies in early childhood education. Play is difficult to define, because it is viewed somewhat differently in different cultural contexts and different early child development curriculum contexts.

1650   1700   1750   1800

The Ontario Early Years Study recommended environments for young children that "offer children an array of opportunities to explore, discover and create…. Play-based, problem-solving with other children and an adult is an early learning strategy" (McCain & Mustard, 1999, pp. 159–60). Problem-based play is activity that captures and engages children in their quest to understand the world.

Play is the context in which children make sense of the world. Play is children's method of learning. Knowledge and skills become meaningful when used in play, as tools for learning are practised and concepts become understood. All elements of learning and development are explored and practised in play. The whole child is unified and supported in environments that support play. A play-based pedagogy is child-directed and purposeful.

In a play-based pedagogy, early childhood educators participate in play to guide children's planning, decision-making, and communication, and to extend children's explorations with narrative, novelty, and challenges. Play encourages learning through interaction with objects, people, and information. Early childhood educators establish play that integrates social, emotional, physical, language, and cognitive development that respect diversity and are inclusive. Play is defined as an activity in which children are actively engaged; it is freely chosen, intrinsically motivated, non-literal, and it serves the child's needs for pleasure, emotional release, mastery, or resolution (Johnson, Christie, & Wardle, 2005). Play-based pedagogy includes activities organized to facilitate movement, activity, choice, autonomy, communication, and social interaction (Bennett, 2004).

Children who thrive in primary school and set trajectories for later academic success are those who enter Grade 1 with strong communication skills, and are confident. These children are able to make friends; they are persistent and creative in completing tasks and solving problems, and they are excited to learn. These are the same qualities that children acquire through high-quality play during their preschool years (Segal, 2004; Ziegler, Singer, & Bishop-Josef, 2004).

Active Play

Active play is play that is physically active; it can be either structured or unstructured. Children are engaged in moderate- to vigorous-intensity activity. Active play develops endurance, control of body movements, and **perceptual–motor** integration. Longer-term benefits are extensive and relate to all aspects

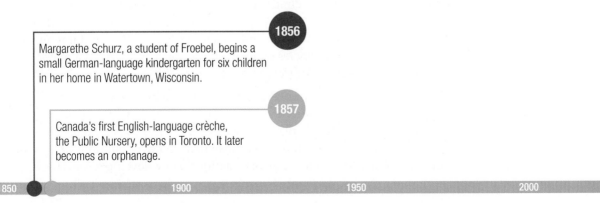

1856
Margarethe Schurz, a student of Froebel, begins a small German-language kindergarten for six children in her home in Watertown, Wisconsin.

1857
Canada's first English-language crèche, the Public Nursery, opens in Toronto. It later becomes an orphanage.

1850   1900   1950   2000

of learning, behaviour, and health. Cognitive abilities, blood pressure and lipid levels, and mental health improve with regular active play.

Active play helps a child learn and practise safety, take care of and respect her or his body, and develop an appreciation and enjoyment of movement and physical activity. And yet, physical activity levels are diminishing amongst pre-school and school-age children, creating long-term health problems (Leitch, 2008). In its 2014 "Report Card on Physical Activity for Children and Youth," the organization Active Healthy Kids Canada reported that while most 3- and 4-year-olds are physically active for the recommended 84 minutes a day, the percentage of school-age children (ages 5 to 11 years) are not.

Active play also contributes to students' physical literacy, which, in turn, is an essential foundation of well-being. Physical literacy is the ability to "move with competence and confidence in a wide variety of physical activities in mul-tiple environments that benefit the healthy development of the whole person" (Physical and Health Education, 2014). Children require regular, frequent opportunities for physical movement and active play.

Five-year-old children are typically ready to start combining skills such as running, throwing, catching, and jumping into games. Older children may seek out structured team games such as baseball, soccer, or field hockey. They may prefer games that involve skipping or running and chasing. At the same time, school age children require unstructured active play time, particularly in programs outside of the school day (Active Healthy Kids Canada, 2014).

Educators can plan active play activities that incorporate physical movement and skill practice across the program, rather than as isolated activities. Through these activities, young children can be encouraged to work co-operatively with others and to persevere with their own physical activities. They can also learn to assess the risk involved in a physical activity and to monitor their own physical abilities to take risks.

Opportunities for physically active play, including play-fighting, help children manage aggressive reactions. In a game of chase, children are physically active and maintain the game by negotiating the rules and agreeing to abide by them. Yet what they value is the thrill of the chase. The rules provide a framework within which the players know that "this is play"; this framework provides a safe place where emotions can be experienced without the consequences they might bring in the "real" world.

Pretend Play

> In [pretend] play, the child always behaves beyond his average age, above his daily behavior; in play it is as though he were a head taller than himself. As in the focus of a magnifying glass, play contains all developmental tendencies in a condensed form and is itself a major source of development (Vygotsky, 1978, p. 102).

Socio-dramatic play is about creating a world in which children are in control and can seek out uncertainty in order to triumph over it. The creativity required and developed in play, the use of imagination and finding one's own solutions to problems, both real and imagined—all help children to develop ways of reacting to a wide range of situations. They develop a repertoire of flexible responses to situations they create and encounter within the safety of the make-believe world they have created.

Socio-dramatic or make-believe play is defined by three components: an agreed-upon pretend scenario, roles, and rules. Together children co-construct and negotiate a pretend situation. They take on and act out defined roles and they follow a set of rules that are shaped by the specific roles. When children take on a particular role for an extended period of time, they have opportunities to pay attention to their choices and not act on immediate impulses.

Preschool children rely on personal experiences for dramatic play and may cooperate with other children and share space with other children. By four or five years of age, children start to develop more complex, interconnected play scenarios, and they differentiate complementary roles. Socio-dramatic play continues into primary school years, often using more fantasy and interconnected, planned scripts. Young school-age children shift from pretend play to dramatic productions with a prepared script drawn from a published story or from one authored by the children.

Socio-dramatic play requires the pretenders to relay their stories and negotiate with each other using language, gestures, and symbolic objects to tell and retell stories. Socio-dramatic play builds a sense of narrative that sets the foundation for moving from learning to read to reading to learn. Children's ability to communicate to a variety of audiences benefits from role-play in socio-dramatic play and then in more structured dramatic arts. They learn to apply their speaking and listening skills for different purposes. Children practise verbal and narrative skills that are needed for reading comprehension.

Socio-dramatic play calibrates emotional responses to the unexpected events that are introduced during play. The ability to regulate emotional responses to disturbance, and to reduce stress levels, enhances the ability to cope with uncertainty and allows for the development of a suite of motor (physical), cognitive, and social skills that can be brought to bear on the situation at hand.

Socio-dramatic play also helps children to develop social responsibility as they interact and negotiate with others. Children learn to see things as others see them and to problem-solve when they role-play at the dramatic play centre. They have the opportunity to experiment with a variety of social roles (e.g., store clerk, bus driver, grandparent).

Pretend play can be hurtful and negative. When children tease, bully or harass other children while playing a role, this is harmful use of imagination. Educators have a responsibility, therefore, to intervene and re-direct the play just as they do in any other situation in the classroom or playground.

1858
The *salle d'asile* Saint Joseph provides care for young children in Montreal.

1859
Charles Darwin publishes *The Origin of Species* in which he explains the theory of natural selection.

| 1850 | 1900 | 1950 | 2000 |

Chapter 2: Early Childhood Education Curriculum

When pretend play entrenches societal inequities, cultural biases or violence educators have a responsibility to step in and redirect in the same way they would if one child hit another child.

Pretend or socio-dramatic play is the primary mode of learning during the preschool years and continues to be important into the primary grades. Pretend play provides practice in choosing, negotiating, planning, thinking, problem solving, and taking risks. In high-quality pretend play, the child is deeply involved and is acquiring and practising skills.

Pretend play also helps children take the perspective of others and promotes later abstract thought. Pretence involves mental representation. A child's ability for joint planning and assigning roles during pretend play with other children is related to their level of **theory of mind**, or their ability to understand that others have beliefs, desires, and intentions different from their own. The understanding that what one believes and what others believe may not be the same is a critical element in the development of theory of mind that is acquired around four years of age (Astington, 1998). Children's development of mental representation is an important cognitive achievement needed for academic skills, such as reading comprehension and use of mathematical symbols.

Pretend play also increases how often children practise **self-regulation**. For instance, children's private speech—speech that helps them regulate their own attention, behaviour, or emotions—occurs more often in pretend play than in less complex play settings, or settings with tasks having predetermined goals and greater teacher direction.

Creative-Constructive Play

Building, painting, or inventing things is creative-constructive play. As children have increasingly complex interactions with others, their ability to represent feelings, intentions, and actions in drawings, paintings, movement, music, and constructions leaps forward. Combined with the exploration and discovery of the properties of different materials, students in early childhood education programs construct and represent their knowledge in a variety of ways. Creative-constructive play is goal-oriented and organized as children transform available materials into something new.

Exploratory play leads to purposeful construction of meaningful objects, structures, and representations. Creative-constructive play often is intertwined with socio-dramatic play in the early years. As children develop more complicated dramatic narratives, creating the settings often becomes a more integral part of the play.

Children's constructive play can lead to figuring out how things are constructed and how they work, and to thinking about what can make them work differently or more efficiently. Solving practical problems that emerge in constructive play involves engineering concepts to design, build, and test solutions. Children have opportunities to experience the added value of tools. Primary students can benefit from access to tools such as screwdrivers, hammers, saws, sewing machines, simple weaving looms, and different types of scissors.

Creative-constructive play also builds enthusiasm, ideas, and skills for children's participation in visual and performance arts. Educators can extend the learning potential of creative-constructive play by providing opportunities for older preschool and school-age children to express themselves in visual arts, music, dance, and dramatic productions. Creative-constructive play and participation in the arts build children's decision-making skills, develops symbolic communication, promotes sensory development, and encourages creative thinking and imagination.

Cultural differences are respected in Canada. Creative-constructive play is an important vehicle for children to understand different cultures as well as to express their own culture. Children experience a sense of accomplishment when they create or construct something new and unique to them. When they collaborate together to create something new, they must share ideas and plans and then negotiate the execution of those plans.

Games with Rules

Rule-based games are play with an external structure. Children learn to how to take turns, share, and resolve differences when they take part in rule-based games with other children.

Simon Says, guessing games, I Spy with My Little Eye, and Red Light/Green Light are examples of classic games that require children to pay attention and remember the rules (working memory). They build children's capacity to get along with each other. Hide and Seek is a game with rules that develops self-regulation as children must wait quietly until they are found.

As children become more skilled, the rules can become more complex. Children become interested in formal games with peers by age four or five and continue into middle childhood. Older children's more logical and socialized ways of thinking make it possible for them to play more complex games together. Games with rules are often the most prominent form of play during middle childhood.

The main organizing element in game play consists of explicit rules that guide children's group behaviour. Some games involve two or more sides, competition, and agreed-upon criteria for determining a winner. Other games require co-operation among children to be successful. Children use games flexibly to meet social and intellectual needs.

Rule-based games provide children with shared activities and goals that build their capacity to collaborate with others. Children learn to negotiate rules in order to create the game they wish to play. They shape the external structure of the game. The fairness of the rules matters to primary grade children.

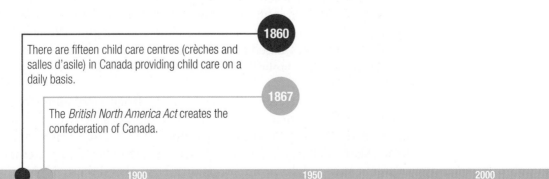

1860

There are fifteen child care centres (crèches and salles d'asile) in Canada providing child care on a daily basis.

1867

The *British North America Act* creates the confederation of Canada.

1850   1900   1950   2000

Strategy games, like checkers, also help children to practise reasoning strategies. In such games, children must consider both offensive alternatives and the need for defence.

Games can also be organized to encourage mathematical understanding and early reading practice in a systematic manner. Games using a number line—Snakes and Ladders, for example—are particularly effective in supporting children's sense of numbers and introducing mathematical concepts.

Play and Literacy

Literacy is the ability to use language in all its form of communication—including listening, talking, reading, writing, music, dance, story-telling, visual arts, drama, numbers, and digital media. Literacy, including numeracy, is an important aspect of communication, critical to successful learning in the early grades and beyond. Thought and language—the representation of words and numbers—are interdependent. Words and numbers are tools for making meaning and are, therefore, integral to cognitive development. Children need time to explore, to reflect, and to make connections between what they already know and new learning. It is essential that children negotiate the transitions from learning to read to reading to learn and from an informal number sense to mathematics in the early grades. The acquisition of these fundamental tools shapes success and well-being for individuals and for society.

Children communicate at birth using sounds and then gestures. Oral language expands their repertoire for communication as they acquire the ability to express their needs, exchange ideas, express feelings, and connect with others. The capacity to express themselves with language offers expanded capabilities to regulate their behaviour and get along with others.

Children's transition from oral language into an understanding of print provides a new way to represent experiences, ideas, and knowledge. Researchers have performed numerous studies of literacy skill development through play that embeds literacy materials within play settings in preschool, kindergarten, and multi-age programs. These studies reveal increases in children's use of literacy materials and engagement in literacy acts (e.g., Christie & Enz, 1992; Einarsdottir, 2000; Neuman & Roskos, 1992; Roskos & Christie, 2004; Singer & Lythcott, 2004; Stone & Christie, 1996). When play-based learning is designed deliberately to involve the integration of literacy props and materials—for example, having newspapers and pamphlets in the dramatic play area—the children's literacy-related play significantly increases. This is particularly evident when adults support the children's interactions with these props during play through modelling, role-playing, or conversation. Literacy-based play has been shown to increase children's emergent literacy knowledge.

Through literacy-based play, children also develop a sense of narrative and the ability to make symbolic representation and actions. They begin to acquire reading strategies.

Numeracy is one type of literacy: it is the language of numbers and the ability to use mathematics in daily life. Children's capacity to interact with mathematical ideas and vocabulary supports their early numeracy development. Mathematical ideas about spatial sense, structure and pattern, number, measurement, and data comparisons can be explored through play.

Pretend play also contributes significantly to a child's acquisition of numeracy. The language of numbers is the ability to see relations about quantity and builds on understandings about amount (e.g., more and less) early in life (Griffin & Case, 1998). Rich pretend play opportunities with other children and adults provide counting systems, including counting words, mathematical relationships, one-to-one correspondence, order, and numbers for the size of a set of objects (National Research Council 2001). Typically, children bring together an understanding about quantity differences between objects (e.g., big and little, large and small, etc.) and a continuum of values in between. Play can consolidate these understandings about numbers. Through play, children can learn how to use a number line for solving number problems that involve addition, subtraction, multiplication, and division. Play that involves games with rules supplements pretend play in mastering and integrating understandings about numbers and number lines. Research has shown that number linear board games (e.g. Ramani, Siegler, & Hitti, 2012) and card games (e.g. LeFevre et al., 2009) contribute to foundational math concepts and numerical skills (Ramani & Siegler, 2011).

Play has long been a well-established feature of early childhood education. But the increasing emphasis on accountability in the education system appears to have led to a corresponding decline in the general understanding of the important contribution that high-quality play—especially pretend play—can make to children's literacy, numeracy, and inquiry skills in the early years. A shift from a focus on play during preschool years to a strong emphasis on formal instruction to learn letters and use phonics can limit children's literacy skills as well as their numeracy and inquiry skills (Barnett, Yarosz, Thomas, & Hornbeck, 2006; Frede & Ackerman, 2002; Kraft & Berk, 1998; Ziegler et al., 2004). High-quality play mediated by adults who are play partners able to inject judicious direct instruction into daily play is an effective pedagogy for emergent literacy, numeracy, and science skills.

◀ Storybooks are part of a print-rich environment and emergent literacy.

moodboard/Thinkstock

Play is a pedagogical strategy that takes advantage of children's natural activity. Effective preschool learning environments embed opportunities for learning in the physical environment and play activities. Play, combined with judicious amounts of direct instruction, creates important learning moments that build children's competencies. Early childhood educators can set up play opportunities that relate to the children's experiences and help them move beyond their current levels of understanding and abilities through a process known as **scaffolding**—offering support from what a child can do on their own to what is possible with assistance or guidance. Children learn best when they can play, explore the world, and interact with expert adults and peers. Their explorations require flexibility and inventiveness. Children react to the outcomes of their investigations and create strategies for discovery.

Play and Inquiry

Inquiry is play-based learning that begins with exploration. Exploratory play (as well as other types of play) leads children to see connections between objects, ideas, meanings, and imagination. Ideas and questions progress to in-depth investigation of a real-world topic that engages children's attention and effort. They move from what they know to what is more complex. Play is a platform for inquiry and exploration. Play engages children's attention when it offers a challenge within the child's capacity to master (McCain & Mustard, 1999; National Research Council, 2001). When adults become involved in children's play, they can help with the difficult spots or sequences in activities in a way that is clear and reinforces learning (Keating, 1998).

Inquiry (sometimes called a project approach) focuses on what children have noticed and their ideas. They build communication and observation skills as well as acquiring new information and becoming experts in that area. As they investigate, ask questions, and expand their capacity to build bridges between ideas, children go through a problem-solving and planning process that encourages them to persist and find alternative solutions. An inquiry may be carried out with an entire class or with small groups of students.

Numeracy and mathematical understanding benefits from exploratory play that evolves into inquiry and involves measurement, space, perspective, and other mathematical ideas. Opportunities present themselves for children to record observations in graphs that represent their findings. Literacy benefits as children document their ideas, experimentation, and findings as a group or individually.

MAKING IT HAPPEN

Extending Learning Opportunities

Some children have been spending time playing with marbles at kindergarten. Today they have set up a spontaneous game, using small blocks to make pathways for their marbles. Recognizing this as an opportunity to build on children's interests and abilities, their teacher, Elmira, collects several empty shoeboxes and brings them out for the children. Nearby are markers, red, blue, and green tape, scissors, string, cardboard tubes, and small slips of paper. Elmira asks the children, "How do you think these boxes could be part of the game?"

1650   1700   1750   1800

Scientific reasoning begins early. Babies notice how objects move and behave, gather information, build patterns of expectations about the world around them, and form general categories. Toddlers experiment with tools and learn to manipulate objects. They learn to solve simple problems they encounter in their environment—how to get an object out of reach or how to make their desires understood. Preschool children use methods of science including data collection, predicting, recording, and talking about findings. Problems to be solved emerge in, or can be introduced to, preschool pretend play. Early childhood educators may introduce problems into the environment, problems that engage children's curiosity and provide opportunities for them to apply and reinforce their problem-solving skills.

ENGAGING FAMILIES

Family involvement and engagement should be built into early childhood education curriculum and pedagogy. Early childhood educators can complement and influence home environments and families, and vice versa.

Families have the strongest influence on children's early learning and development (Sylva, Melhuish, Sammons, Siraj-Blatchford, & Taggart, 2004; NICHD Early Childhood Research Network, 2004). Strong parent–child relationships and the quality of parenting are powerful influences on children's development and learning and can act as an emotional protection for young children (Bornstein, 2002; Centre for Community Child Health, 2007; Kirp, 2007). The family environment is the primary source of experience for children and mediates their contact with the broader environment (Siddiqi, Irwin, & Hertzman, 2007).

Studies have shown, in fact, that home learning environments, shaped by parents and other family members, are more important to positive child outcomes than children's participation in early childhood programs, family structure, or a family's socio-economic status (Sammons, Sylva, Melhuish, Siraj-Blatchford, Taggart & Elliot, 2004; Sylva, Melhuish, Sammons, Siraj-Blatchford & Taggart, 2009; Willms, 2002). In a U.K. longitudinal study of preschool and primary school experiences, maternal education and the home learning environment are strongest predictors of better academic and behavioural outcomes for children at age 10 (Sylva et al., 2009).

1871

In Ontario, the *School Act* makes schooling compulsory for children aged 7 to 12 for four months of the year. Schools in some boards were open six days a week and eleven months of the year.

1873

First public kindergarten in the United States is established in the St. Louis school system, after a letter writing campaign by Elizabeth Peabody. The first teacher is Susan Blow.

| 1850 | 1900 | 1950 | 2000 |

Parents and other family members can be built into the early childhood education curriculum. They can offer feedback about what children do at home and what experiences they are having. They can contribute stories, items, and experiences that contribute to the curriculum. In doing so, families become more involved and engaged in their own children's learning and development.

Involving Families Has a Powerful Impact on Children

In the United Kingdom, a longitudinal study of the impact of effective practice reports that children's home learning environment during the preschool years remains a strong predictor of academic achievement at age 11 years (Sylva et al., 2009).

The Chicago Child–Parent Centers measured parental involvement by aggregating ratings of parental participation in school by children's first-grade teachers. Researchers found that parental participation in preschool programs was associated with higher levels of parental participation in Grade 1 (Graue, Clements, Reynolds, & Niles, 2004).

An extensive international review of early childhood programs identified fourteen studies that included measures of parenting outcomes associated with parental involvement and engagement in early childhood programs (Mitchell, Wylie, & Carr, 2008). The review reported that parental involvement is linked to improved interactions with the child, including greater acceptance of the child's behaviour, positive parenting, activities to help the child learn at home, involvement of the father in the early childhood setting and in parenting, and parental knowledge of early child development.

In a Canadian study of linguistic minority children attending junior kindergarten, parents reported a better understanding of their children's learning and development through the intentional opportunities for communication (Pagani, Jalbert, Lapointe, & Herbert, 2006).

Parental involvement in early childhood settings multiplies children's opportunities for learning as parents reinforce skills and activities in the home environment (Reynolds & Temple, 2008; Sylva et al., 2009; Weiss, Caspe, & Lopez, 2006). Parental support of their children's learning is more likely to lead to more positive experiences in formal schooling (Cleveland, Corter, Pelletier, Colley, Bertrand & Jamieson, 2006; Corter, 2006; Wolanski, 2008).

However, involving parents in early childhood programs needs to go beyond *whether* parents are involved to focus on *how* they are involved and what happens as a result. Parent involvement in school settings includes parenting, communicating, volunteering, learning at home, decision-making, and collaborating with the community. The same strategies may be useful in organizing family involvement in early childhood settings (Epstein & Sanders, 2002; Pelletier, 2006; Corter & Pelletier, 2005; Corter et al., 2006).

Zellman and Perlman (2006) caution that few early childhood program studies have examined parental involvement as a unique concept independent of other parental characteristics, such as parental education, parenting skills or capacity, or commitment to the parenting role. It is possible that more competent parents are the ones who respond to parental involvement strategies.

The relationship between increased parental involvement and better outcomes may be a result of drawing in parents who are already more competent. In fact, one study of morning arrival time revealed that early childhood educators only spent on average 67 seconds with each parent (Perlman & Fletcher, 2008). This is not adequate time either to build parental involvement in the ongoing environment of the program or to exchange meaningful information that would support parents' involvement in their child's learning and development.

Taking Learning Home

Alma is an early childhood educator working in a preschool program that is part of a large multi-service agency. Four-year-old Pedro started the program a month ago. Pedro speaks Portuguese at home, and his mother wants him to know English before he starts kindergarten in six months. Pedro spends time watching other children play. He follows the daily routines and seems to understand what is being said at snack time and group time, but he speaks very little. Pedro's mother asks Alma to help Carlos acquire English. Her own English is limited, but she thinks that she should start speaking only English at home. Alma says, "It is a very good idea to read books with Pedro. What kinds of books to you think would interest him most? If I give you some story-books without text—you and Pedro could tell the story together in Portuguese? We use the same books here and tell the story in English. Pedro's ability to understand and speak Portuguese will help him as he learns English. And he is learning—he already understands a lot of English. When he is watching other children play, he is hearing and understanding more and more of what they are saying. We usually learn to speak a language by understanding before we speak. Could you come early one day next week when you are picking up Pedro? I would like to have you join our group time and introduce all of the children and myself to a few Portuguese words."

Alma demonstrated respect for Pedro and his mother. Her knowledge of how language emerges from understanding produced many points from which Pedro and his peers could continue their language learning.

Strategies for Increasing Family Involvement

The benefits of family involvement are greatest when there is planned programming for children and their families, when relationships between schools and families are based on mutual trust and respect, and when schools are sensitive to family culture, values, language, and composition (Bernhard, Freire, & Mulligan, 2004; Gonzalez-Mena, 2005). Guidelines for culturally responsive parental involvement emphasize respectful dialogue and awareness of cross-cultural communication skills (Daycare Trust, 2007). To include

1877

Ada Maream opens the first private kindergarten in Canada in Saint John, New Brunswick.

1878

The American Froebel Union is established by Elizabeth Peabody. It is the first professional association for those concerned with the education of young children.

| 1850 | 1900 | 1950 | 2000 |

Chapter 2: Early Childhood Education Curriculum

everyone, early childhood settings must encourage healthy dialogue about the principles and shared beliefs that relate to inclusion, diversity, and equity (Moss, 2007; Bernhard, Cummins, Campoy, Ada, Winsler & Bleiker, 2006) and expand communication. When teachers offer a wider range of communication opportunities to parents of linguistic-minority children who are experiencing difficulties with verbal skills, they are more likely to become engaged than other parents, as demonstrated in one Canadian study (Pagani, Jalbert, Lapointe & Herbert, 2006).

Parents want to understand how their children develop and learn (Corter & Pelletier, 2005; Oldershaw, 2002). They benefit from their own experience with children, observations of their own and other children, and information about how to support learning and how to recognize how their children are doing (Bornstein, 2002; Centre for Community Child Health, 2007; Corter & Fleming, 2002). Parents also benefit from having a say in what is offered in the program and what goes into the curriculum (Corter et al., 2006). Effective early childhood programs share child-related information more often, and parents are more involved in decision-making about the curriculum than in less effective settings (Siraj-Blatchford, Sylva, Taggart, Melhuish, Sammons, & Elliott, 2003). Shared developmental and educational aims between early childhood educators and parents encouraged a complementary approach that included sharing expertise and knowledge about the child and the child's development (Siraj-Blatchford et al., 2003; Siraj-Blatchford & McCallam, 2005).

Daily communication with a meaningful exchange of information between parents and early childhood program staff supports children's development and is a measure of program quality (Zellman & Perlman, 2006). Explicit parent education geared to the goals of parents and delivered in ways that respect adult learning principles can be joined with child programming in effective two-generation programs (Cleveland, Corter, Pelletier, Colley, Bertrand, & Jamieson, 2006; Goodson, 2005; Shonkoff & Phillips, 2000). Family literacy studies of programming for parent and child learning suggest that these may foster parents' knowledge about language and literacy development with benefits for children's learning (Pelletier, 2006; Senechal, 2006).

CURRICULUM APPROACHES

Curriculum is an organized system of intentions and plans to promote children's development and learning. It is the sum of experiences, activities, and events that occur within an early childhood program. An explicit curriculum serves other purposes in addition to the child's development: promotion of an even level of quality across programs; guidance and support for educators in their daily practice; and facilitation of communication between parents and staff.

The practical application of a curriculum approach includes guidelines on how to set up the physical environment, structure the activities, interact with children and their families, and support staff members in their initial training and ongoing implementation of the program. The daily schedule and routines define the use of time that sets the architecture of children's daily lives in early childhood programs. Indoor and outdoor physical environments are set up to provide opportunities for children's play, independent problem-solving, and inquiry. Children can learn to make choices and demonstrate responsibility. The available resources and experiences nurture and extend children's learning. Early childhood educators plan opportunities that allow children to explore language and communicate their thinking and learning in meaningful ways in a variety of contexts.

Children benefit from a planned curriculum; having specific goals for children's learning guides decisions about what to include in the environment and embed in children's experiences (Ginsburg, Lee, & Boyd, 2008). Holistic curriculum approaches that support emotional maturity, social competence, cognition, language development, and physical well-being are best in early childhood programs (Miller & Almon, 2009; Shonkoff & Phillips, 2000; Sylva et al., 2009).

Preschool Programs

Preschool programs provide care and education to children in the years before they enter school. They are structured programs with recurrent activities, the content of which is central to supporting and strengthening young children's learning and development. The curricula of these programs form the "front line" of children's experiences—what is taught and what is learned. Find out more in R. E. Tremblay, R. G. Barr, R. De V. Peters, and M. Boivin, eds., *Encyclopedia on Early Childhood Development* (Montreal: Centre of Excellence for Early Childhood Development, 2009), available http://www.child-encyclopedia.com/en-ca/preschool-programs/ how-important-is-it.html, accessed June 10, 2010.

RESEARCH INTO PRACTICE

Early childhood educators intentionally guide and construct opportunities to extend children's learning. This is the "how" or the pedagogy that is part of a curriculum approach. Pedagogical strategies across the continuum from child-directed to teacher-guided approaches provide structure and direction for educators who support the development of capacities and skills while respecting a child's interests and choices (Bennett, 2005; Bertrand & Riehl, 2009; Miller & Almon, 2009). The repertoire of strategies that early childhood educators use includes investigation and exploration; modelling and demonstrating; open questioning, speculating, and explaining; shared thinking and guided learning; and explicit or direct instruction. Curriculum approaches for early childhood programs include pedagogy that offers both intentional and spontaneous opportunities for learning that may be child-directed or adult-guided. Most early childhood programs have elements of both child-directed play and adult-guided instruction, but the balance between the two varies from program to program.

1880
The first teacher training program for kindergarten teachers starts in the Oshkosh Normal School.

1882
Ontario establishes a board of health that promotes public health in the schools.

| 1850 | 1900 | 1950 | 2000 |

Early childhood education programs are social settings that guide children in learning about the world around them. The social context is a critical element to take into account in considering how children learn and develop. Early childhood education curriculum approaches reflect differences in culture. Family structure, social and economic characteristics, community influences, and ethnic and linguistic backgrounds are also part of the social environment and part of learning and development.

There are many different curriculum approaches being used successfully in early childhood education. These approaches include developmentally appropriate practice, the Montessori method, HighScope, the Reggio Emilia approach, and the *Sesame Street* approach.

<table>
<tr><td>

MAKING IT HAPPEN

</td><td>

Direct Instruction

Direct instruction is adult-initiated, planned teaching. It may involve one child, a small number of children, or a large group of children; an early childhood educator or other adult can present the lesson. It may be used to facilitate learning of academic content, physical skills, and social skills. Direct instruction typically starts with clearly stated learning objectives or outcomes. Materials and instructions are carefully sequenced to promote the child's or children's mastery of the content (Beretier, 1972; National Research Council, 2001).

In many early childhood education programs, group time or circle time is an opportunity for direct instruction. Early childhood educators may plan specific content and take advantage of the potential efficiency of the simultaneous attention of a group of children (National Research Council, 2001).

</td></tr>
</table>

Developmentally Appropriate Practice

Developmentally appropriate practice (DAP) is a curriculum approach based on knowledge of the development of children's abilities and observation of individual differences, including abilities, interests, and culture (Gestwicki, 2011). It can be applied in settings with children from infancy through middle childhood. The approach considers that all areas of development—physical, social, emotional, and cognitive—are important and that it is the early childhood educator's responsibility to plan an environment and support experiences to enhance all areas of development.

Programs designed on developmentally appropriate practice contain a number of common characteristics that can be incorporated into related curriculum approaches. Typically, ECEs in a developmentally appropriate program

- support the whole child, that is, all areas of the child's development;
- use observations of children's individual interests and developmental progress to plan the curriculum;
- promote children's active exploration and interactions with others;
- use learning materials and activities that are concrete and part of the lives of young children;
- provide for a wide range of developmental interests that meet the children's individual needs and skills;

- offer increased challenges as children's abilities and skills progress; and
- provide materials and allow time so children can choose activities (Bredekamp, 1987).

Montessori Schools

Montessori schools, which follow the philosophical approach of Maria Montessori, have proliferated in North America since the early 1960s. Montessori schools use unique methods and materials, and they hire specially trained teachers. Sequences of prescribed tasks, using **didactic** Montessori materials, are presented to children in a designated order. Montessori teachers, or directresses, have received specialized training in an institution accredited for Montessori teacher training, which emphasizes observing children and presenting in **sequential steps** the directions for activities for which children are ready. The Montessori philosophy includes introducing children to varieties of **practical life skills**, such as washing dishes, sweeping floors, and watering plants. The curriculum also includes sensorial components, which involve providing materials to help children broaden and refine their sensory perceptions, and it includes conceptual components, which means using concrete academic materials to introduce children to reading, writing, mathematics, and social studies.

There are particular terms that help explain the Montessori philosophy. One of these is the **absorbent mind**, Montessori's term for the ease with which young children learn unconsciously from the environment. Montessori also stressed the use of didactic materials—those that teach children directly by making errors in their use obvious to the child for self-correction. In addition, Montessori was aware of children's **sensitive periods**—the periods of learning during which children are particularly sensitive to particular stimuli. One abiding distinction of the Montessori philosophy is the respect for children and their abilities and accomplishments.

Many Montessori schools are for children ages two through six; in some communities, however, Montessori education may continue through the elementary grades and beyond. In North America today, there are Montessori schools that strictly follow the original techniques, such as schools that belong to the Association Montessori International (AMI), and others that follow practices adapted to North American culture and current thinking, and belong to the American Montessori Society (AMS).

There is further discussion of the Montessori method in Chapter 7.

judwick/iStock/Thinkstock

▲ Developmentally appropriate practices influence all domains of the child's development, rather than focusing solely on the cognitive.

1882

G. Stanley Hall publishes "The Content of Children's Minds" in the *Princeton Review*.

1883

Concerns about preschool-age children being left unsupervised are brought to the Toronto School Board by its chief inspector, James L. Hughes.

1850   1900   1950   2000

Chapter 2: Early Childhood Education Curriculum   **53**

HighScope

Another current model in early childhood education and care programs is the **HighScope** curriculum. This curriculum has developed under the leadership of David Weikart, who was a founder of the Perry Project, one of the best-known intervention programs of the 1960s (see Timeline, p. 181). The HighScope curriculum is based on Jean Piaget's constructivist theories of child development. "The curriculum rests on the fundamental premise that children are active learners, who learn best from activities that they themselves plan, carry out and reflect on" (Epstein, 1993, p. 30). As in most good early childhood programs, children learn in a variety of learning centres with plenty of appropriate materials. Teachers help children actively plan what they will do each day, after which the children carry out their plan during work time using self-selected activities. Then they review what they have done (**plan**, **do**, **review**). Early childhood practitioners join in children's play, asking questions to extend their thinking skills.

The HighScope curriculum identifies five ingredients of active learning for young children:

- materials for the child to explore;
- manipulation of materials by the child;
- choices by the child about what to do with the materials;
- language from the child; and
- support from the adult (Epstein, 1993).

The curriculum is built around early childhood educator- and child-initiated learning activities in five main curriculum content areas: approaches to learning; language, literacy, and communication; social and emotional development; physical development, health, and well-being; and arts and sciences. Within these areas are 58 key **developmental indicators** (formerly called "key experiences")—observable early childhood milestones that guide teachers as they plan learning experiences and interact with children.

The Reggio Emilia Approach

After World War II, preschools opened in the northern Italian town of Reggio Emilia. These preschools continue to operate. The municipal government of Reggio Emilia supports 35 schools, serving children aged 3 to 6 and infants up to age 3. About 47 percent of the town's preschool population and 33 percent of its infants attend **Reggio Emilia** schools (Gestwicki, 2011). This city-run early child development program has captured the attention and imagination of early childhood practitioners in Canada and around the world for several reasons. First, it enjoys a high degree of community support and is viewed as an essential part of a cohesive, healthy, and productive community. Second, the schools' physical beauty and attention to detail are evident to all who visit the program. Third, the program philosophy and curriculum build on Lev Vygotsky's concept of the social construction of knowledge and skillfully integrate other theoretical concepts, including Jean Piaget's theory of cognitive development, John Dewey's concept of progressive education, Howard Gardner's theory of multiple intelligences, and Urie Bronfenbrenner's ecological environment theory (Berk & Winsler, 1995).

Loris Malaguzzi (who was introduced at the beginning of Chapter 1 of this text) was the founder and leader of the Reggio Emilia approach and programs. He based his system of early childhood education on a few key principles:

- child-centred programs, which respect children and emphasize the reciprocal adult–child relationship;
- an "environment as teacher" approach, which organizes space to promote relationships, creates aesthetically pleasing surroundings, promotes choices and activities, stimulates all areas of learning, and reflects children's ideas, values, and culture;
- a curriculum centred on children's interests, reflected in projects that are undertaken in considerable depth and detail;
- a spirit of collaboration between early childhood practitioners and young children in facilitating intellectual discovery through social process; and
- the participation of families as an integral part of the educational experience (Gestwicki, 2011).

Many early childhood educators are turning to an **emergent curriculum** model that allows them to incorporate some of the principles found in Reggio Emilia programs. However, the Reggio Emilia approach is not a curriculum model that can be transported from its roots in northern Italy to Canadian settings. It is a way of thinking and interpreting the immediate surroundings (natural environment and social community) and following the lead of children and their families to create a unique early childhood setting. Emergent curriculum is an approach that encourages early childhood practitioners to respond to their immediate surroundings—physical place and people—and guide children's natural curiosity about their environment to encourage learning.

Emergent curriculum first appeared in the 1970s, and Elizabeth Jones coined the term in the introduction to a curriculum book (Jones & Nimmo, 1994). Many North American ECEs are finding it a useful framework that

A child's own interests are a starting point for a new project.

integrates knowledge about child development and an approach to planning that allows the child's interests to take the lead (Goulet, 2001).

Daily Preschool Curriculum in Action

Mohamed works in a preschool program located in a downtown school in a large city. The children are following the construction of a high-rise office building next door with great interest. During outdoor times children line up at the fence and watch the comings and goings of diggers, front-end loaders, and cranes.

One day, Mohamed moves tricycles, wagons, and some large empty boxes down by the fence. He notices that Carla has sat down on one of the tricycles and is moving it back and forth making a *vrrrrrr* sound. Before long, Carla is joined by three other children and they are orchestrating tricycles and wagons around an area they name "the building site." Mohamed takes an active role in the children's play. He joins the children and asks if they would like to put a large fence up around the building site. Carla says, "Yes, and we will need to make big signs that say 'Danger' and Workers Only".

A week later, the building site is still a popular area of the playground and now includes a digging area in the sandbox, structures made out of blocks, tubes, and boxes, and numerous picture and word signs giving directions for construction vehicles and warning of dangers. The children are asking more and more questions about how the construction vehicles work and debating about what the proper names for each of them are. Mohamed does not know the answers to many of their questions. He has brought in several picture books about construction vehicles. The children's keen interest are the starting points. Mohamed builds on the children's pretend play to elaborate learning, and literacy, opportunities.

Processes of Emergent Curriculum

The Early Childhood Education diploma program and the eight lab centres at George Brown College have adopted an emergent curriculum model. Marie Goulet, a former Early Childhood Education faculty member, prepared the following handout for students, which describes how early childhood educators can support children's learning and respect their interests and explorations.

Provision

Provide materials and space for children to explore and play. Consider the needs of individuals and group development. Environments should be rich enough for each child to find his or her interests represented with opportunities to learn.

Sustain

Learning requires repeated practice to ensure integration and mastery. Provide materials and support to maintain practice at the same level of difficulty (horizontal curriculum). Strategies include open-ended questions, broadcasting, joint-attention, imitation, and parallel play, adding new materials that offer the same practice.

| 1650 | 1700 | 1750 | 1800 |

The *Sesame Street* Approach

Do you remember watching *Sesame Street?*

It is the most successful programme in the history of children's television. It has been broadcast to more than 120 million children in 130 nations and is watched by 77 percent of American preschool children (Gladwell, 2002). *Sesame Street*, derived directly from the 1967 *Public Broadcasting Act*, began broadcasting on U.S. television in 1969 to promote the intellectual and cultural growth of preschoolers (Carnegie Commission on Educational Television, 1967). Television producer Joan Ganz Cooney and puppeteer Jim Henson collaborated to form the Children's Television Workshop, and developed the idea of teaching through the perceptual salience (that is, the focus of the child's attention) of commercial television: quick cuts, animation, and humour with talking puppets and humans posing as narrators.

The historical events and educational policies of the late 1960s shaped *Sesame Street*'s educational goals and audience. One major historical force of the time was the civil rights movement, which focused attention on the crucial role education would have to play if children from low-income circumstances, including disproportionately large numbers of minority-group members, were to escape the cycle of poverty. Head Start and *Sesame Street* were two outgrowths of broad education policies that recognized that special efforts to stimulate the educational progress of children from low-income backgrounds should include an emphasis on school-readiness skills starting at a very early

1886

Chicago Kindergarten College is established.

1887

The Montreal Day Nursery program opens. Ontario becomes the first jurisdiction in the world to officially recognize kindergarten as part of the elementary school system.

1850   1900   1950   2000

(preschool) age. A research study of the era, published by Benjamin Bloom (1964) at the University of Chicago, concluded that more than one half of a child's lifetime intellectual capacity is formed by five years of age.

Sesame Street focuses on improving the social and academic skills of disadvantaged children and helping them succeed at school. The educational or instructional design of *Sesame Street* is based on the premise that learning is a process that takes place from the outside in and moves from simple to complex. Learning-readiness is related to mastering simple patterns, skills, and concepts in preparation for more complex concepts. The plan also sets out to model prosocial skills and introduce specific information and concepts related to early literacy and numeracy skills.

Sesame Street relies on the insight that "if you can hold the attention of children, you can educate them" (Gladwell, 2002, p. 100). It uses the direct instruction strategies that combine specific learning objectives, carefully sequenced images, and matching dialogue into episodes designed to focus the child's attention and master specific content. The high production values and the combination of stable components of the environment (e.g., characters such as Big Bird), isolation and repetition of key concepts in each show (such as the number "6" or the letter "c"), and novel or unexpected events are used judiciously to directly instruct young children.

The approach of *Sesame Street* in using direct instruction embedded in an entertaining format that engages children can be found in many early child development programs. They are typically organized around specific themes that are relevant to children's daily lives and subject areas such as literacy, math, science, social skills, art, and music. Children are encouraged to master specific content such as visual patterns or recognition of colours.

The Best Curriculum Approach?

So you might be thinking: " I want to know what is the best curriculum approach— what benefits children most?"

The answer is … it depends. It depends on you, the children, the families, and the community. There is no magic bullet, no one best curriculum. Fifty years of research reveals that having a coherent curriculum direction is much more important than what that direction is—within some broad boundaries that we will discuss shortly.

Most early childhood curriculum approaches exist along the continuum of adult-guided to child-directed (Bennett, 2005; Miller & Almon, 2009). In adult-guided approaches, ECEs set up the environment and select activities related to a set of learning outcomes or expectations. The Montessori, HighScope, or *Sesame Street* approaches would be considered adult-guided; also most kindergarten curricula follow a teacher-guided approach and are organized to encourage children's attainment of identified learning expectations. In child-directed curriculum approaches, on the other hand, children's interests and emerging skills and aptitudes drive curriculum. The emergent curriculum and Reggio Emilia approaches are child-directed.

The most effective curriculum is custom-designed for each early childhood program. The implementation of ready-made program models might be easier at first but in terms of children's outcomes these programs are usually less effective than programs that construct their own learning environments. Having a clear program direction and specific learning goals for children and families is more important than what program model is adopted. Putting together a uniquely appropriate learning environment creates a more effective setting than trying to transplant a particular curriculum approach.

Research does tell us that some curricula do not support children's early learning. Laissez-faire approaches (sometimes labelled "free play without any structure") don't work well. Children usually run out of ideas, and chaos ensues. Didactic approaches also have drawbacks in that they are based on very specific learning goals to be mastered. Isolated specific skills are thus introduced outside the context of children's lives. Learning goals or expectations drive curriculum, rather than the children's needs.

Curriculum Frameworks

In the past few years, several Canadian and international jurisdictions have developed curriculum frameworks to support programming in early childhood programs (McQuaig, 2014). The purpose of the framework documents is to guide planning without enforcing a particular curriculum approach.

In Prince Edward Island, the document *Early learning framework: Relationships, environments, experiences* is the curriculum framework of the Preschool Excellence Initiative. The framework outlines four broad goals for early learning: well-being; play and playfulness; communication and literacies; and diversity and social responsibility.
[http://www.gov.pe.ca/eecd/eecd_EYFrWrk_Full.pdf]

The *New Brunswick curriculum framework for early learning and child care* provides a foundation for an emergent curriculum for children from birth to five. It aims to "encourage optimum development in an atmosphere of trust, security and respect" (Early Childhood Research and Development Team, 2008, p. 3). Play is viewed as integral to children's learning and richly formative in their capacity for relationships. It is premised on the belief that play must be accorded a key place in the lives of young children. Research and theory support the long-held contention that play is essential to quality of life in childhood and a primary means of understanding the world. Consequently, this curriculum framework articulates ways educators can maximize the potential of play for children's care and learning.
[http://www.gnb.ca/0000/ECHDPE/curriculum-e.asp]

The *Quebec education program: Preschool education* is the guide for curriculum in Quebec's four-year-old kindergarten programs. This document promotes play and spontaneous activities, with a view to getting children to express themselves, experiment, construct their learnings, structure their thoughts, and develop their worldview. They learn to be themselves, to interact with others, and to solve problems. They develop their imagination and creativity. Spontaneous activity and play are their way of mastering reality; this justifies giving play a central place in preschool education and organizing the space and time accordingly.
[http://www.mels.gouv.qc.ca/fileadmin/site_web/documents/reseau/
formation_titularisation/ProgrammeMaternelle4ans_ang_s_02.pdf]

Another document, *Meeting early childhood needs: Quebec's educational program for childcare services update*, outlines the educational program for child care programs in Quebec. It identifies five principles:

1. Each child is unique.
2. Children are the primary agents of their development.
3. Child development is a comprehensive, integrated process.
4. Children learn through play.
5. Cooperation between childcare personnel or home childcare providers and parents is essential for the harmonious development of the child.

The framework stipulates that the educational program should be organized to foster children's overall development, particularly their emotional, social, moral, cognitive, language, physical, and motor development. Also, the program should help children to adapt gradually to life in society and to integrate harmoniously.

[http://www.mfa.gouv.qc.ca/fr/publication/Documents/programme_educatif_en.pdf]

In Ontario, *Early learning for every child today* (ELECT) (Ontario Best Start Panel on Early Learning, 2007) and *How does learning happen? Ontario's pedagogy for the early years* (Government of Ontario, 2014) accommodate a variety of curriculum models and pedagogical methods that are consistent with six guiding principles:

1. Early child development sets the foundation for lifelong learning, behaviour, and health.
2. Partnerships with families and communities strengthen the ability of early childhood settings to meet the needs of young children.
3. Respect for diversity, equity, and inclusion are prerequisites for honouring children's rights, optimal development, and learning.
4. A planned curriculum supports early learning.
5. Play is a means to early learning that capitalizes on children's natural curiosity and exuberance.
6. Knowledgeable, responsive early childhood professionals are essential.

[http://www.edu.gov.on.ca/childcare/oelf/]
[http://www.edu.gov.on.ca/childcare/HowLearningHappens.pdf]

In Manitoba, *Early returns: Manitoba's early learning and child care curriculum framework for preschool centres and nursery schools* is used to develop, describe and enhance curriculum in preschool/child care centres and nursery schools. This document promotes fostering the social, emotional, physical, and cognitive development of children, and the design of play-based, developmentally appropriate interactions, relationships, environments, and experiences to allow all children in the program to develop to their fullest potential. *Early returns: Manitoba's early learning and child care curriculum framework for infant programs* (2014) supports curriculum design in programs for infants.
[http://www.gov.mb.ca/fs/childcare/pubs/early_returns_infant_curriculum.pdf]
[http://www.gov.mb.ca/fs/childcare/pubs/early_returns_en.pdf]

In Saskatchewan, *Play and exploration: Early learning program guide* aims to encourage stimulating and dynamic regulated child care environments that facilitate and guide play in regulated early childhood education programs.

Exploration and discovery are viewed as important processes in enhancing children's holistic development. Early childhood educators are encouraged to support children's learning in an environment that stimulates exploration, curiosity, and interactions with others. Saskatchewan's prekindergarten programs for three- and four-year-old children use *Better beginnings, better futures: Effective practices policy and guidelines for prekindergarten in Saskatchewan, 2008*, a document that serves as a guide to holistic, developmentally appropriate, and caring learning programs. It focuses on the healthy development of the whole child—social-emotional, physical, intellectual, and spiritual. It includes an extensive list of developmental benchmarks for each of these domains. Family engagement and community partnerships are also foundational components. [http://www.education.gov.sk.ca/ELCC/play-and-exploration-program-guide]

In British Columbia, the *Early learning framework* is a guide for early childhood programs, including family support programs and kindergarten. The framework identifies play as vital to children's healthy development and learning. Play is the "work" of children. Children interact with, explore, and make sense of the world around them when they play with each other. Children find joy and fulfillment in play, whether by themselves or in groups. The framework outlines four areas of early learning:

- well-being and belonging,
- exploration and creativity,
- language and literacies, and
- social responsibility and diversity.

[http://www2.gov.bc.ca/assets/gov/topic/57FDB4389CD0FB3F6EC9948B610 A6BA9/earlylearning/early_learning_framework.pdf]

CURRICULUM ISSUES

The curriculum approaches and frameworks are examples of what you are likely to find in early childhood programs n your communities. Many practices—what kinds of materials to make available to children, observing children's interactions with each other, and displaying representations that children have created, for example—are common to a number of approaches, but you can see that there are both similarities and differences among them. Most early childhood educators find themselves more comfortable in one approach than another.

No matter where ECEs are working and no matter which curriculum approach they are using, however, the same issues often challenge them. What is the best way to organize children's groups—same-age or mixed-age? Should early childhood education and care programs try to ensure that children are ready to adapt to school settings, or should the schools adapt to children? How can early childhood programs support children who have developmental challenges or identified special needs? How can early childhood settings respect and support all young children (boys and girls) and their families from diverse cultural, linguistic, and religious backgrounds? Does electronic technology have a place in today's early child development programs?

Mixed-Age Groupings

Children in early childhood programs are not always organized into groups of the same age and stage of development. In home-based programs, for example, it is more common to find children from different ages together in the same setting—similarly to a family with siblings of various ages.

Those of you who have listened to grandparents and great-grandparents reminisce about attending one-room schoolhouses will understand that **mixed-age groupings** in education are not a new phenomenon. But the concept is receiving renewed attention in early education programs and has been used successfully, not only in Canada but also in England, Sweden, and Italy. Rethinking the concept of mixed-age groupings allows early childhood educators to capitalize on the differences in the experience, knowledge, and abilities of children (Corson, 2005).

A mixed-age grouping combines children across at least two, and preferably three, chronological years. Usually, the grouping remains together for much of the time, with the oldest children moving on each year and new children joining as the youngest in the group. This means that children are in a group for at least two and sometimes three years, and remain with the same early childhood practitioner over this time. In child care centres, multi-age groupings "refers to the placement of children of different ages together in activity and learning areas for substantial portions of the daily schedule" (Bernhard, Pollard, Eggers-Pierola, & Morin, 2000, p. 80). Such an arrangement is more like a typical family or neighbourhood setting than grouping children by age.

Such a system has clear social advantages. Over time, children's relationships with one another, and relationships among children, teachers, and parents can develop and provide security and deeper understanding. Another advantage is that older children have opportunities to assume responsibility and to exhibit leadership skills with younger children. Older children in mixed-age groupings increase their own regulation of their behaviour, perhaps taking seriously their roles as models for the younger children. Their pro-social skills (behaviours that help them get along with others) and their caring skills also increase. Younger children benefit by participating in the more complex forms of play developed by the older children and by imitating their behaviours. Co-operative behaviours increase for all children (Katz, Evangelou, & Hartman, 1991).

There are cognitive benefits for children in these groupings as well. Rigid curricula with age-graded expectations must necessarily be relaxed in mixed-age settings. Children are allowed to develop and learn at their own rates without fear of failure and with less competition. Children's unique needs are more easily identified when teachers are not considering group goals; the curriculum is more likely to be matched to children's needs and skill-learning levels. Children whose knowledge is similar but different stimulate one another's mental growth and thinking. Therefore, **co-operative learning** and peer-tutoring situations generally abound in mixed-age settings.

Early childhood educators are key in determining how effectively mixed-age groupings actually work to benefit children. Simply putting children of different ages together does not guarantee these benefits; early childhood practitioners need to carefully structure the environment, plan the curriculum, and play particular roles. As ECEs learn about children's interests, abilities, learning styles, and choices for play partners, they can support individual growth. They plan activities that are child-initiated, so that children can find their own place on the developmental ladder. By freeing themselves from the role of director, ECEs can step in to facilitate as children need their interaction. They may consciously create opportunities for children to work together, make suggestions about how children can help one another, or frame thought-provoking questions that suggest ways of working with others who are younger or older. With adult guidance, children can learn much about democratic practices by jointly solving the problems that naturally arise in a multi-age grouping, such as what to do when the younger ones don't want to listen to the longer books that the older ones love to have read chapter by chapter.

Early childhood educators often resist the move to mixed-age groupings at first, fearing that it will be too difficult to plan for great differences and that individual age–stage behaviours won't mix. However, they usually change their opinions after some experience. The educators discover that they are teaching more responsively and appropriately. They benefit by learning about individual differences in new ways and by questioning their stereotypes and prejudices about behaviours that they may have assumed stemmed from age levels. They discover that the teaching and learning in their classrooms are shared among all participants. Perhaps this innovation will be in your professional future.

Adult and Child Focus

Early child development curriculum is often oriented to parents or other caregivers as well as to children. In some instances, parents or other caregivers attend the program with their children some or all of the time. In other early childhood settings that provide non-parental care, parents do not participate directly in program activities with their children (except during drop-off and pick-up times or at special events). In either situation, the curriculum can be directed to parents or other caregivers and to children at the same time.

A two-pronged approach that is both parent- and child-oriented recognizes the power of early learning within the family and seeks to support parents' and other caregivers' participation in the children's early development. See the Research into Practice box about the Chicago parent–child preschools for an example of how this might work.

Chicago Parent–Child Preschools

RESEARCH INTO PRACTICE

The Child–Parent Center (CPC) Program is a centre-based early intervention that provides comprehensive educational and family support services to economically disadvantaged children from preschool to early elementary school in central-city Chicago. The overall goal of the program is to promote children's academic success and to facilitate parent involvement in children's education.

The CPC program began in Chicago in 1967 based on four principles:

- parent involvement in the early years of school,
- instructional approaches tailored to children's learning styles and designed to develop their speaking and listening skills,
- small class sizes to provide for individual attention, and
- attention to health and nutritional services.

The program practices and structure are based on the assumptions that development is optimized in rich, stable learning environments and when parents are involved in the process of learning. Four components make up the program: early intervention, parent involvement, a structured language/ basic skills learning approach, and program continuity between preschool and elementary school.

Each Child–Parent Center is run by a head teacher and includes a staffed parent resource room, school–community outreach activities, and health services. After preschool and kindergarten, the school-age program in the elementary school provides reduced class sizes, teacher assistants for each class, continued parent involvement activities, and an enriched classroom environment for developing reading and math skills.

The centres make considerable efforts to involve parents in the education of their children, requiring at least one-half day per week of parent involvement in the program. The parent component includes participating in parent room activities, reinforcing learning at home, volunteering in the classroom, attending school events and field trips, participating in vocational and educational training, and receiving home visits from the school–community representative. A unique feature of the CPC is the parent resource room, which is physically located in the centre adjacent to the classrooms. The full-time parent-resource teacher organizes the parent room in order to implement parent educational activities, initiate interactions among parents, and foster parent–child interactions.

The CPC program operates centres throughout the Chicago Public Schools. The centres provide services in preschool (ages 3 or 4) and/or kindergarten. Participation in the CPC program for different lengths of time is significantly associated with higher levels of school achievement into adolescence, consumer skills, and parent involvement in children's education. It is also associated with lower rates of repeating a grade and special education, early school dropout, and delinquent behaviour. Cost–benefit analysis reports that US$7.10 were returned to society at large for every dollar invested in preschool. Excluding benefits to participants, the ratio of program benefits to costs for the general public was US$3.83 for every dollar invested.

Children who have participated longer, with greater family involvement, have had better outcomes. Instructional approaches that blend a teacher-directed focus with child-initiated activities and parental school involvement are origins of the positive long-term effects of participation in the CPC.

Sources: Reynolds, Temple, Robertson, & Mann, 2002; Reynolds, Wang, & Walberg, 2003; Graue, Clements, Reynolds, & Niles, 2004.

Transition to School

Children's coping and competence when they enter formal schooling is related to their academic success—how well they do in school and whether they complete high school and pursue other training and education. There is growing interest in ensuring that all children enter school "ready to learn" as a way of improving academic achievement and social well-being. If the early years set the foundation for later academic achievement (as well as social competence), it makes sense to consider how well prepared children are for school environments. This does not mean, however, that young children should learn to read earlier or that pre-reading, prewriting, or number skills are the only criteria for school readiness.

The desire to improve children's readiness for school learning sometimes leads to an emphasis on **early academics** or the direct instruction of reading and number skills during the early years. Since the modern era of early childhood education began in the 1960s, one issue has generated a good deal of debate: How much academic content and method is appropriate for children in their early years? Although many professional early childhood educators understand and support developmentally appropriate practices for young children, some are less grounded in developmental knowledge. They are more easily influenced by administrators, parents, and policymakers who push for academic experiences for young children that look a good deal like those presented to older children.

What sorts of risks do many experts see in prematurely exposing children to academic learning? There are several:

- Children's self-esteem will suffer if they are unable to succeed at the tasks that seem so important to adults. Many children, especially young children, just cannot learn in the ways academic instruction requires, no matter how hard they try. They cannot sit still, comprehend, or use the material they have learned by rote, or even see its importance. They feel incompetent, as they realize that they have failed to meet adults' standards, without understanding that what they have failed at is alien to their nature and learning style. When these kinds of learning are not meaningful to children, they feel no sense of self-worth, even when they do master some learning.

- A component of healthy development thought to be at risk in academic preschool programs is self-regulation (Shanker, 2010). Learning to make good choices is an important part of self-regulation. In a teacher-directed and teacher-managed environment, young children have few opportunities to make choices. The longitudinal studies of the preschool programs in Ypsilanti, Michigan, suggest more positive social and emotional adjustment in adolescents and adults who participated as children in preschool programs that allowed them to choose and initiate their activities (Schweinhart, Weikart, & Larner, 1986).

- Formal instruction often puts excessive and inappropriate demands on young children, and these demands can result in an overload of stress. A number of studies confirm that there is increased stress on children in developmentally inappropriate learning situations (Burts, Charlesworth, & Fleege, 1992).

- It seems likely that the long-term effects of rushing children prematurely into formal academics may be less than positive. Frequently, children's attitudes and dispositions to learning are negatively affected by the stress and circumstances of those first learning experiences. Evidence also suggests that children whose introduction to academic content and methods has been delayed past preschool and kindergarten have had at least equally positive results in later learning, rather than being handicapped compared with peers whose academics began earlier (Burts, Charlesworth, & Fleege, 1992). This seems to support the notion that waiting until children are developmentally ready for later kinds of school learning is beneficial.

You will need to be prepared to offer a convincing and solid rationale for structuring environments and learning experiences in which children initiate their own active learning through play. These environments and experiences

▲ Making marks—with crayons, pencils, and paints—is a step along the way to learning to print.

萌芽的
読み書き活動
子ども達が実際に読み書きの能力を獲得する
以前の、あるいはまさに獲得しつつある
時期のこと

are supported by facilitators who recognize that teaching based on active learning provides opportunities to develop *all* domains of the child's growth, and is more likely to support readiness for all learning and success in school.

ECEs must recognize that literacy and numeracy 算数 are important skill areas. Individual Canadians need these skills to be successful in almost any workplace and to participate fully in a democratic society. These are basic skills to survival in our society in the 21st century. Therefore, ECEs can understand that families are often anxious that their children acquire the skills necessary for learning to read and compute numbers when they enter formal schooling. We should be concerned too. However, direct instruction in isolated skills such as letter recognition or matching things that are the same and different will not be nearly as effective as other curriculum strategies.

Early childhood educators can provide environments that do prepare children for learning to read and understand mathematics. Early childhood program environments can be structured in a number of ways that support emergent literacy and emergent numeracy during the early years and then early literacy and numeracy abilities as they develop.

Emergent literacy is the development of children's ability to use print forms of language and includes making marks, scribbling, reciting stories from memory, and printing letters. Writing and reading become meaningful, and children understand their purpose even if they cannot read and write themselves. Literacy is related to oral language but is a separate ability; literacy is the symbolic representation of oral language.

We can support emergent literacy by

- understanding that literacy develops in close relationship to oral language;
- speaking with children about things that interest them;
- engaging in reading out loud and storytelling;
- developing a sense of narrative;
- valuing and modelling adult literacy use;
- enriching our environment with books and print;
- encouraging play reading and writing; and
- offering activities that develop visual discrimination, fine motor control, and phonological awareness.

萌芽的
計算活動
1+1=2 という算数
これは少ない、多いという量理解

Emergent numeracy is the understanding of numbers and what they represent. It involves both an understanding of quantity (big and little; two comes before three) and quality (more and less, a little bit, and a lot). Understanding of quantity and numbers begins very early as children explore objects and their properties.

Play is a well-established feature of early childhood education. But the increasing emphasis on accountability in the education system appears to have led to a corresponding decline in the general understanding of the important contribution that high-quality play—especially pretend play—can make to children's literacy, numeracy, and inquiry skills in the early years. A shift from a focus on play during preschool years to a strong emphasis on formal instruction to learn letters and use phonics can limit children's literacy skills as well as their numeracy and inquiry skills (Barnett, Yarosz, Thomas, & Hornbeck, 2006; Frede & Ackerman, 2002; Kraft & Berk, 1998; Ziegler et al., 2004). High-quality play mediated by adults who are play partners able to inject judicious direct instruction into daily play is an effective pedagogy for emergent literacy, numeracy, and science skills.

Inclusion

There likely will be at least one young child with special developmental or learning needs enrolled in the first early childhood program you work in as a student or a graduate. Although the inclusion (also called *integration*) of children began in the mid-1970s, only recently have we seen these programs become common in many communities.

Inclusion means that children with special needs and families in need of extra support or special efforts are accommodated within early childhood programs along with "regular" children. A longitudinal U.K. study found that children with special needs who attended high-quality preschool programs showed benefits in academic achievement and in social/behavioural outcomes at age 11 (Sylva et al., 2009). In addition, research in both Canada and the United States indicates that child care centres that have higher levels of inclusion are associated with higher scores on measures of overall program quality (Buysee, Wesley, Bryant, & Gardner, 1999; Irwin, Lero, & Brophy, 2004).

Successful inclusion is never an accident (City of Toronto, 2007; Lero & Irwin, 2008). Increased education about inclusion and working with children with special needs is necessary at all training levels in early childhood education (Lero, Irwin, & Darisi, 2006).

Early childhood programs that include children with identified special needs also require a supportive funding system. Funding must be sufficient, explicit, and allocated in a timely fashion. Diagnostic assessments need to be made as early as possible. The time when children with special needs transition into early childhood programs from home or early intervention services is a time when supports must be in place to benefit the children and support educators. Designated funding can help maintain inclusion quality and best practices in centres that regularly include a number of children with special needs, while building capacity in centres that have no or very limited experience to date (City of Toronto, 2007). *A partnership for inclusion—Nova Scotia* is an example of an effective program that supports centres and staff to improve program quality and inclusion (Lero, Irwin, & Darisi, 2006).

Benefits have been identified in these programs for all the children involved, both those whose development follows typical patterns and those who require special supports and adaptations. Research shows that children with disabilities in non-segregated settings are able to learn and practise many new skills through imitation of their peers. Children with disabilities demonstrate higher levels of social play and initiate more appropriate social interactions with peers than do children in special education or segregated preschool settings. The gains that children in integrated classrooms make in language, cognitive, and motor-skill development are comparable to those of children in special education classrooms. Therefore, the children are able to take advantage of the activities that promote language, social, motor, and cognitive development while gaining an advantage in levels of play. More realistic expectations are placed on children with special needs who attend the same programs as children with typical abilities. Children with special needs will be perceived as "less different" if they are not excluded from environments with other children and, thus, may be more easily accepted by family, peers, and community.

Children without disabilities also benefit when children with special needs are included in early childhood programs (Irwin, 1995). In addition to making developmental gains equivalent to those that children make in non-inclusive programs, they gain a more realistic view of people with disabilities and develop positive attitudes rather than prejudices toward others who are different from themselves. In inclusive settings, children are able to develop responsive, helpful behaviours and become sensitive to the needs of others.

What has inclusion been like for early childhood educators who have been prepared to work only with children whose development follows typical patterns? Initially ECEs react with caution, fear, or negative responses, wondering whether the placement is wise for the child and fair to all the children. But in two studies (Giangreco and Kontos, reported in Diamond, Hestenes, & O'Connor, 1994), early childhood educators noted that the children had become part of the group, without the disability being identified as their most important characteristic. Those who worked in inclusive classrooms reported they had become more confident and flexible in their teaching, reflecting more on the needs of all the children in their class. Three Canadian studies (Irwin, Lero, & Brophy, 2004) on the inclusion of children with special needs identified multiple factors that contribute to successful inclusion, including

- the director's inclusion leadership—modelling commitment, ensuring staff are supported within the centre, acting as an advocate for inclusion, and marshalling resources to support inclusion efforts;
- staff's attitudes and commitment toward inclusion;
- overall program quality; and
- skilled support staff or in-house resource teachers to enhance ratios.

The support and involvement of resource consultants and a range of specialists are also important to help staff develop skills that allow them to promote the development of children with a wide range of special needs, modify existing curricula, and encourage positive peer interactions among children.

On the other hand, there can be barriers to successful inclusion. One is that there are philosophical and methodological differences between early childhood special education and regular early childhood education. The individualized teaching plans of early special education emphasize skill acquisition, structured use of instructional time, a strong behavioural orientation, and more adult direction than is considered good practice in regular early childhood education.

However, studies have shown that "cooperation, collaboration, and mutual respect between regular and special education early childhood teachers and therapists was an important component of successful integrated programs" (Diamond, Hestenes, & O'Connor, 1994, p. 71). When ECEs have the support of an intervention team that respects their expertise and their educational approaches, most believe that they can meet the needs of the children with disabilities in their classrooms. It is most helpful to successful inclusion if specialists provide intervention work within naturally occurring situations in the classroom setting, rather than disrupting the curriculum and routines; for example, the speech therapist comes in to present a group activity to all the children or to interact conversationally or in a game with small groups during free play time, rather than coming in to remove the young child with special language needs for an individual therapy session. So, too, the physical therapist encourages all the children to try rolling on her giant ball, realizing that the participation of children without physical limitations may encourage the child with cerebral palsy to take part. Besides preventing disruption of the overall program's routine, including all children avoids sending the message to other children that the child is not really a full member of their group. The ECE is more likely to feel supported when the members of the special intervention team share the common framework and goals.

Effective inclusion programs use naturalistic teaching strategies within the context of daily routines. "Activity-based intervention" strategies involve the kinds of teaching we discussed earlier in our considerations of developmentally appropriate practice. When using these strategies, the ECE plans appropriate active learning experiences by taking into account goals for individual children. Thus, a child who is using a variety of fasteners on the dress-up clothes is working on a fine-motor goal, and one who is invited to use the puppets is working on a language goal. Because each child's goals are addressed within the context of daily activities, ECEs have the responsibility of targeting goals, planning materials and activities to further those goals, and regularly assessing progress toward those goals. The planning cycle is part of good practice in every early childhood education setting, no matter what the ability of each participating child. In inclusive settings, ECEs, often with the assistance of other experts, plan modifications in the environment or activity to facilitate involvement of children with special needs.

As early childhood educators understand fully the implications of individualizing programs and curricula, they will see that the inclusion of children with special needs in early childhood settings is simply an extension of this developmentally appropriate practice of individualization. They will be supported in their efforts to help the children with special needs by the active, ongoing involvement of parents, special education teachers and interventionists, and administrators. There has been much learning about inclusion in the past couple of decades. As you enter the profession, your task is to continue learning how to provide education that respects the uniqueness of all children.

Antibias Curriculum

When you first work with young children, you may find yourself working with children and families who look very much like you, having grown up in similar cultural and community settings, and with the same racial heritage, religious beliefs, and historical traditions. However, given the diversity of the Canadian population, it is more probable that your early childhood program will include families with varying structures, including two parents of different genders, two of the same gender, single parents of either gender, and families headed

abuse on 3rct
neglect on 3rct
racial on 3rct
ethnic on 3rct
mental disease on 3rct
delayed

by grandparents, adoptive parents, or foster parents. There will be families of varying income and educational levels. There may be homeless families, families in which children are abused or neglected, and others in which children are well cared for. Families may represent one of any number of the religious, racial, and ethnic groups that live in Canada today. You may also work with children who are learning English as a second language. And, as we have just discussed, you may also work with children whose physical or mental abilities are delayed.

But differences can make people uncomfortable, particularly when those differences seem threatening. Children can feel threatened when no one talks about the reason for the differences they see, or about how similar people are in spite of their differences. This feeling of discomfort is exactly the rationale for discussions in the early education community about the need for an **antibias curriculum** in educating young children. 基本原理

幼児教育 は isolation は存在しない

Early childhood programs do not exist in isolation. They are a product of society and reflect social relations that exist nationally, provincially, regionally, and locally (Daycare Trust, 2007; Robinson & Diaz, 2006). Early childhood programs also reflect the surrounding media and political dialogue. Racial, religious, and ethnic tensions and incidents are often part of the context. Educators can take action to avoid prejudice and to counteract bias when 対抗する it occurs in early childhood settings (MacNaughton, 2006; Siraj-Blatchford, 2006). When educators confront prejudices or biases that emerge as children interact with each other, it is an opportunity to increases the involvement of all children and their families (MacNaughton, 2006).

ECES は 偏見や bias に対抗 する 行動に

子ども が 他人種の子どもとも 交流できるような 環境つくる

Diversity equity inclusion 大事!!

Diversity, equity, and inclusion are prerequisites for learning in early childhood programs. Early childhood programs can be organized to reflect and 前提3/9 respect Canada's ethnocultural and racial diversity. Children grow up with a strong sense of self in environments that support their full participation and promote attitudes, beliefs, and values of equity and democracy (Bennett, 2004). Preconceived notions about children's ethnocultural backgrounds, gender, ability, or socio-economic circumstances create barriers that reduce engagement and equitable outcomes (Bernhard, Freire, & Mulligan, 2004; Centre for Community Child Health, 2008; Robinson & Diaz, 2006).

3rct promote attitudes beliefs values of equity& democracy

To turn belief statements and principles into practice in early childhood programs requires an infrastructure that actively promotes the engagement of all children and their families (Bernhard, Lero, & Greenberg, 2006; Centre for Community Child Health, 2008). Effective strategies begin by identifying the early childhood program needs of families in their communities, and by taking this information into account when planning the curriculum and pedagogy of the program (Ali, 2005; Bernhard, 2003). Curriculum should be applied in the context of how well it enables children's full participation (Bernhard et al., 2006; Bernhard, Lefebvre, Kilbride, Chud, & Lange, 1998; Siraj-Blatchford, 2006).

Early childhood programs can counter racism and stereotypes when educators listen to families and design programs that demonstrate equality, respect, and appreciation for cultures other than one's own—beyond token gestures related to food or celebrations (Ali, 2005; National Research Council 2001; Robinson & Diaz, 2006). Programs can meet the unique cultural or other needs of minority language or new immigrant families.

Very young children are busily constructing their self-identity, as well as attitudes about that identity, by observing the ways they are different from and similar to other people and by absorbing the others' verbal and nonverbal messages about the differences. Young children construct self-identity and attitudes through the interaction of three factors:

1. **Experience with their bodies.** Children are exploring questions about what their bodies look like and how they are different from those of others.
2. **Experience with their social environments.** Children need to know about messages they get, either explicitly or implicitly, about the facts and differences they observe. They need to know about society's evaluation of those differences.
3. **Cognitive functioning.** Young children's methods of thinking produce some confused or illogical conclusions, such as the assumption that genitals or skin colour might be open to change, or that disability is contagious.

In this process of constructing self-identity, children need adults to help them explore some of their questions and curiosity about differences. We know that even very young children can perceive and uncritically absorb the negative messages about diversity in the world, and we know that these messages can be both powerful and harmful in producing bias. Prejudice and bias are destructive forces, and they can hurt all children.

On one hand, struggling against bias that declares a person inferior because of gender, race, ethnicity, or disability undercuts a child's full development. On the other hand, learning to believe they are superior because they are white, or male, or able-bodied, dehumanizes and distorts reality for growing children (Derman-Sparks, 1989, p. ix).

Families come in all sizes and shapes. Early childhood programs can move away from a depiction of traditional, nuclear families as the norm with different family constellations as the "others," to one that recognizes multiple family structures (Shonkoff & Phillips, 2000). Early childhood programs can provide support to all families with awareness of and respect for structural and sexual diversity.

Children growing up with lesbian, gay, bisexual, transgender/transsexual, and queer (LGBTQ) parents are often considered to be "invisible" minorities, although statistics indicate that their numbers are growing across Canada (Janmohamed, 2006). LGBTQ families warrant particular care, consideration, and sensitivity within early childhood programs. Depictions of LGBTQ families within program policies and practices contribute to an environment that includes sexual diversity. Early childhood programs can be proactive in eliminating homophobia and heterosexism (Robinson & Diaz, 2006).

Children need adults who can help them develop positive attitudes about their own identity and that of others. They also need adults who can help them deal with the reality of the world, as well as show them that they can participate in changing ideas from the past to improve their future. The goals of the antibias curriculum are to enable all children "to construct a knowledgeable, confident self-identity; to develop comfortable, empathetic, and just interaction with diversity; and to develop critical thinking and the skills for standing up for oneself and others in the face of injustice" (Derman-Sparks, 1989, p. ix).

Those who see this work as an integral part of what early childhood educators do are quick to explain that the antibias curriculum is an aim and an approach that permeates the existing environment and curriculum, rather than something added on. It is looking at everything ECEs do and say and at the children's interactions and classroom life "through an antibias lens." The attitude of respect for all people that lies behind the antibias attitude is consistent with the sensitivity to individual children and families. Furthermore, cultural diversity and values are declared principles of early childhood education practice. But the thinking behind the antibias curriculum argues that it is important to go beyond respect and create an environment in which children can actively explore questions about disabilities, gender, and race, in order to understand differences, appreciate similarities, and recognize and confront biased ideas and behaviours. One educator expresses this concept in this way:

> As an educator in a community college environment, I encourage students to challenge their understanding of the norm. In class discussions when I raise various forms of discrimination or prejudice, students often respond by talking about the importance of helping children 'get along' and learning to accept all people regardless of difference.…
> I challenge their common perceptions of people living on the street, new refugees, or gays and lesbians.… In order for [ECE] students to articulate and understand systemic barriers, it is the responsibility of educators to create opportunities for transformation … (Janmohomed, 2001, p. 20–22).

In other reading, you will likely come across the term "**multicultural curriculum**." This refers to teaching children about other people's cultures, in the hope that they will learn to respect one another and not develop prejudice. The intent of this approach is positive and is obviously similar to the antibias approach, but those who practise the antibias curriculum suggest that the multicultural approach too frequently deteriorates into a "tourist curriculum" (Derman-Sparks, 1989, p. 7). This negative outcome results from presenting other cultures as exotic and foreign, with different food, holiday celebrations, clothing, and so on, rather than dealing with people's real-life experiences. "Children 'visit' non-White cultures, and then 'go home' to the daily classroom, which reflects only the dominant culture" (Derman-Sparks, 1989, p. 7). The danger here is that such experiences fail to communicate real understanding, and stereotypes about differences may actually be reinforced. In addition, the multicultural curriculum usually focuses on other countries, rather than on the diverse people in our own country whom children actually come in contact with.

The antibias approach tries to avoid some of the dangers of this tourist approach to multiculturalism. It retains some of the positive ideas from the multicultural curriculum and, at the same time, includes more than just cultural diversity. An antibias curriculum addresses ability, age, and gender differences, as well as the problem of stereotypical or biased behaviour in children's interactions.

There are those who feel that it is beyond the capacity of young children to absorb these concepts. Yet others feel that young children are themselves interested in questions about diversity, and that they may exhibit fearful or prejudiced behaviour when they are not encouraged to understand differences in a positive way.

How do early childhood educators prepare themselves to deal with antibias issues with young children? A first and ongoing step is to confront their own attitudes and discomforts, to become aware of how their own identities and attitudes were formed by early experiences. This is a process that may bring pain as well as awareness, but it helps early childhood educators identify their own prejudices, which need to be uncovered before they will be able to do antibias work with children.

Early childhood educators then examine their environments, materials, and curriculum activities to find and eliminate stereotypical messages, and to answer the question "What am I currently doing in the curriculum about gender/race/culture/different physical abilities/stereotyping and discriminatory behaviour?" They observe the children and discover the issues in the community that affect the children's lives, as well as learning the family and community resources for specific antibias activities. ECEs watch for opportunities when children's spoken and unspoken questions show that they need help to understand differences or to be supported in confronting unfair treatment.

Such examinations help early childhood educators discover the steps they will take to slowly make their classrooms into environments where diversity is accepted, and where children know they can explore these important issues with supportive adults. Early childhood educators and parents can work together to explore how to handle sensitive and emotional issues, such as how to celebrate holidays, which holidays to celebrate, or whether holidays should be celebrated at all in early education programs.

These are deeply felt concerns, and it is through dialogue that adults support one another to help children develop healthy self-identity and attitudes of acceptance of diversity. As Canada's diversity grows, children will be empowered and enriched to interact comfortably with those whose lives, appearance, and experiences are unlike their own. Issues raised in the discussion of multicultural and antibias education free all early childhood educators to find new and positive answers. Involve yourself in these dialogues in later reading, course work, and experiences. We will all benefit.

Aboriginal Culture and Communities 先住民の文化&コミュニティ

Effective Aboriginal early childhood programs are generated by Aboriginal communities. (Aboriginal communities include First Nations, Inuit, Métis, and non-status Aboriginal peoples.) Both Aboriginal and non-Aboriginal early childhood settings require programming that values Aboriginal languages and culture and is generated from the community rather than imposed on it. Traditional approaches to measuring successful learning for Aboriginal children have focused on the classroom and have not sufficiently reflected knowledge acquired through experiential learning, including learning from Elders, traditions, ceremonies, family, and the workplace (Ball, 2008; Canadian Council on Learning, 2007; Fearne, 2006).

Aboriginal early childhood programs that are built on the culture of families and the community and controlled by First Nations contribute to the preservation of First Nations' culture (Greenwood, 2006; Native Council of

Canada, 2001). Aboriginal and non-Aboriginal early childhood settings require programming that values Aboriginal languages and culture, programming that is generated from the community rather than imposed on it.

Aboriginal early childhood educators face numerous challenges in designing curriculum. The legacy of residential schools, when children were removed from their parents and placed in institutions, continues to haunt Aboriginal communities (Canadian Institute of Health Information & Canadian Population Health Initiative, 2004; Greenwood, 2001). There are few resources to guide culturally appropriate learning for Aboriginal children (Greenwood, 2001, 2006). Only one-quarter of Aboriginal peoples reported that they had enough knowledge of an Aboriginal language to carry on a conversation (Statistics Canada, 2006). Among children, only 16 percent spoke an Aboriginal language in 2001, down seven percentage points from 1996 (Canadian Council on Learning, 2007). Several reports from Aboriginal organizations highlight the need to honestly acknowledge the history of Aboriginal and non-Aboriginal relationships since European colonization and to respect different perspectives among Aboriginal communities as well as those between Aboriginal and non-Aboriginal communities (Blackstock, Bruyere, & Moreau, 2008).

Non-Aboriginal early childhood programs need staff and curriculum that respectfully incorporate Aboriginal cultures (Ball, 2008; OECD, 2004). The Organisation for Economic Co-operation and Development (OECD) thematic review team noted that, while policy and program goals identified cultural sensitivity, there was little evidence this was practised (OECD, 2004). Australia shares a similar history of British and European colonization of indigenous peoples. Australian researchers (MacNaughton & Davis, 2001) have investigated young children's understanding of indigenous Australians and report that knowledge about Aboriginal peoples was based on past cultural, often exotic, practices. Several research studies suggest early childhood programs can avoid homogenizing Aboriginal peoples into a collective "they" and avoid building knowledge of Aboriginals that positions them as different from the mainstream (MacNaughton & Davis, 2001). In Aboriginal communities, the Elders' understanding of the needs of children and families is incorporated into the curriculum. Children learn their indigenous language and culture.

One successful program was developed through a collaborative partnership between the School of Child and Youth Care at the University of Victoria and the Meadow Lake Tribal Council in Saskatchewan. This partnership developed the generative curriculum for early childhood education (Ball, 2005; Pence, 2005). It is an approach consistent with contemporary and traditional indigenous values, experiences, and goals, while incorporating a sampling of child development research, theory, and practices. A generative curriculum draws as much as possible on the learner's experiences. It prepares early childhood educators to respect the cultures, wisdom, and values of families and communities.

English or French Language Learners

For many children, participation an early childhood education program involves negotiating a new language or unfamiliar cultural experiences. Early childhood educators can make a big difference in raising the comfort level of these children and developing their capacity to become engaged learners. They cultivate relationships when they respond to children's multiple languages as strengths and gifts brought to the group. Across Canada, newcomer children are entering early childhood education programs with a home language that is not English or French. They are, in fact, emergent bilinguals who bring their home language and literacy skills with them (Chumak-Horbatsch, 2012).

Children learning English or French as an additional language benefit when their first language is valued (Ball, 2010; Centre for the Study of Child Care Employment, 2008; Chumak-Horbatsch, 2004, 2012; Hernandez, Denton, & Macartney, 2008; Tabors & Snow, 2001). In order to be able to determine a child's capacity to learn, the child needs adequate opportunities to learn in a language she or he can understand (Tabors & Snow, 2001). Children learning an additional language need to continue to learn vocabulary and conceptual skills in their home language, because without this continued development they will have greater difficulty developing skills in the second language (Office of Head Start, 2008; Tabors & Snow, 1994).

Many children whose home language is not English or French are well positioned to become bilingual (Hernandez, Denton, & Macartney, 2008). Research indicates that children who learn English or French after their home language is established (around age three) are able to acquire full English/French fluency during their preschool and early school years (Office of Head Start, 2008). The bilingual skill leads to long-term cognitive, social, and economic advantages (Hernandez, Denton, & Macartney, 2008).

Many early childhood education programs in Canada will include children and families with multiple home languages. A variety of specific strategies, sometimes called linguistically appropriate practice (LAP) (Chumak-Horbatsch, 2012), can support English/French language learners and educators working with multiple home languages. These learners may need differentiated learning opportunities to benefit fully from early childhood programs (Shonkoff & Phillips, 2000; Siraj-Blatchford et al., 2003). A dual-language approach to teaching can be effective for English/French language learners, and can benefit native English/French speakers (Espinosa, 2007, 2008). Children who are have learned one language—either English or French—can benefit from exposure to another language and can learn ways to communicate that accommodate language barriers. Interpreters can increase the level of effective communication with parents (Office of Head Start, 2008).

TECHNOLOGY IN EARLY CHILDHOOD EDUCATION

Young children today are growing up surrounded by screens: smartphones, iPads, computers, and television. Television and computers have extended their target audience programming down to infancy. Media **technology** is part of daily life for Canadian children in the 21st century. Some programs are specifically designed to appeal to babies and toddlers, and a myriad of others are targeted to preschoolers. While television used to dominate children's media technology, the past decade has witnessed a plethora of new electronic media geared to children—applications for electronic devices, video games, learning activities using electronic technology, and cellphones.

What about the impact of screen time, time children spend with television, videos, electronic games, and computer technology? Parents, educators, and researchers are divided in their opinions about the potential benefits and harm of technology on children's learning and well-being. A central concern is what children are *not* doing—*not* being physically active and *not* interacting with friends—when they are spending so many hours on screens. The Canadian Paediatric Society recommends no screen time for children younger than 2 years, no more than 1 hour for children 2 to 4 years old, and no more than 2 hours of screen time for children over 5 years (Canadian Paediatric Society, 2012). Researchers agree that exposure to television or other electronic media before age two is not beneficial to long-term cognitive, social, or emotional development (Brooks-Gunn & Donahue, 2008).

Most of the research behind the screen time recommendations such as those from the Canadian Paediatric Society is based on research related to television watching. A Quebec longitudinal study found that television exposure at age 2 forecasts negative consequences for children, ranging from poor school adjustment to unhealthy habits (Pagani, Fitzpatrick, Barnett, & Dubow, 2010). Television watching is consistently associated with more sedentary hours and less physical activity.

On the other hand, higher television viewing has been associated with higher literacy achievement in preschoolers from families of low socio-economic status, although this association was not found for children who are advantaged (Searls, Mead, & Ward, 1985).

Others argue that interactive screens such as learning activities on iPads and other electronic games are different than television (Woolridge, 2014). When children, even very young children, are offered interactive screens, they are not passive. They are responsive to what is happening on the screen and they take initiative. Games can be designed to offer opportunities to practise emerging literacy and numeracy skills, to improve attention, and to reduce impulsive responses.

Although interactive media permeate children's lives, their effects are not well understood or well-researched (Cleveland, Corter, Pelletier, Colley, Bertrand, & Jamieson, 2006). Empirical research on the effects of interactive media on young children is still thin; at the same time, technology continues to evolve and pervade children's lives. As the pace of technological change quickens, descriptive studies of young children and technology context are likely to be outdated in a matter of a few years.

Research findings reveal that the actual content of electronic technology is critical to how media influence children (Brooks-Gunn & Donahue, 2008). From more than 50 years of television research, we know that content is significant. In other words, children learn from high-quality television programs, but they do not benefit particularly from solely entertainment content; and they may be harmed by violent content (Houston, 2004). There has been much concern about the negative impact of violence and other inappropriate content in screen media. The literature shows a positive link between violent interactive media, such as video games, and aggressive behaviour (Anderson & Bushman, 2001). It also demonstrates that there is an increase in effectors over time; that is, the games are becoming more violent and they are affecting children more (Anderson & Bushman, 2001; Sherry 2001).

Research on interactivity and learning is mixed. The nature of interactivity itself is not well understood, nor are the specific aspects of interactivity that support learning. Research on the effects of *talking books* on literacy in young children is also mixed. In a 2003 study, while some aspects of literacy seemed to be supported (phonological awareness), others (word reading) were not (Chera & Wood, 2003). Young children are attracted to the interactive elements in talking books, but this can interfere with their interest in decoding text and understanding of the story (deJong & Bus, 2002).

What about having computers or iPads in early childhood education settings? While adults may be struggling to keep up and feel comfortable with technology, young children accept it as a normal part of their environment. Observers note that children are quite comfortable with computers and iPads, exhibiting curiosity rather than fear when given a new software program. Children have increased opportunities for social interaction, since many prefer to work with one or two partners rather than alone, and will more often request help from peers than from the early childhood educator.

Early childhood educators are coming to terms with the idea that technology can be an effective and interesting additional choice in the early childhood education curriculum. Indeed, sometimes it is their own "technophobia" that causes early childhood educators to dismiss computers so abruptly. In fact, research and observation of children using computers suggests that computers offer children another way to play, enhancing social, emotional, and cognitive development. Computers in early childhood education settings can support ideas of child-centred practice and nurture overall child development. They can be used as a social activity that invites two children to work together to take turns or experiment or solve a problem. Computers should not be the only engaging activity, but one of many options. Most importantly, computers should not diminish the amount of time that children are physically active.

Early childhood educators are using electronic technology to record their observations of children's learning. The rapid introduction of user-friendly and affordable digital cameras, printers, and computers has opened up extraordinary opportunities for young children to become active participants in the process, documenting their own learning (Lee & Carr, 2002).

Summary

- The early childhood education curriculum is about time, space, people, and what children do each day in an early childhood program. Theories and knowledge about child development provide ideas about how best to structure the curriculum.
- Theories about childhood build on values and beliefs and shape an early childhood

education program's philosophy, pedagogy, and curriculum.
- A variety of educator-guided and child-directed approaches are used in early childhood programs.
- Concerns regarding early academics include the need to balance the desire to improve children's readiness for school learning

with the recognition of play as a central pedagogical strategy.

- Inclusion (also called *integration)* programs have become common in most communities and seek to include all children's full participation.
- An antibias curriculum balances the needs of individual children and families with those of the group.

- Children in mixed-age groupings benefit from relationships with one another. Older children have opportunities to assume responsibility and to exhibit leadership skills with younger children.
- Young children are growing up in a landscape of interactive media, and researchers do not fully understand the long-term effects. The actual content and its appropriateness for children is an important element.

REVIEW QUESTIONS

1. Describe different types of approaches to the early childhood education curriculum.
2. Describe some of the issues related to early academics and school readiness.
3. Discuss what is meant by "inclusion." List the benefits for the children and adults who are part of integrated early education classrooms.
4. Describe what is meant by an antibias curriculum and the rationale for it. How does an antibias approach differ from a multicultural approach?
5. What is meant by "mixed-age groupings" in early education? List some of the advantages for children and adults.
6. Describe current thinking about the appropriateness of using technology in the classroom in early education.

STUDY ACTIVITIES

1. Visit an early childhood program that is implementing a specific curriculum approach.
2. Use your favourite search engine to search for information about the Reggio Emilia approach.
3. Visit the websites given on pages 59–61 for provincial curriculum frameworks for early childhood programs.
4. Visit an early childhood education setting in your community that includes young children with special learning or developmental needs. Discuss with the early childhood educators the advantages and disadvantages for the children and adults involved. Describe any obvious modifications that have been made in the physical environment to meet the needs of the children, and explain why these alterations were made. List any other specialists involved in planning and therapy for the children.
5. Go to the library and find several books that an early childhood educator might use to help raise children's awareness and positive acceptance of diversity in various forms. Share these books with fellow classmates. There is a helpful list in Derman-Sparks (1989) to get you started.
6. Investigate whether your community has any mixed-age groupings in early childhood education programs or in the school system. If so, try to visit a program or a class to observe the children's interactions and the differences in learning environment and curriculum that distinguish the programs.
7. Try to observe young children using computers—perhaps in the children's section of your local library or in a large bookstore. How does the software encourage creativity, logical thinking and problem-solving, social interaction, and independence? What questions about technology does this observation suggest to you for further study?
8. How many languages are spoken by students in your class? Share your childhood experiences. Brainstorm with each other about how this resource could be used in your community.

9. Dr. Janette Pelletier from the Eric Institute of Child Study at OISE, University of Toronto, points out that dramatic play is a natural context for children's language development. She also notes that children acquire a sense of narrative that contributes to reading comprehension. Read Pelletier's article and find out more about dramatic play and language development: Pelletier, J. (2011, October). *What works? Research into practice: Supporting early language and literacy.* Toronto, ON: Literacy and Numeracy Secretariat, Minister of Education. [http://www.edu.gov.on.ca/eng/literacynumeracy/inspire/research/WW_Early_Language.pdf]

KEY TERMS

absorbent mind: Phrase used by Montessori to describe the active, natural learning style of children in their first years.

antibias curriculum: Philosophical approach developed by Louise Derman-Sparks according to which classroom practices and materials are to be used that foster each child's (1) construction of a knowledgeable, confident self-identity; (2) comfortable, empathetic interactions with diverse people; (3) critical thinking about bias; and (4) ability to stand up for him- or herself and others in the face of bias.

co-operative learning: Learning in which environments and activities are structured so that children can work together.

curriculum: Every learning experience that happens in an early childhood setting, including planned and spontaneous activities and interactions.

developmental indicators: Fifty-eight components organized into eight content areas of the HighScope curriculum.

developmentally appropriate practice (DAP): NAEYC-defined standards that base teaching practices on age-level standards for young children's abilities and on observations for individual differences, including abilities, interests, and cultures.

didactic: Usually refers to materials that teach because they are inherently self-correcting. Montessori developed many didactic materials.

direct instruction: A pedagogical strategy that is initiated by adults and focuses on a specific learning objective to be mastered by the child.

early academics: The introduction of academic content and teaching methods to children before the primary grades.

emergent curriculum: Early childhood educators follow a child's lead by observing his or her interests and needs and then planning the learning environment.

emergent literacy: Awareness of the meaning of print that develops before early reading and writing.

emergent numeracy: Awareness of the meaning of numbers that precedes ability to use numbers in simple computations.

HighScope: Curriculum based on Piagetian cognitive principles, developed after the Perry study model.

inclusion: Placement of individuals with special needs in classrooms with typically developing individuals; special services are provided within the classroom setting.

mixed-age groupings: Arrangements that group children together across several ages and frequently keep them together for two or more years, rather than separating them by chronological age.

Montessori schools: Schools that are based on the philosophy of Maria Montessori; they emphasize sensory learning, practical life skills, and didactic materials.

motor skills: Deliberate movement that involves the brain, the nervous system, and muscles working together.

multicultural curriculum: Curriculum that teaches awareness of the diversity of cultures and of cultural experience.

pedagogy: Deliberate process of cultivating development and learning; closely linked to curriculum.

perceptual–motor: Coordination of sensory and motor skills such as eye–hand coordination.

philosophy: One's beliefs and attitude. Related to early childhood education, one's ideas about how children learn, and how early childhood educators teach.

plan, do, review: Basic methods of the HighScope cognitive curriculum, in which children make activity choices with teachers' assistance, and then carry out the activity and report on it.

practical life skills: Skills used in daily life, such as washing dishes and sweeping floors. Part of the Montessori curriculum.

Reggio Emilia: Early childhood programs in Reggio Emilia, Italy, that are world-famous for their child-centred and extensive project approach to learning.

scaffolding: Process of providing guidance that allows a child to master a concept or skill that he or she could not yet learn alone but can learn with support.

school readiness: State of being ready to attend school. Used in early childhood education, the term indicates a child's ability to learn particular tasks. Readiness tests are frequently used to determine readiness for kindergarten and/or Grade 1 academic learning.

self-regulation: Regulation of one's attention, emotion, and behaviour.

sensitive period: Term used by Montessori to indicate time of readiness for particular learning.

sequential steps: Predictable patterns of development and learning.

special education: Branch of professional study that centres on techniques for working with children with special needs.

technology: Today's electronics-based machines, particularly computers, and the knowledge that drives them.

theory of mind: The ability to attribute thoughts and mental states to oneself and to others.

Suggested Readings

Brennerman, K., Stevenson-Boyd, J., & Frede, E. (2009, March). Math and science in preschool: Policies and practice. In E. Frede & S. Barnett (Eds.), *Preschool Policy Brief, 19.*

Chiarotto, L. (2011) *Building children's understanding of the world through environmental inquiry: A resource for teachers.* Toronto, ON: The Eric Jackman Institute of Child Study, OISE, University of Toronto.

Chumak-Hortbatsch, R. (2012). *Linguistically appropriate practice: A guide for working with immigrant children.* Toronto, ON: University of Toronto Press, Higher Education Division.

Corson, P. (2005). Multi-age grouping in early childhood education: An alternative discourse. *Research Connections Canada, 13,* 93–108.

Lero, D., Irwin, S., & Darisi, T. K. (2006). *Partnerships for inclusion—Nova Scotia: An evaluation based on the first cohort of child care centres.* Guelph, ON: Centre for Families, Work and Well-Being.

McCuaig, K. (2014). *Review of early learning frameworks in Canada*. Toronto, ON: Atkinson Centre, OISE, University of Toronto. http://www.oise.utoronto.ca/atkinson/UserFiles/File/Resources_Topics/Resources_Topics_CurriculumPedagogy/Review_of_Early_Learning_Frameworks_in_Canada-all.pdf

Pacini-Ketchabaw, V., & McIvor, O. (2005). Negotiating bilingualism in early childhood—A study of immigrant families and early childhood practitioners. *Research Connections Canada: Supporting Children and Families, 13*, 109–126.

Shanker, S. (2012). *Calm, alert and learning: Classroom strategies for self-regulation*. Toronto, ON: Pearson.

SpecialLink Newsletters from SpecialLink: The National Child Care Inclusion Network, P.O. Box 775, Sydney, NS B1P 6G9.

Wartella, E., Caplovitz, A., & Lee, J. (2004). From Einstein to Leapfrog, from Doom to the Sims, from instant messaging to Internet chat rooms. *Social Policy Report XVIII* (IV). Society for Research in Child Development.

CHAPTER 3

QUALITY IN EARLY CHILDHOOD EDUCATION PROGRAMS

OBJECTIVES

After studying this chapter, students will be able to
- discuss several specific components of quality in early childhood education programs
- describe specific program and policy decisions that exemplify each component
- identify dynamic, framework, and context components of quality programs
- identify several components that are not found in quality programs

Quality in early childhood settings takes many forms and has unique faces. Yet specific descriptions can be applied no matter what the age group or population served or the structure of the program. It might seem a daunting task to describe and recognize factors that denote quality in early childhood programs. Indeed, it is a task that researchers, scholars, and commissions have laboured over for years, and their combined efforts still precipitate spirited debate. To some extent, the difficulty is that quality is often defined subjectively. If you have visited sites of early child development programs, you have likely been attracted to (or dismayed by) some space in the room or some activity that resonated with meaning for you, often for subconscious reasons.

But standards for quality must go beyond subjective opinion, to find their basis in concrete and observable phenomena that can be discussed and explained. In this chapter, we will explore some of the specific components of quality in early education and describe how these components may manifest themselves. You will be asked to actively consider each component as we move through the discussion, to help you as you begin to construct your own standards of quality in early education. In later course work, you will learn more about how early childhood educators create environments that allow excellent education to occur; for now, it is important that you begin to evaluate child care and learning environments.

THINKING ABOUT QUALITY

High-quality early childhood education can be defined from many perspectives, including those of children, parents, early childhood educators, researchers, employers, and the community. When parents are asked to describe what they are looking for in a program for their children, they often list health and safety as their primary concerns. In a U.S. study of quality in family child care and relative care (care by relatives other than parents), both mothers and caregivers identified health and safety as prime concerns, as well as communication with the family child care provider and the provider's warmth and attention to the child (Galinsky, Howes, Kontos, & Shinn, 1994). ECEs, on the other hand, are likely to define a high-quality program as one that

- "supports and assists the child's physical, emotional, social, language, and intellectual development"; and
- "supports and complements the family in its child-rearing role" (Doherty-Derkowski, 1995, p. 4).

Katz (1993) directs us to consider five different but interrelated perspectives as we consider quality in an early childhood program. The perspectives she describes are those of experts, children participating in early childhood settings, parents who are using early child development services for their children, ECEs and other caregivers who work directly with young children to provide early child development programs, and the community or society at large.

1. The expert perspective is a *top-down* perspective that examines measurable and quantifiable characteristics, such as adult–child ratios and training of ECEs, which set the stage for excellent early childhood education to occur. Many of these things are defined and regulation requirements discussed in this and later chapters. It is important to recognize the correlation between these factors and quality.

2. The children's perspective is a *bottom-up* perspective that describes the quality of life experienced by children within the program. This perspective is obtained when adults take children's point of view; propose whether program practices would help children feel individually welcomed and securely accepted within a program; and find engaging, challenging, and absorbing learning experiences. As we think about stories of children in various early child development programs, we draw conclusions about how those settings would affect children's lives.

3. The viewpoint of staff members (ECEs and others) is the *inside* perspective. Job satisfaction and retention of qualified personnel over time have a major impact on quality. As we consider the components of quality, think about how ECEs would perceive their work if these components were either present or absent.

4. The parents' perspective, or the *outside-inside* perspective, considers the quality and impact of relationships between ECEs and families. The elements that are crucial from the perspective of parents are mutual respect and relationships that allow ECEs to create caring and learning environments that are individually responsive to children.

5. The community or society perspective is the *outside* perspective; it describes the relationship between the early childhood program and its community and the larger society beyond. As programs respond to community needs and expectations, and as social decisions and support mesh, good things can happen for children and families.

ECEs need to be aware of the complex **interrelationships** of all participants when considering quality. There are differences in what is important in quality early child development programs and questions of when one view should be given more weight than another. The values and beliefs that shape perceptions of quality vary in different cultural contexts.

Gillian Doherty (2000) reviewed the "reality of multiple perspectives" on quality and suggests that the level of quality in a particular early child development program depends on who is making the judgement. Doherty states that it is important to recognize that there are different perspectives and to move away from a judgement of quality that is defined by experts only, without the input of other stakeholders. She concludes that "there appears to be agreement that there are some values that are so critical to the well-being of children that they should be a core part of any definition of quality" (p. 4). These values are

- safe care,
- healthful care,
- individualized care that promotes equal opportunity,
- care that provides developmentally appropriate stimulation,
- care that is characterized by positive interaction with adults,
- care that encourages individual emotional growth, and
- care that promotes positive relationships with other children.

Doherty cautions us to keep in mind that there are many ways to support these universal values. Our responses can and should vary to reflect our own cultural realities and those of the children and families we work with in early childhood settings. "Understanding and ensuring quality involves a continuous process of reconciling the perspectives of different stakeholders within the broader context of universal values. It is not a prescriptive exercise" (Doherty, 2000, p. 5).

Be aware of your own perspective on what is essential in a high-quality early child development program as you consider the research on this subject. Your perspective may be challenged or reinforced. Your ideas about quality will most likely change as your knowledge and skills broaden. Pay attention and be aware of the changes (Doherty, 2000).

▶ Sensitivity to children's interests, worries, and passions is central to a definition of quality early childhood program environments.

Hongqi Zhang/iStock/Thinkstock

1650   1700   1750   1800

A Bird's-Eye View of Quality

Let's look at several early childhood education programs to see if our quick glance can yield first clues about quality.

Robin's community child care centre.   Robin Ferguson, a 32-year-old mother of two school-age children and a three-year-old, is an early childhood educator in a child care centre located in a small village. The centre has mixed-age groupings, with a total enrolment of 15 children with 3 ECEs. Her group includes her own preschooler, along with another three-year-old, one two-year-old, and eight-month-old twins. She has cared for children at home since her older two were babies.

This morning finds the three-year-olds busy in a playroom that adjoins the large kitchen shared by all in the centre. One of them is playing with baby dolls in an area with child-sized kitchen furniture, and one is stringing beads and spools. The child with the beads wanders into the kitchen, where Robin is feeding breakfast to one of the babies, while the other infant sits near her on the floor, fitting cups into each other.

Robin helps the bead-stringer tie the beads into a necklace. When he tries to slip the necklace onto the baby on the floor, who protests weakly, Robin redirects him in a conversation admiring the beads, and then changes the topic to the bird feeder on the deck that they filled the day before. The baby on the floor is still unhappy, and Robin gently talks with her as she continues to feed the baby's brother. When this does not soothe her, Robin puts out some Cheerios for the baby she had been feeding in the highchair, rolls the highchair to the doorway, where she can keep an eye on that baby, and scoops up the crying baby. She takes her to the changing table in the family room, commenting to the child playing with the doll that she has to change the baby, and wonders if she has to change her baby, too. She keeps her eyes on the baby's face as she changes the diaper, although her soft conversation includes the older child, as well as the other older child, who has wandered into the room. At Robin's suggestion, he comes over to join her as she sings to the baby, who is now grinning cheerfully.

Sam Cooper's K/1 classroom.   Sam Cooper teaches in a class that includes children who are five to seven years old in a public elementary school. During the few minutes we are in his large, attractive classroom, we see a number of groups, containing three to five children, busy in several areas in the classroom. Three children are talking to one another as they puzzle over a computer game. Four boys are sitting at a round table, busy with notebooks, crayons, pencils, and markers. One boy explains to us that they are writing in their

1889

Hester How allows students to bring siblings to school to reduce student absenteeism.

Fourteen kindergartens are in operation in Toronto schools, with a total enrolment of 981 children.

A kindergarten association is established. It later became the Toronto Early Childhood Association.

1890

William James publishes the first psychology textbook, *Principles of Psychology*, in which he describes the world of the infant as "blooming, buzzing confusion."

1850   1900   1950   2000

journals. Sam arrives at the round table and responds to one child's comment about his work with a specific and enthusiastic response that indicates his familiarity with the child's story. He encourages the child to share his idea with another, and he suggests to a third child that his friend might help him figure out the spelling for the word he asked about.

Sam's glance searches the room, and he moves over to two girls who are in heated discussion about balancing objects on the scale. Sam does not interrupt, listening seriously to each contribution, nodding thoughtfully and supportively, then asking a question. As the girls seem to move into co-operative activity, Sam looks around at other busy children. He notices a child standing by the bookshelf, moves over to discuss his selection, and speaks with him quietly, finally leaving him after giving him a pat on the back and a smile. A child and an adult enter the classroom. Sam moves over to greet them both, and he engages in relaxed conversation with the parent, who seems equally relaxed with Sam. Sam gives the children a prearranged signal to gather at the meeting carpet; the parent has been invited in advance to conduct a mini-lesson about American Sign Language, since the children are interested right now in different methods of communication.

Maia Chen's toddlers.   Maia Chen is one of two early childhood educators for a group of ten children aged 14 months to 24 months in a church-sponsored child care centre in a large city. We find Maia, her colleague, and the children playing outdoors. Their usual playground equipment includes a climber, a low slide, a large sand area, and three small swings. Maia has added several large, sturdy cartons. Four of the toddlers have climbed into the biggest box; Maia sits near them, commenting on their activity. "You climbed right in the big box, didn't you, Justin? Sarah's in the box with you. Oh my, here comes DuJawn; he's climbing in with you. D.H. thinks there's room too—maybe if you scoot over a bit. Look at that—four children in the box. And jumping, too. It's a jumping box." The children laugh with excitement, and Maia joins in. A shriek from the sandbox gets her immediate attention. "Oh, Derek, that looks uncomfortable. I think Jennifer's trying to tell you that you're crowding her," she says as one toddler attempts to sit where another child is already sitting. "How about we find a space for you to dig over here? There—now you both can make big holes. Let me see—oh, that hole is getting big." Meanwhile, Maia's colleague is pushing three children on the swing, and another child climbs repeatedly up the steps and slides down the slide, never far from Maia's gaze and encouraging smile. Maia reaches into her pocket and pulls out a notebook, in which she jots down two words recording a brief observation that she will expand later. Then she turns to the children who are now pushing the boxes around the playground.

Three early childhood programs, three early childhood educators—all serve to illustrate some of the components of excellence. Some fundamental concepts lie behind the practice of each of these early childhood educators. Think about it: What has each educator done that seems excellent to you?

Defining Quality for Early Childhood Educators

Standards for quality early childhood programs have been defined by several professional organizations. These are important resources with which to become familiar as you learn more about early education.

Now we will examine the components of quality in the vignettes just described. These same components will be found in any excellent early childhood program; they are supported by research and consensus among early childhood educators.

Dynamic components. These are the child's daily experiences that are based on the dynamic and interactive relationships that children develop with adults and other children. Dynamic components define the nature of the interactions and activities that ECEs, children, and their families engage in each day. For example, think about Maria's comments with the toddlers in the big box.

Framework components. These are the structural elements that define the social and physical environment in early childhood programs: the number of children, the kind of physical space, the types of play materials and activities available, and the level of knowledge and understanding ECEs have of child development. Framework components are important because they influence the quality of the dynamic components. The actual practice of ECEs can benefit or suffer depending on the framework. An example of a successful framework would be the mixed-age grouping in the community child care centre.

Context components. These are elements outside the immediate early childhood program environment that influence both the framework and the dynamic components of quality. Organizational climate, funding that determines wages and benefits, regulations, and sponsorship, create the structure of the social and physical environment. In turn, they also set the stage for how ECEs relate and connect with children and their families. Sam's classroom, for example, is part of a public school system with policies and practices that will impact on how his program is organized.

In quality programs, these components are interrelated and, sometimes, indefinable as separate entities. But we shall try to identify them individually. As we go through this chapter, keep your pencil and notebook handy. You will be asked to think about your own knowledge and experience with the components of quality. Take your time to see what you already know about good early childhood programs.

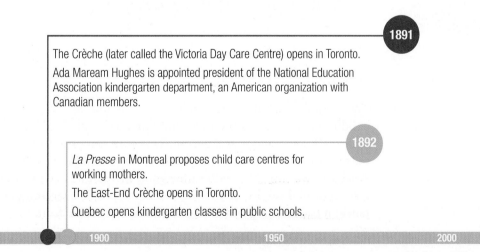

1891

The Crèche (later called the Victoria Day Care Centre) opens in Toronto.

Ada Maream Hughes is appointed president of the National Education Association kindergarten department, an American organization with Canadian members.

1892

La Presse in Montreal proposes child care centres for working mothers.

The East-End Crèche opens in Toronto.

Quebec opens kindergarten classes in public schools.

1850   1900   1950   2000

Quality in Canadian Early Childhood Education and Care Programs

Recent research findings confirm that the quality of children's early environments influences their developmental trajectories. Increased awareness about the importance of the early years puts under a bright spotlight the question of the quality of early childhood programs in general and child care in particular (Beach & Bertrand, 2000; McCain, Mustard, & McQuaig, 2011; NICHD, 2000; OECD, 2001, 2006). While family environments have a larger impact on child development, experiences in child care and other early childhood experiences do affect developmental outcomes as well as immediate and long-term coping skills and competencies (Beach et al., 2004; Brooks-Gunn, 2003; Cleveland & Krashinsky, 1998; Doherty, 2000; NICHD, 2000; Smart Start Evaluation Team, 2003; Sure Start Research Team, 2005).

Findings from Canadian studies are not encouraging. Reports indicate that Canada's child care programs range from programs that support optimal early child development to ones that offer mediocre, custodial services to meet children's basic physical needs.

- The You Bet I Care! (YBIC) Canadian study of child care staff and quality in child care centres used standardized measures of quality to assess 122 infant–toddler rooms and 227 preschool rooms in 234 centres across six provinces and one territory (Goelman, Doherty, Lero, LaGrange, & Tougas, 2000). They assessed curriculum, environment, adult–child interactions, teaching practices, and available supports for improvements to the quality of programs. The findings revealed that the majority of centres provided physically safe environments with caring adults, but only 44.3 percent of preschool rooms and 28.7 percent of toddler and infant rooms offered activities and adult interactions that enhanced early learning.
- The You Bet I Care! study of regulated family child care (Doherty, Lero, Goelman, Tougas, & LaGrange, 2000) collected data from 231 regulated family child caregivers across six provinces and one territory. Similarly to child care centre staff, family child caregivers typically provided physically safe environments with caring staff, but only 36.8 percent provided stimulating activities. The quality tended to be lower for infants under 18 months.
- An international team of early childhood experts reviewed early childhood education and care programs in six provinces in 2003 (OECD, 2004). They reported that quality in Canada's child care programs was decidedly inadequate. However, the review also pointed to some exemplary quality practices and programs in child care and other early childhood programs.
- A study of Quebec-regulated child care settings in 2003 (home-based and centre-based) reported that, overall, 26 percent were good-quality, 61 percent were mediocre, and 13 percent were poor-quality (Japel & Tremblay, 2005).

DYNAMICS OF QUALITY

The central element in the dynamics, or the interactive component, of early childhood programs is the early childhood educator and what he or she believes, knows, and is as a person. This is an important idea to state at the outset, because all of the dimensions in early childhood settings radiate from this basic premise. No matter how good the administration, the education system or philosophy, or the community support, everything of crucial importance in the learning and caring environment comes from the decisions and

1650   1700   1750   1800

actions of the ECE. Some of these components are based in attitudes, values, and ideas, and some are based in areas of knowledge. But *all* translate into specific actions the ECE takes that have far-reaching implications for everyone involved. What an astonishing, humbling thought for all of us drawn to consider caring for and educating young children!

The basic components, which we will discuss separately, include the three R's: **respect** for the uniqueness of individuals, **responsiveness** to children and families, and **reciprocity** of learning interaction. 個人の個性の尊重, 子どもと家族の対応, 学習 の相互作用

3R's
respect 尊重
responsiveness 対応
reciprocity 相互関係

Respect

To respect someone is to honour and to show consideration and esteem for that person. All these phrases suggest that respect is a genuine regard for, and sensitivity to, self and others. How does respect manifest itself in an early childhood program?

移動するペースは、それぞれの子供のために特別にあり ECEの感受性及び応答に値する

Respect for children. There are several key considerations in respecting children. The different interests, abilities, talents, and styles of learning, the range of developmental differences within children, as well as the pace with which children move through development, are particular for each child and deserve the early childhood educator's sensitivity and response.

学習の異なる興味, 能力, 才能, およびスタイル, 子供の発達の違いの範囲, 子どもが 開発を通して

Respect children
· different interests
· abilities
· talents
· styles of learning
· developmental differences

High-quality programs for young children show this respect for individuality in every decision made about children's care and curriculum, from considering what to do about naptime for toddlers to choosing materials for the art table so that preschoolers may find something to whet a particular interest or to guarantee certain success. This is a good time for you to note any practices you are aware of in early care and education settings that demonstrate respect for children's individuality or, conversely, any program decisions that fail to demonstrate this component and that treat all children as if they all had the same needs and interests.

→ 幼児のための質の高いプログラムは, 子どもたちのケアカリキュラムに関する, あらゆる決定においてこのような個性を尊重示す

The need for respect demands that ECEs first acquire knowledge of the children that goes far beyond merely learning characteristics of age-level norms. Such constantly growing knowledge demands that educators continually observe and communicate, as well as avoid the hasty conclusion that they "know the children." ECEs who truly respect children's individuality find themselves always in a suspenseful state of not quite knowing; they are always open to new perceptions and evidence of growth and change.

知覚力

1893

A model day nursery at Chicago World's Fair cares for 10 000 children of sightseeing parents.

1896

John Dewey begins an experimental lab school at the University of Chicago for four- and five-year-olds, called subprimary rather than kindergarten.

In New York, Susan Blow is at Teachers College representing the Froebelian point of view, and Patty Smith Hill represents the newer developmental approach.

The first meeting of the International Kindergarten Union is held in New York City.

| 1850 | 1900 | 1950 | 2000 |

Respect for children also implies recognizing children as capable and interesting people, who are filled with the potential and the desire to learn, grow, and develop. ECEs listen carefully to children, recognizing that their insights are valid and their questions are important. They talk with children individually, about things that are of interest and consequence to both child and adult. These are genuine conversations that follow the same rules as those of adult communication; they are not just "pop quizzes" or questions such as "What colour is the ball?" or "How many bears do I have in my hand?" ECEs talk *with* children, not at them.

Quality early childhood educators enjoy children as people, rather than seeing them as entertaining because of their less-developed abilities and under-standing of the world (*not* as in "Did you hear that? Isn't that cute—he called the lobster a monster"). ECEs accept children's feelings and social interactions with seriousness, but they also recognize children's need for guidance and assistance in moving toward greater emotional maturity (*not* as in "It's nothing to get upset about. He probably doesn't even understand much about moving to another province"). ECEs see this need for help and guidance not as a defect, but as part of the progression of learning (*not* as in "I'm sick and tired of hearing toddlers yell"). Respectful guidance of young children means that educators use techniques and communication that safeguard positive feelings of self-esteem. Guidance methods that humiliate or cause feelings of shame and doubt are not seen in excellent programs.

Adults with this kind of respect for childhood are not in a hurry to move children to more advanced learning or behaviours that they are not yet ready for. Instead, they recognize that childhood has an importance of its own, not just as a preparation stage for a later time. This is an important question to consider: How do adults convey to children that their childlike abilities and characteristics are appreciated, enjoyed, and accepted?

Respect for families. Early childhood educators also respect children's individuality when they help children learn to recognize and comfortably acknowledge the **diversity** of race, culture, religion, socio-economic experiences, gender, and physical ability that exists within Canadian communities and in early childhood education and care settings. Play materials, visitors, activities, and conversations all help children accept their **self-identity** and that of others. Each child identifies with a specific family and its background. As ECEs interact with children's parents, welcoming them into communication and collaboration, children perceive that their own family culture is respected. When parents are drawn into partnership, they are able to help ECEs truly understand their children. Parents can also guide ECEs in creating a curriculum that is responsive to their needs and goals for their children. Without dialogue between parents and ECEs, the educators are in constant danger of overstepping the boundaries of appropriateness in the multicultural world in which we live. Respect for individuality includes this acknowledgement of family needs and preferences and the active attempt to work with families. Genuine respect comes when parents and ECEs recognize that each has a role in children's lives—roles that are different, but complementary, rather than cause for antagonism. What are some of the

◀ Every child has unique interests.

practices in early childhood programs that convey respect for different cultures and that reach out for collaboration with families?

In essence, showing respect means that programs and early childhood educators are child-sensitive; that is, they notice that children are unique, acknowledge this as important, and use this knowledge as a significant basis in planning the total program. "Respect" may be a more descriptive term than the frequently used "child-centred," which can seem rather one-sided or totally indulgent toward children. Respect demands responsiveness.

Respect for self. Early childhood educators who have self-respect recognize the right and personal obligation to be authentic to the values and principles that drive their lives. This begins as educators consider the philosophy and practices of potential employers, to determine whether these are compatible with their own deeply held personal convictions. Nothing more quickly destroys the joy of personal or professional life than working in a setting that creates cognitive dissonance. Sometimes ECEs feel they can make compromises that

1899
John Dewey publishes *The School and Society*, outlining his philosophy of progressivism—that is, that education is a means of social reform.

1903
In Ontario, legislation is passed allowing municipalities to purchase land for public parks.

1906
Montreal begins the first regular and systematic medical inspection of school pupils in Canada.

1850   1900   1950   2000

would allow them to keep their job while balancing with their principles. It is true that there are, as yet, few perfect worlds, and that ECEs will likely have to live with some situations that are less than ideal. Nevertheless, to be able to maintain congruent feelings of personal and professional integrity, ECEs will need to identify those ideals and issues for which there is no room for compromise.

Such insights sometimes come slowly, after experience, as with the early childhood educator who left her first job after several months, saying ruefully, "I didn't realize how strongly I felt about teamwork. I now know that being part of a supportive community of adults and children is necessary for my ability to grow and see myself as a real contributor in the small world of the child care centre. I will never again take a job that doesn't emphasize that feeling of community." Some ECEs might want to be able to express their religious beliefs in their daily work; they will need to find programs that permit them to do so. The same is true for ECEs who believe so strongly in being able to espouse particular lifestyles that they would be uncomfortable working with other adults who deem them unacceptable. ECEs must identify their own defining principles.

Beyond being aware of who they are, ECEs also need to value the worth of their ideas and abilities. Humility is an important characteristic for professionals. But this is not a self-effacing humility; rather, it is a confident recognition of one's strengths and capabilities, coupled with an understanding of the need to join with others for maximum effect. In other words, ECEs do not have to be all-knowing, able to answer any question; they can draw on the strengths of others, both adults and children. ECEs who value their own worth are confident that they have a contribution to make in early care and education. They know that their passions and ideas are worth sharing, that their presence is valuable. Such confidence leads toward excellence.

▶ This early childhood educator is listening to the child's explanation of her drawing.

alexsokolov/iStock/Thinkstock

Responsiveness   対応力

Good quality child care provides emotional security, frequent communication and encouragement to play and explore. It begins with a nurturing, stimulating relationship between the child and the caregiver, and extends to positive relationships and appropriate activities with other children (Human Resources Development Canada, 1994, p. 11).

Doherty-Derkowski (1995, p. 26) states that the concept of responsiveness combines

- age-appropriateness,
- appropriateness for this particular child at this time, and
- appropriateness in this particular situation.

Effective early childhood programs recognize that learning takes place in the context of responsive relationships.

Responsive adults are able to read children's verbal and nonverbal signals, and they react promptly to children's needs and requests. Responsiveness is a sensitivity to a child's emotional state and mood, as well as attention to his or her physical needs. Children's trust emerges when adults are emotionally and physically available and reliable in meeting their needs. Infants and young children are more likely to form a secure attachment to responsive early childhood educators than they are to less-responsive caregivers.

Responsive early childhood educators are good for children. Research findings in both centre-based and home-based programs reveal that children who interact with responsive early childhood educators

- are more likely to get along with their peers (Rubenstein & Howes, 1979, 1983; NICHD, 2000; Sylva et al., 2004; 2009); and
- have higher cognitive and language skills (Cleveland, Corter, Pelletier, Colley, Bertrand, & Jamieson, 2006; Mitchell, Wylie, & Carr, 2008; NICHD, 2004; Sylva et al., 2009).

Responsive adults bring out better social skills and higher levels of intellectual skills in children (Clarke-Stewart, 1987; Cleveland, Corter, Pelletier, Colley, Bertrand, & Jamieson, 2006; Shonkoff & Phillips, 2000). Effective early childhood education programs recognize that learning takes place in the context of responsive relationships. In a quality program, much time and effort go into building and sustaining significant relationships. These relationships form complex webs that extend in many directions: from ECE to child; from child to child; from ECE to parent; from ECE to ECE; from parent to parent; and, most importantly, from parent to child. The ultimate statement on the importance of relationships in early education comes from the late Loris Malaguzzi (1993, p. 9), of the Reggio Emilia programs in Italy:

1906–1908

Playground associations are established in Hamilton, London, Ottawa, and other centres in Ontario.

1850   1900   1950   2000

Although (from our experience in Reggio Emilia) we know how strongly children represent the centre of our educational system, we continue to be convinced that without attention to the central importance of children and families, our view of children is incomplete; therefore, our proposition is to consider a triad at the centre of education—children, early childhood educators, and families. To think of a dyad of only an early childhood educator and a child is to create an artificial world that does not reflect reality...

We strive to create an amiable early childhood setting where children, early childhood educators, and families feel a sense of well-being; therefore, the organization of the school, contents, functions, procedures, motivations, and interests, is designed to bring together the three central protagonists—children, early childhood educators, and parents—and to intensify the interrelationships among them.

"Intensify the interrelationships"—what a strong image! Those who offer good early childhood care and education make procedural and environmental decisions based on their potential for encouraging relationships to flourish. The current practice of assigning **primary caregivers** for the youngest children is based on this concept. Mixed-age groupings (in which children remain together and with the same ECEs over two or three years), are also based on this concept, and many schools and programs are exploring them for continuity of relationships. How different this is from making decisions based on efficiency; for example, if an ECE had a feeding-table device that allowed her to feed six infants simultaneously, time might be saved, but the quality of personal and physical interaction that promotes emotional attachment would suffer. Consider the benefits to interrelationships when children in primary grades face one another at tables, to interact and work co-operatively, rather than working in silence at separate desks. Or consider the effects of changing the common policy of having the fewest staff members available at the beginning and end of the day, so as to permit time for ECEs to talk with parents and with one another. What other specific decisions in the procedures, functions, and environment of early childhood settings can you imagine that could enhance the quality of the relationships within the programs?

Reciprocity of Learning

If early childhood educators believe that learning takes place in the context of many complex adult–child relationships and does not result solely from one-way pronouncements and instruction, learning becomes a reciprocal relationship, in which every participant within the system shares responsibility. Most early childhood educators find this concept exciting, as it removes from them the burden of being the sole resource for learning.

Children construct their own increasing understanding of the world by interacting with materials and people in their environments. High-quality programs understand that individuals construct their own reality, with all participants playing both teaching and learning roles. An ECE aptly stated this idea to

Margaret Yonemura (1986, p. 50) when she said, to quote Yonemura, "'We all have some learning to do from each other,' expressing her underlying view that we are all resources with practical knowledge ... the 'all' was inclusive of all children and adults."

non-reciprocal 非相互的せ

An image that conveys the concept of a *nonreciprocal* learning environment is that of pouring liquid from a pitcher into an empty cup. The ECE is the pitcher, the cup is the child. The action is all one-way, with the child taking in knowledge from the ECE and giving nothing back, and with no one else involved in the transaction.

An image that <u>exemplifies</u> a reciprocal learning environment, on the other hand, is that of a game in which many balls are being thrown at random around a group. A ball leaves one hand, flying across the room to another hand, crossed by the flight of another, which goes from a different hand to still another. Another ball suddenly surprises the first thrower, and so on. Learning is multi-directional rather than following a single line. The possibilities of connections and combinations are limitless. This is the richness of a reciprocal learning environment, in which all participants can teach and learn from one another through interaction.

What might a reciprocal learning environment be like from an early childhood educator's point of view? One of the best descriptions comes from Vivian Paley (1990, p. 136), who continually marvels at how she learns from the children themselves how to present ideas they can comprehend. Her mistakes with using adult logic are gently changed as she listens carefully to the children and has new insights into the world they have constructed. As Paley also points out, the children learn from one another in ways she cannot teach. Here she is reflecting on a child's words:

> Samantha's explanation, "You're really a helicopter really but you're pretending a baby," could never be used by an early childhood educator. The statement can only be made by another child, because it must stay within the child's context of reality. . . . In this single exchange between two young children there are important implications for classroom teaching at all levels. Children are able to teach one another best if they are permitted to interact socially and playfully throughout the day.

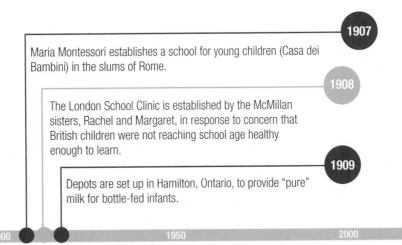

1907
Maria Montessori establishes a school for young children (Casa dei Bambini) in the slums of Rome.

1908
The London School Clinic is established by the McMillan sisters, Rachel and Margaret, in response to concern that British children were not reaching school age healthy enough to learn.

1909
Depots are set up in Hamilton, Ontario, to provide "pure" milk for bottle-fed infants.

1850   1900   1950   2000

Read some of Paley's work, such as *Mollie is three* (1986), *Bad guys don't have birthdays* (1988), *The boy who would be a helicopter* (1990), and grow into your own understanding of how good early childhood educators learn from children. Janet Gonzalez-Menza also reminds us, in *Multicultural issues in child care* (1993), how early childhood educators can change their limited perspectives as they learn reciprocally by listening to parents who have very different views about raising children.

One of the most important, and often undeveloped, reciprocities in early childhood programs is the interaction that should exist between early childhood educators and colleagues. Professional growth and learning does not take place in a vacuum. Opportunities for supportive dialogue and shared reflections, and for joint observation and goal-setting, provide early childhood educators with stimulation and challenges. Excellent programs provide encouragement and environmental supports for forming real collegial systems. Reciprocal learning is possible only when ECEs show attitudes of respect for all, and when they recognize the importance of relationships and nurture them.

Think about this concept of reciprocity in good learning environments. What evidence of reciprocity have you encountered in your own learning experiences?

FRAMEWORK OF QUALITY

The framework of a quality program is constructed from basic building blocks, including an underlying knowledge of child development and early education practices, the number of children for whom each early childhood educator is responsible, the interrelationship and integration of learning experiences, and environments prepared for active learning.

Underlying Developmental Understanding

When early childhood educators make decisions based on facts and **theories** drawn from child development knowledge and research, they are using standards of developmental appropriateness. The question is always this: Is our practice supported by what we know to be true about children in general, and these children in particular?

Early childhood educators in quality programs work from a base of knowledge of child development. They are aware of children's abilities and interests at various stages, and so are able to structure learning experiences in which children can find their own developmental level, guaranteeing success without fear of failure. They recognize that children, even within a particular chronological grouping, may be far apart in their actual development; and they provide materials that children can use with increasing levels of sophistication and skill.

An appropriate curriculum in a good early child development program is created through the interaction of children and all the involved adults, including parents, and through early childhood educators' careful observations of children and knowledge of developmental tasks and goals. ECEs are acutely aware of the direction they will help children move toward because they recognize the sequence of development in all domains. Children's interests direct the actual activities, themes, and projects. Children are free to make choices; with support and challenge from the ECE, they find the activities they are ready for.

What We Know about Child Care

Non-parental care or child care can be defined as the care of children in the child's own home, in someone else's home, or in a centre, where care and education are provided by a person other than an immediate family member. As child care programs vary in location and design, so do the levels of quality.

The provision of quality in child care centres is mainly determined by three factors:

- low child–adult ratios,
- highly educated providers with specialized training, and
- stimulating environments.

Source: R. E. Tremblay, R. G. Barr, R. De V. Peters, and M. Boivin, eds., 2009.

Early childhood educators recognize that young children's learning styles are active and hands-on, and so the strategies they use to support active learning may look quite different from what many think of as typical teaching strategies. ECEs in good programs for young children will not be found instructing or lecturing from the front of the room; indeed, you would have a difficult time finding a front to the room! They interact with individuals or small groups busy at work or play. Embedded in their interaction may be challenges or suggestions of new directions to take in exploration, questions that may stimulate more activity or extend thinking, and comments that reinforce or provide information. This is subtle and supportive teaching, adapted to each situation. Occasionally, you will see ECEs working with the whole group, but there is much less direct instruction even in this form, as children and adults interact. As they listen to children's responses and ideas, ECEs are continually

1910

The University of Manitoba introduces a child development component to the Faculty of Home Economics.

The Ottawa and Toronto school boards establish "forest schools" to maximize the time "sickly" children spend outdoors.

1911

Rachel and Margaret McMillan establish the Deptford School, an open-air nursery school in London, inventing the term "nursery school."

The Ottawa Day Nursery opens.

The Vancouver Infants Centre opens at the infants' hospital.

The first Montessori school in the United States is established.

| 1850 | 1900 | 1950 | 2000 |

assessing their progress and seeing what new learning they can facilitate. Teaching styles and strategies are shaped by knowledge of how young children learn and develop. How does this description of ECEs' strategies match your image of what you would do as an educator of young children?

Educational qualifications matter—for the most part, research confirms that the more early childhood–related post-secondary education, the better the practice (Pascal, 2009b). Related post-secondary education increases the likelihood that all caregivers have an understanding of development to guide their work with young children.

Research findings consistently back up the recommendation that early childhood educators prepare for their work by participating in ECE studies at the post-secondary level. In Canada, staff with post-secondary ECE qualifications are more likely to be associated with high-quality early child development settings and better child development outcomes than those without these qualifications (Doherty & Stuart, 1996; Goelman & Pence, 1987; Lyon & Canning, 1995).

Education in early child development and pedagogy assists the adult to understand children's developmental stages and needs. This, in turn, increases the likelihood that the adult will provide activities that are both stimulating and appropriate for the child's developmental level, and will not impose unrealistic expectations. Early childhood educators cannot know the child's developmental level and needs as well as a parent, but an understanding of typical sequence child development enables the early childhood educator to make "educated guesses" about what is appropriate and desirable for the child. It also assists early childhood educators to understand and manage the more complex group dynamics and processes among unrelated children who may not have the same history of familiarity and compromise as do brothers and sisters.

Do you think your own studies in a post-secondary early childhood education program will affect your understanding of young children's development? Take a moment to reflect on what you are learning about children's development and how this might be changing some of your behaviours.

Earlier we discussed the dynamic components of quality in early childhood programs—respect, responsiveness, and reciprocity. Your capacity to respect, respond, and reciprocate with young children is clearly the crux of the issue of quality. Of course, your own values, attitudes, and other personal characteristics have an important role in your capacity, but so does your underlying understanding of development. As you become more knowledgeable about the principles of child development and developmentally appropriate practice, your capacity to respect, respond, and reciprocate with all children increases.

College and university early childhood education programs recognize the importance of both theoretical and practical knowledge in preparing early childhood educators. Theoretical knowledge encompasses child development principles and learning theory. Practical knowledge focuses on varied strategies and when to use them in guiding children, making decisions that take the immediate situation into account, and following appropriate rules of thumb in day-to-day routines (Vander Ven, 1994). We will examine the curricula offered in Canadian college and university programs further in Chapter 5.

Early Child Development Research in Canada

Early childhood educators can find out about how Canadian scientists are studying early child development. For example:

Atkinson Centre on Society and Child Development

The Atkinson Centre promotes research on child development, and the development of early learning policy and practice that serve young children and their families. The Centre carries out basic and applied research projects, through university–community collaborations and professional/graduate training. The Centre aims to build societal supports for young children and families. Central to the work of the Atkinson Centre is the integration of diversity, equity, and inclusion in its research agenda. **http://www.oise.utoronto.ca/atkinson/index.html.**

Better Beginnings, Better Futures

Better Beginnings, Better Futures is Canada's most ambitious community-based research project to date on the long-term impacts of early childhood development programming. The model is designed to prevent young children in low-income, high-risk neighbourhoods from experiencing poor developmental outcomes, outcomes which then require expensive health, education, and social services. The model has been implemented in eight socio-economically disadvantaged communities in Ontario since 1991. **http://bbbf.ca.**

Institute of Human Development, Child and Youth Health (Canadian Institutes of Health Research)

The CIHR Institute of Human Development, Child and Youth Health will support research to enhance maternal, child, and youth health and to address causes, prevention, screening, diagnosis, treatment, short- and long-term support systems, and palliation for a wide range of health concerns associated with reproduction, early development, childhood, and adolescence. **http://www.cihr-irsc.gc.ca/e/8695.html**.

Centre for Families, Work and Well-Being

The Centre for Families, Work and Well-Being is an interdisciplinary research and educational centre, responding to dramatic changes in family patterns, paid work, and broader economic and political structures. Research topics include organizational health, family dynamics, social support, and community development. **http://www.worklifecanada.ca.**

Centre of Excellence for Early Child Development

The Centre of Excellence for Early Childhood Development (CEECD) disseminates scientific knowledge on the social and emotional development of young children and the policies and services that influence this development. It also includes formulating recommendations on the services needed to ensure optimum early childhood development.

CEECD has prepared the Encyclopedia on Early Childhood Development, a compilation of papers from leading experts that covers 33 topics related to the social and emotional development of young children, from conception to age five, and addresses three perspectives: development, services, and policies. **http:// www.excellence-earlychildhood.ca**.

Childcare Resource and Research Unit

The Childcare Resource and Research Unit (CRRU) is a policy- and research-oriented facility that focuses on early childhood education and care. CRRU provides, synthesizes, analyzes, and disseminates extensive information resources on early childhood education and care policy and research.

CRRU periodically assembles pan-Canadian data to produce the country's most complete snapshot of early childhood care and education. The eighth edition of *Early Childhood Education and Care in Canada* presents 2008 data. Together with data compiled for earlier editions, the report reveals trends in early childhood development over more than a decade. **http://www.childcarecanada.org**.

Canadian Institute for Advanced Research (CIFAR)

CIFAR launched the Child & Brain Development (formerly called Experience-Based Brain and Biological Development) program in 2003 to explore the core question of how social experiences "get under the skin" to affect human biology and set early trajectories for development and health. The program delves into exactly how, when, and under what circumstances early social experiences change neural, endocrine, and immunological systems. **http://www.cifar.ca**.

Human Early Learning Partnership

The Human Early Learning Partnership (HELP) is an interdisciplinary research partnership, based at the University of British Columbia, that is directing a world-leading contribution to new understandings and approaches to early child development. HELP explores the ways in which different early environments can influence the development of children, and helps apply this knowledge in the community by working directly with government and communities.

The Provincial Early Child Development Mapping Unit increases awareness and understanding of healthy child development in neighbourhoods across British Columbia. HELP produces maps that combine Early Development Instrument (EDI) data, socio-demographic factors, and community assets and resources. By networking with local coalitions, HELP assists communities in interpreting maps and assessing factors that influence children's development. **http://www.earlylearning.ubc.ca**.

Manitoba Centre for Health Policy

MCHP is a research unit in the University of Manitoba's Faculty of Medicine. MCHP examines patterns of illness in the population and studies how people use health care services. The primary focus is on the question "What makes people healthy?" and includes consideration of social factors such as income, education, employment, and social circumstances. MCHP sorts out the contribution of each of these factors. Some of their work focuses on the determinants of health in early childhood and the impact of early childhood development on later health and well-being. **http://www.umanitoba.ca/centres/mchp**.

Offord Centre for Child Studies

The Offord Centre for Child Studies conducts research on healthy child development in order to improve the quality of life and the opportunities of the Canadian children and youth who suffer from serious social and emotional problems (one in five in Canada). The Centre led the development of the Early Development Instrument to measure children's early social, emotional, cognitive, language, and physical development at a population level. **http://www.offordcentre.com**.

Science of Early Child Development

The Science of Early Child Development (ECD) is an online curriculum resource, presented in a flexible, interactive multimedia format, inspired and informed by the following questions:

* What is the new framework for studying child development?
* Why is it important for early childhood educators to understand the science related to young children?
* How can we narrow the gap between research and practice?

http://scienceofecd.com/index.php.

Number of Children

It is common sense that the total number of children a caregiver is responsible for will affect the quality of care and education children receive. Can you imagine the quality of care or child development outcomes in situations in which one ECE is responsible for six infants? Basic safety is missing in this situation, let alone an environment of respect, responsiveness, and reciprocity.

Optimal child–adult ratios in early childhood settings allow ECEs to interact frequently with each child, respond promptly to children's needs, and observe individual children and the group dynamics. The overall size of the group is another important component. If the total group size becomes too large, even when the number of children each ECE is responsible for is small, quality deteriorates. The adults must pay more attention to overall group organization and schedules, taking away from their individualized attention and flexibility in following the lead of children's activity. In large groups, children's play and daily routines must fit into a group schedule and pattern. It becomes much more difficult to respond to individual children without creating chaos in the group.

Research studies help us to understand the optimal adult–child ratios and maximum group sizes for different ages of children for centre-based early child development programs.

Where a multi-age grouping exists, the adult–child ratio and group size requirements can be based on the age of the majority of children in the group. When infants are included, the ratio and group size for infants should be maintained.

Think about your experiences in early childhood settings during field placements or while working. Can you remember times when you were responsible for more children than is recommended by the research? What was it like? Were you able to engage in conversations? Could you respond to children's nonverbal signals? Did you observe their activity and the dynamics of the group? Or were you mainly focused on "crowd control" and on the safety of children? Was your communication mainly directed at the whole group, rather than at individual children?

Integration of Learning Experiences

High-quality programs consider the **whole child**; there is equal attention paid to needs and growth in all domains of development: **physical**, **cognitive**, **emotional**, **social**, and **moral**. Physical competence, including both **gross-motor** and **fine-motor** skills, and emotional, social, and intellectual development are recognized as important areas of growth that occur simultaneously in young children. "Simultaneously" does not mean at an equal rate; rather, it means that all of this learning is occurring in the child at the same time. Furthermore, what is happening in one aspect of development has an effect on what is happening in other aspects. For example, success in learning within the cognitive curriculum of the early elementary years can be predicated on the child's comfort in social situations and ability to respond to the directions and guidance of a new adult. Infants' language development parallels their acquisition of motor abilities to explore the world first-hand. Toddlers' frustration and temper outbursts may be directly related to their limited vocabulary for expression, and so on.

Considering the whole child also means taking into account the child's family. The world at a school or centre makes up only a part—a small part—of a child's life experiences. Family life is included in the classroom, and the child is recognized at all times as a family member and participant.

Those who sponsor good programs know they cannot expect children to learn in a fragmented way, with learning or subject matter broken up into individual, isolated lessons. Imagine how nonsensical it would be to plan an infant's day to include a time to practise the physical skills of crawling on the mat, followed by a short period of language instruction, with an experience in emotional closeness and bonding to come next! Instead, ECEs sit near babies crawling on the mat, while smiling, talking, encouraging, and interacting. Development in all domains is being nurtured simultaneously—learning is integrated.

In the same way, a good curriculum for older children consists of an **integrated curriculum** of whole activities, rather than separate subject lessons. Instead of providing a language period, followed by math and then science, teachers have children participate in a cooking activity that allows children to learn all of those concepts in a meaningful activity, as well as to develop and use the skills involved.

Integrated learning for children in high-quality programs does not happen by chance. Early childhood educators who observe children continually come to know their abilities, their strengths, and the areas of development that need particular support. They assess individual development in the light of their knowledge of the predictable sequence of developmental abilities, so that they have, for each child, a sense of where the child is now and what the next steps will be. These **assessments** are always enhanced by the ECE's dialogues with parents, so that objectives are based on the best available information. In good programs for young children, ECEs have a clear sense of direction to guide them in planning the most appropriate learning experiences for each child. The learning may look spontaneous and involve choices and action on the child's part, but it is part of a careful overall plan for each child.

Another factor that contributes to unified rather than fragmented experiences for children and families is the wholeness of the early childhood program itself. Such wholeness is achieved only when a clearly articulated common philosophy connects all participants to an understood framework. The framework is, in turn, translated into daily actions. Defining common beliefs is crucial to full participation for both staff and families, so that adults knowingly commit themselves to the stated fundamental beliefs that will bind them. Quality programs have clearly stated and understood philosophies to guide their decision-making.

Physical Environment for Active and Co-operative Learning

The physical **environment** is a powerful influence on our behaviour. Think about how you change your behaviour in different spaces. Large, open spaces encourage big movements. Cozy, small spaces encourage quieter activity. The physical environment gives us messages about what kinds of behaviours are expected. An early childhood education environment that is organized to include defined spaces for big movements, quiet retreats, and messy play give children cues about how to behave.

1650   1700   1750   1800

Excellent programs for young children have environments structured so that early childhood educators are able to continually observe children. Can you think of environmental arrangements, curriculum methods, and pedagogical practices that allow educators to continually observe the children in their care? Specific practices include encouraging individual exploration or small-group interaction, rather than whole-group activities led by ECEs; providing **open-ended** materials that do not require adult instruction or assistance; and defining observation formats and record-keeping templates as important tasks for ECEs.

The physical environment is an extension of the pedagogical approach of the program. The arrangement of furniture, objects, and materials may reinforce a coherent approach with considerable attention to the details of colour, light, and shapes. A chaotic physical environment usually signals a lack of an intentional pedagogy and points to a more custodial type of program.

Quality early childhood education provides language-rich environments, with stimulating materials, in which children feel included and valued. The indoor and outdoor spaces provide safe opportunities for children's play, independent problem solving, and inquiry. The staff plans opportunities that allow children to explore language and communicate their thoughts and learning in meaningful ways. How the environment is set up influences how children explore, learn, and express their understandings of the world around them. The environment can be structured to encourage positive experiences of play creating an interest in further learning and exploration.

Some environments may focus and calm children, while others agitate and overstimulate them. Environments may excite and motivate or they may simply bore children. The arrangement of the physical environment can define or limit children's choices and encourage or discourage the process of learning.

Programs designed for children to learn by interacting with materials and people structure the time and space environment for active learning. Classroom environments reflect early childhood educators' beliefs about children and how they learn, about the form and content of the curriculum, and about the importance of social connections. When early childhood educators see environment as an important component of quality, they create physical arrangements for opportunities that encourage "encounter, communication, and relationships" (Gandini, 1993, p. 6).

Ingram Publishing/Thinkstock

▲ Building blocks are essential in quality early childhood programs.

1913

Caroline Pratt, frustrated with the Froebelian-based teacher preparation at Teachers College, begins an experimental school for five-year-olds in New York City.

John Watson introduces the term "behaviourism" in *Psychology as the Behaviorist Views It*.

1914

Caroline Pratt designs the first set of unit blocks.

The school nurse is moved into the central position in school medical programs.

Jost Mission Day Nursery opens in Halifax.

1850   1900   1950   2000

▶ Outdoor environments can extend the curriculum into the playground all year round.

Monkey Business Images /Shutterstock

Because ECEs know that children learn through direct manipulation, play, and work with varieties of materials, furniture is used to display the available choices in a logical and organized way, encouraging children's choices and productive use of materials. The environment is organized into logically separated **learning centres**, so that children may decide to work or play alone, with a few other children, or with a larger group. The coherence and unspoken messages of invitation, challenge, and order allow children to feel a measure of control over their learning activities and methods. In quality learning environments, children have opportunities to make choices about which activities they are interested in, how they will structure their learning activity, and whom they will play and work with, and where.

Environment conveys messages. It can say, "This is a place where you can decide some things that you are going to do today" or "The early childhood educator will always be the one in charge of telling you what to do." It can say, "Work with a friend if you like" or "Stay in your seat and work by yourself." It can say, "Here are some things that will allow you to succeed" or "This stuff is really hard and the early childhood educator thinks you won't be able to learn it without her." It can say, "They care about your work here" or "What you do isn't really very important." It can say, "What you do, think, and communicate with your play is significant" or "After you play then we'll do the important things." It can say, "Your rights to work undisturbed and undistracted will be protected" or "This is not a peaceful place." It can say, "Childhood is valued and appreciated as a separate and distinct time of life" or "Childhood is merely a superficially cute stage." It can say, "You can do as much as possible for yourself here" or "You'll need to depend on grownups to do things for you." It can say, "There are some limits on things that aren't safe or acceptable" or "You'll have to make mistakes and then we'll stop you." It can say, "You belong here as a member of this classroom community" or "Your individuality is not respected."

Think about it—in what ways might the design and placement of classroom furniture and materials, the decoration on the walls, or the classroom schedule and routines reflect these messages? What other messages have you been aware of in physical environments? Programs that understand children's active involvement in discovery learning support this involvement with the way they arrange time and space.

High-quality programs for young children emphasize materials and experiences, knowing that children learn through doing, not through simply being told about concepts. Excellent early childhood education and care programs include enticing materials that invite touching. This variety of "loose parts," to use Nicholson's term for open-ended materials (1974), allows children to explore, invent, combine, create, and communicate. Materials are and in good repair, and they match the children's manipulative abilities. As well, they have been carefully selected for the learning environment to correspond with the early childhood educators' goals and children's interests. Think of some of the materials that have been part of any good early childhood program you know. What were some open-ended items that children used in interesting ways?

Large blocks of uninterrupted time are needed for children to become meaningfully involved in their play. The daily schedule will be organized to permit participation, practice, and repetition as children's repertoire of skills and knowledge grows, rather than fragmenting the day into defined times for separate activities, with many confusing **transitions**. When programs recognize that children's self-esteem and confidence as learners result from meaningful, personal involvement in activities, the daily plan permits such involvement.

Quality programs for young children recognize the importance of environmental decisions and create environments that support interaction and activity. The physical environment can greatly enhance early childhood educators' abilities to respect, respond, and reciprocate.

CONTEXT OF QUALITY

The *framework* of an early child development program sets the stage for the *dynamics* that occur among children and early childhood educators each day. The *context* of quality describes the elements outside the immediate early

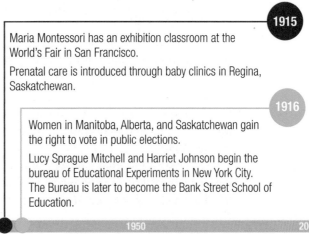

1915

Maria Montessori has an exhibition classroom at the World's Fair in San Francisco.

Prenatal care is introduced through baby clinics in Regina, Saskatchewan.

1916

Women in Manitoba, Alberta, and Saskatchewan gain the right to vote in public elections.

Lucy Sprague Mitchell and Harriet Johnson begin the bureau of Educational Experiments in New York City. The Bureau is later to become the Bank Street School of Education.

| 1850 | 1900 | 1950 | 2000 |

childhood setting that influence both the framework elements and the children's day-to-day experiences. Early childhood education programs are influenced by funding, government regulation, non-regulatory measures, and the sponsorship of early child development programs.

Think about your field placements. How did the work environment vary from one setting to another? Did the roles of the director or supervisor? differ between settings? What kind of remuneration did ECEs receive? Was there a difference in the level of government funding compared to the fees paid by parents? Who was ultimately responsible for the care and education of the children? Did any of these arrangements and practices make a difference to how ECEs worked with young children?

The context of quality in early childhood education programs is a complex and sometimes confusing array of details that seem to have little to do with the actual work of providing quality nurturing and stimulation to young children. But these details are important, and they either contribute or present barriers to your capacity as an early childhood educator. We will consider the various elements of the context of quality, including the work environment, funding, regulation, and voluntary standards and the impact of these standards on quality.

Work Environment

A number of interrelated elements make up the work environment of a child care centre, nursery school, home-based setting, or kindergarten classroom. These elements include the style of administration and supervision, organizational climate, compensation, working conditions, and **staff turnover** rates, all of which influence early childhood educators' interactions with young children and their ability to organize the physical environment and learning experiences.

Administrative style.   In centre-based early childhood education and care programs, the role of the director or supervisor includes program and professional leadership; information, financial, and personnel management; parent and community relationships; and legal compliance. All of these functions underlie the early child development program. Like a building's foundation, the elements are often invisible if they are effective. But ineffective administration and management, like cracks in a building's foundation, have noticeable negative effects.

Program and professional leadership.   Child care centre directors, nursery school supervisors, and public school principals share common ground in the influence their leadership has on the early childhood educators and teachers they supervise.

A director's involvement in curriculum planning and in the professional community of early childhood education is linked with higher levels of overall quality.

Canada's first child care sector study reports that the director in a centre-based early childhood education and care program "is a gatekeeper to program quality who establishes standards of practice and expectations for others to follow" (Beach, Bertrand, & Cleveland, 1998, p. 99). School principals who provide academic leadership to teaching staff are a critical component of quality in kindergarten and primary grade classrooms (Pascal, 2009b).

In other words, a competent leader demonstrates and encourages practices that support the dynamics and framework elements of quality, increasing the likelihood that ECEs who are working directly with the children will do likewise.

Information, financial, and personnel management. Directors and supervisors in centre-based programs manage information systems, monitor finances, and supervise ECEs and other staff members. This role involves myriad details and technical skills. It also involves the ability to set clear job expectations, monitor staff performance, and provide constructive feedback. The director's success in carrying out these responsibilities determines the effectiveness of the centre's organization. A well-run centre pays staff members on time and makes accurate deductions, keeps children's records updated and within easy access in case of emergencies, and provides clear, written expectations of job responsibilities.

Parent and community relationships. The director is an important link in establishing partnerships with parents and with other groups in the community.

Legal compliance. All early child development centre-based programs that provide non-parental care are subject to numerous regulations and requirements. The director needs to ensure that these obligations are met and that the necessary records are available for verification. A good information system will go a long way toward fulfilling these obligations.

In family child care settings, as in centre-based child care programs, the administrative style shapes the work environment. In family child care, an early childhood educator sets his or her own expectations for program standards, manages information and finances, develops parent and community relationships, and ensures compliance with all legal requirements. The ability to carry out these responsibilities sets the administrative style and influences the quality of the family child care program.

In in-home child care settings as well, the working relationship between the early childhood educator and the employer is the basis of the administrative style. Both verbal and written communication are key components of the working relationship. The ECE can enhance the administrative style by ensuring that written employment agreements outline both parties' responsibilities and expectations. Because in-home child care takes place in the child's family home, clear communication practices help to maintain personal boundaries. Communication includes the ongoing exchange of information, as well as the discussion of problems and the exploration of solutions. The important

1916–1920

Mother's allowances/pensions are introduced in four provinces (British Columbia, Alberta, Manitoba, and Ontario). This provides financial assistance to poor, single mothers and their young children.

1850   1900   1950   2000

exchange of information between family members and an ECE is helped by written daily logs, opportunities for daily verbal reports and transitions, regular parent–ECE conferences, and job performance reviews. Early childhood educators can work with employers to establish these kinds of practices. If an employment agency is involved, the agency is likely to provide administrative support in these areas.

Compensation and working conditions.   The income, benefits, and working conditions ECEs receive in early childhood settings are important components of the work environment. These context components have an impact on job satisfaction and turnover, which, in turn, influence the dynamics of quality. We will discuss these issues further in Chapters 6 and 9.

Funding

It is fairly simple to determine the cost of a child's participation, whether in a home-based or centre-based setting. The biggest expense (usually 80 to 90 percent) is the cost of the early childhood educators who provide the services; other expenses include the costs of the physical environment, food, supplies, and play materials. To calculate the cost per child, the total expenses are divided by the number of children enrolled in the program. In Canada, funding for the costs of early child programs comes mostly from two sources: parents who pay fees and public money from governments, which may fund early childhood programs or subsidize the parent's fees.

The impact of funding on the quality of early child development programs is also easy to determine. Quality early childhood programs depend on skilled early childhood educators. Reasonable compensation levels help to attract and retain competent ECEs in early child development programs. To offer reasonable compensation rates, early child development programs require higher levels of funding, either from higher parent fees or from higher levels of government funding. The dilemma is that higher funding reduces the affordability of child care, both to parents and to governments, making it less accessible to children and their families.

The cost of early childhood programs to parents.   Parents are responsible for most of the costs of child care centres, nursery schools, regulated and unregulated family child care, and in-home child care. Some parents receive subsidies, which are intended to help low-income families meet the costs of regulated child care. Parents do not pay, however, for the cost of kindergarten programs within the school system, most early intervention services, or early childhood services offered within family resource programs.

The cost of child care centres, nursery schools, and regulated family child care varies from one provincial/territorial jurisdiction to another. ECEs and other caregivers receive different levels of compensation, and there are differences in the types of direct funding to these programs by provincial/territorial governments. Also, there are significant variations in the amount of fee subsidies available to parents.

The cost of early childhood programs to government.   Governments' contributions to the funding of early childhood programs are complex and subject to frequent change. Governments at all levels contribute to the cost of early childhood programs in different ways. Some governments fund the programs directly, covering partial or full operating costs. Public funding to programs also provides fee assistance to low-income families. Other government funding goes to parents to cover the costs of child care, usually as part of employment assistance and training programs. Kindergarten programs operating within the education system are publicly funded as part of the school system and do not charge fees to parents. Finally, governments also fund child care expenses through the income tax system in the form of the Child Care Expense Deduction.

The level of public funding influences the compensation levels of early childhood educators across all early childhood settings; compensation rates, in turn, affect the education qualification levels and turnover rates of ECEs. Consistent, qualified ECEs are more likely to provide respectful, responsive, reciprocal, and reliable daily experiences for young children in early childhood settings. Early child development programs that receive higher levels of funding are likely to offer better compensation to ECEs.

Regulation

Of the variables that can be regulated (i.e., those with set standards), three that affect positive child outcomes in early childhood programs are adult educational qualifications, group size, and adult–child ratios (Cleveland, Corter, Pelletier, Colley, Bertrand, & Jamieson, 2006; Shonkoff & Phillips, 2000). These factors determine the quality of relationships within the program.

In Canada, these factors are regulated by provincial/territorial legislation for regulated child care settings. There is considerable variation from one jurisdiction to the next; and no one jurisdiction has regulations for educational qualifications, adult–child ratios, and maximum group size that meet recommendations for quality programs (Beach, Friendly, Ferns, Brabhu, & Forer, 2009; McCain, Mustard, & McCuaig, 2011; Akbari & McCuaig, 2014).

Kindergarten programs operate within the legislative framework for education in each province and territory. Kindergarten teachers in public school programs are required to meet provincial/territorial qualification requirements for education and certification. In all jurisdictions outside the Northwest Territories, requirements include an undergraduate university degree and specialized teacher preparation education. In many instances, these requirements are combined in a bachelor of education degree, sometimes with specialization in primary education required. In the Northwest Territories, an undergraduate degree is not required, although this is under review, and classroom assistants and Aboriginal-language specialists are qualified to teach kindergarten under

1917

Women with property are permitted to hold office in Saskatchewan. Women in British Columbia and Ontario gain the right to vote in provincial elections.

Caroline Pratt's Play School (later to become the City and Country School) is growing. Lucy Sprague is one of its teachers.

1850   1900   1950   2000

the supervision of a certified teacher. Kindergarten teachers are not required to have ECE credentials or experience, but primary teacher preparation programs and employers (school boards) often prefer that teachers have this background.

Four provinces and territories stipulate maximum class size for public kindergarten programs. In Yukon, the maximum group size is 23 and the ratio is 1 adult for every 23 children; in New Brunswick, the maximum group size is 20 and the ratio is 1 to 20; and in Quebec, the ratio for junior kindergarten is 1 to 17 with a maximum of 34 children per group, while senior kindergarten has a maximum group size of 20 and a 1 to 20 ratio. In Ontario, the maximum group is 26 children—with an early childhood educator and a teacher.

Voluntary Standards

Government regulations establish minimum standards only to support the framework and dynamic elements of quality. They can influence important structural elements of quality—in particular, requirements for early childhood educators with ECE post-secondary qualifications, maximum group sizes, and the maximum number of children for every adult. But there are limitations: requirements vary from one jurisdiction to another, monitoring and enforcement cannot ensure full compliance, many of the crucial dynamic elements of quality cannot be regulated, and many early child development settings operate outside the system of regulation.

Voluntary standards offer another mechanism to support and ensure the presence of dynamic, framework, and context elements of quality. The standards are established outside legislation and regulations. In most instances, voluntary standards for early child development programs are established by professional organizations outside the government.

Accreditation. Accreditation is a process by which a recognized independent body establishes standards for services and evaluates programs on the basis of those standards (Doherty, 2000). Accreditation or operating criteria are often based on indicators or benchmarks of what is considered effective practice based on research findings, professional judgment, and community values. To date, large-scale accreditation processes have not been linked with improvements in quality, independent of other factors (e.g., salaries, ratios, leadership) (Mustard, 2008; OECD, 2006; Whitebook, Sakai, & Howes, 1997). Most accreditation processes are based on self-evaluation strategies.

In 1985, the National Association for the Education of Young Children (NAEYC) established and administered a national, voluntary **accreditation** system for child care programs in the United States. The accreditation process is based on ten factors: the physical environment, health and safety, nutrition and food service, administration, staff qualifications and development, interactions among staff and children, staff–parent interaction, curriculum, staffing, and evaluation, with specific criteria defined in each factor (Bredekamp, 1990). The process involves self-study guided by the NAEYC publication *Accreditation criteria and procedures*.

Administrators, parents, and staff work on constructive improvements to create high-quality programs; excellence is then verified by visits and assessment from representatives of the NAEYC. The 1987 **position statement** on developmentally appropriate practice (DAP) made some of the desired outcomes regarding self-study and validation visits more explicit. The National Academy of Early Childhood Education Programs is a body within the NAEYC that administers the voluntary accreditation system for child care programs.

Accreditation of Regulated Child Care Programs

In Alberta, all licensed and approved child care programs (day care centres, family day homes, nursery schools, and out-of-school programs) have to meet a minimum set of provincial standards. In 2002, Alberta introduced the Child Care Accreditation Program, which establishes standards that exceed provincial standards. These higher standards have been developed by members of the child care sector, together with Alberta Children and Youth Services. An accreditation agency works with accredited programs to make sure the standards are met. This voluntary program is the only one of its kind in Canada.

Funding for programs is tied to meeting the established accreditation standards. Child care centres are able to receive two types of funding:

- staff support funding—monthly funding for staff based on certification level; and
- quality funding—based on the licensed capacity and whether the centre generally or consistently is in compliance with licensing requirements.

The Alberta Resource Centre for Quality Enhancement (ARCQE), established in November 2004, is a non-profit agency that provides technical assistance to the ECEC sector through provision of supporting quality and building capacity to those it serves. As a provincial organization, ARCQE is unique in designing support and resources specific to the needs of the Alberta child care community.

In 2009, Alberta Children & Youth Services contracted with ARCQE to provide pre-accreditation of up to 20 hours of support for new child care programs/agencies enrolling into accreditation. This support involves assistance with steps of the self-study process. Unsuccessful programs can receive up to 20 hours of support.

Sources: Alberta Children and Youth Services, 2009; Beach & Flanagan, 2010b.

EVALUATING QUALITY

Evaluating the quality of early childhood education is important to ECEs, to parents, and to policymakers, who might ask the following questions:

- What is the level of quality offered by an individual program?
- What type of early childhood service offers the best experience for my young child?
- What is the most effective use of public funding to promote quality early childhood education programs?
- How can the impact of changes in staff qualifications, funding, or daily routines be monitored?

But quality can be looked at from different perspectives, as we saw at the beginning of this chapter. We have considered the various dynamic, framework, and context elements of quality in early childhood settings. Which of these elements is most critical in evaluating the quality of early child childhood programs?

The first step in answering all of these questions is to consider which aspect of quality to measure. Policymakers and researchers use three different possibilities:

1. program ingredients or characteristics, which are mostly the framework and context quality elements;
2. child or parent outcomes, which include the achievements, behaviours, and characteristics of children or parents; and
3. program outcomes, which attempt to measure what children actually experience, or the dynamics of quality.

Evaluation Tools

Researchers and early childhood educators have developed tools to evaluate early child development programs. The Early Childhood Environment Rating Scale (ECERS) (Harms & Clifford, 1980, Harms, Clifford & Cryer, 1998) provides a scale with which to review preschool centre-based child care programs. The scale focuses on the physical environment and looks at the use of space, play materials, and learning experiences, as well as at adult–child interactions. There are 43 items on the scale, with a continuum of possible performance. ECERS is the most frequently used measure of quality for research studies in Canada and is also useful as a tool to assist individual program development. In addition to the scale for preschool ECERS settings, there are comparable tools for infant and toddler settings, school-age settings, and family child care settings.

The Classroom Assessment Scoring System (CLASS) measures the quality of the learning environment in prekindergarten to Grade 5 classrooms (Pianta, La Paro, & Hamre, 2008). It includes ten dimensions organized within three broad categories—emotional support, organizational support, and instructional support. The tool focuses on what teachers do to stimulate reasoning, problem-solving, and depth of thinking about materials or experiences. The CLASS assessment is used in early childhood education research in Canadian programs and often used by early childhood education programs in the United States and Australia (including child care centres, prekindergarten, and kindergarten).

NOT FOUND IN QUALITY

Before we finish this discussion about what quality early childhood education programs look like, it may be useful to identify what you will *not* see in a quality program.

Institutionalization

When decisions in programs are made to fit adult needs or preconceptions, children are often expected to behave and learn in ways that fit with the requirements of the institution, rather than in ways that nurture their growth and development. What do we mean by this? As you search your memory for early childhood education experiences, you may recall occasions when children have had to do things that were not necessarily good for them, their learning, or their self-esteem, but were deemed necessary for the good of the institution. Examples of this might include keeping exhausted toddlers awake so they can eat their lunch at the time convenient for the kitchen staff, insisting that first-graders eat a silent lunch so they can finish in twenty minutes and allow the next group to use the cafeteria, demanding that three-year-olds all sleep on their tummies at naptime so they won't look around the room and prolong time for falling asleep, and insisting that two-year-olds give up all pacifiers.

Quality Child Care

What Is Quality Child Care About?

It's about warmth and caring and interesting things to do. It's about high self-esteem and genuine concern about the quality of everyone's day. It's about playing games and singing songs and playing house and holding hands and laughing and having a nice time. It's about everyone being accepted and respected without reservation—and telling each other this in lots of ways. It's about overlooking transgressions so we can get on with things that really count. It's about children and adults spending the day together and looking forward to spending tomorrow together, too.

What Is Poor-Quality Child Care About?

It's about criticism and harsh voices and stern faces and frowns. It's about battles of will between children and adults. It's about threats and time-outs for everything. It's about too many rules and bribery and adults who always stand up so no one can sit in their laps. It's about not much that's interesting going on and waiting for time to go home and wishing you didn't have to come back tomorrow.

Source: Allen, Jeannie. (1991).

Sometimes inappropriate practices exist because "that's the way we've always done it," and no one is applying the test of developmental appropriateness to it. Sometimes inappropriate practices exist because the adults in charge are thinking about adult convenience, efficiency, time, or budgets. Sometimes they exist because the adults lack child development knowledge or awareness of current thinking about appropriate practices. And sometimes they exist because adults believe that children need to endure negatives to strengthen their character. Whatever the reason, practices that do not nurture development and learning through emphasis on support and acceptance of individuals are bad for us all and dehumanize society.

Failure

If early childhood education programs stand ready to adapt to children's individual needs and achievements, there will always be opportunities for children to find a comfortable learning level and style and thus to succeed. But when programs apply their own arbitrarily drawn standards for success to children at various ages, there are too many occasions when children will have to fail, since arbitrary standards allow no room for individual timetables. For example, readiness testing before gaining admission to kindergarten is going to exclude some children who have failed to meet the school system's standard for readiness. Proof of having completed toilet training before moving on to the next preschool classroom will negatively characterize those children who are not yet ready. Not yet being ready to move from two to one nap per day may mean that some toddlers will be denied moving on to the wonderful stimulation of the next class. Standardized testing at the end of Grade 2 will label deficient those children who are learning at a less-standardized rate. As long as schools and programs apply firm and arbitrary standards, with no room for individual needs or developmental patterns, children will fail; and they and their parents will be burdened by a negative evaluation that may have a lasting impact on future learning and development (Kamii, 1990).

Indifference

Quality early childhood education depends on adults who have visions of wonderful worlds to support children and families, and who are unwilling to accept mediocre facilities, policies, or curricula as the way it has to be. If early childhood educators are not knowledgeable enough to be able to know the mediocre from the excellent, if they become overwhelmed by the discrepancies between what they know should be and what is, or if they become indifferent to lack of quality, too many less-than-wonderful situations for children will exist. Indifference is an enemy to good early childhood education.

This is a good time for you to consider other conditions that you believe you should not find in good early childhood programs. Write them down for later discussion. Recognizing what is the opposite to excellence in early childhood education and care will help you define your personal standards.

Summary

- Quality in early childhood education involves many different components, but the relationships among and between ECEs, children, and families is the most important component.
- Program decisions about schedules and use of space influence quality, as do policy decisions that affect compensation and regulatory requirements.
- The dynamic components of quality include respect, responsiveness, and reciprocity. The framework components include child development knowledge, pedagogical practices, child–staff ratios, integration of learning experiences, and the physical environment. The context components are the working conditions and the internal and external policy decisions that shape that environment.
- Institutionalization, failure, and indifference are not part of quality early childhood programs.

REVIEW QUESTIONS

1. Describe several components to be found in quality early childhood education. Why are these elements necessary?
2. For each component described above, discuss several practices that might be included in program structure or function.
3. Review the items in the Early Childhood Environment Rating Scale—Revised. Observe a preschool program and assess the environment using ECERS-R.
4. Identify several components not found in quality programs. Explain why these practices should be avoided.

STUDY ACTIVITIES

1. In small groups, discuss with classmates the statements and experiences you reflected on and recorded in your notebook throughout the chapter. Identify experiences that seem to support components discussed in the chapter. Identify experiences that seem at variance with the components.
2. Write a personal statement of your belief or philosophy of quality early childhood care and education, based on your thinking and reading to this point.
3. Prepare a statement to deliver at a school board meeting. Your statement is about whether to exclude from kindergarten five-year-olds who fail to achieve a specific score on a readiness test given before admission.
4. Prepare answers to the following questions from parents:
   a. Why do the children spend most of their time playing in your classroom?
   b. Why are some of the two-year-olds beginning toilet training, and some not?
   c. Why doesn't my four-year-old bring home artwork every day, as my neighbour's child does?
   d. Why do you call it teaching when you're not doing reading or math lessons or anything like that?
5. Explore websites that present perspectives on quality early childhood education. For example, you might want to look for the Canadian Child Care Federation's document, *National statement on quality early learning and childcare*. Another useful document is *Starting strong III: A quality toolbox for ECEC*, published by the OECD.
   What can you find out about different perspectives on quality?

KEY TERMS

accreditation: System of voluntary evaluation of excellence in early childhood centres, administered by the National Academy for Early Childhood Education and established by the NAEYC.

assessment: Evaluation of abilities, skills, and knowledge when referring to persons, or evaluation of components when referring to environments.

child-sensitive: Also called *child-centred*. Programs whose practices are responsive to knowledge and observations about children.

cognitive development: Related to mental functions of thinking, perceiving, and learning.

diversity: Variety of differences that exist in a classroom, community, culture, or country. Diversity may refer to ability, gender, age, race, culture, and so on.

emotional development: Related to feelings and expression of feelings.

environment: Everything that surrounds the children that, therefore, affects their lives. Includes physical arrangements of time and space, materials, and activities within the environment, and the people available for interaction.

fine motor: Related to the smaller muscles of the body and limbs, such as those in the fingers, toes, face, and sphincters.

gross motor: Related to the whole body and to the larger muscles such as those in the legs, arms, and trunk.

integrated curriculum: Centres on activities that address many aspects of development and knowledge, rather than separating curriculum into numerous skill areas.

interrelationships: Connections between one aspect of development and another, and between people.

learning centres: Also called *interest centres*. Program areas arranged for particular activities that can be chosen by children. Examples are art, block, and book centres.

moral development: Related to acquiring a sense of right and wrong behaviour and to the ability to control one's actions according to these internalized standards.

open-ended: Activities, materials, or communications that permit various responses and reactions, rather than one fixed correct response.

physical development: Related to growth and coordination.

position statement: Statement of philosophy of a professional organization, used to guide the practice of professionals.

primary caregiver: Person assigned responsibility for a small subgroup of children within a larger group.

reciprocity: Mutual give-and-take.

respect: Recognition of, and sensitivity to, self and others.

responsiveness: Being sensitive to a child's emotional and physical needs, and taking actions to meet those needs.

self-esteem: Sense of self-worth, or value placed on the self.

self-identity: Image of self, constructed by feedback from others and cognitive understanding of gender, race, ability, and the cultural messages about these components.

social development: Steps in learning appropriate social interaction with peers and adults.

staff turnover: Rate at which practitioners leave their place of employment and seek other work.

theory: Set of ideas, principles, or explanations that explain phenomena.

transition: Period of change. The daily classroom schedule contains several transitions, for example, when children change classrooms.

whole child: Theory that supports recognizing the separate and interrelated aspects of the individual, including the domains of the physical, cognitive, language, emotional, and social development.

Suggested Readings

Canadian Child Care Federation. (2007). *National statement on quality early learning and child care*. Ottawa: CCCF.

Doherty, G. (2000). Issues in Canadian child care: What does the research tell us? *Research Connections Canada 5*, pp. 5–106. Copyright © Canadian Childcare Federation.

Doherty, G. (2001). Regulations as a strategy for promoting quality in child care settings. *Research connections Canada: Supporting children and families*, 6.

Friendly, M., Doherty, G., & Beach, J. (2006). *Quality by design: What do we know about quality in early learning and child care and what do we think? A literature review*. Toronto: Childcare Resource & Research Unit, University of Toronto. Available at http://www.childcarequality.ca, accessed May 15, 2006.

Greenman, J. (2008). *Learning spaces, caring places: Children's environments that work*. Redmond, WA: Exchange Press.

Katz, L. (1993). Five perspectives on quality in early childhood programs. Perspectives from ERIC/EECE. [Monograph series, 1]. Urbana, IL: ERIC Clearing House on Elementary and Early Childhood Education.

Moss, P., & Pense, A. (Eds.). (1994). *Valuing quality in early childhood services*. New York: Teachers College Press.

Penn, H.(2011) Quality in early childhood services: An international perspective. Berkshire, England: Open University Press.

Jupiterimages/Stockbyte/Thinkstock

SECTION

THE EARLY CHILDHOOD WORKFORCE

In Section One, we examined the organization of early childhood education and related programs in Canada. We also discussed quality in early childhood education settings. From this framework, it is time to look at the roles of ECEs, who make up the early childhood workforce. Chapter 4 will highlight the roles and responsibilities of those who are part of the early childhood workforce. Chapter 5 will examine ECEs' motivations for entering the field and the education options available to a student interested in becoming an ECE. Chapter 6 will look at the work environment and the opportunities and challenges that lie ahead for the early childhood workforce.

Be prepared to think honestly about yourself in relation to the early childhood workforce. Could this be your life?

EDUCATORS MATTER

Encounters between people are fluid and never the same twice. For this reason, it is important for all educators to be reflective practitioners, sensitive to children and knowledgeable about how they develop. Skilled ECEs match their interactions and responses to what is required to best assist a child's learning….

ECEs ask questions to promote problem-solving and challenge children's thinking and reasoning. Children acquire numeracy skills from birth, first recognizing the patterns in people's faces, then in repetitive games like "patty-cake" and "peek-a-boo." Even very small children know two cookies are better than one. Young children acquire the language of numbers when they understand how to put things in order and the relationships between big and little, more and less, tall and short. With experience, their understanding of qualitative and quantitative relationships deepens and children develop abilities to measure time, temperature, length and mass….

Bringing children to learning opportunities is part of the supportive relationship between educators and parents and between educators, parents and children; the child learns through active involvement, not through passively receiving information. Adults open up learning opportunities for young children when they respect children as confident and competent learners. These expectations encourage young children's hopefulness in their own capabilities.

Source: From McCain, Mustard, & McCuaig (2011). *The Early Years Study 3*, p. 54.

CHAPTER 4

EARLY CHILDHOOD EDUCATORS

OBJECTIVES

After studying this chapter, students will be able to

- define the terms "early childhood workforce" and "early childhood educators"

- describe the characteristics of early childhood educators who work with young children in early childhood programs
- identify several distinct roles played by early childhood educators

Over 320 000 individuals work with young children in early childhood programs and home settings across Canada. This chapter will focus on those people who are trained and educated as early childhood educators and who may work in child care centres, nursery school programs, home-based child care, family resource programs, and kindergartens.

EARLY CHILDHOOD WORKFORCE AND EARLY CHILDHOOD EDUCATORS DEFINED

You are preparing to become an early childhood educator with specific training and education in child development and in early child education practices. As an early childhood educator, you will have several roles in caring for and educating young children. You will ensure that children are safe and that their basic physical needs are met. You will provide opportunities for learning by creating the framework for good programs and curricula. You will make connections with the larger community that supports children and their families. But your most important role will be to know, understand, and relate to each child and his or her family.

Ingram Publishing/Thinkstock

▲ Early childhood educators work with young children and their families.

The early childhood workforce describes the sector of individuals who work with young children and their families in early childhood education and related programs. ECEs are the core professionals within the early childhood workforce. ECEs may also work in related settings including family support programs and recreation and leisure programs as well as in unregulated family care and in-home care. ECEs may work in any of the early childhood education programs described in Chapter 1.

TABLE 4.1   A Profile of the Early Childhood Workforce

	Total (All Staff)	ECE or Related Post-Secondary Credential	Average Income Full Time ($)
Early Childhood Education Programs			
Child care centres/preschool	180 000	78%	$37 000
Early intervention staff	9 500	n/a[1]	n/a[1]
Kindergarten teachers teachers (5-year-olds)	50 000	98%	$82 000
Pre- or junior kindergarten or –school-based family literacy (children <5 years old)	12 000	85%	n/a[1]
Related Programs			
Family support programs	7 000	n/a[1]	n/a[1]
Family child care/in-home child care	60 000	45%	
Recreation and leisure programs	n/a	n/a[1]	n/a[1]

1. Not available

Sources: Adapted from Beach & Flanagan, 2007; Centre for Spatial Economics, 2009; Child Care Human Resources Sector Council, 2009; Ferns & Friendly, 2014; McCuaig & Akbari, 2014.

Over 320 000 individuals work with young children and their families. They have different job titles, earn different salaries and benefits, and spend each day in different kinds of environments. Table 4.1 introduces you to some of the similarities and differences among those who work with young children in Canada. Within each of the groups of individuals who work with young children and their families, there are early childhood educators who have specific post-secondary qualifications in early child development, usually an early childhood education (ECE) credential. Kindergarten teachers have a university degree and teacher education credentials that meet their provincial/territorial requirements.

A DIVERSE WORKFORCE

Demonstrating diversity in the workforce to children through the visibility of men and women . . . alongside the visibility of people of colour, is an important goal for enhancing the quality of childcare (Cameron, Moss, & Owen, 1999, in Moss, 2000 p. 14).

Is Canada's early childhood workforce a workforce that is representative of the population at large? Look around your class, and consider your field placements.

The first observation that you are likely to make is that the early childhood workforce in Canada is predominantly female—about 97 percent. Early childhood workforces in other countries—Sweden, United States, Australia, Britain, New Zealand, Spain, France, Denmark, Italy, etc.—are also predominantly female

(Moss, 2000). The care, education, and development of young children remain women's responsibilities. The early childhood workforce is probably the most gendered workforce in North America, Europe, Australia, or New Zealand (Moss, 2000).

Early childhood educators and early childhood programs do, however, represent Canada's cultural, linguistic, religious, and ethnic diversity. This diversity is an enormous strength of the early childhood workforce. In urban centres, immigrants, newcomers, and visible minorities make up a large proportion of the population. Approximately 20 percent of early childhood educators and assistants are immigrants, which mirrors the makeup of the Canadian workforce overall (Beach, Bertrand, Forer, Michal, & Tougas, 2004; Child Care Human Resource Sector Council, 2009). Immigrants are under-represented among kindergarten teachers and over-represented among in-home caregivers (e.g., nannies, babysitters, and parents' helpers).

Men in the Early Childhood Workforce

If you are a male entering the early childhood field, there are additional issues of respect for you to consider. At this time, men constitute only a small proportion of all early childhood educators in Canada, probably about 3 percent (Beach, Bertrand, & Cleveland, 1998). Professional attitudes and practices may have been defined too narrowly as a result of the dominance of females in the field; but it is likely that men avoid the field for specific reasons related to status, economic conditions, and bias.

Most cultures convey to men the idea that they have to compete in the job field as a measure of their worth. Many men are reluctant to enter a field that is accorded so little recognition. Men also report that family, friends, and even academic counsellors strongly discourage their working with young children, as they feel it is far beneath their talents. When considering long-term career opportunities, as most men have been socialized to do, the early childhood field appears to have relatively little opportunity for advancement.

The poor salaries in early childhood education and care programs probably discourage both men and women to look for other employment opportunities. Because men in general earn more money than women, the low salaries are even lower compared to what are other men are earning. It is possible that if more men entered the field, the low salaries accorded to a mostly female profession would increase.

In the decades since the women's movement, more men play an active role in parenting, indicating their abilities and interest in **nurturing** young children. But there is still widespread gender bias. This bias translates into both overt action and covert attitudes that prevent males from feeling acceptance in early childhood centres and in schools, to say nothing of within ECE post-secondary education programs. Early childhood education is associated with the role of mothering, and men, who obviously cannot be mothers, are seen as less capable of caring for young children. The teaching role is associated with a variety of characteristics generally classified as female traits, such as patience, gentle nurturing, and emotional sensitivity, as opposed to aggressiveness and emotional control. Men who are willing to take on these roles are unfairly subjected to conjecture and suspicion about their masculinity.

◀ Few men work in early childhood education and care programs.

A few widely publicized cases of sexual abuse in the past decade have added fuel to this discriminatory fire, to the point where men are often subjected to humiliating questions and restrictions. There have been instances when directors have refused to allow male students in rooms where diapers would be changed or have refused employment to well-qualified candidates on the basis that "the parents would be uncomfortable." Men report bias directed toward them by directors, parents, and even female co-workers. Small wonder that few choose to become uncomfortable minorities within the early childhood field.

This is a pity. Men in early childhood programs have much to offer. Seifert (1988) refers to a "compensation hypothesis," meaning that male early childhood educators could perhaps compensate for the lack of male involvement in the lives of many young children, as well as offer children of both sexes a model of a caring, nurturing male. Seifert also speaks of a "social equity hypothesis," suggesting that the presence of men in these programs would help

1918

The Canadian National Committee for Mental Hygiene is established and transfers ideas on child study from the United States. Women gain full federal franchise.

Women in Nova Scotia gain the right to vote in provincial elections.

1919

Women in New Brunswick gain the right to vote in provincial elections.

Margaret McMillan publishes *The Nursery School*. (Her sister Rachel had died in 1917.)

Harriet Johnson establishes the Nursery School of the Bureau of Educational Experiments, in New York City.

1850   1900   1950   2000

society in general, and children in particular, to discover the many options available to men and women. Little research has been done on male early childhood educators; however, it is clear that their presence in the workforce could add a stronger voice for the emergence of a true profession, in which colleagues are not restricted by current stereotypes of "women's work."

As a male, are you willing to recognize the stereotypes and counter them with your own personality and ideals? As a female, are you able to support males as true colleagues, who can work with you for the nurturing and care of young children, as well as for the growth of the profession?

Aboriginal Early Childhood Educators 先住民のECEs

Aboriginal communities identify the need for Aboriginal early childhood educators to work in programs on- and off-reserve (Anderson, 2005; McIvor 2005; OECD, 2004). Many Aboriginal communities are not able to employ their members as early childhood educators, because they have not had access to training. Aboriginal people need to have training that is accessible and culturally relevant so that there are sufficient early childhood educators to meet the needs of Aboriginal children and their families.

The barriers surrounding the recruitment and retention of qualified staff that challenge child care services across Canada are magnified for Aboriginal communities. Several studies point to the need for new approaches to the training of Aboriginal teachers (Beach & Flanagan, 2007; Greenwood, 2001; Native Council of Canada, 2001).

ECEsの特徴

CHARACTERISTICS OF EARLY CHILDHOOD EDUCATORS character 性格 気質

It is impossible to list all the characteristics of a perfect ECE. But we do know that good early childhood educators are a combination of particular dispositions, knowledge, and experiences that contribute to their abilities to care for and educate young children.

A disposition is an attitude or a tendency to behave in a certain way (Carter & Curtis, 1994; Katz, 1995). Disposition is closely linked to personal characteristics that typify how an individual thinks, relates to others, and deals with daily life. Some characteristics that we expect from adults who will spend their days working with young children include patience, energy, enthusiasm, and a sense of humour.

The Canadian study on quality (Beach, Bertrand, & Cleveland, 1998) asked early childhood educators and other caregivers working in child care settings what they thought were the most important characteristics for those who work with children. Patience topped the list, followed by respect for children and the ability to communicate.

We know that children learn best when they take initiative, make their own choices among interesting possibilities, manipulate materials, and interact with people. So, too, adults construct their increasingly sophisticated new ideas by interaction with the concepts and experiences they encounter. Whether

| 1650 | 1700 | 1750 | 1800 |

your past learning environments have encouraged you to play this active role as a learner or not, allow yourself now to assume an active role.

If you are to be a successful ECE, you must create your own way of interacting with young children; you will use the knowledge and experience you gain, and you will reflect on your own experiences. You will come out of your professional preparation program ready to assume your own identity as an early childhood educator, but only if you have done more than passively meet the assigned requirements, by creating your own knowledge and increasing your self-understanding.

Begin inventing your own way of interacting with children now, by framing some of your own questions and using some of the additional resources suggested at the end of each chapter to delve further into the material. Use every encounter and opportunity to create your expanded understanding of what it means to be an ECE, and how you will do it.

Dispositions

Commitment to self-discovery. Effective ECEs recognize that the preparation for their work is an ongoing, never-ending process. Just as they recognize that their work with children is a process of facilitating development over time, rather than achieving specific, easily observable, and quick goals, so too do ECEs acknowledge that they continue to develop their teaching skills, their understanding of what they do and how they do it, and their personal perspective. They continue to question, to puzzle, to set goals, to remain open to new learning. In so doing, they model for children the active process of becoming better human beings. "The good early childhood educator is not a finished product, but a human process" (Combs, Blume, Newman, & Wass, 1974, p. 144).

Being committed to self-discovery allows ECEs to grow. ECEs must recognize and welcome their constant state of growth and change. They must realize that they do not yet know what lies ahead and what directions they will take. This uncertainty should not be regarded as daunting, but as intriguing with its wealth of possibilities and unknowns. Good ECEs are curious about themselves, as well as about much else in their worlds. In addition to curiosity, early childhood educators need an ability to engage in self-criticism, to uncover the new challenges and demands that call for growth.

Self-confidence. Competent ECEs accept themselves and feel comfortable with who they are. Basic feelings of adequacy allow early childhood educators to perform their daily tasks with the confidence and maturity to focus on the

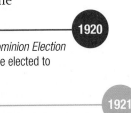

1920

Uniform franchise is established through the *Dominion Election Act*, making permanent the right of women to be elected to Parliament.

1921

The first Canadian maternity protection legislation is introduced in British Columbia.

Patty Smith Hill begins a lab nursery school at Columbia Teachers College in New York City.

1850   1900   1950   2000

他の人からの評価, や答えに
頼るのではなく.
自分に気をくばり + 他にも気をくばる

子どもと関わる
＃
愛情・気を引く

ECE = focused on the needs
of others

小さい事から大きい事柄まで
いくつも決めなければいけない
↓
すぐに判断する
柔軟さも可欠

多軟な考え

job at hand, rather than constantly evaluating their own ability to perform or others' responses to them. ECEs need to be able to transcend their own needs and pay attention to those of others. 越える

Working with young children is not about meeting the early childhood educator's needs for attention and affection. This is not to say that there are no emotional rewards for early childhood educators from their interaction with children and their families; rather, these emotional rewards are not sought to adjust early childhood educators' feelings of inadequacy. The ECE must be focused on the needs of others, not self-indulgent in pursuit of satisfying personal needs. わがまま

Flexible thinking. Every day, ECEs are required to make hundreds of decisions, both large and small. They have to select responses and methods that are appropriate to complex and unique circumstances. Often they are faced with situations that they have not encountered before and with behaviours that require them to adapt existing ideas and techniques to fit complicated circumstances. They must move beyond theories to create their own answers to immediate questions.

The child care environment demands that ECEs depend on their own problem-solving abilities, rather than resorting to an approach based on rigid and predetermined solutions. ECEs work from a solid knowledge base but are able to fit the knowledge of children, philosophy, and goals to the immediate situation and discover the best course of action.

flexible manner —

規律
Autonomy. ECEs who have developed autonomy are able to function in the flexible manner described above. They do not heavily depend on others' opinions to guide their actions or decisions. They understand their own goals and motivations and feel comfortable functioning independently. To be able to make choices, ECEs must have a healthy sense of autonomy, which allows them to accept ultimate responsibility for their work and their decisions. Being autonomous does not necessarily mean being solitary, however. ECEs can assume responsibility and leadership, while still being able to work as a member of a team.

children parents staff

共感
Empathy. ECEs require the ability to identify with others, including the children with whom they work, their parents, and other team members. Empathy is based on understanding the complexity of human development, and on respect and concern for others' personalities and feelings. Empathy grows as ECEs are able to focus on others' needs and feelings, an ability that arises from the ECE's maturity and willingness to transcend issues of self. This allows ECEs to be really tuned in to both children and adults, to recognize and accept their differences. ECEs gain this knowledge of others by observing others and making connections that allow others to reveal themselves.

Empathy → bias
prejudice
とりのぞく
narrow thinking
になる

Empathy prevents ECEs from exhibiting biases or prejudices; they are able to get past narrow thinking, as they take another person's perspective, rather than shying away from others who are different.

A sense of the "big picture." ECEs need to have a philosophy that connects their work with young children to the important issues in their lives, so as not to get bogged down in the minutiae of early care. This larger philosophy is likely

にきままる

what Almy (1975) referred to in her list of important personal characteristics of ECEs as "world-mindedness," an interest and a view that extend beyond the family child care or group care setting and connect the early childhood educator to webs of deeper meaning and social relevance. When ECEs understand the values and themes that are important in their lives, they find ways of embodying these ideas in their early childhood settings and practices.

Attitudes

Attitudes will guide you as you become an effective professional ECE. In general, you will need to have a positive attitude toward yourself, the children you work with, their parents, your supervising teachers and other administrators, and your colleagues—now, as a student, and later, as an employee. A positive attitude allows you to see the potential in any situation or person, rather than narrowly focusing on limits and restrictions. ECEs who nurture this perspective find less frustration and greater pleasure in their working situations.

In acknowledging that there is no one right way to educate young children and that there are always unknowns, the disposition of remaining open to new ideas and possibilities develops. It is important that you realize that completing a professional preparation program is not the end of something, but only another step along the path. So many students seem to feel that graduation means the learning part of their career is over, and they are now moving into the practice aspect. It is vital that you understand that continual learning comes from the practice, if, as an ECE, you remain able to grow and adapt to new demands. Learning becomes a passion for open, growing teachers. "The exceptional teachers I know are passionate about learning.… They see connecting points everywhere" (Perrone, 1991, p. 117).

Along with an attitude openness to insights and learning goes the attitude of risk-taking. You have to dare to try new things, to risk the mistakes and failure that sometimes accompany new directions, and to learn from what you have risked. These are characteristics you will want to cultivate. Students are often unnecessarily hard on themselves, expecting the polished performances they see when visiting the classrooms of mentor teachers. Recognize now that much of your learning as a student will come in evaluating experiences afterward and figuring out what you will do differently the next time. Mistakes and less-than-positive experiences are a necessary part of this learning.

Closely related to risk-taking is restlessness: the inability to accept and drift with the status quo. For your healthy professional future, it is important that you avoid being pulled into any rut; rather, you must maintain a perspective of

1922

Women in Prince Edward Island gain the right to vote and to hold elected office.

1921

Arnold Gesell writes *The Preschool Child*, which describes his naturalistic studies of motor and cognitive milestones in young children.

| 1850 | 1900 | 1950 | 2000 |

restless searching for what step, idea, or experience comes next—for you and for your early childhood program.

Another attitude to develop is what Van Arsdell (1994) describes as "seeing themselves less as managers of learning and more as witnesses to learning" (p. 94). Being able to see the excitement in others' active learning, and not to feel the need to control the directions of that learning, allows teachers to retain true excitement about children's learning and growth.

Perhaps the most important attitude is the capacity to be passionate about what you do. To retain the edge of excitement and freshness, early childhood educators develop strong convictions about what is appropriate for children's healthy growth. That underlying passion propels teachers with determination that doesn't falter, even in the face of frustrating circumstances. Care about what you do, and keep caring. These attitudes and dispositions will be indispensable as you travel your professional path.

Collegiality and Connection

Your growth and learning as a professional will have to be in the context of dialogue with others in the early childhood workforce. For those of you planning to do family child care, this will be harder than for the others, but the principle remains the same. It is within those professional relationships that you will find the support, the challenges, the ideas that you will need. When you find yourself within a community of others who care about common issues, as well as for each other's welfare, you will be encouraged in the difficult periods and fortified in the good times of teaching. Where are you going to find these connections?

First, deliberately seek employment in a setting that values collegiality. You will be able to tell if this is so by asking questions about staff meetings and staff development opportunities, by looking at the staff bulletin board, reading job descriptions, and talking with teachers. Some programs make collegiality and team teaching a vital part of their day-to-day life, and it is evident in the relationships of the co-workers.

When newly employed, convey an attitude of openness to others by asking for your co-workers' assistance and opinions about issues that come up. New ECEs are often so anxious to prove themselves and their competence to others that they put up invisible barriers that prevent them from getting the support and assistance they really need. Seek out the experienced ECEs whose programs you admire, and let them know you would value their ideas and help in designing your practice. Find out if there are formal mentoring programs available; many communities have designed such pairings to support new ECEs in their first year or two of teaching. If there is such a system, volunteer to become involved. Not only will this relationship foster your developmental growth as an ECE; it will also benefit the experienced colleague. If such systems do not exist, read about and promote discussion of mentoring systems.

Make sure you get involved in whatever local professional organization is available to you. Here you will find a ready-made group of individuals who have similar interests and commitment to children's issues. You will find members with a cross-section of experience, job description, and training; within such diversity you will find others to support you. Take the initiative to seek out what you need. If you gain more by talking with experienced ECEs, do so. If it is more helpful to talk with other novice ECEs who are undergoing the same kinds of adjustments that you are, create opportunities to do so.

There are several ways to form ECE support groups. If a number of graduates from your program are working in the same area, you may be able to form the core of a group for regular meetings to discuss common concerns. Or the professional association may offer such options. Both new and experienced ECEs benefit from the exchange of questions and ideas in such a group. Sometimes groups read and discuss a common book; others simply raise issues of personal or program concern. Sometimes such groups work on community early childhood issues, finding a common voice; but for beginning teachers their main benefit is support for professional growth. Whatever form this process takes, teachers who expect to grow and learn, through good times and bad, will discover that they must find ways of networking, or making connections with colleagues.

Reflective Practice

Throughout this text, you are encouraged to discover the importance of reflection on your relationship to teaching and caring for young children. **Reflective practice** is the process of thinking about your daily interactions with young children. As you move into early childhood education settings, it will be important for you to use your daily experience as material for you to consider, muse, meditate, and speculate upon. "The basic and comprehensive question during reflection is, 'What am I doing and why?'" (Valverde in Cruickshank, 1987, p. 3).

Award for Excellence in Child Care

Every two years the Canadian Child Care Federation's Award for Excellence in Child Care honours individuals who have made an outstanding contribution to the field of child care. It recognizes achievements in caregiving, new initiatives, quality, research, education, policy and advocacy.

Typically, recipients have considerable experience as practitioners working directly with young children and their families and have also moved into leadership positions in child care programs as well as in advocacy, research, and professional learning. Many have moved into early childhood education faculty positions.

For more information: http://www.cccf-fcsge.ca.

MAKING IT HAPPEN

Many ECEs find that recording events and questions to reflect upon in a personal journal allows them to gain different perspectives for approaching their work. Finding a few minutes when children are napping or at the end of the day may seem too difficult for new ECEs, who are overwhelmed with program plans, material preparations, and physical environment maintenance. But it is likely one of the most important things you can do to help keep your focus on your professional development. Through using a reflective journal, ECEs record their "experiences within and outside of the classroom that bear directly on classroom life" (Cruickshank, 1987, p. 10). This record of thoughts, actions, beliefs, and attitudes will help teachers learn from the children and the classroom. When ideas and experiences are recorded, they provide a frame of reference for ECEs to refer back to and see growth, or see patterns of questions that will identify needs for additional research. Make it your resolution to begin a journal on the first day of your new job, and to write in it regularly. Keeping a journal forces an ECE to assume the posture of reflection. The ECE asks, "How did I come to do it this way? What might I do differently?" ECE growth and development lie in the answers.

Self-Evaluation 自己評価

One of the most difficult things for many new ECEs is to develop the skill of self-evaluation (Duff, Mac, & Van Scoy, 1995). Perhaps because so many life experiences depend on others' telling us how well we are doing (or not), most beginning ECEs have had little experience in evaluating their own performance. Any well-run program will provide you with evaluation from your supervisor, but usually such feedback is so occasional that ECEs must, instead, rely on their own evaluation of their performance to determine their strengths and to set their own goals for improvement. Your personal reflections and your journal can be helpful in starting this process. You will likely discover a number of evaluation tools in the course of your studies and as you visit various centres. Some examples were given in Chapter 3, such as Early Childhood Environment Rating Scale; or centres may have developed their own evaluation tool. Don't hesitate to evaluate yourself honestly and fairly; your professional growth depends on it.

Personal Philosophy of Early Childhood Education

To evaluate how close you are keeping to your personal pathway, it is important that you have a guideline of your personal philosophy of early childhood education. As your last act in this preliminary examination of early childhood education, organize your thoughts about what you believe about teaching and learning into a written statement. (Study Activity #5 at the end of this chapter provides some guiding questions to get you started.) This document will undoubtedly grow and be adapted as you proceed through subsequent course work in your professional preparation. Plan to review it at the end of each semester or each year, and take it with you, making it something you refer to and reflect on as you complete each year, evaluation session, or some regular period in your professional life. As you evaluate your day-to-day practice in the light of your vision and philosophy, you may be able to keep your ideals and realities aligned.

EARLY CHILDHOOD EDUCATOR ROLES

We need reflective and well-informed practitioners, who do not assume there is one best practice which suits all, but who are able to recognize, explore, and discuss the arc of human possibilities (Penn, 1999, p. 4).

When we refer to ECE roles, we are referring to the particular functions and behaviours that ECEs are expected to perform and exhibit. If you were to ask experienced ECEs what they do on any given day, they might respond with a list of nouns associated with particular actions. That list might include nurse, diplomat, housekeeper, artist, musician, judge, cook, friend, bookkeeper, entertainer, and instructor. They might add some specific skills that have been handy: repairing toys, detecting guilt or sources of strange odours, restoring physical order from chaos, unstopping toilets, and determining fair solutions to playground conflicts.

As we discussed in Chapter 3, ECEs are critical to the provision of high-quality early child development. Above all else, early childhood educators recognize their roles and responsibilities in supporting optimal child development and respecting family relationships. A recent review of research studies in neuroscience, social sciences, education, health, and child development identified four broad determinants of optimal child development: protection, relationships, opportunities, and communities (Guy, 1997). These provide a framework for identifying an ECE's key roles in supporting children's optimal development in early childhood education settings.

Providing Protection

ECEs meet children's physical needs for safety, nutrition, health care, and hygiene; they are caregivers. **Caregiving** means ensuring that children eat healthy foods, get enough rest, and are in safe, secure physical environments. Ensuring children are safe and healthy and have good nutrition is all part of the ECE's role in providing protection.

ECEs working with younger children will find that they spend a great deal of time changing diapers, feeding children or helping them learn to feed themselves, serving food and cleaning up afterward, helping with hand-washing and face-wiping, and changing clothes after spills or accidents. Through such commonplace daily acts, adults provide children with gentleness and demonstrate skills that children can eventually acquire themselves. Physical care is a core part of the daily routine and is not something to rush through. Daily routines are opportunities to provide responsive care and learning moments.

Providing protection also means protecting children from harm. Safety must be a priority for all ECEs. You have an obligation to be aware of situations that put children at risk of harm. You also have an obligation to take action if you suspect any form of child maltreatment.

Building Nurturing Relationships

Interactions with parents and other adults are central in a child's life and evidence shows that these relationships actually shape brain circuits and lay the foundation for later learning, behaviour, and health (McCain, Mustard, &

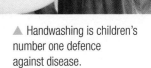

▲ Mealtimes are important. Safe and healthy daily routines protect children.

▲ Handwashing is children's number one defence against disease.

McCuaig, 2011; National Scientific Council on the Developing Child, 2004). Children begin life ready for the relationships that drive early brain development (Greenspan & Shanker, 2004). Primary caregivers mediate experiences that encourage the baby's brain to become highly attuned to the quality of those early experiences. The abilities of children to regulate their own emotions, behaviours, and attention increase over time with maturation, experience, and responsive relationships. Support for self-regulation is a central focus of early childhood, because self-regulation skills lead to physical, social, emotional, behavioural, and cognitive competence. The brain's capacity for higher-level human functions, such as the ability to attend, interact with others, signal emotions, and use symbols to think, build on this platform.

With the youngest children, the warm physical contact and responsiveness that accompany the providing of physical needs is an interrelated and inseparable part of establishing relationships. The gentle stroking and soft crooning that accompany the cleansing bath or the warmly enfolding arms that hold a nursing or bottle-fed baby nurture overall development. Young children's healthy social, emotional, and cognitive development depends on their involvement in warm, supportive relationships with caring adults.

The most important relationships, of course, are with their parents and other family members. The parent–child relationship is the most powerful influence on children's early development, particularly in the first two years. Learning to respond to and stimulate children from birth builds core competency and coping abilities.

ECEs are also very important in this process. Often, ECEs are the first people outside the family with whom children have caring relationships. Nurturing care for infants and toddlers in early childhood education programs is essential. And the need for warm, responsive relationships does not disappear with infancy and toddlerhood; preschoolers and school-age children also look for affection and responsiveness from ECEs.

Early childhood educators establish relationships with children through sustained positive interactions. In positive interactions, adults are responsive to children's verbal and nonverbal communication and encourage two-way or turn-taking conversation. Some children enjoy a lot of physical contact, whereas others do not. ECEs can demonstrate warmth and emotional responsiveness to children in many ways: in gentle smiles and eye contact, in a warm tone of voice, in personal attention and shared moments. The exact manner of interaction that builds relationships is individual. Children know when they are genuinely cared for, even though the message may come in different ways.

For babies and toddlers, positive interaction may include being "smoothers of jangled feelings … comforters … facilitators of parent–child separations" (Balaban, 1992, pp. 69-70), as well as rockers, singers, and tummy-kissers. For preschoolers, care may include touching a child on the arm when passing, offering moments of quiet conversation, and bestowing a special hug to say good morning. For school-age children, care may involve offering a joke that the child can appreciate, teasing gently about private secrets, and giving a personal wink or a thumbs-up sign. All of these interactions tell children that ECEs know and like them as unique individuals.

Another part of an ECE's role in creating positive relationships is setting limits and guiding behaviour. Young children slowly understand which behaviour is acceptable in their homes and in other environments. Sometimes what is acceptable varies from one environment to another. Children gradually internalize this understanding to regulate their own behaviour. In the meantime, they need adults who understand how difficult a process this is, and who can guide them positively and effectively as they learn to live within limits.

Young children need to have adults around them who are using their power with warmth, support, and encouragement, and who explain clearly the reasons for the limits they must impose. As ECEs base their guidance decisions on their developmental understandings of how children think, learn, and develop impulse control, they are more likely to guide as firm and friendly adults. Within the context of caring relationships, children come to trust that adults will help them regulate their behaviour.

ECEs use both direct and indirect guidance in their relationships with young children.

- **Indirect guidance** refers to the behind-the-scenes arrangements that early childhood educators make in the environment that not only prevent problems from occurring but also help children learn appropriate behaviour. Indirect guidance actually reduces the number of conflicts or problem situations that arise, making the atmosphere more positive and reducing the need for direct adult intervention.
- **Direct guidance** includes either verbal or nonverbal messages that ECEs send to children about appropriate behaviours. These messages include explanations of what the children's limits are, the reasons for them, and what changes in behaviour are necessary. ECEs learn to communicate clearly, in terms that children can understand. They are careful to use words and techniques that teach without shaming or demeaning children. They are less concerned with merely stopping the undesirable behaviour or disciplining the child, and more concerned about what the child can learn about behaviour. Children need to discover that their behaviour affects the way others respond to them and that they should not hurt other people or ignore their rights. They need to learn that some ways of expressing feelings are unacceptable, especially when they infringe on the rights of others. They need to learn that they can discuss differences and disagreements and do not have to rely on physical force to solve problems. Children need to learn that adults will keep them safe while helping all the children in the group to learn to live within limits.

Building positive relationships with children means both directly and indirectly guiding children's behaviour, based on an understanding of children's development. Positive relationships do not include harsh or punitive measures or the withdrawal of warmth and affection. Besides undermining both the adult–child relationship and the child's self-esteem, these actions are ineffective in either changing behaviours or supporting children's abilities to regulate their own behaviour.

Designing Learning Opportunities

Children whose physical and emotional needs are met are primed to learn from the world around them. They are active and ready receptors for stimulation from new experiences, which provide them with the learning they need for later competencies.

► Early childhood educators set up the environment to extend and enrich play.

Stockbyte/Thinkstock

As resource persons who help children as they construct their own continually shifting knowledge of the world, early childhood educators facilitate children's active learning. They provide time, space, materials, and support for children's active explorations to promote development and learning. They choose to make specific opportunities available based on their knowledge of individual children, child development, and family and ethnocultural goals and needs.

Environments with play materials to put together and take apart, storybooks, examples of literacy in daily living, occasions for exploration and problem-solving, regular joint reading times, and engaged conversational exchanges offer developmental opportunities that boost early learning (Siraj-Blatchford & Taggart, 2009). Early language exposure predicts vocabulary growth and has a significant effect on later verbal skills (Hart & Risley, 1995) and literacy skills (Dickinson & Tabors, 2001; Hart & Risley, 1999; Snow 2007). In one study, by age four children in affluent families had heard 30 million more words and had vocabularies that were three times larger than those of children in low-income families (Hart & Risley, 1999). ECEs can apply these research findings by working to ensure that all of the children are exposed to rich vocabulary throughout the day.

In designing learning opportunities that contribute to optimal development, ECEs are continually learning more about educational theory and practice in general; and, in particular, they are learning about the children and families with whom they work. They seek out new information and experiences of others, gather information about their own group of children through observations, and set specific goals for supporting children's development and learning.

ECEs organize and create the environment for children's active learning. They decide on the aesthetics of the environment, creating a look that invites children to participate. They set the order and organization of the children's

environment, placing objects where they will attract notice and can be used most effectively. They consider what materials, toys, and objects will enhance the environment for particular children.

ECEs match their interactions and responses to what is required to best assist a child's learning. Adults can help children to stretch their abilities in their learning through scaffolding: to help a child take the next step, the adult provides a bridge. The term "scaffolding" describes the process of helping children reach new levels of understanding (Berk & Winsler, 1995). Russian psychologist Lev Vygotsky used this term to describe the kind of assistance that adults give children in their learning. "If the children have gone from [point] A to B and are getting very close to C, sometimes to reach C, the child needs to borrow assistance from the adult at that very special moment" (Filippini, quoted in Edwards, 1994, p. 153). In helping a child take the next step, the adult functions rather like a scaffold, providing support that allows the child to reach further than would be possible unassisted.

Bringing children to learning opportunities is part of the supportive relationship between an ECE and a child; the child learns best through active involvement, not through passively receiving information.

ECEs also open up learning opportunities for young children when they expect children to become confident and competent. These expectations encourage a young child's hopefulness.

Connecting with Communities

ECEs are part of broader communities—neighbourhood, faith, ethnocultural, school, professional, and workplace communities. They can connect the families they work with to the resources and supports available in various communities. They can connect children to other services to meet their health or developmental needs or to programs that offer specialized opportunities for recreation, sports, and cultural activities.

Early childhood education settings offer daily opportunities to connect families with each other and create a community of families. Families have strengths, experiences, and skills that they can share with one another (Centre for Community Child Health, 2007; Wilson, 2010). Several studies report that families form social networks, make cultural connections, and participate in their communities (contributing to social cohesion) as a result of their early childhood program participation (Corter et al., 2006; McCain, Mustard & Shanker, 2007; Mitchell; Wylie & Carr, 2008). Families who are newcomers to Canada, and who share similar cultural traditions or speak languages other than English or French, benefit from meeting each other. Families also benefit when they learn about childrearing practices from families of different backgrounds. Informal social networks among families with young children can become valuable resources that promote children's health and well-being (McCain & Mustard, 1999; Moran, Ghate, & van der Merwe, 2004; Weiss, Caspe, & Lopez, 2006).

Children and their families are also part of broader communities. Children bring traditional practices, values, and beliefs and the experiences of family and community to early childhood education programs. Their sense of inclusion increases in environments that allow their full participation and promote attitudes, beliefs, and values of equity and democracy (Bennet, 2005).

Early childhood education programs live alongside other institutions including public media and political dialogue. Racial, religious, and ethnic tensions and incidents are often part of the context. Confronting prejudices and taking action to avoid discrimination and biases increases the belonging of all children and families (MacNaughton, 2006). In Canada, there are currently a number of exciting initiatives that provide a holistic view of community. They have incorporated early childhood education into a continuum of services and programs founded on principles of community decision-making and autonomy. In Chapter 1, on page 24, Toronto First Duty is described. This is a good example of a community-based initiative that combined public health, education, child care, family literacy, and early intervention.

Across North America, there is a trend in child and family services, to improve the coordination and integration of a continuum of services at the local level (Benner, 1999; Corter et al., 2006). Early childhood education has an important place within this continuum, but ECEs will need to be actively involved in planning, delivering, and evaluating these services. Child care centres, nursery schools, and other early childhood education programs cannot best serve children and families if they remain outside this continuum, which includes players from education, health, and social services.

Many communities are trying to draw together and integrate different early childhood education to support young children and their families. Both public awareness and the overall number of early child development programs are growing.

Across Canada, communities are taking advantage of the climate of opportunity and experimenting with community-based models. Some of these initiatives grow out of the federal Community Action Program for Children (CAP-C) collaborations (discussed in Chapter 1 in the section on family resource programs).

While each community-wide early childhood and family program is unique and efforts reflect local context and provincial/territorial policies, two main strategies stand out:

- community-wide mobilization to improve environments for all young children; and
- weaving together of different types of early childhood programs to create a seamless early childhood program to meet the needs of young children and their families.

RESEARCH INTO PRACTICE

Community Connections

Better Beginnings, Better Futures

Better Beginnings, Better Futures, located in Ontario, is a unique community-based early child development project. The project focus is on children up to eight years of age living in eight low-income communities in Ontario. The communities themselves have defined what services they need to promote their children's development and to alleviate the impact of economic disadvantage. Each Better Beginnings, Better Futures community is unique, but most offer early childhood intervention services, such as home visits, family support programs, and school and child care centre enrichment, which are coordinated with other early child development services in each community. The project has an exciting research component, whereby the impact on children, families, and communities is monitored and a group of children and families will be followed for twenty years to measure the long-term effects of the program. Short-term outcomes reveal that "where programs for children 0–4 were sustained from infancy (home visiting) through the preschool period, with parent–child playgroups and quality child care, children started school with less anxiety, fewer behavioural problems, and more ready to learn" (Peters, 2001, p.3).

Understanding the Early Years—Building Community Capacity for Early Child Development

Understanding the Early Years (UEY) is a national research initiative. It is based on the belief that communities will use community-specific research to make the case to allocate resources to provide opportunities for young children. The project, developed by the Applied Research Branch (ARB) of Human Resources Development Canada (HRDC), emerged in response to a growing recognition that, in order to ensure the best possible start for Canada's children, it is crucial to (1) increase our understanding of the factors that help or hinder child development and (2) increase community tracking of how well children are developing.

One of the main purposes of UEY is to help determine the extent and nature of community influences on child development and how this might vary from child to child. Data is collected in the community about what resources are available, children's readiness to learn at school entry (using the Early Development Instrument), and child, family, and community context using the National Longitudinal Survey of Children and Youth. The three independent but complementary data collection components allow for more detailed monitoring and reporting at the community level. Together, all this information helps fill in gaps in our understanding of the community factors that affect early child development and the ways a community can best support the growing needs of young children and their parents.

Putting together the information collected from these three components provides a framework for analysis that will not only tell us more about *what* is working well, or less well, but also give some indication of *why* services and neighbourhood resources work the way they do. This analysis will also provide the basis for community-wide discussions on how to develop community strategies and allocate resources with the goal of optimizing child development outcomes.

The Chagnon Foundation and the Quebec government created the Early Childhood Development Fund in April 2010—$400 million over ten years ($250 million from the Foundation and $150 million from the Quebec government). *Avenir d'enfants*, a Quebec non-profit organization, administers the fund and supports local community mobilization to promote the overall development of children under five living in poverty to ensure that every child has a chance to benefit from a good start in life. *Avenir d'enfants* offers guidance and financial support to collective actions and community projects, connecting schools, community organizations, public health programs, and *centres de la petite enfance* (CPEs). It also supports initiatives that reinforce the knowledge and skills needed to promote the well-being of children and their families. The EDI (Early Development Instrument) will be used to monitor progress and support mobilization.

Sources: Janus & Offord (2000); Human Resources Development Canada (2001); McCain, Mustard, & McCuaig (2011).

Community Monitoring

The Offord Centre for Child Studies in Hamilton, Ontario, developed and validated the Early Development Instrument (EDI) as a broad measure of children's development or readiness to learn at school entry (Janus, 2007). The EDI is based on the concept of readiness to learn that includes all areas of development. It measures children's ability to be cooperative and attend to the teacher, to benefit from educational activities, and to get along with other children. The instrument consists of five domains (or scales): physical health and well-being, social knowledge and competence, emotional maturity, language and cognitive development, and general knowledge and communication skills. Kindergarten teachers complete the EDI for each child, but the results are reported at the population level for individual communities and schools. This means that all of the scores for the children in a kindergarten class are grouped together to give a picture on the overall readiness for school of that group of children living in that community (Kershaw, Irwin, Trafford, & Hertzman, 2006).

The Early Development Instrument (EDI) is an excellent tool for assessing community early child development levels. It allows us to monitor how well children are doing, at the community or neighbourhood level, when they enter school. Community EDI levels can be used as an indicator of children's health in a community, because the EDI reflects a broad concept of developmental health and provides a population-level indicator (Janus, 2007). The EDI is also a measure of how well the community is doing to support early development. It is not intended to identify individual children's developmental problems or delays.

Low birth weight is a universal marker that serves a function similar to that of the EDI. It is a measure of maternal health and reflects the conditions surrounding pregnancies. It also points to problems in the physical and social environment and is a point of reference to monitor to see if changes to prenatal supports or social conditions are making a difference. Kindergarten is the next point following birth when it is possible to get a measure of the whole population of children.

In British Columbia, the Human Early Learning Partnership (HELP) has implemented the EDI in every school district in the province, incorporating the results into an Atlas of Child Development (Kershaw, Irwin, Trafford, & Hertzman, 2006). Coloured maps depict information about median family income, ethnic diversity, available child care spaces, hospital utilization rates, and other variables relevant to young children's environments. Preliminary findings reveal strong correlations between median family incomes and population EDI scores across communities. The EDI holds promise as a community mobilization and engagement tool, and as a common outcome measure that can be understood by families, service providers, and policymakers and used to drive system change at the neighbourhood level.

Used with local demographic characteristics, EDI results can help a community assess the use of local early childhood programs (e.g., see Corter et al., 2006; Wolanski, 2008; Yau, 2005) and plan new programs that meet the needs of vulnerable populations (Mort, 2004; Wolanski, 2008). Many British Columbia school districts note that (1) EDI reporting was their first exposure to hard data indicating that they should become involved in discussing the pre-school agenda and (2) they now felt confident to apply the findings to the real-location of funding for early years programming (Mort, 2004).

WHAT EARLY CHILDHOOD EDUCATORS DO

We have discussed the attitudes and dispositions that are important for ECEs. But what is it that ECEs actually do? What skills and competencies do they need? The 1998 Child Care Sector Study (Beach, Bertrand, & Cleveland, 1998) described the skills and competencies early childhood educators need to work with young children. These have been widely adopted by ECE post-secondary programs and professional organizations.

An ECE will

- ensure that the physical environment and daily practices of caregiving promote the health, safety, and well-being of children in care;
- establish a working partnership with parents that supports parents' responsibilities to their children;
- develop and maintain a responsive relationship with each child and with the children as a group;
- plan and provide daily learning opportunities, routines, and activities that promote positive child development;
- observe and think about children's activity and behaviour;
- act in a manner consistent with principles of fairness, equity, and diversity to support the development and learning of individual children within the context of family, culture, and society; and
- work in partnership with other community members to support the well-being of families (Beach, Bertrand, & Cleveland, 1998, p. 4).

What Is This Early Childhood Educator Doing?

Before we leave this discussion of roles, it will be useful for you to read the following story of a family child care provider and identify the various roles she is playing in her morning of interaction with her group of children. Although not all of the roles just discussed are represented in this account, it will be useful to see the integration of the roles in a typical scenario of good practice, and, not incidentally, representations of the high-quality practice we discussed in the preceding chapter.

A Puzzle, a Picnic, and a Vision: Family Day Care at Its Best

Not long ago I was fortunate enough to be present during an extraor-dinary drama between a family day care provider and the children in her care.

It was late morning. A three-year-old and a four-year-old were racing small, cast-iron cars along a homemade highway running from the arm of a comfortable chair to the living-room wall. A willing tod-dler retrieved the cars that had met their demise on the moulding. A mobile eight-month-old infant followed in his wake.

Chapter 4: Early Childhood Educators

In the kitchen, oblivious to the noise and excitement, Joel, a four-year-old boy, sat at the table, intently working on a 100-piece puzzle.

After some sixty cars had wrecked themselves on the wall, the older children tired of the game. Hungry and ready for lunch, they advanced toward the kitchen table.

Absorbed in the puzzle, Joel was unaware of the danger headed his way; but the caregiver could see what was about to happen. Scooping up the infant, she placed herself between the group and the kitchen. "Joel is working at the table," she said. "I'll go and see how he's doing. You wait here."

She stood over the boy a moment before she said, "The other children are hungry. Are you ready to stop for lunch?"

Joel looked up, but only for an instant. "I'm not," he said.

Passing me on her way to the children, the provider explained, "He worked on a different puzzle for over an hour yesterday. When he was finished, he picked out this one to do today."

To the children she said, "Joel is still working on the puzzle." She gave out the information evenly, the way someone might read a telephone number from the phone book.

"So?" asked the four-year-old.

"Let's take a minute and think about what we should do." The caregiver released the infant and sat down on the floor with the children. "Let's see. We could wait and give Joel time to finish what he's doing."

"We're hungry now!"

"Well, then that won't work. What else could we do?"

The infant shrieked, but no one else said anything.

"I can think of things," the caregiver said in the kind of voice that lets children know something special is about to happen.

"Like what?"

"Well, we could fast. We could skip lunch for today and see how we felt." The provider dangled this as bait, but the preschoolers knew enough not to bite.

"All right, we could make Joel stop. We could tell him it isn't fair for him to keep working when we're hungry. We could mess up his puzzle because he's kept us waiting."

Unaware of the momentousness of this suggestion, the infant and the toddler were making their way back to the cars. Transfixed, the older children held their breath.

"We shouldn't do that," the four-year-old finally said.

"I agree, Sara. I'm glad you said that." The caregiver smiled at Sara and then, with a flourish, pulled the rabbit out of the hat: "We could have a picnic, instead, in the living room."

"A picnic! A picnic! We want the picnic!"

Looking down from his observation post in his highchair, the infant watched as the caregiver, the toddler, and the two preschool children spread a blanket, a plastic tablecloth, sandwiches, milk, and fruit on the rug.

When everyone was seated, Joel left the table and joined the group.

"How come he gets to have a picnic with us?" the three-year-old asked.

"Why?" the caregiver returned the question.

"Because he wasn't finished with the puzzle."

"Is it finished now?" she asked Joel. She couldn't see the tabletop from the floor, where she was kneeling.

"Not yet."

"You'll be able to work on it again later, after the picnic, if you want to," she said.

"Yeah. Because we're having a picnic and you didn't have to move it!" the three-year-old exclaimed.

This whole drama took no more than five minutes, and yet, so inspired was this caregiver's nurturing, the moment lives with me still. She had a vision of what a child—a person—could become. She nurtured the children's highest qualities—the ability to listen to their own conscience, the ability to talk about their feelings, the ability to correct their mistakes, and go on. She was looking for more than good behaviour from them; she had a commitment to the human spirit.

She knew intuitively how to guide them. "We could mess up Joel's puzzle," she said in a voice so beguiling it caused my heart to skip a beat. Only a moment before, the children had been on their way to do just that. But the caregiver knew what she was doing. The children didn't take off for the kitchen; they paused and considered. "We shouldn't do that," Sara said. And this time Sara knew that she was right.

The same skill is evident in the provider's conversation with Joel. She could easily have decided whether or not to let him continue with the puzzle. But more is at issue here than lunch. It is important for Joel to learn to recognize his feelings and speak on his own behalf. And so the caregiver invites him to consider the problem. His answer reveals her nurturing—he knows that he matters.

As I left this home, I thought of how fortunate these children were to have this adult for their caregiver. Her vision was profound, her instincts were true, and her touch was light. Child care can't get much better than that.

Source: Amy C. Baker, "A puzzle, a picnic and a vision: Family day care at its best," *Young Children*, 47(5) (1992), 36–38. Copyright © 1992 NAEYC®. Reprinted with permission.

Consider the effectiveness of the various roles this teacher played. These are the roles you too will play as you become an ECE.

Summary

- Early childhood educators take on numerous roles and responsibilities in various early childhood education settings.
- Motivations to enter the early childhood workforce include enjoying children, wanting to make a difference to families, desiring variety and challenges, and seeing a demand for early childhood educators in the workforce.
- Competent early childhood educators bring together personal characteristics and dispositions with knowledge and experience.

REVIEW QUESTIONS

1. Identify several of the roles of ECEs discussed in this chapter.
2. Discuss briefly your understanding of the rationale for each role, including specifics about what that role might look like in particular settings.
3. Discuss the interrelationships among the various roles.

STUDY ACTIVITIES

1. Identify the ECE roles that you find in the following examples. Remember that the various roles are interrelated, so you may find more than one role.
   a. An ECE in a preschool writes a newsletter describing some of the children's recent learning activities. In the newsletter, she includes a copy of her philosophy of discipline and invites parents to comment on it. She also solicits donations of old kitchen utensils.
   b. An ECE working with infants displays family photos, under clear plastic paper, above the baseboards in the room.
   c. A preschool ECE prepares for her fall conferences with families by organizing the anecdotal observations the two teachers in the room made on each child and noting questions that she wants to ask each parent.
   d. A kindergarten teacher clips newspaper articles on pending local legislation that will affect adult–child ratios in child care centres. She posts them on her parent bulletin board, along with the addresses of local representatives.
   e. A Head Start ECE arranges for her director to observe a child in her group. This child frequently hurts other children.
   f. An ECE working with toddlers creates a cozy area in her room with piles of soft pillows and stuffed animals. She frequently sits here with children.
   g. A kindergarten teacher adds several new containers of objects to his counting centre.
   h. An ECE working with infants rocks a fussy baby, then places him on a mat with some colourful objects just out of his reach. He's been crawling for a week now.

2. Go back to the scenarios that began this chapter. Now what roles do you find?

3. Complete the following statements:
   a. When I first thought about becoming an ECE, I thought that educating meant _____.
   b. Now I'm beginning to think that educating also means _____.
   c. One ECE role that appeals to me a great deal is _____.
   d. One ECE role that concerns me at this point is _____.

4. Observe in an early childhood education setting for a morning. Take detailed, objective notes on one scenario. Later, label each ECE role and define its purpose.

5. To get started on a personal philosophy, try completing these sentences:
   I believe that the purpose of early childhood education is _____.
   I believe that children learn best when _____.
   Parents and families are important because _____.
   A curriculum for young children should include _____.
   The elements of a quality early childhood education environment are _____.
   Parent involvement means _____.
   The basic needs of young children are _____.
   Qualities important for ECEs are _____.

KEY TERMS

caregiving: Physical nurturing and protection of young children.

direct guidance: Teaching children appropriate behaviour through direct methods, including verbal and nonverbal messages. An alternative term, *discipline*, is used infrequently because of its negative connotations.

indirect guidance: Arrangements teachers make in the time and space environment that influence children's behaviour by both preventing problems and creating a positive learning environment.

nurturing: Providing care and fulfilling needs to promote development.

reflective practice: Process of thinking back and reconsidering actions based on knowledge and expertise, and refining practices accordingly.

Suggested Readings

Beach, J., & Costigliola, B. (2005). *A snapshot of the child care workforce.* Ottawa: Child Care Human Resource Sector Council.

Cameron, C. (2004). Building an integrated workforce for a long-term vision of universal early education and care. *Leading the Vision Policy Papers*, 3. London: Daycare Trust.

Duckworth, E. (1987). *The having of wonderful ideas and other essays on teaching and learning.* New York: Teachers College Press.

Feeney, S., & Chun, R. (1985, November). Effective teachers of young children. *Young Children, 41*(1), 47–52.

Ferguson, E. E. (1995). *Child care . . . becoming visible.* Halifax: Child Care Connection.

Toronto First Duty. (2005). A guide to early childhood service integration. http://www.toronto.ca/firstduty/guide/index.htm.

BECOMING AN EARLY CHILDHOOD EDUCATOR

OBJECTIVES

After studying this chapter, students will be able to

- identify and discuss some motivations for entering the early childhood workforce

- identify stages of development as a student and as a practising ECE
- discuss the different types of educational preparation available that lead to a career in early childhood education

Why do individuals choose to be ECEs and make a career in early childhood education? We will look at the motivations of several people who decided to work with young children. Then, we will explore the range of post-secondary education programs that prepare individuals to become ECEs.

なぜ "ECEs educator になるのか?

WHY BECOME AN EARLY CHILDHOOD EDUCATOR?

In Canada every year a few thousand women and men enter the field of early childhood education through college or university programs. Many do not end up working in early childhood education or related settings, however; many who begin a career in child care centres, kindergartens, or early intervention programs leave their work for other employment. Why do they come to early childhood education, and why might they decide to leave? Clearly, educating and caring for young children demands much of those who accept the task. So the education and care of young children is not an endeavour that can be entered into casually or accidentally—not if the ECE is to remain satisfied and productive and stay in the field.

ECEs — many tasks demands

大学で勉強することで自分にあっているか motivation own intension expectations

Your participation in an early childhood education post-secondary education program represents your own intention to examine issues of early childhood with some seriousness. As you read about ECEs who decided to work with young children, think about your own motivations and expectations. What do you think working with young children as a career can offer you?

Motivators toward a given profession are both major and minor. Some are related to human characteristics, including the emotions and meaning for the individual; others are related to structural aspects; that is, the way the profession is organized. We will consider the human motivators first—enjoyment of children and making a difference to children and their families—and then we will look at the motivators related to the structure of the early childhood education sector.

子供の教育に携わりたい!! などmotivation = human motivation enjoyment of children making difference to children & families

ここではまず、人間的な動機、すなわち子どもを学ぶことと子供と家族に変化をもたらすことについて考える — それから幼児教育セクターの構造に関する動機をみる

◀ Being with children and guiding their development is strong motivation for many ECEs.

Enjoyment of Children

For most ECEs, the fact that they genuinely enjoy being with young children is the main reason they consider a career in early child education and care, and it is definitely the reason they stay.

> What other job can you have that lets you play with kids, and watch them playing? They're great—I mean really fun. Amazing things come out of their mouths. They know so much, and they're learning so much. And never, I mean never, boring. Kids are so real.—Connie

> I'd never really paid much attention to children until I had my own. Then I was blown away. There's these little people, and every single day they find something new. And the world is really brand new for them, and their eyes are so wide, taking it all in. And I get to look at it all again too, because I'm with them. It's like getting a second chance at the world.—David

> I just like being with kids. They're honest and funny and smart, and they love your singing, even if nobody else does. I can just let myself go and be silly right along with them. Nothing else is so much fun.—Laura

> Hutch was a year old and my first day with him I was hooked.... Hutch was just a joy to be with.... I remember one time early on, it just happened that I had Hutch and Eric on the same day because their mothers asked me, and I was fascinated by the interaction between them. It wasn't some kind of underdeveloped, superficial play that you might read about. I was amazed at how full and engaged it was.—JoAnne

A deep and genuine enjoyment of children and a desire to be with them is a primary motivator for early childhood educators. They recognize

Chapter 5: Becoming an Early Childhood Educator

that children are interesting and valuable in their own right, and they don't approach children primarily as persons in need of change or instruction. This enjoyment goes beyond the sentimental view that is frequently phrased as "I just love children; they're so sweet." ECEs can enjoy young children while still being quite realistic about their developmental characteristics. These characteristics may include stubbornness, illogical thinking, uncontrolled outbursts, and a tendency not to care about other people's needs or rights. They recognize that children are not always sweet—they can scream, whine, and kick, and are frequently smelly and sticky! But ECEs enjoy them anyway.

Canadian surveys (Doherty, Lero, Goelman, LaGrange, & Tougas, 2000) identify enjoyment in working with children as the primary source of satisfaction for staff working in child care centres. Family child caregivers echoed this sentiment in the Child Care Sector Study (Beach, Bertrand, & Cleveland, 1998), in a survey of regulated family child care (Goss Gilroy, 1998), in a labour market update (Beach, Bertrand, Forer, Michal, & Tougas, 2004), and in a survey that included family child caregivers (Flanagan & Beach, 2010).

Making a Difference to Children   子どもは様々

Can you remember how a particular adult made a difference in your life when you were a child? As an adult, have you been able to touch a child's life with lasting impact? How was that important to you?

Another primary motivation for most early childhood educators is the tangible evidence that they are making a difference in the lives of children and their families. Every ECE knows of some specific impact she has had on children, and that impact has a lasting effect on these children's lives. Research proves it. **Longitudinal studies** of children show that participating in early education contributed to their later school success and social adjustment.

One review of the impact of early child development programs on later development shows that the results of multiple longitudinal studies point in the same direction (Pascal, 2009b; Shonkoff & Phillips, 2000; Tremblay & Craig, 1995). Children who participated in early childhood programs tended to complete higher levels o education, have fewer social problems, and more easily find employment than their counterparts who did not to participate in early education programs.

A particularly well-known longitudinal study in the United States shows that early education programs have a dramatic impact in the lives of children who are at risk. For 37 years, the Perry Preschool Project of Ypsilanti, Michigan, followed participants of a compensatory preschool program as well as contemporaries who did not have the benefit of a early education program (Schweinhart & Weikart, 1993; Schweinhart, Montie, Xiang, Barnett, Belfield, & Nores, 2005). Researchers found noteworthy differences between the two groups of participants at age 40 years, not only in school success, but also in social factors such as involvement with crime, marriage, and job and salary levels. The researchers found specific positive correlations between participation in early childhood learning experiences and later positive accomplishments. "It was the development of specific personal and social dispositions that enable a high-quality early childhood program to significantly influence participants' adult performance" (Schweinhart & Weikart, 1993, pp. 11-12).

In France, all children may attend preschool programs, which are part of the public school system, and most children attend at least two years of full-time preschool education before entering formal schooling in Grade 1. Researchers and educators have found that children from all socioeconomic and family backgrounds are likely to be more successful in elementary school if they have at least two years' preschool experience (Bergmann, 1996).

These studies, and others, testify to the fact that early childhood education has positive impacts on children and their futures, and this significance to children is another reason why people are drawn to early childhood education as a career.

Making a Difference to Families   家庭も様々

子ども = 家庭との関わり大

Of course, children do not come to early childhood education settings as independent beings—they are part of families. Early childhood educators have an important role in supporting families, and this significant role also draws people to the profession. ECEs reach beyond the confines of their settings to support the lives of families, acknowledging that strong and stable families mean healthy communities. Parents of the youngest children need information and emotional support to best nurture their children's development. They need the security of knowing they can leave their children in the hands of trusted and competent early childhood educators while they go to work. They need connections with community resources that will help them perform all the tasks of parenting. They need to trust ECEs to help their children become interested in learning and in school. They need to be welcomed into the early childhood education program and understand that they can contribute to their children's lives away from the family home. Parents need to feel respected by other adults and by society as a whole for their primary importance in their children's growth and development. It is a tall order, but when ECEs respect and listen to families, they can contribute to valuing the role of parents and families in the lives of young children.

ECEs are on the front lines between parents and the society at large. ECEs are often the first people outside the family who have prolonged contact with children and parents. Their support and relationships may be crucial determinants in families' optimum functioning. They have the power to help parents understand, accept, and value their children's skills, abilities, and dispositions and to support parent–child relationships.

1924

Lawrence Frank, administering the Rockefeller Foundation grant, is the first to begin using a multidisciplinary approach to studying children at Columbia University.

St. George's School for Child Study (later the Institute of Child Study) at the University of Toronto and McGill Day Nursery are founded through a grant from the Laura Spellman Rockefeller Foundation.

| 1850 | 1900 | 1950 | 2000 |

The Ideal Teacher and How She Grows

This was written in 1920 by Jessie Van Stanton, who would later become director of the Bank Street Nursery School, after one year of teaching at the City and Country School. It was an assignment to write an exposition about the ideal teacher. She said she wrote it while "oppressed by a sense of dreadful inadequacy, convinced that I could never learn to be a teacher." This summary recognizes that there is no ideal for an early childhood educator.

The teacher of young children should have a strong physique and a strong well-balanced nervous system. She should be plump and round and have curly short hair. Her cheeks should be rosy and her teeth pearly white. She should have a pleasing personality and a quiet firm manner. She should be poised and of a high moral character. She should have sentiment but not sentimentality. She should be gentle but not sloppy, strong but not impetuous when bitten or scratched.

She should have a fair education. By this I mean she should take a doctor's degree in psychology and medicine. Sociology as a background is advisable. She should be an experienced carpenter, mason, and plumber and a thoroughly trained musician and poet. At least five years' practical experience in each of these branches is essential.

She should be a close observer and a judge of character and should be able to deal with young and old. She should be able to hypnotize the parents of her young pupils and to cause them to change life-long habits of thinking in two mothers' meetings.

Tested at birth and found to have an I.Q. of 150, she was taken from her parents and brought up in totally disinfected surroundings. She was given a cold bath and a globule of gland each morning and her health was carefully watched.

From early childhood she was given every sort of tool and taught to practise close observation. She spent every morning seeing and sawing. In the afternoons, her time was spent on music, hearing, howling, and handling. She spent her evenings practising manners, masonry, mechanics, mesmerism, and musing on metamorphosis. Thus she acquired early in life the inestimably useful habit of using every second to its highest capacity. Now, at 63 she is ready!

But, added to all the virtues and attainments for a teacher, the ideal director should have a spine of steel—to stand the long hours and the tremendous demands made upon her. Her spine must bend easily, however, so that she can crawl under radiators with the cleaning man to dig out the dirt—or put away blocks for two-year-olds on shelves close to the floor. She should have feet of iron so that she can go up and downstairs tirelessly all day long from kitchen to roof to classroom to office.

Now she has studied. Now she has taught. Now, at 83—she is ready to direct!

Source: Van Stanton (1990). Used with permission of New York State Association for the Education of Young Children (NYSAEYC). Originally published in *New York Nursery Education News* (Winter 1954).

Variety and Challenge

Some people are attracted to work that is never predictable, in which challenges and questions arise continually, and every day is likely to be different from the one before. Life in early childhood education settings with children from birth through elementary school is just that—and then some.

As you read the descriptions of quality programs in Chapter 3, you probably realized that the active, hands-on learning required means that ECEs live

1650   1700   1750   1800

in a world of movement, noise, choice, and activity. In such an environment, an infinite number of tasks call for attention simultaneously. A typical scenario is four children splashing at the water table, while another needs assistance in the bathroom, and yet another is crying quietly in the book area, when the phone rings and a parent walks in the door. Working with young children demands energy, knowledge, patience, and creativity, as well as the capacity to be flexible in the face of diverse demands.

Much of the variety in an ECE's day comes from the children and their families. With rapidly developing children, change is the operative word. Today's crawlers are tomorrow's walkers; abilities to use a spoon, catch a ball, or climb stairs are acquired in quick spurts; and the use of language often seems to explode overnight. The diversity of potential and environmental experience offered by each family means that a roomful of three-year-old children will have stunningly different interests, needs, and ideas.

ECEs have to develop the skills and intuition to adapt to a great many unknowns in the course of a day. Sometimes the small events indicate larger happenings: the six-month-old baby seems unusually fussy, until you find a new tooth about to pop through; the six-year-old cries because he's "forgotten" his library book, then reveals that he left it in the car when Dad picked him up from Mom's house after the weekend visit.

You learn to make adjustments to children's individual styles and idiosyncrasies, as well as to new skills and abilities. The variety and challenges of working with unique children and families should motivate you, rather than frustrate you. ECEs who are stimulated and excited by this part of the work environment are continually challenged to learn new things and develop new skills.

ECEs encounter beings who are constantly changing and becoming, and they themselves are challenged to continue to grow.

Demand for Early Childhood Educators

One motivator for people considering a particular occupation or field is the availability of job opportunities—that is, the need for employees in the sector. The good news about early childhood education is that there appears to be no end to the demand for competent early childhood educators. Whether you are drawn to work with school-age children or with younger ones, there are many opportunities in every community across Canada.

1925

Women over 25 gain the right to vote in Newfoundland.

Sigmund Freud's theory of personality development, stressing the importance of the early years and relationships, is published.

1926

Jean Piaget publishes *The Language and Thought of the Child*, outlining his theory of the four periods of the growth of intelligence.

Canada's first nursery schools open at the St. George School for Child Study in Toronto and at McGill University in Montreal.

The Canadian Council on Child Welfare sponsors prenatal and preschool letters to mothers eager to find out the most up-to-date childrearing advice.

| 1850 | 1900 | 1950 | 2000 |

Chapter 5: Becoming an Early Childhood Educator

▶ The demand for early childhood educators to work with young children and their families is growing.

2009は ECEEりで
5000の仕事夢早あった

In 2009, economists estimated that there is a workforce shortage of about 5000 qualified early childhood educators across Canada in regulated child care programs alone (Fairholm, 2010). The recent expansion of public education into early childhood education has increased the shortage of qualified early childhood educators, as ECEs are finding employment in these programs (Flanagan & Beach, 2010; McCuaig, Bertrand, & Shanker, 2012; Mehta, Janmohamed, & Corter, 2011). Also, the recent spotlight on early child development as a determinant of later learning, behaviour, and health (e.g., McCain, Mustard, & Shanker, 2007) has spawned a growth of niche programming, such as music and movement classes, preschool creative groups, or infant–mother yoga, for young children and their parents. ECEs are well positioned to fill positions in these programs as well.

GROWING AS AN EARLY CHILDHOOD EDUCATOR   *ECEsの成長*

"A good teacher is first and foremost a person, and this fact is the most important and determining thing about him" (Combs, Blume, Newman, & Wass, 1974, p. 6). If you think back on the good educators you have known, you will likely confirm this statement. No doubt each educator stands out in your mind as a unique person, with a particular personality, values, beliefs, methods, and techniques.

Think about what you bring to early childhood education. This is the beginning of how you will grow into an ECE.

← Self-Knowledge   *自己知識*

- character
- experiences
- thought
- learning ⇓
子どもに影響

A good ECE is the sum of her or his character, experiences, thoughts, and learning, all of which interact with the environment in which she or he works

| 1650 | 1700 | 1750 | 1800 |

with young children. Since the self is the tool with which ECEs fulfill their caring and educating roles, both new and experienced members of the early childhood workforce benefit from an understanding of themselves—both a self-awareness and a self-acceptance.

ECEs who examine their personal lives, including the experiences that have helped shape their values and the ways they live and relate with others, take part in an ongoing, important process. A word frequently used to describe educators who take the time and effort to analyze their actions and evaluate their experiences is *reflective* (Kochendorfer, 1994). We discussed reflective practice on page 129 in Chapter 4. An effective ECE extends this concept to reflect on her whole life.

Take a moment to reflect on your own life. Here are some questions to get you started: What early influences made you the person you are today? Who were the important people in your life? What picture comes to mind as a place you liked to be? What were you like when you were ten? Who gave you your name, and why?

What strong childhood memories do you have? How do these memories influence you as you think about working with children? Do you see an influence from your family on your decision to care for and educate young children? How have you been influenced by colleagues or mentors? What outstanding educators do you remember? What were their central teaching and caring ideas and styles?

When did you decide to work with young children? What was it about early childhood education that attracted you? Were there any chance factors that led you to consider early childhood education? How did you feel after you had made the decision? What are your goals for children?

What is important to you beyond early childhood education? What do you do about it? What concerns you most about the state of the world and about the state of children and families? What have you read recently that was important to you? What do you see yourself doing five or ten years from now?

Stages of Early Childhood Educator Development

As and ECE is beginning his or her career in early childhood education, it is interesting to learn that the various sequences of professional development and growth of ECEs has been studied. Recognizing the common emotions and experiences and their needed supports at the various stages may be helpful. Katz (1995) discusses four distinct phases, with unique developmental tasks and training needs. The stages are generally linked to experience acquired over time.

1928
John Watson publishes *Psychological Care of Infant and Child*, which suggests that parents not hug or kiss their children, or let them sit on laps.

1929
Women are deemed "persons" and can therefore be appointed to the Senate.

1850   1900   1950   2000

Stage I: Survival. During this period, which may last at least a year, ECEs are mainly concerned with surviving—getting through the day or week in one piece, doing the work, and being accepted without doing something dreadful. Many early childhood educators feel inadequate and unprepared as they face the realities of a classroom of energetic, developing children. ECEs at this stage need direct help with specific skills, as well as encouragement, reassurance, comfort, support, and understanding, as they develop basic concepts of what young children are like and what to expect of them.

Stage II: Consolidation. After some time, ECEs believe they will survive the immediate crises and stay in the profession. They are now ready to consolidate their overall achievements and to concentrate on learning specific new skills. They begin to focus on individual children and situations that are troublesome and to look for answers to questions for children whose behaviour differs from the norm. ECEs at this stage benefit from discussion with more experienced colleagues about possible alternatives for action and resources.

Stage III: Renewal. After several years of teaching, ECEs frequently get tired of doing the "same old things" and the same activities for successive groups of children. They become interested in learning about new developments in the field. It is often useful for ECEs at this stage to meet colleagues from other programs, to attend local and regional conferences, to read more widely, and to set new learning goals for themselves. Supports to your participation—such as reduced fees for conferences, access to professional publications aimed at practising ECEs, and informal online networks with other ECEs—are helpful.

Stage IV: Maturity. After several years of teaching, many ECEs have reached a comfortable level of confidence in their own abilities. The questions they ask are deeper, more philosophical, and more abstract. ECEs at this stage search for insight, perspective, and realism. These ECEs are ready to interact with other educators as they work on problem areas on many different levels. (See more about these stages in Katz, 1995.)

Stages of Student Early Childhood Educator Development

You might also be interested to know that someone has organized some typical patterns that student early childhood educators often experience. It is comforting to know you are not alone when some of these feelings and situations occur during your first practicum (field placement) and teaching experiences. If you read through them all, you will see light at the end of the tunnel, even though on some days that seems very far off.

Phase I: Anxiety/euphoria 不安 / 幸福

- Worries about interacting with children and the responsibility of caring for them.
- Easily identifies with children—because it is important to be liked by them.
- Starts making friends with other students and ECEs working in the program.

Phase II: Confusion/clarity 悩い / 明確

- Thinks, "I don't know anything about planning curriculum."
- Asks, "What are the rules?"

1650   1700   1750   1800

- Asks, "How should routines proceed?"
- Wonders, "When should I intercede between children?"
- Sometimes avoids situations out of fear or not knowing whether it is part of the ECE's role.
- Positive experiences in intervening and guiding children bring a feeling of confidence.

Phase III: Inadequacy/competence 不十分 / 能力

- Needs strong reinforcement from supervisor. Even though progress has been made, still feels everyone else seems to "know it all."
- Feels there's so much to learn.
- Wonders, "Will I ever be that good?"
- Still finds it difficult to be a controlling figure or disciplinarian.
- Feels triumph in guiding children.
- Comes up with a good idea during planning.
- Gets a hug.

Phase IV: Criticism/new awareness 批判 / 新い感付き

- Says, "If it were my classroom, I would do it differently."
- Begins to notice imperfections.
- Starts to find fault with practicum.
- Starts to question as part of the growth process.

Phase V: Greater inadequacy/more confidence 不十分 / 自信

- No longer questions—has acquired a sense of stability.
- Knows she'll make it.
- Experiences success more frequently.
- Wants more responsibility.
- Has doubts about her own ability to take full responsibility.

Phase VI: Loss/relief 不安 / 安心

- Has to depart from children with whom she's become close.
- Puts standards of performance in proper perspective.
- Finds returning to classes somewhat difficult.
- Feeling of satisfaction of progress in acquiring ECE skills (adapted from Caruso, 1977).

1929

Susan Isaacs writes *The Nursery Years*, interpreting Freudian theory for teachers and suggesting applications for early education schools in their work with children.

1930

Over 1500 registered public health nurses are at work in Canada organizing and conducting well-baby clinics, visiting families at home to inspect school-age children, and sponsoring Little Mothers Leagues and Junior Red Cross branches.

The McGill University Nursery School closes.

The Fisher-Price Toy Company is established.

1850   1900   1950   2000

Students will notice that individual variations during the phases may range from experiencing success and confidence to discovering this may not be the field that best matches student capabilities. Many student ECEs find that keeping a **journal** during their experiences helps them express their feelings and keep track of their learning experiences (Surbeck, 1994).

In fact, this may be part of your field placement assignment. Journals provide an opportunity to reflect on what works and what does not work. You can also think back to your reactions to situations and develop an awareness of how your responses influence how children react. For example, being aware of what behaviours annoy you may result in thinking about why they annoy you and recognizing that your responses influence the children.

POST-SECONDARY EDUCATION FOR EARLY CHILDHOOD EDUCATORS

As you prepare to join the early childhood workforce, you will want to know what education and professional experience you need to work with young children in early childhood education settings. As you can imagine from what you have already learned about early childhood education, the answers to this question are not simple.

Different educational requirements are necessary for the various kinds of settings. The requirements for regulated early childhood education/child care centres are summarized in Chapter 3. Kindergarten teachers are required to have a university degree and teacher education credentials. Early intervention programs and family literacy include as part of their staff teams ECEs who typically have early childhood education and additional educational qualifications.

Post-secondary early childhood education programs prepare students to work with children, their families, and other professionals in a variety of early childhood education settings. Students develop the attitudes, knowledge, and skills necessary for them to fill the multidimensional roles of an ECE. Graduates of the program demonstrate their ability to meet the program outcomes through their academic studies and fieldwork performance. In collaboration with the community, post-secondary early childhood education programs support the development and education of students, enabling them to make a positive contribution in their work with children and families.

Common Elements of Early Childhood Educator Programs

The post-secondary early childhood education program curriculum is typically based on current relevant theory and research, drawing on evidence from the fields of biology, psychology, sociology, and health and well-being (Bertrand & Michals, 2007). Programs consider the best available scientific evidence in evaluating and adjusting curriculum. As provincial and territorial governments identify and develop early childhood education program policies, post-secondary early childhood education programs will respond and adapt to entry-level and post-diploma initiatives.

The pedagogy threaded across post-secondary early childhood education curricula is guided by three overlapping instructional strategies—inquiry/research, problem-based learning, and applied practice:

1. Inquiry emphasizes systematic questioning. ECE students become active participants in constructing their own knowledge and skills. Observation and documentation of children's learning and development are opportunities to collect systematic data and use it to create the curriculum. An understanding of the scientific method and its application in early childhood research contributes to students' growing capacity to assess the relevance of academic studies in their practice. Self-reflection and practitioner or action research are also valuable research strategies.

2. Problem-based learning is inquiry-based learning that is applied in post-secondary early childhood education programs. Problem-based learning prepares students for professional practice in cross-disciplinary teams. Students collaboratively solve problems and reflect on their experiences. ECE students often work in small groups, and faculty are facilitators of learning.

3. Application is the primary goal of post-secondary early childhood education programs. Graduates are prepared to enter the workforce as professional ECEs in early childhood programs. Field experiences are aligned with course content. Students demonstrate their abilities to apply their learning, translating theory into practice.

▲ ECE students learn to engage small groups of children and extend their learning.

Diversity in Early Childhood Educator Preparation

Cheryl W. is currently a student at a community college, where she will earn a diploma in Early Childhood Education. She plans to work in a child care program with preschool children. The centre where she hopes to teach has two ECEs with four-year degrees in ECE and teacher certification credentials, one who has a bachelor's degree with a major in abnormal psychology, two who have earned a certificate in Early Childhood Education offered through continuing education at a community college, and four who have no related training.

Christy S. is a university student, completing a bachelor of education degree, with a major in primary education. When she graduates, she will be eligible to apply for certification as a school teacher. She hopes to be a

1931

The Mothercraft Society is introduced to Canada-trained well-baby nurses.

1933

Commission des assurances sociale (Social Insurance Commission) du Québec proposes establishment of public-funded child care.

About twenty day nurseries exist in Canada, serving approximately 2500 children.

1850 1900 1950 2000

kindergarten teacher. After high school, Christy took a year off school and worked in a YMCA kindergarten child care program as an assistant. During that year, she participated in the professional development activities offered by her employer, such as a recreation leadership course, creative movement workshops, and conflict resolution sessions.

Why are there such differences in the educational paths these women took? What do these differences in education and training mean to their performance in early childhood education programs and, ultimately, to the question of quality in programs for young children? Today you will find differences like these in every program for children, in every province or territory and location you visit. What do you already know about the provincial/territorial requirements where you hope to work?

One reason for the multiplicity of educational paths is that there are also several typical routes by which people become early childhood professionals: the traditional route, the parent route, and the "serendipitous" route (Bredekamp, 1992). When ECEs come into the profession via different routes, the profession must respond with different kinds of training and education:

- Pre-service training and education refers to professional education acquired before entering the early childhood workforce.
- In-service training and education refers to professional education and development acquired while employed in an early childhood setting.

College and University Early Childhood Education Programs

In Canada, post-secondary education, like regulated child care, is the responsibility of the provinces and territories. The federal government transfers funding to provincial and territorial governments for post-secondary education, and to support research; it also participates in initiatives to coordinate education across Canada. But it is the provincial and territorial governments that establish post-secondary institutions and policies for their governance. So, like the delivery of regulated child care and other early childhood programs, each jurisdiction sets up its own system. This adds to the diversity of early childhood workforce across Canada.

Most of the professional education of ECEs is offered through two types of post-secondary institutions: colleges and universities. There are approximately 120 colleges and 15 universities delivering post-secondary ECE programs at the certificate, diploma, and degree level (Bertrand & Michals, 2007). The majority of these institutions are publicly funded. A minority are private not-for-profit or commercial organizations. Post-secondary institutions are within provincial/territorial jurisdiction and may be directly operated by government (such as in New Brunswick), or they may be autonomous entities with individual governing structures (such as in Ontario). Provinces and territories establish broad guidelines and procedures for both college and university programs.

The length of programs varies from two-semester certificate programs to three- or four-year degree programs. Degree programs are usually offered in universities, although there are a few colleges that now have degree-granting status. Some programs are full time, while others are available part time through continuing education or distance education programs.

ECE Certificate and Diploma Programs

Canadian colleges and Quebec's CEGEP programs offer 135 ECE certificate and ECE diploma programs (Beach & Flanagan, 2007; Beach & Flanagan, 2010) and graduate approximately 4000 early childhood educators every year. A certificate program is generally one year long, and a diploma program is two years. The programs prepare early childhood educators to work with young children in early child education settings, particularly child care centres and nursery schools. Specific curriculum content for ECE certificate and diploma programs is shaped by the particular institution, by provincial/territorial post-secondary education requirements, by provincial/territorial requirements for regulated child care, and by the early childhood workforce and its organizations in that jurisdiction.

In spite of differing institutional and provincial/territorial requirements, surveys reveal remarkable similarities across all Canadian ECE certificate and diploma programs (Beach & Flanagan, 2007):

- All programs include course content related to child development, teaching/caregiving practices, and behaviour guidance.
- Most (about 90 percent) include course content in health, safety, nutrition, observation skills, interpersonal communication, and the foundations or history of early education theory.
- Ninety percent focus their program's course content on centre-based settings, whereas only 10 percent include specific curriculum content related to other early childhood settings, such as family child care.
- All certificate and diploma early childhood education programs include field placement requirements.
- Early childhood education certificate and diploma programs contain general education content, in addition to the professional education related to early childhood education.

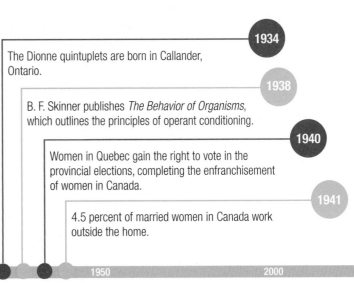

1934

The Dionne quintuplets are born in Callander, Ontario.

1938

B. F. Skinner publishes *The Behavior of Organisms*, which outlines the principles of operant conditioning.

1940

Women in Quebec gain the right to vote in the provincial elections, completing the enfranchisement of women in Canada.

1941

4.5 percent of married women in Canada work outside the home.

1850   1900   1950   2000

▶ Field experiences are an essential component of early childhood education post-secondary programs.

Ingram Publishing/Thinkstock

[handwritten notes in left margin:]
certificate & diploma 返い
↓
2年生 infant toddler 足3

4年大学は kindergarten elementary school

A number of gaps in ECE certificate and diploma programs have been identified, including the need for a more family-centred approach, more content related to infant/toddler and school-age care, inclusion of children with special needs, and greater attention to cultural, linguistic, and racial diversity (Beach & Flanagan, 2007).

University Degree Programs

Universities provide degree programs leading to certification for teaching kindergarten and elementary grades in the school system. Teacher education programs are driven by provincial/territorial policies and curriculum guidelines with little consideration of the early childhood education sector.

Early childhood education university degree programs. There are about a dozen early childhood education degree programs offered at Canadian universities, programs which can extend ECEs' career opportunities. Some of these university programs are offered as bachelor of arts programs; others are bachelor of child studies or child and youth studies. A few programs have been developed in collaboration with early childhood education college-level programs or offer concurrent early childhood education degree/diploma programs.

Admission requirements and curriculum. A few degree programs require an early childhood education diploma or other post-secondary education, and others may give advanced standing for college-level early childhood education credentials.

The curriculum of early childhood education degree programs often focuses on working with children with special needs and on early intervention strategies in specialized and regular early childhood education and care settings. Many programs offer students specialization options. Some early childhood education degree programs emphasize preparation for further graduate study.

Other Professional ECE Preparation Programs

Specialized post-certificate and post-diploma programs. A number of post-secondary education institutions in British Columbia, Manitoba, and Ontario offer post-certificate or post-diploma programs specializing in child care management and administration, children with special needs, infants and toddlers, and school-age children.

Teacher education programs. Teachers in the school system in Canada complete a university degree and specific teacher education programs to be eligible for provincial/territorial teaching credentials. Teacher education programs usually lead to a bachelor of education degree. B.Ed. degrees may be earned as a first university degree or as a second degree. A few professional education programs in Canada offer joint ECE and teacher education programs. Early childhood educators who complete these programs are qualified for either system.

A first-degree B.Ed. program takes four to five years to complete and is open to students with a secondary school diploma. It is often offered as a conjoint, concurrent, or integrated program and includes study both in professional training for elementary or secondary education and in an academic discipline area. Students then graduate with both a B.Ed. and another degree such as a B.A. or a B.Sc.

Students with early childhood education certificates or diplomas are usually eligible for admission to these programs, even if they do not have the required secondary school diploma. In a few instances, there are articulation agreements between a B.Ed. program in a university and an early childhood education program in a college that allow for advanced standing into the second year of the teacher education program.

Other teacher education programs are organized as a second degree (a B.Ed.), after the completion of another university degree program, including a degree in early childhood education or child studies.

1942

The Dominion-Provincial Wartime Day Nurseries Agreement is established. The federal government passes an order-in-council authorizing the Ministry of Labour to enter into cost-sharing agreements with any provincial government willing to establish daycare services.

1942–1945

Six community-based preschool child care centres are established in Montreal to support the war effort. Ontario establishes 28 preschool and 42 school-age day nursery programs.

1850   1900   1950   2000

Program Standards for Post-Secondary Early Childhood Programs

To prepare ECEs, post-secondary education programs have to expose students to general knowledge and specific competencies associated with all groups within the early childhood span—infants, toddlers, preschoolers, and primary-aged children. Students have to learn about children with needs beyond those of the typically developing child. They must also have course work and placements that particularize their knowledge about some of these age groups.

In addition to this general knowledge, some professionals in particular roles—such as a director of an early childhood program, an early interventionist, or an ECE working with children with special needs or with language delays—require specialized knowledge. Because of the complexity of their roles, ECEs have to reach beyond child development and early childhood education and learn the communication skills that will allow them to work effectively with colleagues on the teaching team and on more extended professional teams, with parents and others in families, and with the community beyond. At each successive level of preparation, from the introductory courses and certificate programs through to graduate degree levels, professionals become increasingly able to apply, analyze, and refine the core knowledge to improve practices. Higher levels of general education are linked to quality in programs for children, as professionals are able to apply their knowledge. General knowledge also helps early childhood educators to create learning experiences for children that draw on the broad content of studies in the arts and sciences.

Six provinces have adopted provincial standards for post-secondary early childhood education programs: Newfoundland and Labrador, Nova Scotia, Quebec, Ontario, Manitoba, and British Columbia (Beach & Flanagan, 2010b).

▲ When early childhood educators nurture children, children nurture each other.

MAKING IT HAPPEN

Red River College, Winnipeg, Manitoba

Red River College is a post-secondary institution located in Winnipeg, Manitoba, that offers a two-year ECE diploma program. Graduates from this program are eligible for classification as Early Childhood Educator II by the Manitoba government, and are thus qualified staff members in Manitoba's licensed child care centres and nursery schools.

The ECE diploma program was first offered at Red River College in 1971. Since that time, the program has continuously evolved to remain current and to meet the needs of its community.

The detailed, thoroughly developed curriculum has made the program very portable, providing flexibility for various delivery modes and communities. As well, with course content organized in learning packages and multiple delivery modes, students can choose the delivery mode that best fits with their life circumstances and to move to a different mode if needed.

Currently, the ECE program is offered on-site on a full-time basis as well as through Distance and Continuing Education (online and traditional classes) and Recognition of Prior Learning. The program also offers a workplace model delivery that enables employed child care assistants to complete the diploma within two years while continuing to work. This highly successful approach was developed to help alleviate the shortage of trained ECEs in Manitoba. ECE Workplace students are experienced child care employees who work three days a week, attend classes two days a week ten months a year, and do most of their practicum in their workplace while receiving a full salary. RPL, workplace practicum, Gap training, and regular classes are all components of this accelerated program. A recent rural expansion initiative has enabled the ECE Workplace program to be "streamed" to several regional campuses. The on-campus cohort in this group have their classes in the college television studio which are live-streamed to regional classrooms where on-site facilitators support learning.

Red River College's ECE program has a history of partnering with communities to deliver the program in Winnipeg neighbourhoods and in First Nations communities, and it developed a partnership with Urban Circle, an Aboriginal community-based training centre in Winnipeg's north end. The diploma program is delivered in the community under the cultural guidance of Urban Circle elders and will include a demonstration children's centre, Makoonsag (Many Little Bears), for Urban Circle students and community members. In the past, the program was delivered full time in ten First Nations communities outside Winnipeg, including several remote fly-in communities. These projects enabled many students who would never have been able to attend classes in Winnipeg to graduate.

Most ECE graduates go on to join the early childhood workforce and find employment in a child care centre or nursery school. With a shortage of trained ECEs in Manitoba, graduates enjoy a healthy employment record. The college also has several articulation agreements with universities enabling graduates to obtain credits toward degrees in the areas of developmental studies, family studies, and human services. Some return to Red River College to participate in one of its post-diploma programs (Studies in Aboriginal Child Care, Studies in Special Needs Child Care, or Infant Care). With experience and this additional professional education, a number of graduates achieve an ECEIII classification and move on to positions as directors of child care centres or in early childhood intervention services. The ECE graduates from Red River College meet the requirements for staff qualifications in most jurisdictions across Canada.

The ECE program at Red River College has had a longstanding interest in developing media to enhance learning and often addresses content not widely available. These are some of the materials developed by the program:

- *Our children, our ways.* A six-part DVD series illustrating culturally relevant exemplary ECE practices in First Nations and Inuit community programs across Canada.
- *Family resource programs.* A four-part DVD series highlighting diverse family resource programs in Vancouver, Winnipeg, Montreal, and rural Newfoundland.
- *The science of early child development (SECD).* A multi-faceted, media-rich, online curriculum resource that focuses on translating recent research, much of it neurobiological but also within an ecological perspective in a user-friendly, accessible, interactive medium. This resource has also been developed in an international version. *SECD* has been developed in partnership with the Atkinson Centre of Society and Child Development, OISE, University of Toronto (www.scienceofecd.com).
- *Training the eye.* A series of DVD clips that follow one child over a year in a Winnipeg child care centre, focusing on play.

The DVDs are used widely across Canada, and *SECD* is also used in many other parts of the world. With the exception of *Training the eye*, all these projects have been externally funded.

Over the years, RRC's ECE program has been involved in several international projects. The program has two international projects related to *SECD*: a partnership with the Aga Khan Foundation (Geneva-based but active in many countries in East Africa, the Middle East, and Central and South Asia) to develop a contextualized version and an online course, and a partnership with BRAC University in Dhaka, Bangladesh, to also develop and deliver courses on location. Previous international projects have been in Pakistan, Vietnam, the Philippines, and Peru.

The ECE program at Red River College continues to innovate and evolve to maintain currency and quality in teaching and learning, and to meet the needs of its community.

Source: Based on interview with Janet Jamieson, Chair, Community Services, Red River College (2010).

MENTORING

During the past several years, a new pattern has been added to opportunities for professional growth and learning in many early childhood communities. It is possible that you will have an opportunity to benefit from a mentoring program, either as a student or as a professional. In mentoring programs, experienced and effective early childhood educators are given specialized training to help early childhood educators who are beginning their careers to gain skills and become more effective practitioners. Students or beginning early childhood educators, called *protégés*, *mentees*, or *apprentices*, are paired with the **mentor** early childhood educator, generally in the mentor's early child development program. Here, during experiential learning, mentors act as backup support, offering feedback that allows the beginner to move to a higher level of skilled performance.

RESEARCH INTO PRACTICE

Mentoring Programs in Canada

Mentoring Pairs for Child Care (www.mentoringpairsforchildcare.org) was a province-wide study in Ontario that aimed to improve child care quality by matching more experienced child care supervisors with less experienced child care supervisors in their own communities. Child care supervisors' knowledge of and application of the Human Resources Sector Council's Occupational Standards for Child Care Administrators (http://www.ccsc-cssge.ca) was emphasized. Once the mentor/mentee pairs were established, participants attended special training and monthly study groups offered by the participating colleges. They met on a weekly basis and communicated regularly through experiential learning, journalling, and dialogue. The program used specific professional learning pedagogical strategies including group learning, guided communication, site visits, and one-on-one coaching and interaction.

The study findings included improved centre quality through increasing supervisor administrative knowledge and skills (Doherty, 2011).

Earlier initiatives in Canada studied the effectiveness of a mentoring approach in ECE field placements:

- Pollard (1996) examined both mentor and supervisory roles involved in the relationship between an early childhood education student and the child care centre staff member who is a co-operating teacher in field placement situations. The study concluded that early childhood education students in field placement benefit from a mentor–mentee relationship with the sponsoring/co-operating teacher.
- Singleton (1997) tried out a mentoring model with ECE students completing field placement at the lab centres at the College of the North Atlantic in St. John's, Newfoundland. The mentors planned scheduled conferences and journal writing for students to reflect on their practice experiences. The study reported benefits for both the mentors and the students because the mentoring process led both to examine, reflect on, and improve their childhood care practices.

Obviously, both participants gain from such arrangements. Experienced ECEs receive recognition, advanced education, and increased salaries when they act as mentors. They can remain in their early childhood education settings with children, using their developed skills and expertise, and yet know that they have advanced in their own professional careers, taking on new positions of leadership in their centres and communities. They are more likely to remain in the field, with the new status and enhanced salaries, as well as with the new interest in leadership and professional development. Their own practice is likely to improve, as the mentors increase their reflection on their teaching to share with the protégé.

Protégés also gain a great deal from the mentor–protégé experience. They too are more likely to remain in the field over time, having been given the opportunity to develop the skills needed to prevent the overwhelming frustration of the unskilled. Having formed a relationship with an experienced early childhood educator, they see that early childhood education is a viable profession over time. They have received the coaching, guidance, and counselling that help during the initial adjustments to any new experience.

It is not only the participants who benefit from mentoring programs. In lessening the probability of staff turnover and in developing more educated and skilled practitioners, mentoring programs are making important contributions to communities and early childhood programs. Therefore, the quality of services to children and families is directly affected by the development of such opportunities.

Summary

- ECEs are motivated by enjoyment of children and families, by the knowledge that they can make a difference, by the variety and challenges of working with children, and by the many and varied employment opportunities available to them.
- ECEs develop through the stages of *survival* and *consolidation* and on to *renewal*, and finally they reach *maturity* as ECEs.
- During field placements, student EC[E] typically develop through stages fro[m]

continuum of anxiety to euphoria to the continuum of loss to relief during field placements.

- Different types of educational preparation allow students to pursue early childhood education studies part time or full time, in person or online. Many ECE students pursue educational qualifications while working as assistants in early childhood programs.

REVIEW QUESTIONS

1. Identify and discuss the motivators described in this chapter. Why do young men and women choose to study early childhood education?
2. Which of these motivators have personal meaning for you?
3. Why is self-knowledge important to the development of an early childhood educator?
4. Describe several attributes that are important for ECE growth and optimum functioning.
5. Describe several characteristics of the various stages of ECE and student ECE development.
6. What post-secondary education should you consider before embarking on a career in early childhood education? Why are there so many diverse ECE preparation requirements?
7. Discuss the concept of mentoring as it is currently being used in ECE professional development.

STUDY ACTIVITIES

1. Interview ECEs about why they chose this field, and then ask them about their reasons for staying. Also ask them about the characteristics they feel workers in this field need, and about things they dislike about the field or their job.
2. Many of the following questions are for your consideration in your private notebook or journal. Some are appropriate to share with a partner.
   a. List ten words that you would use to describe yourself, to yourself only. List ten words that someone who knows you well would use to describe you. List ten words that an acquaintance would use to describe you. List ten words with which you would like to be described. Reflect on these lists. What do the similarities and differences mean?
   b. How have you changed in the last three years? What would you like to accomplish in the next three years? What thing that you don't know how to do right now would you like to learn in the future? What skill would you like to acquire?
   c. What is your favourite thing to do alone? With others? What is something that is special to you that you would like to share with a child?
   d. Complete these sentences:
   I want to be an ECE who _____.
   I want to be an ECE who believes _____.
   I want to be an ECE who feels _____.
   I don't want to be an ECE who _____.
   I don't want to be an ECE who believes _____.
   I don't want to be an ECE who feels _____.
   I feel most competent when _____.
   I feel most unsure of myself when _____.
   It really bothers me when children _____.
   I love it when children _____.
   e. Ask your ECE faculty to describe their educational background.
   f. What stage of ECE or student ECE development do you think you have reached at this time? What makes you think so? What would be most helpful to your growth as an early childhood educator right now?
   g. Are there any other ECE-related programs offered at your college? Is your ECE program eligible for advanced standing or special consideration for admission into an ECE degree program?

KEY TERMS

journal: In early childhood education, notes made by a student ECE to document her or his own progress or the progress of children.

longitudinal studies: Research that follows the same individuals over a long time.

mentor: Experienced individual who supports someone with less experience.

Suggested Readings

Ball, J. (2005). Supporting First Nations' constructions of early childhood care and development through community–university partnerships. *Research Connections Canada: Supporting Children and Families*, 13, pp. 21–40. Ottawa: Canadian Child Care Federation.

Beach, J., & Costigliola, B. (2005). *The future child care workforce: Perspectives of early childhood education students*. Ottawa: Child Care Human Resources Sector Council.

National Research Council. (2001). *Eager to learn: Educating our preschoolers*. Washington, DC: National Academic Press.

THE WORK ENVIRONMENT

In this chapter, we will juxtapose the positive aspects of a career in the early childhood workforce with the challenges faced by the early childhood workforce in Canada today. The early childhood workforce offers opportunities for a variety of career directions, and options for skilled ECEs in Canada are expanding. The words and stories of ECEs who find fulfillment and satisfaction in their work suggest that the early childhood workforce can allow you to achieve your personal and professional goals. As the field is expanding and becoming more visible, recognition of the value of the early childhood educator in working with young children and supporting families is growing.

Nevertheless, there are challenges, and ECEs are often overworked, underpaid, and undervalued. Some of the challenges must be accepted as things that cannot be changed. Others you can remedy through your own efforts and commitment as you become increasingly competent in your role as an ECE.

CAREER DIRECTIONS

As you look ahead to your career, you may be looking toward 30 or more years. During that period, you may be involved in different kinds of work in the early childhood field. Today, as the field continues to grow and expand, there are numerous possibilities for those who choose to focus their life's work on early childhood.

As larger numbers of children live in families where both parents work, more ECEs are needed to care for and teach these children. Families also need people to help them find care, and they need assistance paying for this care.

In addition, our society has become more concerned with how this care affects young children and what quality child care really means. These concerns have led to more jobs: we need more family and early intervention specialists to help families find the kind of care they need, more researchers to find out what produces quality child care programs, more trainers and consultants to ensure child care programs are meeting the quality requirements, and more administrators to help organize all these people and projects.

Careers in the early childhood field include those who serve children directly, those who serve families directly, those who organize services for children and families, those who provide information about children and families, and those who provide goods and services to businesses and governments that, in turn, affect children and families. As public education offers more programming for children prior to entry to kindergarten, employment opportunities for early childhood educators are opening up. We will explore some of these careers here.

Remember that within each type of position, there are many different job positions; and the particular responsibilities and requirements, as well as salary ranges, will vary across specific organizations.

▲ Across Canada, early childhood educators work in many different settings and under many different working conditions.

Careers That Serve Children Directly

Centre-based programs. Child care centres or nursery schools will likely be a starting point for many of you. Almost every other related career requires that professionals have some direct experience with young children. Many of you may decide this is where you want to stay for many years; others may consider the experience an important foundation for other goals. From your reading of earlier chapters, you will know that there are many different kinds of centre-based programs to choose from, depending on your educational preparation. These may include public programs, such as kindergartens or primary grades in the school system; before- and after-school care programs; Head Start programs; child care centres that may be operated by churches, not-for-profit corporations, or for-profit organizations or owners; employer- or government-sponsored agencies; and part-day preschools. Some early childhood educators may operate out of a centre-based program but work as home visitors either in family child care or an early intervention service.

Home-based programs. ECEs may work with young children in their own home or in the child's home. In-home early childhood educators, sometimes referred to as nannies, may be hired by individual families. Family child care programs may be regulated or may operate outside provincial/territorial child care requirements beyond adhering to the maximum number of children. Many early childhood educators choose to work with young children in their own homes for reasons of convenience for their own families and preference for the types of relationships fostered in the home setting.

Resource teacher. ECEs may decide to work with children with special needs and their families to ensure that the children are able to participate fully in early childhood education and care programs. As the special needs of each

Handwritten margin notes:

Centre-based program
- kindergartens
- primary
- before-and-after school care program
- Head Start

Home-based programs
- nannies
- own home or the child's home

Resource teacher
special needs

Chapter 6: The Work Environment   167

child and the concerns of the family are identified, resource teachers and other service providers work with the family to create a plan to meet those needs. This plan is called an Individualized Program Plan (IPP) or Individualized Family Services Plan (IFSP), depending on the age of the child. (You will learn more about this terminology and this process in your later coursework on children with special needs.) Resource teachers work with other early childhood educators to implement the plan and include the child in the daily program. Resource teachers often help families access other support and remedial services as needed.

Child development specialist on health team. Professionals with a background in child development are often included on the assessment and education teams that provide services to children with special needs. Education specialists may interact with children during screening or assessment sessions, may help provide appropriate stimulation for children in small group therapy sessions, or may provide appropriate knowledge and guidance for family members. Some health departments include child development specialists on their teams to provide information about typical development of young children for parents. Other child development specialists may be part of the staff facilitating children's play in the play therapy room of hospital pediatric units. Some health agencies, such as the Red Cross, employ early childhood educators in their community education programs.

Recreation leader. Some recreation facilities, such as city park and recreation programs and residential camps, employ early childhood educators to staff and administer their recreation programs for children. There are companies that sponsor exercise, dance, and fitness programs for children, and others that provide child care for parents who participate. Some library systems employ individuals with early childhood backgrounds to be storytellers and provide other services in children's rooms.

Careers That Serve Families Directly

Family support program staff. Family resource programs, parenting centres, and family literacy programs usually have a multidisciplinary team that includes ECEs. In these programs, ECEs will work directly with young children and their family members and other caregivers. They plan and carry out curriculum that is both adult- and child-focused and strives to actively involve parents and other caregivers in their children's early development and learning.

Family specialist. Family specialists include a broad spectrum of early childhood professionals who help families gain access to the services they need to care for their children. Many community agencies support families in the complex tasks of parenting and help find them the resources they need. A family specialist may provide information and education, refer families to services, help them gain access to funds to pay for services, or give direct support services. Family specialists may deliver services in agency offices, in child care programs, or in the family's home. Some have specialized expertise, such as child care referral counsellors, social workers, or family counsellors. Examples of programs that employ family specialists are child care resource and referral agencies, Head Start programs, community mental health and child abuse prevention agencies, and health departments.

Early childhood resource teacher. Early intervention is an interdisciplinary field that includes health, human services, and educational services for young children with special needs and their families. Early childhood resource teachers are early intervention specialists who work directly with children and their families, in both homes and child care programs. They also work with other specialists who provide direct services to children and their families, such as child care providers, speech and language diagnosticians and therapists, physical and occupational therapists, medical personnel, and social workers. Early childhood resource teachers often develop the IPPs or IFSPs that are used by early childhood educators (described in the previous section). Early intervention specialists coordinate activities between the family and the other professionals working with the child, and they help plan and deliver services. These duties require specialists to use their knowledge of child development, assessment, and family needs. They must also be skillful in working with other professionals, in communicating with parents, and in applying techniques for working successfully with children.

Vitalinka/Shutterstock

▲ Early childhood resource teachers design individualized programs to support the development of children with special needs.

Careers That Organize Services

Early childhood program administrator. Program administrators usually have several years of work experience in early childhood education and care, as well as specialized studies in administration and business matters. Administrators have responsibility for ensuring that programs offer developmentally appropriate experiences for children and meet all legal standards. They are also responsible for helping teachers to grow and develop professionally; supporting the needs of families and involving them in their children's lives at the centre where the program is being offered; and supervising the daily flow of all centre operations, including maintaining staff, collecting fees, meeting nutritional needs, and

1943

British Columbia becomes the first province to license child care centres under welfare legislation.

Representatives from the government, the Children's Welfare Council, and the Institute of Child Studies attend a conference to establish guidelines for the wartime day nurseries in Ontario and Quebec.

Ontario establishes the Day Nurseries Branch, Canada's first provincial child care authority.

Junior kindergartens are introduced into Toronto Public Schools.

The Marsh *Report on Social Security in Canada* recommends that maternity leave and benefits be extended to Canadian women.

| 1850 | 1900 | 1950 | 2000 |

ordering equipment, materials, and supplies. Fiscal management is an additional challenge, and some may also have responsibilities for fundraising. Because the director is usually the one who handles crises, the job may include plumbing, first aid, social work, and counselling on any given day. The differences in centre-based programs help determine what is expected of directors. Some very large centres also have an assistant director to help meet these responsibilities.

In large early childhood education settings, program administrators may have responsibility for arranging wider goals and priorities rather than for dealing with the day-to-day minute details of operating a program. For example, an upper-level manager may be the executive director of a child care resource and referral agency or a director of a multi-site Head Start program. Program or project coordinators often manage a single specialty area: examples include the education coordinator of a program or a child care coordinator in a local department of social services.

Regulator. Regulators, or licensing specialists, visit early childhood programs in order to ensure that they comply with government requirements. In addition, many regulators provide directors and teachers with technical assistance and training to help them meet the government standards. The knowledge required by regulators is comprehensive: they must know child development, appropriate programming and curriculum, effective guidance strategies, and health and safety precautions. In addition, regulators must have the communication skills necessary for working in the often difficult situation of monitoring others' practice. Most regulators are employed by provincial or local government agencies. Some monitor child care centres or homes; others monitor food programs or complaints of abuse or neglect.

Consultant. Early childhood consultants provide assistance and information to businesses, communities, and other organizations to help them develop child care programs or meet various standards. Usually, consultants work on-site to help the organization assess its current program, resources, and future plans. There is a growing need for consultants to help the corporate community work out methods of providing for their employees' child care needs. In addition to knowledge of child development and child care program administration, consultants who work with the employers in the corporate community need specialized knowledge about market research and employee benefits.

Careers That Provide Information

Resource librarian/information officer. The expanding knowledge base about the science and practice of early child development creates new opportunities for early childhood educators. Resource centres, research institutes, early childhood organizations, and governments are exploring ways to make new knowledge and information readily available to the early childhood workforce, parents, and communities. Early childhood educators understand the daily lives of front-line staff and families in early childhood settings and can explain what new policies and research findings may be relevant.

Researcher. As programs and policies regarding children continue to expand, there is an ever-increasing need to understand all aspects of children's development and programming. Researchers generally focus attention on specific service aspects, such as child care, health services, early intervention programs, and nutrition. Much research focuses on children at various stages of development, and on family variables and needs. Possible employers include colleges and universities, research institutes that may be affiliated with universities, government agencies, foundations, professional associations, and advocacy organizations. In addition to having a wide background in child and family development knowledge, many researchers need knowledge of observation and other data collection methods, as well as data analysis techniques. Many researchers begin their careers as part-time research assistants or interns.

Trainer or instructor.   Those who work with practitioners have the important responsibility of helping those adults gain the knowledge and skills they need to work effectively with young children and their families. In addition to having a depth of knowledge in child development and all aspects of effective early childhood education and programming, they have to understand adult development and learning as well as useful teaching strategies. Effective trainers and instructors have generally had considerable first-hand experience in early childhood settings with children. Many experienced early childhood professionals train others part-time in addition to working in the classroom with young children; they participate in workshops, take part in local conferences, or teach part-time at a local college. This is a satisfying way of making a larger contribution to the field, while still maintaining the connection to early childhood education and care programs.

You will recall from the discussion of mentoring that many early childhood educators work in their own programs with children while supporting students and other new practitioners in learning effective practice. Others, such as regulators, family specialists, and early intervention specialists, also occasionally provide training as part of their jobs. Still others, such as college and university ECE faculty or high school child development teachers, teach other practitioners full-time. Some large child care programs with multiple centres employ their own educational specialists to work with their staff.

Author or editor.   There are a number of local and national publications devoted entirely to children's and family issues. These range from the large, glossy magazines sold nationally on newsstands and by subscription, to local publications sometimes distributed free of charge in doctors' offices and schools. All of these publications offer professionals opportunities to share their knowledge about children and families, in print.

1945

Attachment theory is discussed by René Spitz in "Hospitalism: An Inquiry into the Genesis of Psychiatric Conditions in Early Childhood."

The federal Family Allowance Program is introduced.

Quebec closes wartime centres. Ontario tries to do the same but is stopped by the effective public campaign mounted by the Day Nursery and Day Care Parents' Association.

| 1850 | 1900 | 1950 | 2000 |

Careers That Provide Goods and Services

Merchandiser. There is a large consumer market for developmentally appropriate toys, books, teaching materials, clothing, and other items used in the care and teaching of young children. Merchandisers may sell their products in stores or at local or national conferences. Many corporations prefer to have their items marketed by individuals with knowledge of child development.

Politician or advocate. Although a background or experience in child development is not a prerequisite, gaining a voice in elected local, provincial/territorial, or federal government is one way individuals who care about children's and family issues can be effective. Legislators have a direct impact on creating the laws and policy that influence the lives of families and of childhood education programs. In our modern world of increasingly large organizations set up to deal with the complexities of the legislative process, some people with early childhood interests may find there are opportunities to influence others by working with advocacy groups. Here, again, child development and other professional knowledge can make legislators and advocates far more effective.

The ECE Career Lattice

A conceptual framework of ECE post-secondary education and development has to achieve a balance between inclusivity and exclusivity. It has to embrace the diversity of roles and levels of preparation of ECEs providing high-quality services for young children. It also has to recognize that individuals enter the profession with diverse educational qualifications and experience, and promote a system that encourages ongoing professional development for individuals at all levels and in all roles. The framework should also set high standards for professional performance and distinguish the specialized skills and knowledge of the early childhood profession from those of other professions. (See Johnson & McCracken, 1994, p. 11.)

The multiplicity of career possibilities for an early childhood educator can be represented as a **career lattice**. Picture a graph: The vertical strands represent the various settings where ECEs work, while the horizontal strands represent the various roles and levels of responsibility in each setting. The X axis represents, therefore, the different entry points at which an ECE can embark on a career, and the Y axis represents increasing responsibility and compensation. The lattice allows for the possibility of upward movement with increasing responsibility and compensation within each role, as well as lateral or diagonal movement across the various roles. This lattice image seems a better representation for a field as diverse as early childhood education than the more traditional career ladder, which implies that there is just one clearly defined path to professional development and which also indicates that one must step over others to advance.

One scenario illustrated by the lattice is the following: A young woman is employed as a child care assistant without any pre-service training. After two years of experience, she earns a promotion to lead early childhood educator and enters a program at a community college, where she completes a two-year diploma program in early childhood education. Some time later, she seeks employment as a lead early childhood educator in a Head Start program, where she is encouraged to continue her education in a degree program. A number of years later, she applies for position of assistant director at her original child care centre.

The career lattice concept also allows for the scenario where a parent in a Head Start program is hired as a bus driver/aide. He takes an introductory course in ECE at a local community college, then completes an ECE certificate through continuing education and, after a number of years, becomes a lead teacher in a Head Start program. While teaching in the program, he continues his education to obtain his teacher's certification, and he later becomes a kindergarten teacher in a local elementary school.

The lattice allows for the entry of people like these into the profession, and it allows them to continue their professional growth and move into various roles. It allows entry, as well, for those who followed the more traditional routes of enrolling in a diploma program, a teacher certification program, or a degree program immediately after high school graduation, obtaining credentials before gaining employment in the field, and then, perhaps, making several changes in the early childhood settings chosen for employment.

The lattice distinguishes the early childhood field from the early childhood profession; the field includes anyone engaged in providing early childhood services, whereas the profession includes those who have acquired some professional training and are on a professional path. It defines distinct categories on a continuum of professional development.

◀ The working conditions in early childhood programs set the climate for children and staff.

The Organizational Climate of Early Childhood Programs

International and Canadian research findings point to the school principal or program manager, supervisor, or director as the gatekeeper of quality who sets the organizational climate (Fullan, 2001; Goelman, Doherty, Lero, LaGrange, & Tougas, 2000; Mill, Jacobs, Mill, & Jenning, 2002; National Research Council, 2000). School principals are expected to be leaders of learning, knowledgeable about curriculum and pedagogy and able to assess and develop teacher skills. They are also expected to provide working conditions for teachers that allow them to practise their profession (McElgunn, 2006; Mort, 2007; National Association of Elementary School Principals, 2005; Phillips, 2003). Early childhood educators need the same kind of leadership in all early childhood programs.

Skilled management and leadership in early childhood programs creates a positive organizational climate. ECEs have opportunities to be involved in decision-making. A coherent administrative framework supports early childhood educators working together in teams. In family child care, support and contact with other caregivers is part of a positive organizational climate.

Effective leadership practice in early childhood programs includes pedagogical and curriculum leadership and outreach to families and communities (Bennett, 2008; Bertrand & Michals, 2007; Best Start Quality and Human Resources Expert Panel, 2007; Siraj-Blatchford & Manni, 2006) in addition to necessary financial and human resources management skills. Pedagogical leadership contributes to good practice (Bertrand & Michals, 2007; Siraj-Blatchford et al., 2003) and encourages staff stability (Whitebook & Sakai, 2004). In early childhood programs, leaders and managers who are pedagogical leaders enhance program quality and the overall climate of the program. Managers who have higher educational levels seem to be better able to provide curriculum and pedagogical leadership to ECEs.

Leadership, innovation, creativity, and a strong knowledge base are essential (Friendly, Doherty, & Beach, 2006). As early childhood programs in Canada expand and expectations for their achievements grow, the complexities of providing high-quality programs will require highly skilled people at all levels. Appropriate training for leadership roles is a critical element in providing high-quality early childhood education programs, particularly as more complex, multi-professional teams of staff come together to provide more integrated programs (Corter et al., 2006; Siraj-Blatchford & Manni, 2007).

WORKING CONDITIONS

A discussion of working conditions includes the employee's income, benefits, and workload, as well as characteristics of the social and physical environment.

賃金, 有休休暇, 何Hour 働く
は働く場所におて様々

Although provincial regulations and legislation about employment standards set the basic requirements for a minimum wage, mandatory vacations, and maximum numbers of hours of work per week, for ECEs all these factors vary depending on the setting in which they work and their role. ECEs may be employed by parents, non-profit organizations, local or provincial governments, businesses, or school boards; or they may be self-employed. The type of early childhood education setting affects the employment status of ECEs and the related working conditions.

| 1650 | 1700 | 1750 | 1800 |

The working conditions in each setting create a climate for both the adults and the children in that setting. A positive work climate helps create a quality setting for young children and their families. (See Chapter 3 for further discussion about quality.)

If the salary and benefits are reasonable, job responsibilities and obligations are clear, health and safety are protected, and ECEs are valued, the working climate is positive.

Compensation 補償

ECEs and assistants earn much less than other workers and less than most women in other occupations. Table 6.1 compares the full-time average salaries of teachers employed in public schools and ECEs employed in early childhood education settings (McCain, Mustard, & McCuaig, 2011).

TABLE 6.1 Teacher–ECE Remuneration by Provinces

	Teacher salaries 2008/09	ECE salaries $ 2009/10	ECE salaries as % of teachers'
NL	67,720	25,500	38
PEI	67,950	31,200	46
NS	66,540	30,180	45
NB	63,440	34,715	55
QC	60,180	38,790	65
ON	75,295	36,179	48
MB	73,035	34,403	47
SK	59,070	33,945	58
AB	80,375	38,355	48
BC	76,315	34,590	45

Sources: Brockington, R. 2010; Provincial/territorial profiles, available at www.earlyyearsstudy.ca.

Reprinted with permission from Margaret and Wallace McCain Family Foundation.

1946

The Common Sense Book of Baby and Child Care is published by Dr. Benjamin Spock.

Arnold Gesell, doing child development research at Yale, establishes the first descriptions of children at different chronological ages, using normative data.

The withdrawal of federal government funding leads to the closure of all 42 school-age programs in Ontario.

1850	1900	1950	2000

Chapter 6: The Work Environment

On average, ECEs with post-secondary qualifications working with young children in child care centres earn approximately $30,146 annually and child care directors earn $40,194 (Flanagan, Beach, & Varmuza, 2013). The salary differences between teachers and ECEs persist, and in many jurisdictions the gap is growing (Akbari and McCuaig, 2014).

The still too-low income levels of ECEs are a major issue for the sector. Recent studies report that low remuneration remains a significant problem for those working in early childhood education settings as well as for government officials, representatives from provincial/territorial and national sector organizations, and faculty members from colleges and universities (Beach & Flanagan, 2007; Flanagan & Beach, 2010; Doherty, Lero, Goelman, LaGrange, & Tougas, 2000; Akbari & McCuaig, 2014).

It is difficult to compare income levels for ECEs in different settings. ECEs who work with children in centre-based programs or care for young children in the child's own home are usually employees. But ECEs in regulated or unregulated family child care settings are self-employed. Wages earned as an employee are subject to different deductions and taxation than income earned through self-employment. Nevertheless, it is quite clear that both groups receive remuneration that fails to reflect the responsibilities and skills involved in working with young children.

The large wage gap between ECEs and teachers is emerging as a major issue as early childhood education programs become integrated into the education sector and into schools (Flanagan & Beach, 2010). ECEs want a role as programs become part of the education system, and they want to see comparable compensation. ECEs currently working in early childhood programs operated by schools (such as family literacy programs in British Columbia and Ontario) or as educational assistants typically earn higher hourly wages than other ECEs working in child care centres in the same region.

Centre-based early childhood educators. ECEs with a college diploma or certificate working full-time and for the full year in licensed child care programs received less than 75 percent of the annual income of the average full-time, full-year female worker with the same level of education (Child Care Human Resource Sector Council, 2009).

You Bet I Care! (Doherty, Lero, Goelman, LaGrange, & Tougas, 2000) was a major study of the wages and working conditions of staff employed in licensed child care centres across Canada in 1998. *You Bet We Still Care* (Beach, Flanagan, & Varmuza, 2013) updated the survey. Between 2000 and 2012, provincial/territorial government policy and funding initiatives that influence human resources included wage subsidies, educational support, bursaries, and incentives, and revised policies regarding recognition of post-secondary early childhood credentials. Higher education, more experience, unionization, and non-profit status were factors found to be related to higher income levels, even within the same province or territory (Beach, Flanagan, & Varmuza, 2013). *You Bet We Still Care!* also reported on benefits that staff in child care centres received. In 1998, only 25 percent of full-time staff reported pension benefits, and 26 percent did not have sick leave benefits. About half of the staff members in the survey reported that they did not have long-term disability benefits. In 2012, 38 percent of child care staff reported pension benefits—a slight improvement—while 36 percent did not have sick leave benefits—a decline from earlier levels (Beach, Flanagan, & Varmuza, 2013).

Early childhood educators in regulated family child care. Most family child caregivers are self-employed, and their programs are set up as small businesses. They are able to deduct reasonable expenses from the child care fees they receive, either directly from parents or through government fee subsidy programs.

The income of ECEs in family child care is affected by the number of children in the settings. The maximum number of children is determined by the provincial/territorial regulations and varies from one region to another (as discussed in Chapter 1), but many family caregivers provide care for fewer children than is allowed by government regulations.

ECEs working in family child care are self-employed, and therefore would have to purchase benefits on their own. As of January 2011, self-employed individuals can register for the federal Employment Insurance plan, to be eligible for unemployment, parental leave, sickness coverage, and compassionate care benefits. Family care providers can opt into the program if they have a minimum of $6515 (in 2013) in earnings and have paid the premiums for one year (Service Canada, 2014).

Employment Contracts

A contract of employment outlines the terms or "rules" of an employment arrangement (Bertrand, 2008). It is an agreement between the employer (e.g., the early child development setting) and the employees (e.g., early childhood educators). In a unionized setting, it is called a collective agreement and is negotiated by a process of collective bargaining.

A contract of employment usually includes

- job title;
- employment status;   契約內容
- salary;
- benefits;
- work requirements; and
- employment procedures (hiring, termination).

1946

The American baby boom begins.

Ontario legislature passes the *Day Nurseries Act.* Federal funding for day nurseries ends.

1947

The Canadian baby boom begins and continues until 1964.

1850   1900   1950   2000

Health and Safety

Your early childhood education studies emphasize the issues of health and safety of children in various early child development settings. Policies and practices ensure that the physical environment is safe. There are also significant issues related to early childhood educators' health and safety in their work environments; for example, ECEs are particularly vulnerable to infectious diseases and musculoskeletal disorders.

Getting sick is an occupational hazard in early childhood settings. Young children get colds, with runny noses and crusty eyes. They get gastrointestinal viruses and may vomit or have diarrhea. ECEs who are exposed to these germs, and other common childhood diseases, risk becoming sick. Personal health care and preventive measures, as well as excellent hygiene practices in the early childhood setting, help to reduce the likelihood of illness. But, compared to most work environments, there is increased exposure to infectious diseases in work with young children.

Working with young children is physically demanding. Babies, children, furnishings, and equipment are carried or moved throughout the day's activities. An ECE's back, knees, and other joints can suffer, leading to musculoskeletal disorders.

Health and safety challenges are reduced by good working conditions that minimize the risks. As well, when illness or injury happens, sick leave and extended health care benefits can make a big difference.

Stress and Isolation

ECEs are exposed to several sources of stress in their daily work environments, including the need for constant attention to keep children safe; frustrations connected to a lack of resources; too many demands from too many people; children's unpredictable interests, emotions, and behaviours; and emotional involvement with children and their families. Although the variety of situations and constant interactions with people are what attract and motivate many early childhood educators to work with young children, these same characteristics can be overwhelming.

Often in early childhood settings, resources—human and physical—are in short supply. There may be too many children and too few adults to provide optimal experiences for the children. The quality of materials that the ECE can provide for children is constrained by the program's budget. ECEs know what they should do with children and what they would like to do, but they are often unable to do so because of situational constraints.

Beach, Bertrand, Forer, Michal, and Tougas (2004, p. 129) report that "the demands for, and expectations of child care are changing and often the caregiver bears the brunt of the inability of the sector to respond adequately to these changes. The sector is having difficulty responding to the needs of parents and offering high-quality care. Yet parents are becoming more aware of the importance of quality care and early experiences to their child's development, and are expecting more of caregivers." As resources become tighter and family expectations grow, early childhood educators feel the squeeze in trying

to meet increased expectations with fewer materials, and with cutbacks in
public health, social services, and public school programs.

Another factor contributing to stress is isolation. As an ECE, you will
spend most of your time in the company of young children from infancy
through to twelve years of age. ECEs often work with other colleagues and
assistants, but most of their conversations and contacts will be with the children. Even when parents and other family members are invited to spend
time in the early childhood setting, the amount of time they spend there will
be a small fraction of the workday. Though working with young children is
rewarding and satisfying, it is also isolating. Family caregivers identify isolation
and lack of contact with other adults as a work challenge (Beach, Bertrand,
Forer, Michal, & Tougas, 2004; Best Start Quality and Human Resources
Expert Panel, 2007).

We will examine some of the characteristics of the ECE's work
environment that often contribute to stress and isolation.

Variety and unpredictability. There is constant change in work with young
children; no two days are the same. Although a moderate amount of variety is
stimulating and exciting to most people, a constant barrage of unpredictable
events may result in psychological overload. The need to adapt continually can
be exhausting, both physically and emotionally, even while it is exhilarating.

Imagine the adjustments an ECE needs to make when she discovers that her
co-worker's car has broken down so she is running late; that two of the children
in her class have just been diagnosed with chicken pox, and the other ten families need to be informed; that there is no red paint for the planned art activity
this morning and the child who is painting at the easel is demanding a substitute
for the blue paint provided; that the puzzle table that is usually quite attractive to her group of children draws only uninterested glances this morning; that
the birthday party scheduled for lunchtime will have to be moved to morning
snack time to accommodate working parents' schedules; and that the child
who usually separates from her grandmother easily has chosen today to run
after her with heartbroken screams. After order is restored, the ECE may feel a
boost in self-confidence as she realizes that she has coped with these and other
impromptu decisions and situations; but at the time, she has undoubtedly experienced a good deal of the stress that comes with having to adapt quickly.

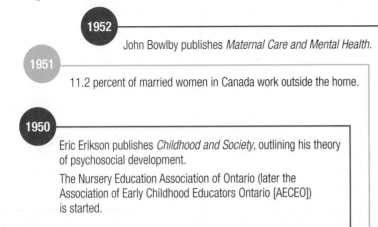

1952
John Bowlby publishes *Maternal Care and Mental Health*.

1951
11.2 percent of married women in Canada work outside the home.

1950
Eric Erikson publishes *Childhood and Society*, outlining his theory
of psychosocial development.
The Nursery Education Association of Ontario (later the
Association of Early Childhood Educators Ontario [AECEO])
is started.

1850   1900   1   2000

Let's analyze the reasons behind the stress in such a scenario. One reason is that ECEs are inextricably bound to a variety of other adults, both co-workers and the parents of the children. Their schedules, needs, and wishes, to say nothing of values, all have to be acknowledged and have an effect on the ECE's actions and schedule. A second reason is that ECEs have so many roles to play, and play simultaneously. Concurrently, this ECE is concerned with ensuring the health and safety of children, communicating with parents, planning and providing appropriate learning resources and a daily schedule, and providing emotional support. Small wonder that she experiences stress.

Yet another reason for stress in the early childhood classroom is that young children are "predictably unpredictable" (Hyson, 1982, p. 26). Fast-changing interests, emotions, and behaviour mean that teachers are never quite sure how children will react to activities or situations, as in the case of the unexpected separation distress. With emphasis in the early childhood education curriculum on children's choice and independent exploratory play, ECEs regularly have to adapt to children's preferences in the use of materials. The unpredictable process of responding to children's choices means that ECEs face stress in trying to provide appropriate curriculum activities and materials, often without advance planning.

For many ECEs, this spectacular lack of limits—the variety, freedom, the open-ended and unpredictable nature of the early childhood education setting—is attractive. For others, this same variety and freedom may create anxiety and stress.

Frustrations. ECEs have often chosen their profession because of their high ideals and their desire to influence children's development in important ways. "They impose upon themselves the responsibility for unlocking each child's potential" (Hyson, 1982, p. 27). Each child comes with a particular background and cultural context and with unique abilities, interests, and needs. There are enormous differences in what each child needs from the ECE and in the ECE's ability to respond to each child. Good ECEs try their best to rise to each specific challenge and to find the resources to help when they are unable to do the job themselves. They spread themselves around as much as they can, often painfully aware that although there are one or perhaps two adults in a setting, there may be three, five, or even ten times as many children, all demanding and deserving of help. There is never enough time to do all that ECEs feel should be done, and it is frustrating to feel unable to meet that need.

Frustration also comes from the complexities of the ECE's tasks. The children are the main focus, of course; but every ECE would like to have more time to talk with parents, to share ideas with colleagues, to prepare new play materials, and to reach out to educate the community about young children's needs. The multiplicity of aims and goals may be daunting. Time just does not permit a sense of completion in all these activities, and early childhood educators can feel frustrated in knowing that they could do their jobs better, "if only …"

Frustration comes not only from being unable to accomplish everything you would like with children or families, but also from the fact that resources are often inadequate to support the work of early child development. In times of tight budgets, it is extremely rare to work in settings that provide all the materials and equipment that ECEs feel are essential to their task. Indeed, the programs that serve the needs of children and families often seem to be the first to feel the sting of budget cuts. On a day-to-day basis, limited resources mean constant efforts to stretch inadequate staff, learning materials, and supplies, in ways that are frustrating and sometimes downright humiliating. "I'm sorry," apologizes the infant ECE, "We've run out of diapers, so I'll have to ask you to bring some in for your child." "Only one cup of juice; we'll get seconds of water." "Just one dot of glue."

Frustration is a part of many occupations today that are stretched to do complex jobs with inadequate supports or resources. If ECEs are to avoid the **burnout** that comes with ever-mounting frustration, they will need to find the satisfaction that outweighs the frustrations in their work.

Changing times.   One challenge for ECEs is that their roles, which have always been somewhat loosely defined, are even more nebulous as society's demands and needs for the care and education of young children grow and multiply. ECEs sometimes feel that they are asked to become counsellors, psychologists, and social workers, as they tend to the stresses of both children and parents. In addition, there are many other changes taking place in the profession; for example, child care regulations are under review in many parts of Canada (e.g., Ontario, Prince Edward Island, New Brunswick, and Nova Scotia), and public education is taking on early childhood education programming, creating changes in how families are using child care centres.

Attachment and loss.   In many early childhood education settings, children leave and move on to new relationships with other teachers at least once a year. ECEs work by creating warm and nurturing relationships with the children in their care and with their families. Especially in child care situations with very young children, they are intimately involved with the daily care that leads to closeness and with the momentous events that bring satisfaction to both child and adult. Those mutual relationships often lead to strong attachments, which also fulfill some of the early childhood educators' emotional needs. ECEs often discover that the severing of ties with children and families on a regular, cyclical basis is difficult.

Some ECEs protect themselves from the pain of loss by not forming meaningful attachments to the children under their care; however, they are then unable to be truly effective with children, as they have not created reciprocal relationships. ECEs have to learn, instead, to recognize the temporary, though important, nature of their work with children. The inevitable sense of loss will be tempered by the knowledge of what they have accomplished through the relationship. ECEs also must learn to have most of their emotional needs met outside of classroom relationships, lest they become too dependent on those relationships. The following quotation is from an ECE student who was leaving her field placement:

> It was all connected, I realized, to a feeling of loss. Cathy and I were not only leaving the children, we were losing the

1953

Arnold Gesell publishes *Infant Development.*

1954

B. F. Skinner publishes *Science and Human Behaviour,* applying behaviourist theory to parenting and education.

1957

Sputnik is launched by the Soviet Union (USSR), precipitating much discussion about the effectiveness of American and Canadian education.

1960s

Many boards of education in Ontario establish junior kindergartens.

1850   1900   1950   2000

▲ Working with young children can be isolating.

先生どうしが かたまって 話しをしたり
して、子ども と 関わらない
すぐに 休憩する。スマホ いじる
→ 経営者 不満
子ども を きちんと みてほしい

結果 でなく プロセス
先生は 子どもの 最終的 結果みれない
子どもの 親ではないので 成長結果は
分からない
その プロセス をみる

ability to influence their lives. Who would these children talk to when they left us? Would their parents continue our work? Would their next caregivers love them as much as we did? There were no answers to these questions. In the end, we told ourselves that it didn't really matter. We had done our best: we had given the kids a good beginning. No one could take that away from them—or from us, either (Wollman, 1994, p. 269).

Adult isolation. Many administrators complain that their staff congregates together on the playground. Rather than being a sign of indifference to the need for supervising children, this congregating probably speaks of ECEs' needs for adult communication. Infrequent staff meetings or quick breaks are often the only chance early childhood educators have to speak with other adults for any period. And the isolation of adults who work alone means not only that they are often hungry to talk and share ideas with other adults, but also that the total responsibility for the care of the children rests on them. It is not unusual to hear caregivers in home child care settings comment that they never even have anyone to leave the children with so they can use the bathroom or make a telephone call. Such continuous on-duty time and lack of privacy can be physically and emotionally exhausting.

Family caregivers in regulated settings report dissatisfaction with the long and irregular hours, which interfered with their personal and family lives.

Process rather than product. Perhaps one of the most stressful parts of being an ECE is that there is not necessarily a finished product to show for all the effort. What results there are may be intangible and virtually unobservable. Human development is a process of being and becoming. Parents get the rewards, as well as the headaches, of being able to watch the unfolding results of their efforts over long periods of time. In the best scenario, their child eventually becomes a responsible, caring adult; parents are able to see the result of their efforts and worries. ECEs, on the other hand, function for a relatively brief period in children's lives. Although they may see progress during the time they work with each child, they usually have no way of knowing what the final outcomes will be in that child's life. The doctor knows when the medicine that was prescribed cures the symptoms; the TV repairperson knows when the correct wire has been connected to fix the problem; the painter sees the appearance of the house improve with a new coat of paint. Much of what ECEs do is based on hope and belief in the future benefits of their present efforts.

Ideals versus realities. Few ECEs enter the profession without some images of what it will be like and without ideals that drive their efforts. Though you may have imagined working with children who are always delightfully smiling and responsive, your studies and practical experience will likely replace this image with a more realistic one before you have finished your program. But this is not to suggest that your ideals also need replacing. One of the most

1650   1700   1750   1800

disillusioning things that ECEs often encounter early in their careers is that some people will try to strip them of their ideals. Although it is certainly true that beginning early childhood educators have to adapt to the real situations in which they find themselves, this by no means implies that they have to discard the ideals and goals that drive them. In fact, those ideals allow ECEs to continue to grow, develop, and demand the best of themselves, their colleagues, and their schools. "It is important to be both a dreamer and a doer, to hold onto ideals but also to struggle continually to enact those ideals in concrete situations" (Ayers, 1993, p. 131).

Respect and Recognition

In Canada, the early childhood workforce struggles to be recognized as a valued occupation and it struggles to be adequately compensated. Unfortunately, there is a societal lack of respect for those who educate and care for young children. It is widely viewed as work that is an extension of women's traditional roles as mothers and homemakers. "Caring—the looking after, responding to and supporting of others—has traditionally been carried out by women and is often viewed as women's natural role" (Beach, Bertrand, & Cleveland, 1998, p. 123).

Surveys and consultations with early childhood educators working in child care centres, nursery schools, family child care, and in-home child care identify lack of respect as a significant problem and a barrier to recognition of the value of their work (Beach & Flanagan, 2010a; Bertrand & Michal, 2007; Bertrand, Beach, Michal, & Tougas, 2004; Best Start Human Resource Quality Expert Panel, 2007). The lack of respect is related to low compensation levels throughout the sector. If Canadians valued early child development, public investment and pay levels would be higher, and ECEs would have more incentives to stay in the field and to continue expanding their knowledge and skills related to child development and early childhood education practices.

In Canada (and elsewhere), teaching of the youngest children, even in the early grades in elementary schools, has always been primarily women's work, and thus is linked with a sense that it is somehow inferior and requires little skill or knowledge. Some related terminology implies that the work is not very important. Who wants to be called a "babysitter" when the term implies a temporary, and purely custodial, function?

Provincial/territorial legislative bodies undermine the value of early child educators, as well. The training requirements for regulated child care programs set by these legislative bodies suggest that not everyone requires special preparation. Part of this attitude is no doubt a side effect of the sexist assumption in society that work primarily carried out by mothers and other women is not very valuable, and that it is easy to master. It is an interesting paradox that our North American culture pays vehement verbal respect to the importance of children and the power of mothering, yet finds few concrete ways to translate this rhetorical tribute into real support (Modigliani, 1988).

1960

20.8 percent of married women work outside the home.

1961

Pampers disposable diapers are introduced in a test market, along with an advertising campaign to promote their use.

1850　　　1900　　　1950　　　2000

FACING CHALLENGES 課題、挑戦

As you prepare to enter the early childhood workforce, it is important that you face the less attractive aspects of the sector. There is no question that the work is important and necessary and the field needs many new early childhood educators every year. But those who are entering the early childhood workforce will also face some challenges.

When Christie S. announced to her friends and family that she would major in early childhood education and planned to be an ECE, she was dismayed by their responses. Rather than congratulating her on her choice of doing meaningful, important work, as she saw it, her parents kept asking "Why?" To Christie, their question seemed to imply "Why do this work, when you obviously have a good deal of intelligence and could do something more important?" And "Why be a teacher of young children, when other work could be far more profitable for you?" Her father put it rather bluntly: "I'm afraid I'll still have to support you after you are finished with college." And one friend said, "You call that educating—what can you possibly teach those little kids?" Perhaps you have also encountered these responses; they are indeed discouraging, since they imply a lack of respect for the work that you have decided is meaningful and important to you. And, even more discouragingly, these questions reflect some of the issues and attitudes that trouble the early childhood profession today.

When Christie turned to ECEs who were already employed in early childhood education centres and schools for reassurance and support, she was dismayed to discover that here, too, were numerous rumbles of discontent. One spoke to her of his frustration with the gender bias he encountered; another complained of the stress of dealing with too many conflicting needs and unmet goals. Several stated that they would be moving on to work that allowed them to earn salaries that would reflect their education. It took a number of conversations with an ECE who had also experienced frustration and stress, but who still felt that the satisfactions of the work were strong enough to outweigh the negatives, before Christie was reassured that her decision was a good one. She continued with her plans to become an ECE, knowing that there would be financial, physical, emotional, and social hurdles ahead. It is interesting to note that some of the advantages that were discussed in earlier chapters also contribute to the stress and frustration ECEs experience.

Solutions to many of the challenges are intricately connected with challenges of quality, affordability, and accessibility in early child development programs. We will consider these challenges and how we can take action in Chapter 9.

Now, let's examine the five central challenges that ECEs face today:

1. ECEs are subject to many sources of stress and often work in isolated settings.
2. Financial compensation is low compared with other occupations, and benefits are scarce.
3. ECEs face health and safety risks in their work environments.
4. ECEs are often confronted by those who do not recognize their skills and the value of their work with young children.
5. Men who choose to work with young children face gender-bias challenges.

1650   1700   1750   1800

The first challenge listed is inevitable for those who choose to work in early childhood education settings. This challenge is an unchangeable reality, which ECEs must come to terms with as an integral part of the occupation. The next four areas of challenge can be changed and, indeed, are slowly changing, through the efforts of ECEs, families, communities, and Canadian society as a whole. In the final chapters of this book, we will examine those efforts, but here we will simply consider the challenges themselves.

There will be subtle and not-so-subtle pressures on you to give up the idea of caring for and educating young children, and to leave it to someone else to change the world, while you are urged to grow up and recognize harsh realities as unchangeable facts. You, and you alone, know how you feel as you contemplate these challenges and how you think about them as they will affect your future teaching. Think long and hard about the difficulties involved in early childhood education. There is a long line of ECEs, past and present, who hope that you, too, will decide this is worthy work and that you will take up the challenge.

You are encouraged to take every opportunity to discuss these ideas with experienced ECEs, to hear about their real experiences and how they have made their choices to stay in the profession in spite of its challenges. Let us consider some of the ways you can face the challenges of your chosen profession.

Knowledge

Opportunities to learn and develop skills will help ECEs deal with the pressure of decision-making and adaptation; take advantages of all the enrichment opportunities that come your way. The more you learn about current research and practice in early childhood education, the more confident you will feel in the face of challenges and opposition.

You are now embarking on a program of pre-service education. But you also will continue to acquire knowledge after you have completed that initial qualification. The challenges will keep coming; it is important that your learning continues also.

Support

Challenges seem less overwhelming when early childhood educators are not attempting to face them alone. Forming connections with colleagues allows ECEs to release feelings and get emotional support, to generate more solutions to problems both large and small, and to decrease feelings of isolation. ECEs can obtain this collegial support from several sources. It is important to choose employment in a setting where collegiality is encouraged and facilitated by administrative support for teamwork and opportunities for collaboration. Membership in local professional organizations also can provide a sense of collective purpose and strength. A source of support often overlooked by ECEs is parents. Taking the time to form relationships and communicate with parents not only decreases many challenges but also increases insights and strength for meeting existing challenges.

1962

Jean Piaget publishes *Play, Dreams, and Imitation in Childhood* in English.

Dr. Susan Gray establishes Early Training Project in Tennessee, which includes centre-based programs and home visitors.

David Weikart and associates establish the Perry Preschool Project in Ypsilanti, Michigan.

1963

The IDS Harlem Project is established by Martin and Cynthia Deutsch in Harlem.

1850   1900   1950   2000

► Early childhood educators often find support from their colleagues.

Networking 先生同志のネットワーク etc

The challenges that can be changed—those primarily related to social attitudes and social policy decisions—require the work and effort of all early childhood professionals. The energy and sense of optimism that result from joining forces and working together contribute to early childhood educators' sense of professional well-being, as well as producing concrete results. The progress made in the past decade in terms of political support for children's issues proves the efficacy of joint efforts when trying to educate the public or garner legislative or corporate support. Meeting challenges requires networking with other ECEs and forming coalitions with others who value early childhood education; it is virtually impossible to go it alone. We will come back to the question of coalitions in Chapter 8.

Supervisor Support 上司、先輩のサポートも大事
チーム大事、団結力

In early childhood education settings, supervisors can either add to or ease caregiver stress and frustration. It is important that ECEs communicate openly with their supervisors, who can be a positive source of support; supervisors can develop opportunities for ECEs, both as individuals and as members of a team. ECEs need to avoid distancing themselves from their supervisors and to recognize that their supervisors share their interests. Supervisors and ECEs are all on the same team.

As one ECE stated, "All of my good feelings [about the ECE role] are to a large extent due to the fact that my supervisor is a person who goes out of her way for all of us. She trusts her staff in making decisions, is always searching for new ways of improving the program, and is open to ideas for these changes. Most important she listens.… Our parents respect her, because they know they can depend on her honesty and integrity. As a result, the atmosphere is friendly and warm and it's a good place to work" (Carson, 1978).

Summary

- The work environment in early childhood education programs is characterized by the rewards and challenges of working with young children and families. Making a difference in the lives of young children is meaningful and fulfilling. The demands of the work environment are constant and require full engagement and high energy.
- A career lattice for an ECE includes the idea of the multiple roles and levels (horizontal strands) and early childhood education and related settings (vertical strands), as well as diverse entry points and bridges between roles and settings in terms of professional preparation and responsibility (diagonals).
- The working conditions for an ECE include relatively low compensation and a high level of responsibility and personal reward.
- Knowledge about early childhood education practices, support from colleagues, alliances with other ECEs, and a supportive supervisor help early childhood educators address workplace challenges.

REVIEW QUESTIONS

1. Identify six of the challenges discussed in this chapter, including at least one that is being slowly changed by the efforts of early childhood professionals.
2. Describe at least three of the conditions that help ECEs face challenges.
3. Discuss what is meant by a "career lattice" and its significance for the early childhood workforce. Draw a career lattice that shows some of the opportunities you will have after your complete your ECE program.
4. Discuss various career options within the early childhood field, under the following headings: working directly with children, working directly with families, organizing services for children and families, providing information about children and families, and providing goods and services to children and families.

STUDY ACTIVITIES

1. Think about any negative responses others had about your decision to become an ECE (Record these comments in your journal). How do you now feel about these responses?
2. Reflect on the challenges of the field. Are there any that may seriously influence your wish to become an ECE? Are there any that you feel will not be a particular problem for you?
3. Work with classmates to identify people in as many of the careers listed in this chapter as you can. Choose three careers that you would like to investigate further. If possible, make an appointment to discuss the work with someone currently involved in it.
4. Conduct a short survey of your classmates to identify what you think are the emerging issues for the early childhood workforce. Consider
   a. Salaries and benefits
   b. Access to further post-secondary education
   c. Working conditions
   d. Trend toward integration of early childhood programs into public education
   e. Respect and recognition
5. What will be your role in the early childhood workforce in five years? What kinds of work experiences will support your goals?

KEY TERMS

burnout: Physical and emotional weariness caused by stress related to work.

career lattice: Diversity of educational backgrounds, entry points, and employment opportunities within the early childhood field.

separation: Process of a child learning to be apart from someone he or she feels attached to; a developmental task of toddlerhood.

stress: Physical and emotional responses associated with coping with situations beyond one's control.

Suggested Readings

Beach, J., Bertrand, J., Michal, D., & Tougas, J. (2004). *Profiles and case studies: Working for change: Canada's child care workforce.* Ottawa: Child Care Human Resources Sector Council.

Beach, J., & Flanagan, K. (2010). *Examining the human resource implications of emerging issues for the early childhood education and care sector.* Ottawa: Child Care Human Resources Sector Council.

Beach, J., Flanagan, K. & Varmuza, P. (2013) *You Bet We Still Care! A Survey of Centre-Based Early Childhood Education and Care in Canada: Highlights Report.* Ottawa, ON: Child Care Human Resources Sector Council. http://www.wstcoast.org/pdf/YouBetSurveyReport_Final.pdf

Doherty, G., Lero, D., Goelman, H., LaGrange, A., & Tougas, J. (2000). *You bet I care! A Canada-wide study on: Wages, working conditions and practices in child care centres.* Guelph, ON: Centre for Families, Work, and Well-Being, University of Guelph, Ontario.

THE EARLY CHILDHOOD CHILDHOOD WORKFORCE COMES OF AGE

SECTION

3

Having considered personal motivations and challenges in becoming an early childhood educator, we now will consider the workforce at large. In this section, we will consider the early childhood workforce: what it has been, what it is now, and the directions for the future. Chapter 7 looks back at the historical roots of work with young children. Chapter 8 discusses the early childhood workforce as a modern profession that creates philosophical bases for a discussion of common ideals, practices, and ethics. Chapter 9 describes the role of advocacy in addressing the challenging issues facing the workforce and the sector, and it leaves students to embark on their personal journeys as early childhood educators and passionate early child development advocates. Again, you are challenged to see yourself taking a place within the ranks of this workforce.

CHAPTER SEVEN
The Roots of Early Childhood Education in Canada

CHAPTER EIGHT
The Modern Profession

CHAPTER NINE
Advocacy

Courtesy Ontario Archives.

STRATEGIES TO ADVOCATE FOR A PROFESSIONALLY RECOGNIZED WORKFORCE

Jamie Kass, National Childcare Coordinator for the Canadian Union of Postal Workers, made this presentation to the June 2014 Summer Institute at George Brown College in Toronto. These are her speaking notes.

I am a 62, a feminist, a professional, an Early Childhood Educator and trade unionist. None of these roles are contradictory. I have spent my working life advocating for a national child care program.

I started working as a "child care worker" right after university in 1976, first as a supply teacher at a municipal school-age program operated by the City of Ottawa, and then as an educator at a non-profit community-run child care centre. I worked with preschool children, then as the centre cook (probably my favourite job), and then as the coordinator of the centre. I returned to school at Algonquin College to take ECE.

We had 51 children from infants to kindergarten age with different abilities, from different economic backgrounds, diverse cultures, and many new immigrants with a range of languages.

I was paid $7000 a year, with few health benefits, and my salary was lower than when I worked as a supply at the municipal centre.

My salary remained stagnant through those first few years of work. Any increased funding went to heat, hydro, and the rising cost of food and program supplies. Inflation hovered at 8% in those days. Increasing wages were the last on the list.

By 1978, frustrations were growing. We couldn't afford to live on our own. There was a revolving door of staff. We couldn't purchase many of the toys and equipment we needed.

The parent Board of Directors was supportive and united with staff. Parent fees kept increasing; families languished on long waiting lists and couldn't find care, or lost their government subsidy and couldn't afford to keep their care.

It shouldn't have had to be this way for parents or for workers.

Why were our wages so low? It was important for us to understand why it was so difficult to make a living wage. It was and still is to keep the cost of care down. It is a system based on the private market—a market that is fundamentally flawed, and pits increasing parent fees against higher wages. The system doesn't work as a user-fee service—and we would be hard pressed to find any other education or social services operating this way.

Perhaps it was the sense of injustice that spurred us on.

So back in 1978, we decided enough was enough. If we wanted change, we had to do something. So we started talking UNION—what it was, how it could help us.

We found the Canadian Union of Public Employees (CUPE) and joined. And our understanding of what goes into a collective agreement, making decisions about wage and benefit proposals, bargaining strategies, priority-setting, lobbying governments, and engaging all the workers in these issues was a learning curve.

Our understanding of solidarity shifted forever.

I also realized that making gains was more than an issue in any one centre or even all the centres in Ottawa, but we were plagued with low wages across the province.

In 1981, I was there for the founding of the Ontario Coalition of Better Child Care. Women's, anti-poverty, and social service organizations, and public and private sector unions joined with child care groups to form a new coalition and something new for Ontario: an activist advocacy group was born! I met many of the Toronto advocates who were working to change the child care system. They were talking policy and action. I liked the combination. Over the years, we focused a lot of our work provincially—with cross-province tours, campaigns for the Wage Enhancement Grants and Direct Operating Grants (direct government funding for wages), increased funding, quality enhancement and expansion, and pay equity. And we developed many position papers calling for the overhaul of child care in our province. I was also involved in Queen's Park lobbies with the provincial politicians meeting with us in a room of over 400. I had to learn public speaking quickly to get rid of the fright of asking a question. Skill-building was certainly integral to my union and advocacy work.

In 1982, I went to Winnipeg for a national child care policy conference. I realized we were far from alone—things were happening across the country; and our issues were very similar even with different legislation and public policy in all the province and territories.

Out of that conference, we formed a national advocacy group—the Child Care Advocacy Association of Canada—to push the government to change. The Canadian Child Care Federation was also born with a focus on professional and quality workforce issues.

We felt we were part of a growing movement. We started collecting data and research to be able to make better arguments. We had to understand Canadian federalism (not an easy feat!). We started to better understand social programs and make international comparisons.

We refined our policy debates.

What did we want? A universally accessible, affordable, not-for-profit, publicly funded, comprehensive child care system! Imagine how many times we had to say that! (The times of calling for free daycare were over!) We pushed ourselves to describe what it would look like and how a system could be phased in.

And then our campaigns—this is when I realized the creativity of our movement:

- Sending cookies to the government saying, "No more crumbs for child care"
- Sign On for Child Care with a petition of over 100 000 signatures
- Numerous fights against big box corporate and for-profit care
- Code Blue for Child Care leading into Federal elections and Death March for the Child Care Program after Harper was elected
- We headed to Parliament Hill in Ottawa and to Queen's Park in Toronto enough to wear the rubber off our shoes!

We did it to make the system better for children, families, women, and the staff working in the centres.

So the years passed, but my commitment never waned. We have had our victories and also our defeats. I have learned and changed along the journey.

I started to look more at the quality of programs. What was quality? Did it look like what we were practising? What could we do better to make sure our programs were inclusive of all children?

Our union had always advocated for quality, but what did that really mean? I remember seeing the results of the quality assessment for the You Bet We Still Care survey of wages and working conditions. It highlighted some real issues around the quality of care across the country.

I got involved with the Canadian Child Care Federation, an organization committed to understanding quality and developing an educated and skilled workforce. I was often called into discussions as the "token union rep." I felt an enormous weight to represent the union movement and to show that we cared about the child care program, real inclusion of all children, and training. I started to realize how important education and a sound body of knowledge was for our practice.

I was pulled into developing occupational standards for the workforce. I was appointed to the Ontario government's Expert Panel on Human Resources. I started working with a group of people from ECE organizations, advocacy groups, post-secondary ECE instructors, employers, and unions to form the Child Care Human Resources Sector Council, a federally funded organization to look at HR issues in the sector. The Sector Council developed a national training strategy, pathways to credentialing, occupational standards for ECEs and Administrators, an HR tool kit for supervisors, boards of directors, and employees. We also developed a labour market information research agenda and funded research to predict upcoming labour shortages in our sector and the broader socio-economic benefits (cost benefits) of good quality care.

We worked together over 15 years until the federal government pulled the funding last March [2013]. Today, what we have left is a website that hosts all the documents [http://www.ccsc-cssge.ca]. We also have a sector that has made advancements in many provinces, in quality resources and enhancements, introduction of provincial curricula and accreditation, direct government funding to increase wages, and recognition and improvement in pre-service and in-service training.

But as we all know, things are far from perfect. The federal government has reneged on its leadership role, and our ability to track provincial initiatives is weaker. In Ontario, provincial politics meant few gains in increasing wages and keeping the number of child care spaces. Policy advancement during those years was limited.

But in last 10 years, changes have been taking place—in Ontario, a College of ECEs formed; provincial-wide curriculum implemented; child care moved into the Ministry of Education; the introduction of full-day learning in junior and senior kindergarten with good paying jobs for ECEs and more partnerships and recognition for ECE in the school system.

Front line staff, supervisors, instructors, and students need to be part of the change and part of the solution. We have much work to do. Changes are happening in the services supporting children under 3. We need changes in the DNA [Day Nurseries Act] and the regulations. Wages in the ECEC sector have stagnated for some, but they have improved for ECEs in the new full-day kindergarten programs. Being part of the "public sector" has made a difference. But we can't leave behind other ECEs doing the same work.

So what does this mean for us as a profession? We have three pillars to making progress and we must ensure that we are part of the solutions for children, families, and staff. These pillars include professional organizations, unions and advocacy organizations for policy, and action.

First off, experience has showed us that any profession who has advanced to promote themselves, such as nurses, teachers, and social service workers, have strong a professional organization and have often unionized and been part of broad advocacy organizations.

So how do we build on what is happening in Ontario? Define and understand your goals as a professional and for your profession.

Is the primary goal to promote a quality universal service that supports all children and families, and to ensure that the people working in the system are well compensated and well trained to provide the best care and education of young children?

Organizations who represent ECEs must be well positioned to make a case for our professional development needs, the needs of the sector users (families, children), the linkage between public policy and practice, and to fully promote these to the public, the media, and the government. In other words, the sector itself has to promote itself. No one else is better positioned to do this work, but it doesn't just happen. There is a need for a united voice.

Be open to broad policy debates. Don't be afraid of engaging and talking policy. Government policy affects all our services—who has access to care, who can afford it, and what are our conditions of work. Make the links. Understand issues of training and education and policies that promote further education. Deepen your view of how government policies affect services: Does the expansion of for-profit care matter? Should services be universal? How do we support inclusion? And what role should local, provincial, and federal governments play? Expect and welcome differences in approach and ideas.

Join and promote and fund organizations that support your goals. Recognize that professional organizations, trade unions, and broad-based advocacy groups all can be critical vehicles for ensuring advancement. Professionals have a key part to play. These organizations are not mutually exclusive, and their goals can be complementary. There can be endless opportunities for collective work for change.

Broaden and expand who we see as part of our movement—today, the education sector plays a key role, but also health, family resource, post-secondary, provincial/territorial policy-makers. Look across broad spectrums. Let's break down "silos" and get rid of territoriality. Find out what are the debates in your sector and get involved. Also, let's look at and acknowledge the role gender plays in our strategies, organizations, and goals.

And you can have fun and use your creativity. It is not all hard work.

So, to finish my story, I am now getting ready to retire. I have had a hugely rewarding career. I've made lifelong friends and met incredible colleagues. I have learned a huge number of skills from children themselves, from our program development and design. I've learned to appreciate good research and policy analysis, and what it brings to advocacy for system change. I have learned how to organize, promote, and inspire parents, other workers, and the ECE workforce in seeing the potential of good quality early learning and care. I have learned how to chair meetings, facilitate conversations, and mediate differences, and to speak publically. I have learned how to listen. I've learned resiliency.

Source: Jamie Kass, National Childcare Coordinator, Canadian Union of Postal Workers (CUPW). Adapted from a presentation at Summer Institute: Investing in the Early Childhood Workforce, June 12, 2014.

THE ROOTS OF EARLY CHILDHOOD EDUCATION IN CANADA

OBJECTIVES

After studying this chapter, students will be able to

- discuss several reasons for examining the history of early childhood education
- identify contributors to beliefs about early childhood education and childrearing
- recognize the role of psychology in current early childhood education practices

- discuss social context in the history of early child development
- consider the beginnings of early childhood education systems, education systems, and recreation systems
- identify contributors to early childhood education practice and public policies

Many eyes glaze over with a section on history. Those who are beginning in a profession today may feel that learning about what people did in past decades or centuries has little relevance to them. But the roots of early education beliefs and practices have connections to conditions, patterns, and beliefs that you will encounter in your immediate experience. George Santayana, an author of the late 19th and early 20th centuries, once commented that "Those who cannot remember the past are condemned to repeat it" (*Life of reason, reason in common sense*, Scribner's, 1905, p. 284). In the case of early childhood education, we also study history to understand how it has created our present and to understand the work to be done in the future. As we examine contemporary conditions in early childhood education, some of the reasons these conditions exist may become clear in the light of history.

In this chapter, you will look at the historical roots of work with young children in centre-based settings and the patterns that have developed into the present. You will find out how our understanding of early childhood has evolved since the 1700s. We begin by developing further the reasons that it is important to understand the roots of the early childhood profession. We continue by examining two divergent philosophical approaches to how children develop and learn. We then move to an overview of last century's study of psychology and its influence on early childhood education and childrearing practices. We will also consider how cultural, technological, political, and economic contexts have shaped how we view children's growth and development during their early years.

You will then learn the story of Canada's earliest child care, kindergarten, and recreation programs, trace the development of nursery schools and related teacher preparation from the 1920s on, follow the development of day nurseries during World War II, and note the explosion of child care centres during the 1980s.

UNDERSTANDING THE HISTORY OF EARLY CHILDHOOD EDUCATION

There are important reasons to understand the roots of the multiple traditions that have created the complex world of early childhood education. First, it is worthwhile to recognize that the ideas and passionate efforts of many people live on today in the daily practice of contemporary early childhood educators. The significance of play in children's active learning, for example, is an idea that was formed before the defining of developmentally appropriate practice in the late 20th century. The concept of uniqueness in learning styles and the need for early childhood programs to include families also have earlier roots, as we shall see. "The lack of historical perspective leads us to interpret too much of what passes for reform as new when, in fact, much of the reform had an earlier history" (Perrone, 1991, p. 120). There is a sense of continuity, of being in a long line of people who have cared about young children, that is some-what humbling, as well as uplifting, for today's professionals. So, on the time-line, and in this and the next two chapters, you will learn about people who have contributed to the theory and practice of what we do.

Second, it is crucial in appreciating the importance of early childhood education to understand that real events in history and sociological trends shape a profession and its practitioners; changes take place in response to particular events and needs in society. As you continue to read the timeline included in each chapter of this book, you have noted statistics that suggest changes in family structure and resulting needs, as well as events that have focused national attention on children's early education. These events, which make up the social context of early child development in Canada, are discussed in this chapter.

Third, it is important for ECEs to be able to articulate the theoretical basis for their practice—the *why* that undergirds the *what* of our daily practices. The contributions of the various thinkers and researchers in the field of early childhood education have been noted on the timeline and will be discussed in this chapter in con-nection with the educational trends they influenced.

Fourth, our understanding of our diversity in how early childhood edu-cation programs are organized in education, in social services, and in public health, and the related differences in professional preparation, social status, and attitudes comes with recognizing the separate forms of early childhood educa-tion that developed in North America in the last decades of the 19th century and into the 20th and 21st centuries. These forms are only recently coming together, and not without difficulty; each has developed its own approach, practices, and culture. In fact, this last idea may be the most compelling reason to examine our historical roots: to help us see that the difficulties in getting

▲ This baby was having a bath before the days of running water.

Jean Bertrand

professional consensus and public support for early childhood education result from differences in how programs and professionals are organized, rather than from a lack of will or ability to work together. Once we understand the original separations, it may be easier to remove them. It is this last idea that will focus our discussion in this chapter, as we identify questions and trends that divided early education professionals and separated professionals from policymakers.

Philosophical Views of Early Childhood

The establishment of the first European and North American early childhood programs extends back through the lines of philosophical thinking about children and education.

The English philosopher John Locke (1632–1704) wrote of the importance of early experiences and was one of the first in Western societies to point out the individuality of children. He noted the importance of children's learning through play and emphasized natural education, rather than the harsh discipline more common in his time. Locke believed that children were born as a blank slate, or *tabula rosa*, and were shaped by their experiences.

Another who wrote of the importance of natural methods of childrearing was the French philosopher Jean Jacques Rousseau (1712–78). In *Emile*, his fictional account of raising a child, he discussed the need to protect children from the evils of society and the importance of planning educational experiences that were directly related to children's interests. Rousseau believed that children were shaped by nature and that it was best to let them grow naturally without interference.

Both Locke and Rousseau influenced the thinking of Johann Pestalozzi (1746–1827), who is known as the first early childhood educator, since he opened a school for young children in Yverdon, Switzerland, in 1801. He believed that children are capable of making their own discoveries, and he encouraged his teachers to respect each child's individuality. Pestalozzi was influential because he allowed others to observe his school and to see his theories in practice. Robert Owen, who opened the first infant school, visited his school; Friedrich Froebel, who introduced the concept of kindergarten, taught at Pestalozzi's school.

The Study and Science of Psychology

By the middle of the 20th century, the study of child development had grown into a respected academic field in North America, Europe, Britain, Australia, and New Zealand. In North America, three theoretical approaches dominated:

1. *Psychoanalytic theories* emphasize the role of the unconscious, or factors which are beyond our awareness, in human development.
2. *Learning theories* are based on the assumption that development is a result of learning, which is a long-lasting change in behaviour based on experience or adaptation to the environment.
3. *Cognitive theories* of child development emphasize children's conscious thoughts. They focus primarily on the structure and development of an individual's thought processes and how thinking affects an individual's understanding of the world.

Throughout the 20th century, several psychological theories shaped early childhood education.

Behaviourism was a new perspective on human development that emerged during the early part of the 20th century. This approach to development is concerned with behaviours that can be directly observed and objectively measured. It continues to influence researchers and practitioners working with children and youth today. Behaviourism views human development as continuous, rather than occurring in stages.

Early behaviourist researchers and psychologists considered that children were shaped by external forces in the environment and that all behaviour, including cognitive activities, can be learned through experience.

Ivan Pavlov. Russian physiologist Ivan Pavlov (1849–1936) carried out a number of studies of animal learning (Cleverly & Phillips, 1986). Pavlov realized that the dogs would salivate before they actually tasted food. In fact, Pavlov observed that the dogs would start to salivate when the trainer came into the laboratory and headed toward the food storage cupboard. Pavlov decided that the dogs had learned to associate a neutral stimulus (the trainer) with another stimulus (food) that produces a reflexive response (salivation). Because the dogs had learned this association, the neutral stimulus (the trainer) could bring about the response by itself. Pavlov went on to design experiments in which dogs learned to salivate at the sound of a bell that rang when they were fed.

John B. Watson. The American behaviourist John B. Watson (1849–1958) applied the classical theories of learning to young children. He argued that a child is shaped completely by his or her experiences. Watson described a newborn as a "lively squirming bit of flesh, capable of making a few simple responses.… Parents take this raw material and begin to fashion it" (Watson, 1928, p. 46).

B. F. Skinner. B. F. Skinner (1904–1990) was the most prominent theorist of **behavioural theory**. Behaviourists believe that children are shaped by external forces in the environment and that almost all behaviour can be learned through experience. Specific behaviours can be strengthened or weakened by the responses children are given following the behaviour. Skinner became interested in the effects of reinforcements of particular types of behaviours.

Albert Bandura. Social learning theory evolved from behaviourism as an explanation of children's social behaviour. American psychologist Albert Bandura (b. 1925) is recognized as the main architect of social learning theory. Bandura believes that cognitive processes are important mediators of environment–behaviour connections. His research focuses on observational learning, or learning that occurs through watching what others do. Observational learning is sometimes referred to as imitation or modelling. Bandura proposes that people cognitively represent the behaviour of others and then try to adopt this behaviour for themselves.

1964

Benjamin Bloom publishes *Stability and Change in Human Characteristics.*

1965

Project Head Start is established in the United States on May 18 by President Lyndon B. Johnson, as part of the War on Poverty.

A summer program of Head Start is held in the United States, serving 536 108 children in programs that run two to six weeks.

1850   1900   1950   2000

Sigmund Freud. Sigmund Freud (1856–1939) was the creator of psychoanalytic theory. His work with adults with psychological problems led him to believe that childhood is the source of difficulties in personality formation. His work describing the stages of emotional development in childhood forever changed our thinking about the nature of the child. Freud's ideas were more readily adopted by the **nursery school** movement than by those in kindergarten education, partly because of the work of Susan Isaacs (1885–1948). In 1929, her book The Nursery Years interpreted Freudian theory for teachers and suggested how early education schools should apply this new insight about the unconscious to their work with children.

Freud believed that we form our basic personality in the first few years of life. He identified five stages of personality development from infancy to adolescence during which the individual must deal with conflicts between their biological and sexual urges for pleasure and the demands of society. According to Freud's psychoanalytic theory, the urge for pleasure shifts from the mouth to the anus and then to the genitals. Freud proposed that adult personality is formed by the way conflicts between the early sources of pleasure and the reality of social demands are resolved.

Erik Erikson. Erik Erikson (1902–94) further developed Freud's thought into a **psychosocial theory** of personality development, extending through the life span. He theorized that each stage of life offers a specific psychological struggle that contributes to a major aspect of personality. Erikson was one of the first to suggest that children develop in the context of their societies' expectations and prohibitions. His theory continues to influence our understanding of the environmental responses and supports that help children achieve healthy development.

Erik Erikson worked as a Freudian psychoanalyst in Vienna, before fleeing Nazism and coming to United States in 1933. His professional and personal experiences influenced his views and extended and expanded Freud's theories. He became the most important neo-Freudian in the field of child development.

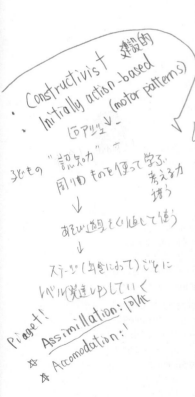

Jean Piaget. Swiss psychologist Jean Piaget's (1896–1980) substantial body of work has greatly influenced early childhood education today, with his focus on the cognitive development of children. His theory explained how children's understanding of the world continues to grow through adaptations made as a result of interaction between the individual and the physical and social environment. Piaget has influenced the way we believe children think and learn, with implications for our educational settings.

Piaget stressed that children actively construct their own knowledge as they manipulate, experiment with, and explore their world, and that their cognitive development takes place in stages. He believed that children adapt their thinking to include new ideas and that the additional information furthers understanding. Perhaps his greatest insight was that studying the development of human children was one way to integrate philosophical speculation with the scientific approach (Gopnik, Meltzoff, & Kuhl, 1999).

Since the 1960s, Piaget's theories have dominated both developmental child psychology research and educational practices. They provide a framework

1650　　　　　1700　　　　　1750　　　　　1800

of understanding that has matched North American's attention to improving environments and intellectual achievement of all children.

Lawrence Kohlberg.   Lawrence Kohlberg (1927–87), influenced by the work of Piaget, developed his own theory of moral reasoning. Both Piaget and Kohlberg believed that children form their own moral views on the basis of their development of reasoning; unlike Piaget, however, Kohlberg differentiated between the moral reasoning of children and adults. He believed that children's moral development occurs in three fixed and invariable developmental levels— which he termed pre-conventional, conventional, and post-conventional. All children pass through these stages, though perhaps at different rates.

Lev Vygotsky.   Russian psychologist Lev Vygotsky (1896–1934) was one of Piaget's contemporaries, but his work has been translated into English more recently. Vygotsky also believed that children construct their own understandings of the world. He differed from Piaget in that he emphasized that social interaction and experience with others is the major learning process for children. For Vygotsky, the development of language is the primary task of learning. Vygotsky's theory has important implications for early educators, because it stresses the adult's role in assisting children with collaborative learning. Vygotsky recognized that children's cognitive and language development do not happen in isolation.

Vygotsky's ideas and theories did not gain much prominence in North America until toward the end of the 20th century. Vygotsky's sociocultural theory of human development focuses on how culture (the values, beliefs, customs, skills, and tools of a social group) is transmitted or passed on to the next generation. Vygotsky's short life (he died at 38 years of age), and his isolation within the young Communist world in Russia, both contributed to the delay before his theories became of interest to North American researchers and practitioners. The current attention to cross-cultural studies brings Vygotsky's theories and ideas into focus for many ECEs.

Information processing theorists.   Influenced by modern technology, information processing theory studies how individuals process information about their world compared to the way computers analyze and process data. A human baby is capable of synthesizing new information in ways that are beyond the capability of the most advanced computers; however, information processing theorists propose that we can study and understand step-by-step mechanics of human thinking just as we learn to program computers for various tasks. They suggest that if we learn to understand the mechanics of thinking, we will be better able to understand cognitive development (Siegler, 1994).

Information theory is interested in mental activities that involve noticing, mentally manipulating, storing, combining, retrieving, or acting on information. Like computers, humans must store large amounts of information, get access to that information when it is needed, and analyze problems to get correct solutions. Information processing theorists believe that human cognitive development, including early childhood cognitive development, is a continuous process of learning to take in and understand information.

1966

Bereiter and Engelmann develop a direct instruction program, marketed under the trademark DISTAR.

The Canada Assistance Plan makes federal funds available for subsidized daycare.

The *Ontario Day Nurseries Act* is amended to allow school-age children to participate in licensed group child care.

1850 — 1900 — 1950 — 2000

Urie Bronfenbrenner.   Ecology is the study of the relationship between organisms and their environment. One of the most influential theories of human development emphasizes how the environment influences a child's development and how the developing child influences his or her environment. Urie Bronfenbrenner's (1917–2005) ecological theory of human development (Bronfenbrenner, 1979) has received considerable attention over 50 years.

Bronfenbrenner proposed a framework for organizing sets of environmental systems. He conceived that the child's world is organized "as a set of nested structures, each inside the next, like a set of Russian dolls" (1979, p. 22). These environmental systems range from the most immediate setting, the family, to more remote contexts that do not directly involve the child, such as society's legal system or beliefs.

Howard Gardner.   American theorist Howard Gardner (b. 1943) has received attention with his theory of **multiple intelligences**. Rather than measuring intelligence from one perspective, Gardner identifies seven intelligences: linguistic, musical, logical–mathematical, spatial, bodily kinesthetic, interpersonal, and intrapersonal. This theory has interesting implications for the individualizing of learning experiences and expectations.

Developmental health.   Moving into the 21st century, the focus has shifted to more integrated perspectives on early childhood education, perspectives which recognize the complex interactions between individuals and their environments. Psychological theories continue to inform early childhood education, particularly those of Vygotsky and Bronfenbrenner. Neuroscience and understanding of early brain development, population health, and attention to the rights of young children bring new influences to early childhood education.

Canadian scientists Dan Keating and Clyde Hertzman (1999), along with their colleagues at the Canadian Institute for Advanced Research, have marshalled evidence to support the **developmental health** theory, a 21st-century conceptual framework for understanding human development. It integrates knowledge from the biological sciences with knowledge from developmental psychology and other sciences. Developmental health explains how our earliest social and physical experiences shape the brain's development and set the foundation for learning, behaviour, and health. Developmental health was popularized in the *Early Years Study* (McCain & Mustard, 1999), *Early Years Study 2* (McCain, Mustard, & Shanker, 2007) and *Early Years Study 3* (McCain, Mustard, & McCuaig, 2011).

BEGINNINGS: EARLY CHILDHOOD EDUCATION IN THE 19TH CENTURY

Ideas about early childhood and psychological theories of child development and early learning do not occur in a vacuum; they are products of the larger social context, which includes the structure of families, work, governments, and communities; the dominant political and economic systems; and the values and beliefs of a particular society.

| 1650 | 1700 | 1750 | 1800 |

Different communities and societies often have different perceptions about children, childhood, and the purposes of early child development programs. They produce significant variations in ideas about quality in those programs. But communities and countries with varying histories and circumstances also have many ideas in common. The core elements of quality seem to cross cultural, community, and country borders (Friendly & Beach, 2005) and begin with a clear understanding of the purpose and goals of the program (Moss, 2004).

Today's Canadian early childhood education programs find their beginnings in the 19th century. In the early 1800s, Canada as a nation did not exist. Instead, the British colony struggled to bring together the worlds of French- and English-speaking people, or Upper and Lower Canada. The birth of Canada as a nation within the British Empire took place in 1867 with the passage of the British North America Act.

In the mid-19th century, industrialization grew in Canada. Commercial and manufacturing development brought rapid growth in urban centres, such as Montreal and Toronto. In the early part of the 19th century, women and children, as well as men, were sought by employers to work outside the home in factories. However, by the middle of the 1900s, the supply of workers exceeded the jobs available.

Immigration had increased to meet the demands of populating the new nation and filling its workforce. The resulting pressures of rapid population growth and industrialization brought problems for children and their families. Children from working-class and poor families were now often idle, without supervision or direction. Child advocates and charitable organizations looked for ways to organize and structure young children's time and activity.

Infant Schools

In the early 19th century, Robert Owen, a factory owner in Scotland, wanted to increase the number of workers available in the local community to work in his factory. His strong commitment to the education of young children led him to establish infant schools to educate very young children and to provide supplemental care while parents worked (Pence, 1990).

The infant schools were popular, and the early experiment in early childhood education and care tied to labour participation spread to North America (Pence, 1990; Prochner, 2000). Infant schools were introduced to Canada in the 1830s by factory owners in Halifax who wanted to attract women and older children to work in their factories. These infant schools and others located in Canadian urban centres were based on the models developed in Scotland. The philosophy of infant schools promoted the notion that these early education settings were beneficial to all children— particularly in North America. By the middle of the 19th century, however, Victorian attitudes and beliefs about the sanctity of motherhood brought about the demise of infant schools in Britain and the United States (Pence, 1990), although in Canada some infant schools continued to operate into the 1870s (Prochner, 2000).

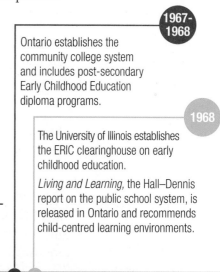

1967–1968

Ontario establishes the community college system and includes post-secondary Early Childhood Education diploma programs.

1968

The University of Illinois establishes the ERIC clearinghouse on early childhood education.

Living and Learning, the Hall–Dennis report on the public school system, is released in Ontario and recommends child-centred learning environments.

1850   1900   1950   2000

Crèches, Day Nurseries, and *Salles d'Asile*

In Canada in the 1800s, work was the only alternative to starvation for many mothers who were poor, widowed, or deserted. Many women who had young children were employed as domestic servants or wet nurses.

Beginning in the mid-19th century and continuing into the 20th century in Montreal and Toronto, and then in other Canadian urban centres, philanthropic organizations, churches, and settlement houses founded institutions to care for the children of poor working mothers. These institutions were established to encourage the poor to help themselves through their own labour (Prochner, 2000). The early child care centres were called *salles d'asile*, crèches, nurseries, or day nurseries. Crèches, first established in France, provided custodial care for the children of poor, working women. In Britain, these programs were called day nurseries.

Roman Catholic nuns opened Canada's first crèche in Montreal in 1850 (Schulz, 1978). In 1857, a group of wealthy Toronto women started the Public Nursery, which was the first English crèche (Prochner, 1996). Its initial focus was to provide infant day care but later became an orphanage for girls. *Salles d'asile* in Quebec were primarily educational programs for young children both from the working poor and from wealthier families. Roman Catholic nuns in Montreal established numerous *salles d'asile* in the 1850s (Schultz, 1978).

In the late 1800s and early 1900s, crèches or day nursery programs expanded across English-speaking Canada (Schultz, 1978). They provided care, sometimes into the school years, to young children of poor, working mothers or of mothers physically unable to care for their children. In 1887, the English-speaking Montreal Day Nursery programs opened, and were followed in the next twenty years by crèches in Toronto, Ottawa, and Halifax.

Canada's early crèche and day nursery programs were typically funded by private charities and sponsored by well-to-do women volunteers or by churches, missions, or settlement houses (organizations that provided services to new immigrants to Canada). Mothers were usually asked to pay a small fee for the care of their children. Government involvement in either funding or monitoring these early programs was minimal.

The development of early childhood centres in Vancouver was one instance that did involve government participation. In 1910, the Infants Hospital in Vancouver opened a crèche for infants and preschool children of working mothers, and the Associated Charities and the City of Vancouver jointly organized another crèche. In 1916, both programs were put under the jurisdiction of the Health Department of British Columbia (Schulz, 1978). The *salles d'asile* also government support in the form of grants from the Quebec government, as well as charitable donations and parent fees.

Children experienced custodial care at most crèches and day nurseries at the turn of the century. Physical space was often limited to a couple of rooms. The staff included untrained nannies and housekeepers, usually supervised by a matron. In one report, a matron, a nanny, and a cook were responsible for 45 infants and children (Schultz, 1978). For school-age children, care usually included a hot lunch and loose supervision by a housekeeper

| 1650 | 1700 | 1750 | 1800 |

after school (Young, 1994). Hygienic practices and routines to encourage obedience and moral development kept children physically safe, clean, and behaved. This kind of care was often thought to address the dangerous side effects of poverty and neglect faced by many of the children living in urban poverty (Schultz, 1978).

The crèches and day nurseries did provide other types of services to children and their families, including health care; the distribution of free milk, food, and clothing; and social events. But perhaps the most notable service apart from the care of young children was their employment assistance.

The primary stated purpose of many crèches was "to enable struggling and deserving women to help themselves, by taking care of their children by the day, or the week, and by so doing make it easier for the parent to earn the necessary means of support for her family" (ref. 16 in Schulz, 1978, p. 140).

In addition to the provision of care for the children of working mothers, many of the early crèches operated as employment agencies for the mothers themselves. The crèches that operated to provide employment for destitute young mothers were usually provided by charitable organizations, efforts of upper-class women, and private donations. Young women who found themselves alone with a child to support in urban settings used these services to care for their children while they worked.

The majority of the women using the centres were domestic servants, and a chronic shortage of domestic help throughout the early part of the 20th century made these agencies very useful to the same class of women who were members and managers of the centres. Annual reports consistently outline the number of days of care provided for children, and the number of days of employment provided for parents in the same paragraph (Schulz, 1978, p. 141).

The institutional records of the early crèches also reveal examples of job training for young mothers. For instance, during World War I, the West End Crèche in Toronto set up a laundry so that the women could do soldiers' washing and offered night classes in how to do laundry. By the end of the Depression, mothers with young children could usually find regular employment, so the employment agency aspect of these centres was discontinued (Schulz, 1978).

1970
The White House Conference on Children identifies child care as one of the major problems facing the American public.

Toy libraries are introduced in Canada through community programs such as public libraries and community centres.

The HighScope Educational Research Foundation is incorporated.

1969
The Report of the Royal Commission on the Status of Women recommends universal child care.

Sesame Street begins on public television on November 19.

1850   1900   1950   2000

The Crèche, Toronto

Hester How taught Grade Four in downtown Toronto in the 1880s at Elizabeth Street Public School. She became concerned that many of her students, particularly the girls, were frequently staying home to look after younger siblings. She allowed them to bring the young brothers and sisters to class. Once the problem became more visible and unmanageable, How convinced the school trustees to support the establishment of The Crèche in 1891. The Crèche was operated by a group of women volunteers as a charitable service. It cared for preschool children and for school-age children outside school hours.

Courtesy Archives and Museum, Toronto Board of Education

▲ Hester How taught in her Grade 4 classroom with her students' young siblings in attendance.

Public Schools

During the early 19th century, a variety of schools flourished in local communities throughout Upper and Lower Canada. They were supported by families, churches, and concerned public benefactors. Wealthy parents sent their children to private schools, and "ragged schools" were set up by individuals or charities to provide education and clothing for poor children.

Universal education was proposed as the answer to the ills facing a changing society. In order to be available to all children, it had to be free. Common or parish schools had emerged in communities during the first half of the 19th century, partially subsidized by government grants in most provinces. School reformers proposed that these schools be entirely sustained by a combination of provincial grants and assessment on local property. Egerton Ryerson, in his *Report on a System of Elementary Public Instruction for Upper Canada*, published in 1847, stated that "a system of general education amongst the people is the most effectual preventative of pauperism, and its natural companions, misery and crime."

The campaign for universal education was based on

- the realization that an educated population would stimulate economic growth and ensure social stability;
- the recognition of education as a means of achieving desired social and political attitudes in support of the status quo, that is, loyalty to Britain and British institutions;
- the promotion of education as an equalizer that could break down barriers between classes, and could increase social harmony; and
- the view of schools as agents of social control, which could influence the development of loyal citizens.

The mid 19th-century shift of education as a responsibility of families, churches, and communities to that of being public institutions free and distinct from social and denominational interests was dramatic. Schools were becoming part of an educational system, instead of programs created by communities. (Accommodation of both Protestant and Roman Catholic interests resulted in two public systems of education in most parts of Canada.) Egerton Ryerson was the superintendent of education for Canada West in the Province of Canada (Canada West was formerly called Upper Canada and later became Ontario, after Confederation in 1867). He, along with Alexander Forrester in Nova Scotia and John Jessop in British Columbia, worked to establish universal, publicly funded elementary education (Gaffield, 1991). The *School Acts* from 1841 to 1871 in what is now Ontario set out the foundation for Ontario's school system and for more education acts in most other parts of the country.

The 19th Century: The Century of Schooling

MAKING IT HAPPEN

1816 **Introduction of Local Boards of School Trustees**

- Loose governmental involvement in administration of local schools (schools are private and voluntary; some are aided by government grants or church assistance; and all are supported by student fees)

1841 *Common School Act*

- First legislation to provide a uniform school system for United Province of Canada

1843 *Second Common School Act*

- Increased centralization

1844–76 **Egerton Ryerson**

- Appointed superintendent for schools in Canada West

1846 *Common School Act* **(Canada West)**

- Standardization of curriculum, textbooks, and teachers

1850 *Great Charter of Common School Education*

- Recognition of principle of universal property assessment

1867	**British North America Act**
	• Confederation of Canada
	• Provisions made for Roman Catholic separate schools
1871	**School Act**
	• Ontario government compels communities to provide free common schools; attendance is compulsory for children aged seven to twelve for at least four months each year. Other provinces follow this direction.

Sources: Adapted from Corbett, B. (1989); Young (1994); Mathien (2001).

The new educational system responded to industry's growing demand for skilled labour and for scientific and technological advances. During the second half of the 19th century, the curricula introduced manual training, as a means of preparing students to enter the workforce, with an emphasis on **rote learning**. School inspectors ensured standardization of curriculum, textbooks, and teachers.

Kindergarten

Friedrich Froebel (1782–1852) is known as the originator of the kindergarten, a German word meaning "children's garden." He believed that children could grow and flourish like plants in the right environment, developing internal impulses that would unfold naturally. Kindergarten was designed for children between the ages of three and six. Froebel's curriculum emphasized language, numbers, forms, and eye–hand coordination, and it aimed to train children in ways that would establish courtesy, punctuality, neatness, and cleanliness, as well as respect for others. The most notable elements of his tradition were the curriculum materials that he called "gifts" and "occupations." The gifts were a series of ten concrete, manipulative materials, such as wooden balls, wooden shapes and cubes of various sizes, tablets, wooden sticks, and a variety of natural objects, all presented to children at defined intervals with specific skills and symbolic concepts to learn. The occupations included sewing, perforating paper, weaving, working with clay, and cutting paper. As Froebel said, "What the child tries to represent, he begins to understand." Although this idea seems very familiar to us, it was considered quite revolutionary to educate children in a group outside the home and use play materials.

During the 1870s, Froebel kindergartens first appeared in Canada as private institutions supported by parent fees or charitable donations. Egerton Ryerson's work in establishing the school system in Ontario did much to lay the groundwork for acceptance of kindergartens in schools in Ontario and other provinces (Corbett, 1989). He added Pestalozzi's object lessons to the curriculum and accepted Christianity (but not specific formal religions) as central to the school curriculum. By 1871, school attendance was compulsory

1650	1700	1750	1800

for children from seven to twelve years for at least four months a year; but children often attended for considerably more time. Particularly in urban areas, children younger than six years were often in attendance.

The first Canadian public school kindergarten program opened in 1883 at Louisa Street School, in Toronto. James L. Hughes, the chief school inspector for the Toronto School Board at the time, had studied the writings of Pestalozzi and Froebel and was convinced of the value of education to support the whole child. Faced with concerns about growing numbers of preschool children left unattended while their mothers worked, Hughes (who supported Hester How's efforts to initiate The Crèche to care for young children left on their own) introduced Froebel kindergartens. The program, which responded to concerns about young children's environments, was also a vehicle for promoting curriculum innovation (Mathien, 1990, 2001).

Ada Maream (who later married James Hughes) was the first teacher, or **kindergartener** (the term used for a Froebel kindergarten teacher), in the Toronto public school kindergarten. She had studied Froebel education in the United States and opened private kindergartens, first in New Brunswick and then in Toronto, in 1878 (Corbett, 1989). Her first public school kindergarten was a class of eighty children. Seven kindergarteners-in-training assisted her. Maream's professional education and her strong connections with American kindergarten activities provided the basis for her leadership in Ontario's and Canada's kindergarten programs as part of school systems.

In 1885, Ontario officially recognized kindergartens as part of the public school system. In 1887, the province began to provide grants to school boards to establish kindergarten programs for children three to seven years old. Kindergarten was introduced in several schools in Toronto and in towns and cities across the province. By 1900, there were 120 public school kindergartens across Ontario (Mathien, 1990). Quebec established kindergartens within its school system in 1892.

In 1885, a kindergarten course was introduced at the Toronto Normal School (a teacher-training facility); and in 1889, the Toronto Kindergarten Association for kindergarteners was established.

Courtesy Ontario Archives

▲ The Froebel kindergarten at the Toronto Normal School, circa 1890, is very different from today's kindergarten class.

1970–1973 Federal funding through Local Initiatives Projects for child care centres and advocacy groups encourages expansion of community-based child care as well as daycare advocacy activities across Canada.

| 1850 | 1900 | 1950 | 2000 |

Kindergartens in the United States

Froebel's ideas and model of the kindergarten were imported to the United States primarily by German immigrants who had been trained in Froebelian principles in Germany. In 1856, Margarethe Schurz opened the first German-language kindergarten in her home in Wisconsin and was the person who explained the Froebelian principles to Elizabeth Peabody. Elizabeth Peabody (1804–1894) opened the first English-language kindergarten in Boston in 1860, and is generally credited with gaining acceptance for the kindergarten movement in the United States. It was Peabody who influenced the superintendent of the St. Louis schools to sponsor the first public kindergarten in the United States in 1873. At one of her lectures, Milton Bradley, the toy manufacturer, first learned of Froebelian methods; he later began to manufacture the gifts and materials for the occupations (such as stitching and threading). Kindergarten normal schools followed, including the Oshkosh Normal School in 1880, the Chicago Kindergarten College in 1886, and the Wheelock School in Boston in 1888. In 1878, Peabody founded the American Froebel Association for interested kindergarten teachers.

The first public school kindergarten opened in St. Louis, Missouri, in 1873. But public school sponsorship of kindergartens came slowly; during the late 19th and early 20th centuries, many were sponsored by churches, charitable organizations, and settlement houses. Patty Smith Hill, writing in 1926, said, "When the kindergarten was introduced into this country more than a century ago, it survived as a philanthropy long before it was accepted as an organic member of the educational system" (Hill, 1987, p. 12). This was the time of heavy immigration, when slums were developing in major cities, accompanied by the social problems of crime, delinquency, and other difficulties associated with rapid increases in foreign population. Settlement houses were created in major cities to combat the problems and to help new citizens assimilate. The philanthropists adopted kindergartens in the hope that improving the lot of young children could improve society. Richard Watson Gilder, first president of the New York Kindergarten Association stated, "The kindergarten age marks our earliest opportunities to catch the little Russian, the little Italian … and begin to make good American citizens of them. The children are brought into a new social order" (Youcha, 1995, p. 148).

The standard kindergarten schedule of morning classroom programs left the kindergarten teachers free to visit in the afternoons, essentially functioning as social welfare workers, "seeking work for the unemployed; space in hospitals for ill mothers, sisters, and brothers; physicians who would remove adenoids and tonsils; or dentists who would extract diseased teeth" (Hill, 1987, p. 13). Gradually, the philanthropists turned to the schools to ask them to accept the kindergarten "as a member in good and regular standing" (Hill, 1987). They usually asked to be able to use an empty room in the school, and the philanthropic agencies still paid for the teacher's salary and the program expenses. Gradually, the boards of education were persuaded to take full responsibility for the kindergartens, and, so, the kindergartens became part of the public school systems.

But there were problems in their acceptance within the school systems. Kindergarten teachers had been trained in normal schools, which were separate from other teacher-training schools. They used curricula, materials, and methods—encouraging children to "talk, sing, dance, dramatize, model, paint, draw, build, and construct"—that seemed quite foreign to teachers who used a curriculum "based upon the acquirement of the three Rs in their baldest and most barren form" (Hill, 1987, p. 14). The kindergarten method of handling behavioural problems was considered soft and sentimental, and it certainly did not prepare the children to enter Grade 1. Hill comments that kindergarten children were not welcomed by Grade 1 teachers, through

1650　　　　　　　1700　　　　　　　1750　　　　　　　1800

no fault of either the kindergarten or the teachers. "It was due to the fact that children were supposed to pass on from one teacher to another with continuity of work when the two teachers were trained in diametrically opposed philosophies, curricula, and methods" (Hill, 1987, p. 14).

The Canadian introduction of kindergarten was influenced by the American experience. James Hughes was inspired to open public school kindergartens after visiting the St. Louis World's Fair demonstration. Canadian kindergarteners, including Ada Maream, joined the American kindergarten organizations.

MOVING INTO THE 20TH CENTURY

The first two decades of the 20th century witnessed the ongoing evolution of early child care and education. The early crèches and day nurseries continued with a few additions, but the majority of working women relied on family and neighbourhood arrangements, rather than on organized child care programs. In urban settings across Canada, organized playgrounds responded to the needs of school-age children for out-of-school hours, and kindergarten programs continued to expand. Interest in child study heightened attention to different approaches to early education, including Montessori and nursery schools. Early educators looked to progressive education and psychological theory for answers on how best to educate young children. Some crèches and day nursery programs began to employ teachers with kindergartener training or those who were knowledgeable about child development.

World War I reminded Canadians of human vulnerabilities and the destruction that comes from hate and violence. After the war, people wanted to benefit from growing modern conveniences and health advances, including new understandings of mental hygiene (the term used for mental health) from Freud and others. They wanted to get on with the business of earning a living and raising children in a safe, secure world.

1971

The *Unemployment Insurance Act* provides fifteen weeks of maternity benefits after twenty or more weeks of full employment.

The Mothercraft infant caregiver training program begins in Canada.

Health and Welfare Canada begins to collect statistical information on Canadian daycares.

There are 17 391 regulated daycare spaces in Canada.

The Child Care Expense Deduction is introduced through the income tax system in Canada.

French immersion kindergartens are introduced into Toronto public schools.

The first National Day Care Conference is organized by the Canadian Council on Social Development and helps to focus on child care as a national issue.

1970s

The introduction of legislated standards and limited funding for each province signals the beginning of the modern era of child care.

| 1850 | 1900 | 1950 | 2000 |

The suffrage movement, led by middle-class women, never took issue with the notion that a woman's place was in the home. The movement did not demand the right of women to work or the right of children to high-quality child care. Their campaign for support to single, widowed, and deserted women did, however, result in the introduction of Mother's Allowance (social assistance or welfare) in the 1920s. Once women had gained some support for their children without having to enter the workforce, the need for crèches and day nurseries actually decreased.

Across Canada, the 1930s were difficult economic times for children and families. The Depression dragged on, with high levels of unemployment and little in the way of social support networks. There were drops in both women's participation in the labour market and in the birth rate. Many of the crèches and their related employment agencies for women were forced to close.

Children's Playgrounds

At the beginning of the 20th century, there was considerable interest in camping and fresh-air experiences. Settlement houses acquired properties for family camping outside urban centres and made this a specific service available to supported children and their parents. The value of organized play programs for children in kindergarten was extended to older children. As well, concerns about unsupervised children on city streets and their enticement into criminal activity gave rise to the development of children's playgrounds, which offered supervised, outdoor play spaces for children outside school hours. Their development became connected to local governments and community organizations (Young, 1994). Here are a few examples of early 20th century playground initiatives:

▲ These children are playing in a supervised Toronto playground, circa 1910.

Courtesy Metropolitan Reference Library, Special Collections Centre

- in 1900, inner-city settlement houses in Toronto operated summer playgrounds and provided noon-hour meals;
- in 1903, Ontario allowed municipalities to purchase land for public parks;
- in the 1900s, playground associations were established in Toronto, Hamilton, London, Ottawa, and other urban centres.

James Hughes viewed playgrounds as an extension of kindergartens and led the Toronto School Board's establishment of supervised playgrounds in eighteen of its schools; the Toronto municipal government took responsibility for programs in municipal parks (Young, 1994).

Public Health

Public health developments began in the 19th century and continued into the 20th century. Public health outreach programs played a role in helping to support mothers and their infants and young children. Immigration, urbanization, and industrialization brought larger numbers of people together, increasing the risk of infectious disease and mortality. Diseases that thrived in crowded, dirty living conditions could not be contained, and the transmission of disease to upper-middle-class environments was inevitable. Therefore, prevention of diseases attracted attention and interest from all socio-economic groups.

Research evidence identified health prevention measures that could greatly reduce the spread of infectious disease and reduce mortality, particularly among infants and children (Sutherland, 1976). Canadian historian Neil Sutherland identifies three events in 1882 that shaped the direction of public health: "Louis Pasteur proved the effectiveness of immunization for anthrax in sheep, Robert Koch discovered the tuberculosis germ, and Ontario established a board of health" (1976, p. 40). Other provinces followed Ontario in establishing public health boards. The emerging public health movement in Canada built upon the achievements of 19th century improvements in sanitation and on the dramatic bacteriological discoveries of the 1880s and 1890s.

Public health initiatives brought prenatal and well-baby clinics, milk depots, and home visiting to communities throughout the province (Sutherland, 1976; Arnup, 1994). These measures reduced infant deaths and improved maternal health (Sutherland, 1976).

The public health nurse's responsibilities for well-baby clinics and home visits encompassed a parent education role. In many instances, the public health nurse became a friendly advisor who was able to suggest changes in caregiving practices and promote healthy habits (Sutherland, 1976). The approach to parent education was often patronizing and didactic (Kellerman & Kyle, 1999), but it was typically directed at all families with young children, not just those living in poverty, consistent with the notion that everyone was vulnerable and that it was in everybody's best interest to avoid or prevent disease.

1973

West Side Family Place, a parent–child resource program, opens in Vancouver.

In the United States, the Children's Defense Fund of the Washington Research Project is established by Marian Wright Edelman, later to become the Children's Defense Fund.

There are only 28 000 regulated daycare spaces in Canada.

1972

Home Start programs are established in the United States to provide Head Start's comprehensive services to children and families at home.

The first National Canadian Conference on daycare is held.

| 1850 | 1900 | 1950 | 2000 |

Chapter 7: The Roots of Early Childhood Education in Canada

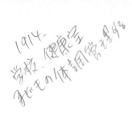

By 1914, the public health nurse's role in the schools was becoming central in school health programs (Sutherland, 1976). School nurses dealt with preventive health—routine inspections, maintenance of medical records, and teaching healthy habits (including nose-blowing and tooth-brushing drills). They also often led health clubs after school such as the Little Nurses League in Winnipeg or Little Mothers in Vancouver, Regina, Victoria, and Stratford (Sutherland, 1976). Such clubs provided after-school activities for school-age children while promoting health prevention.

Public health initiatives in the early part of the 19th century are the historical roots of many early child development programs for children and their families.

First Nursery Schools

Nursery schools evolved from British and European experiments at giving children from disadvantaged backgrounds an early head start (Prochner, 2000). Maria Montessori and Margaret and Rachel MacMillan established programs specifically designed to intervene in children's early lives and ameliorate the effects of poverty and poor housing conditions.

Maria Montessori. Maria Montessori (1870–1952) was the first Italian woman to earn a medical degree. From her observations of children, Montessori recognized the uniqueness of each child. Her phrase "the absorbent mind" captures her philosophy of children educating themselves, actively, in a prepared environment, using carefully selected didactic (self-correcting) materials. From the opening of her Casa dei Bambini (Children's House) in the tenements of Rome in 1907 until the present, Montessori's philosophy has had an impact on early childhood education, although not universal acceptance. Her book The Montessori Method was translated into English and became available in North America in 1912. There were Montessori schools in Canada and the United States within the next decade, but the real popularity of Montessori education in North America did not develop until the resurgence of interest in early childhood education in the 1960s. Nevertheless, kindergarteners and others working with young children were, in the meantime, exposed to her approach and did absorb some of her ideas and practices.

The lasting contributions of the Montessori philosophy include

- an attitude of respect for children;
- the idea that young children are essentially self-didactic, or learn through their own activities and adaptations;
- the concept that teachers learn through their interaction with children;
- the emphasis on a prepared, attractive environment, with child-sized furniture; and
- the focus on the quality of manipulative materials (Elkind, 1983).

On the other hand, some contemporary educators suggest that much Montessori practice may not fall within the guidelines for developmentally appropriate practice due to

- its emphasis on work and the absence of fantasy;
- children's lack of freedom to experiment with materials, once they have been introduced to their appropriate use;

- the discouragement of co-operative and collegial planning and conversation;
- the strictly sequenced series of activities; and
- tight teacher control of how space, time, and materials are used (Greenberg, 1990).

Because Montessori philosophy and training have been maintained so separately from other institutions within early education, Montessori and her schools maintain a unique place in our history.

The McMillan Sisters. Meanwhile, in England, another form of early education was evolving for even younger children. A British government report in 1908 had pointed out that although most children were born healthy, about 80 percent arrived at school age in poor health. In response, that same year, Rachel and Margaret McMillan established the London School Clinic for children under five years of age. Then in 1911, in Deptford, they established the Deptford School (later renamed the Rachel McMillan School) as an open-air nursery school. This was the first time that the term "nursery school" was used. The Deptford School emphasized healthy living for children, as well as nurturing for the whole child.

Throughout the early 20th century, the McMillan sisters operated fresh air camps in Britain with a strong emphasis on hygiene, health, and physical activities to strengthen children's bodies (Prochner, 2000).

Other tenets of the nursery school philosophy were that schools should develop close links with children's families and communities and that teachers of young children should be well trained. Therefore the nursery school also functioned for many years as a teacher-training laboratory. Although Rachel McMillan died in 1917, Margaret continued her influential work in nursery education. She published *The Nursery School* in 1919, and her advocacy of government support for nursery schools led to the establishment of public nursery schools in England as part of the national education system.

Progressive Education and the Child Study Movement

The original Froebelian methods found in the early kindergarten programs began to be perceived as too rigid and abstract, centred as they were on

1975

Two parent–child resource programs—the Parent Preschool Resource Centre in Ottawa and the Children's Storefront in Toronto—are established.

The National Association of Toy Libraries is established.

William Greenough publishes animal studies that suggest experience is critical in brain development.

1974

Margaret Birch, a minister in the Ontario government, proposes cutbacks to regulated child care programs in Ontario. The Day Care Reform Action Alliance is established in Toronto to fight back.

1850   1900   1950   2000

prescribed methods and symbols with precisely ordered activities. During the 1920s, new learning about children was emerging from university-based scientific research on child development, known as the **child study movement**. The "progressives" that felt the kindergarten curriculum should be based on scientific knowledge, rather than the tenets of Froebelian philosophy.

Americans John Dewey and G. Stanley Hall, whose ideas about appropriate education for young children were influencing educators in both the United States and Canada, initiated the child study movement. With his progressive philosophy, John Dewey (1859–1952) believed that education was a method of social reform, that information and knowledge would enable individuals to improve the quality of their lives, and that schools must represent life. He opposed the idealistic philosophy of Froebel and his concept of "unfolding"; he wanted to base the education of young children on scientific knowledge about their abilities. He also opposed the traditional method of teaching children by **rote learning**, which is a form of learning by repetition, memory, and habit, rather than first-hand understanding. Dewey wanted the active involvement of the whole child as well as interaction among the children, as described in *My Pedagogic Creed*, published in 1897. In 1896, he and his wife opened a laboratory at the University of Chicago for four- and five-year-olds, which he called "subprimary," rather than a kindergarten, possibly to distinguish it from the Froebelian model. Dewey's influence on the growing early childhood education movement was profound, as was his influence in North America on the whole scope of **progressive education**, which promotes active involvement of the child in learning.

G. Stanley Hall (1844–1924) is credited with beginning the scientific study of children. His book *The Contents of Children's Minds* (1883) focused on descriptions of children's concepts of their understanding of the world around them, and the educational implications of these findings for teachers. "Hall criticized Froebelian kindergarten theory as being superficial and fantastic—he considered that young children needed large, bold movements rather than the sedentary activities of gifts and occupations and asserted that free play could serve their developmental needs" (Spodek & Saracho, in Osborn, 1991, p. 76). Hall's influence on the movement away from the Froebelian kindergarten was eventually profound, although at a seminar in 1895, most of the kindergarteners who assembled to hear his child development research left infuriated (Osborn, 1991).

At the same time, the mental hygiene movement was launched in the United States (Prochner, 2000). The movement shifted from treatment and prevention of mental illness to the promotion of mental health. Researchers and practitioners in mental health disciplines agreed that the roots of mental health were found in early childhood. Attention turned to the need to understand how children develop and what conditions are necessary to promote mental health.

The theories and practices of progressive education, the child study movement, and the mental hygiene movement converged to influence emerging kindergarten and nursery school programs in both Canada and the United States.

| 1650 | 1700 | 1750 | 1800 |

The Child Study Movement in Canada

In Canada, establishment of child study and nursery school programs was stimulated by the progressive education, child study, and mental hygiene movements in the United States, and by the new social science known as psychology. The experiments of the McMillan sisters in Britain and Maria Montessori in Italy did not find a direct translation in Canadian nursery schools that first appeared in the 1920s. However, they did offer powerful examples of how early child development programs could be targeted to disadvantaged children.

Because of the widespread interest in the development of young children generated by the child study movement, nursery schools were established in laboratory settings as part of child study programs. The will of Laura Spelman Rockefeller in 1923 provided funds to establish child study centres in major research universities, such as Yale, the University of California, the University of Minnesota, the University of Iowa, and Columbia University.

The impetus to start a nursery school in Toronto came from this interest and from concerns about mental hygiene. Clare Hincks, a Toronto physician and a leader of the mental hygiene movement, worked closely with E. A. Bott, who headed the psychiatry department at the University of Toronto. They were successful in securing a grant from the Laura Spelman Rockefeller Fund to establish the St. George's School for Child Study at the University of Toronto in 1925. The St. George's School later became the Eric Jackman Institute of Child Study at Ontario Institute for Studies in Education at the University of Toronto, a site of extensive child studies, as well as a working model of early childhood care and education practice.

McGill University also secured funding from the same source to establish the McGill University Day Care in Montreal, which operated from 1925 to 1930. In other university settings, child development studies, often including nursery schools, were introduced as part of psychology and home economic departments.

William Blatz, a physician who graduated from the University of Toronto and then pursued a Ph.D. in psychology at the University of Chicago, is recognized as the founder of Canada's child study movement. In 1926, he opened a nursery school at St. George's School for Child Study. Because he did not have direct experience with either kindergarten or nursery school settings, he worked with the school staff to develop the program. Della Dingle, who had studied at the College of Home Economics at Cornell University in

1977
All provinces pass legislation enabling their governments to take advantage of the federal funding.

1976
Lawrence Kohlberg describes his view of the states of moral reasoning in *Moral Stages and Moralization*.

1850   1900   1950   2000

New York, was the first nursery school director. From the beginning, in addition to the nursery school, parent education, early educator training, and child development research were major components of the St. George's School for Child Study.

In the first year of operation, four adults developed a program for eighteen children at the school. Blatz's recent studies in psychology had introduced him to Watson's theory of behaviourism, Dewey's progressive education, and psychoanalytical ideas about mental hygiene. Blatz and his team did not have a cohesive understanding of young children or a theoretical framework to guide their practice. Instead, they were eager to explore new ideas about child development and took a "let's watch the children and find out" approach (Raymond, 1991). The nursery school was a laboratory.

▲ Children follow their lunch routine at St. George's Nursery School, circa 1930.

Blatz encouraged a smooth-running routine that promoted the habit of regularity in the lives of young children. Blatz experimented with precise organization of children's time and daily routines. He believed this approach helped to develop regular habits and a strong sense of security for the young child. The nursery school also established such practices as staggered enrolment and a staff timetable that covered every situation in a nursery school day. Within the parameters of daily routines (such as eating, washing hands, using the toilet, and napping), children were encouraged to explore environments designed for open-ended play activity. Blatz created a program of guidance and education for children from two to five years of age that influenced practices and regulations in early childhood care and education across Canada for decades.

Over the years, the research of Blatz and others also explored environmental influences on child development and the importance of adult–child relationships in developing emotional security. The focus of the St. George's School for Child Study was not just child-oriented; parent education was championed from the start. Blatz began an infant–mother drop-in program and promoted parent training in his frequent lectures broadcast on CBC radio (Raymond 1991). Parents whose children attended the nursery school program at St. George's School for Child Study participated in parent education classes (Wright, 2000) and were encouraged to read Blatz's publications for parents.

A dramatic event in the 1930s propelled William Blatz and his approach to child studies and parent education into a very public international spotlight. In 1934, the Dionne quintuplets were born to a French-Canadian couple living in rural northern Ontario. The babies were made wards of the province and cared for in a controlled environment (Wright, 2000). Blatz and his colleagues were given the opportunity to study the children for over two years. It was a horrific situation for the young children (Berton, 1977), but it did offer a unique opportunity to study environmental influences and development among five children who were thought to have identical genetic inheritance (Wright, 2000).

The Dionne Quintuplets and Scientific Childrearing

The Dionne quintuplets, Yvonne, Annette, Cecile, Emilie, and Marie, were the first group of identical quintuplets to live beyond a few days after birth. Their Franco-Ontarian parents found themselves at the centre of public interest and media attention. They struggled to care for the vulnerable infants in a northern Ontario farmhouse without central heating or running water. The parents signed over guardianship of the infant girls to the provincial government. A specially designed hospital/laboratory, complete with observation rooms open to the public, was built in Callander.

In 1936, William Blatz was put in charge of how the babies were raised. Nurses and teachers implemented his model program with instructions for minute-by-minute routines. Habit reinforcement through repetition and praise were blended with a structured play program following the model that Blatz had developed at St. George Nursery School. Blatz was conducting a scientific experiment in a controlled laboratory with more precision than could ever be possible in the St. George Nursery School.

Blatz had good intentions. He wanted the girls to be treated in a rational and scientific manner that was considered progressive at the time. Blatz hoped to send the girls to school along with other children their age. However, the fame of the quintuplets and the provincial government's unwillingness to disappoint fans (or lose out on the funds raised by this lucrative attraction) interfered. Blatz's involvement and the high-profile modern psychology experiment ended in 1938.

Eventually the girls were returned to their parents' authority. Catholic family values, francophone culture, and religious order replaced the psychologists' approaches. Their future was generally unhappy. The well-intentioned but intrusive early interventions disrupted the family relationships. Blatz and his colleagues' failure to establish a working relationship with the parents seems astonishing now.

Their birthplace in Ontario illustrates many of the controversies that surrounded the upbringing of the girls. The Dionne farmhouse was in a rural area between two towns, Corbeil and Callander in northern Ontario. The parents registered the birth in Corbeil, which was predominately home to Franco-Ontarians. Callander, a larger and mostly English town and the location of Blatz's laboratory, reaped most of the commercial benefits, and some sources say they were born there.

Sources: Strong-Boag (1985); Wright (2000); Beach & Bertrand (2000).

In 1938, the St. George's School for Child Study became the Institute of Child Study, and within a year began to offer courses to kindergarten teachers. During the next two decades, it remained a leader in the development of early childhood care and education programs. Today, the Eric Jackman Institute of Child Study continues to offer a lab school from nursery through grade six. The lab school offers an enriched curriculum and opportunities for applied research and field placements.

Other nursery schools followed the lead of the St. George's Nursery School, beginning to open in the late 1920s. They joined private kindergarten programs (operated outside the public school system) in offering educational programs to young children. For example, by 1928, there were several private nursery school/ kindergarten programs operating in Calgary. Most were half-day programs for middle-class children from age two to five years, and they relied on parent fees. Many were unable to survive the economic depression of the 1930s.

FROM DAY NURSERIES TO EARLY CHILDHOOD EDUCATION AND CARE IN THE 21ST CENTURY

Over the past 60 years, early childhood care and education have been repeatedly brought to the forefront of social policy, education, and employment initiatives. The types of programs vary, but their relationship to women's employment in the labour force has remained constant. Periods of strong demand for the participation of women in the workforce resulted in government support of full-time early childhood care and education. However, during periods of women's decreased participation in the labour force, the emphasis shifted to part-time early childhood programs that focused on children's development and education needs.

Wartime Day Nurseries

World War II created an acute labour shortage in Canada, and the government began to recruit women to work in industry. The government first recruited single women, then married women, and finally married women with children. As women were recruited for work in war-related industries, the image of the perfect Canadian woman changed from being the foundation of hearth and home to the industrious beauty on the assembly line. The recruitment drive made it necessary to consider alternative care for children. In 1942, the federal government passed the *Dominion-Provincial Wartime Day Nurseries Agreement*, authorizing the Ministry of Labour to enter into cost-sharing agreements with any provincial government willing to establish day nursery services.

Quebec and Ontario were the only provinces to take advantage of the scheme—the other provinces maintained that the need did not exist. The federal government stipulated that at least 75 percent of day nursery spaces had to be given to children whose mothers worked in essential wartime industries. In both provinces, day nursery operating standards were established. In Ontario, the St. George's School of Child Study provided a model for a rapidly expanding system and established short training courses for staff.

By the end of the war, there were 28 nurseries for preschoolers and 42 programs for school-age children in Ontario; in Quebec, there were five community-based centres. The Ontario centres were located in Toronto, Ottawa, Hamilton, and Windsor. The cost was $1.05 per day, shared roughly equally between parents and the federal and provincial governments. There was no provision for infant care.

After the war, attention turned to maintaining a prosperous economy in peaceful times, and social policies were introduced to ensure basic protection for families from the economic devastation of the Depression era. The consumption of goods and services, combined with the baby boom, created the conditions for economic expansion and the expansion of government social programs.

3개념경7

Governments also undertook a campaign to get women back to hearth and home and introduced Family Allowance ("baby bonus") benefits. In Quebec, the government closed all five centres, despite enrolment to capacity and long waiting lists. In Ontario, all three governments (federal, provincial, and municipal) tried to close the centres, but they met with strong resistance through the Day Nursery and Day Care Parents Association. Federal funding ceased, but the Ontario government then passed the *Day Nurseries Act*, which included provisions for licensing day nursery and nursery school programs and 50 percent provincial cost-sharing of fee subsidies to municipalities. The regulations were based on routines and practices in place at the Institute of Child Study (formerly called St. George's) nursery school. Sixteen of the 28 preschool centres survived, but all 42 school-age programs closed due to lack of funding and political support (Schulz, 1978).

Day Nurseris Act Ontario

Establishing a Day Care Centre in 1944

MAKING IT HAPPEN

Procedure in establishing and operating day care centres is gradually becoming crystallized. The School Board investigates the need by a prepared questionnaire sent to the parents. Upon receipt of twenty or more applications, a plan and budget are set out to meet the specific requirements of each school setup. These are submitted by the Board to the Provincial Advisory Committee, and thence to the Department of Labour, Dominion Government. Upon approval, they are returned to the Board for administration. Officers of the Wartime Day Nursery Branch of the Department of Public Welfare act to advise and assist in establishing each centre.

Fitting day care into a school organization is a challenge in ingenuity. Even its most obvious aspects of time, place and personnel have required considerable forethought. Adequate care necessitates a program from 7:00 a.m. until 6:00 or 6:30 p.m. Space in crowded school buildings is difficult to spare. Assembly halls, gymnasiums, music rooms, and even classrooms, are variously used. In a few cases the ideal has been reached—namely, provision of a room of their own. Here, surroundings can be made attractive and conducive to easy, enjoyable but busy living. A sense of belonging and possessing can be achieved, and thus, more basic objectives of the program approached. A demonstration has been attempted in one Toronto school. The room—an empty classroom—is decorated in soft green; gay curtains relieve its classroom severity; coloured tables and chairs built to suit recreational needs break the monotony; a reading corner furnished with comfortable chairs is conducive to relaxation.

Serving lunch at school has presented, on first glance, insurmountable difficulties. In a majority of centres, it has been possible through community co-operation to arrange meal service in a nearby church or other community building. The Board remains in charge of this service, providing adequate facilities where these are lacking. The child's well-being is built up and maintained by a nutrition program planned through the Provincial Department. Staff from the Nutrition Department of the University of Toronto give directions to this program.

For staff to carry out the daycare program, authorities have turned, in the first instance, to those whose work they know and value—namely, the teachers. These have given their services regularly and unstintingly in overtime hours. It is recognized, however, by those participating, that time is required for planning a daycare program, time not possible to the busy teacher. In a few centres, a regular staff has been provided whose one responsibility it is to plan for the needs of a particular group of children.

Source: Millichamp, D. (1944). *Toronto Day Nurseries*. Toronto: Institute of Child Study, OISE.

The Baby Boom ベビーブーム (1950-1960)

The campaign for women to remain with *küche* and *kinder* continued through-out the 1950s and early 1960s. To the extent that day nurseries existed in Canada, they continued to operate mostly as charitable institutions for women in need. However, with increased numbers of births and growing numbers of young children, nursery schools offering part-time enrichment programs for children (and breaks for full-time mothers) were popular throughout Canada.

Parent co-operative preschool programs, which had surfaced in Canada as part of the nursery school movement, expanded during this period. In 1950, Vaughan Road Nursery School was established in Toronto. Daisy Dotsch was the teacher in charge, and she became a leader in the development of preschool philosophy in Canada (Stevenson, 1990).

The Nursery Education Association of Ontario (which later became the Association for Early Childhood Education, Ontario) started up in 1950. An organization for nursery school and day care teachers, it offered extension courses and began a voluntary system of certification for early childhood education staff.

The preschool curriculum during the 1950s reflected an emphasis on the personality development of young children. Blatz's theory of security guided the focus on the interaction between adults and children in preschool settings. The development of children's emotionally healthy relationships dominated preschool programs, and skill development was a less dominant goal (Millichamp, 1974).

Times A-Changin'

The 1960s and 1970s saw enormous changes in Canadian society. Women were receiving higher levels of education and had greater employment opportunities. At the same time, lone-parent families, the need for more than one income to sustain family standards of living, and the consciousness-raising efforts of the women's movement led many women with young children into the workforce.

A growing awareness of poverty and the importance of the early years led to increased attention to early childhood education research and curriculum methodology. Education reform became an important issue throughout school systems and universities. Federal legislation was introduced to provide assistance to low-income Canadians, including provision for daycare fee subsidies. The booming economy created thousands of new jobs in the service sector, and the participation of women began to increase rapidly. In 1967, fewer than 20 percent of women with children younger than six years were in the labour force; by the end of the 1970s, 40 percent of women with children under six were in the labour force (Ferrao, 2010).

To meet the need for affordable child care, the federal government made daycare a cost-shareable welfare service under the terms of the Canada Assistance Plan in 1966. By 1977, all provinces had passed legislation enabling their governments to take advantage of the federal funding.

Several provincial/territorial governments introduced legislation to regulate daycare and nursery school programs and to improve quality. As a result of funding and demand, the number of licensed daycare centres began to rise.

During the 1960s and into the 1970s, preschool education began to emphasize early academic skills, based on Jean Piaget's theory of cognitive development, and the direct instruction theories, which come from a behaviourist orientation. The makeup of childhood care and education in Canada at this time was influenced by campus programs, government employment programs, and compensatory education initiatives.

University campuses across Canada established daycare centres for infants and toddlers, often as outgrowths of students' or women's organizations. Typically, these programs involved parents as participants. They set up collective decision-making structures, and they attempted to provide an environment free of gender stereotypes. University child care centres were often operated at odds with the prevailing licensing and professional standards and guidelines; however, many of the campus child care centres are still in existence because they changed ECE post-secondary education programs and government regulations by illustrating support for full-day child care for very young children as a viable choice for families, not just for those in social need.

The federal government launched a number of employment programs such as the Local Initiatives Programs (LIP) during the late 1960s and early 1970s. In the winter of 1972–73, 215 children's programs, mostly daycare centres, were created. LIP provided these programs with funds for workers to organize daycare centres for neighbourhood children. Many LIP-initiated child care programs set up community/parent boards of directors and sought fee subsidies from provincial governments to continue operation after the LIP grants ran out.

Throughout the 1970s, daycare activists across the country continued to campaign for more and higher-quality day care, pointing to the enormous gap between demand and supply. In 1973, there were only 28 000 regulated daycare spaces in Canada. Although this rose to over 125 000 spaces by 1982, it in no way kept pace with need.

Compensatory Preschool Programs

During the 1960s and 1970s, child development research studying the importance of early experiences on later abilities, as well as the growing movements to end racial segregation and poverty in the United States, pointed to early childhood care and education solutions.

Child advocates, policymakers, and researchers pursued early child development initiatives with high hopes that enriched early childhood experiences could change the life course of disadvantaged children, especially African-American children. Head Start, the Perry Preschool Project, and *Sesame Street* are three initiatives that attempted to improve disadvantaged children's developmental outcomes and ameliorate the effects of poverty, social marginalization, and racism.

Head Start. This program was established in 1965 as part of President Lyndon Johnson's War on Poverty to expose young children (ages three to five years) living in disadvantaged environments to experiences that would minimize the effects of poverty and racial discrimination. The purpose of the program was to improve children's health and well-being; develop physical skills, social

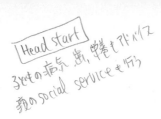

opportunities, and cognitive functioning; and involve parents in their children's educational experiences. In addition, the program offered medical, dental, and nutritional screening and services for children and social services for their families.

Perry Preschool Project. The Perry Preschool Project was a carefully designed experimental longitudinal study on the effects of compensatory preschool education programs for children three and four years old in the 1960s. Preschool teachers worked closely with child development and educational experts to develop a cognitive–developmental program based on Piagetian theory of cognitive development. The findings dramatically endorsed the financial and social benefits of compensatory preschool education as an intervention for disadvantaged, marginalized children (Schweinhart & Weikart, 1993). The follow-up studies found that children who attended the half-day program were more successful in school, less likely to be involved in the criminal justice system, and less likely to be on social assistance. The cost–benefit analysis of the results illustrated a seven-dollar savings for every dollar spent on the targeted program delivered to at-risk children and their families (Schweinhart, Montie, Xiang, Barnett, Belfield, & Nores, 2005; Pascal 2009b.).

The *Sesame Street* approach. *Sesame Street*, the best-known children's educational show in North America, began in 1969. The Children's Television Workshop produced the daily program to foster intellectual and social development. The initial program proposal stated that *Sesame Street* would respond to "the national demand that we give the disadvantaged a fair chance in the beginning" (Liebert & Sprafkin, 1988, p. 219). The creators drew on both ideology and research to design a show that would bring stimulation and opportunities for learning into disadvantaged children's homes through the television to compensate for resources presumed to be available to affluent families. Both earlier assessments (Liebert & Sprafkin, 1988) and others (Wright & Huston, 1995) report positive benefits for low-income children who regularly view the show. *Sesame Street* as a curriculum model is discussed in Chapter 2.

Other compensatory programs. A number of smaller-scale programs based on Head Start and the Perry Preschool Project emerged in Canada during the 1970s. Several of the programs funded by the federal government's youth employment program (Local Initiatives Program), mentioned earlier in this chapter, launched preschool compensatory programs for poor children. The programs often adapted the cognitively oriented curriculum of the Perry Preschool Program and a Head Start approach that combined enriched early childhood education experiences with additional family supports.

In 1974, Moncton Headstart Inc. began as a free daycare for a few children whose parents could not afford outside care and were having difficulties in their parenting role (Bradshaw, 1997). It quickly adapted the Perry Preschool Program's curriculum and included programs to support families. Parent participation in the children's program and in parent sessions was required. Adjunct programs that met families' basic physical needs (food, shelter, and safety) and adult education activities were also offered.

The University of Western Ontario Preschool Project, begun in 1973, was another experiment to assess the impact of compensatory preschool education on low-income children (Howe, Jacobs, & Fiorentino, 2000). Mary J. Wright, who headed the project, developed a curriculum with an emphasis on cognitive development (similar to the HighScope curriculum) as well as a focus on the development of social competence and emotional control (derived from her work with William Blatz at the Institute for Child Studies). Children from economically disadvantaged families attended the University of Western Ontario [now Western University] Preschool for one or two years alongside children from middle-class families. Low-income children who attended the program for two years demonstrated greater cognitive and self-management skills than low-income children who attended for only one year. Follow-up assessments after Grade 3 found that 82 percent of the low-income children who attended for either one or two years were at grade level compared to only 58 percent of a low-income control group of children who had not attended any preschool program. "Overall, the findings of the UWO Preschool Project supported the idea that compensatory education can have long-term beneficial outcomes for low–socioeconomic status children, particularly if the preschool experience is two years in length. A word of caution is in order: the study was based on a very small number of subjects, and it is difficult to generalize the findings" (Howe, Jacobs, & Fiorentino, 2000, p. 226).

Association of Early Childhood Educators, Ontario

MAKING IT HAPPEN

The Association of Early Childhood Educators, Ontario (AECEO), is a professional organization concerned with the quality of care and education for young children. It provides leadership and vision as the unified voice of early education in Ontario. Its mission is to promote the profession of early childhood educators.

The organization was established in 1950 as the Nursery Education Association of Ontario (NEAO). It evolved from the increasing demand for child care and nursery schools after World War II, as well as the absence of government regulations and the lack of formal training in child care studies.

In the early years, the NEAO worked tirelessly to foster the development of training programs. Co-operating with the Institute of Child Studies at the University of Toronto, Ryerson Polytechnic Institute (now Ryerson University), and the Ontario Agricultural College (now University of Guelph), the NEAO began some of the first courses in child studies. Later, under AECEO sponsorship, the extension departments of six Ontario universities began offering evening and summer training programs for those already working in the field. Parent resource centres were also set up in some localities.

In the 1960s, NEAO was a major help in the development of the two-year diploma program for the new community colleges. The diploma course is now the standard for qualification and registration as a professional early childhood educator in Ontario. In 1964, NEAO established a certification process to encourage individual achievement in formal early childhood education studies and practical experience.

In 1969, the organization changed its name to the Association for Early Childhood Education, Ontario (AECEO). In 1980, the AECEO held its first annual Week of the Young Child promotion, following the UN International Year of the Child in 1979. Every October, a broad series of public events and professional development activities are sponsored across Ontario during the Week of the Young Child.

In 1993, the Association once more changed its name and became the Association of Early Childhood Educators, Ontario (still abbreviated AECEO), to better reflect its current mission, which is "to be the leader in promoting the professional development and recognition of early childhood educators, on behalf of the children of Ontario."

The AECEO has more than 2500 members distributed across 24 branches and representing the entire province. It is governed by a board of directors with representation from the membership. Its strategic goals are

- to continue to strengthen the organization and base of the operations;
- to pursue legislative recognition for ECEs; and
- to enhance public education and awareness of the importance of quality early childhood education.

In 2005, the AECEO joined with the Ontario Coalition for Better Child Care and other provincial organizations to establish the Common Table for Childhood Development and Care, to promote collaboration in advocacy and delivery of services to children and families in Ontario. The Common Table signals a new era of co-operation among early childhood educators in Ontario. The two organizations co-hosted a conference in 2006, and continue to work together to influence the provincial government's establishment of a College of Early Childhood Educators.

Sources: AECEO (2005); Beach, Bertrand, Forer, Michal, & Tougas (2004); Thomas (2000).

The 1980s—The Child Care Decade

Action Day Care was established in Toronto in 1979 to advocate for free, high-quality, non-profit child care for all families, with demands for a universal child care system. It grew out of a decade of rapid expansion of both regulated child care programs and the labour force participation of women with young children. Action Day Care developed the neighbourhood hub model to deliver comprehensive child care programs. With the help of other daycare and early childhood advocates, labour groups, women's organizations, parents, and other concerned citizens, the new agenda for child care spread across the country. During the 1980s, provincial organizations with similar demands sprang up.

The 1980s saw rapid growth in other early child development programs. Several provinces introduced regulations for family care, and kindergarten within the school system expanded. Family support programs, such as toy-lending libraries, family resource programs, and parent–child drop-in programs expanded in many parts of the country (Beach & Bertrand, 2000). Some of these programs were aimed at high-risk families and focused on enhancing parenting skills. Others offered opportunities for informal child care providers to get together with each other, and to take part in training activities. Others offered group play activities for the children. And some were provided to more advantaged at-home parents.

The 1980s also witnessed the initiation of two national child care organizations. In 1982, the second Canadian Conference on Day Care brought advocates, early childhood experts, and policymakers from across Canada together, for the first time in ten years. The tumultuous conference grabbed media attention and had several concrete outcomes. It passed resolutions calling for the enactment of national legislation to create a universally accessible, high-quality, non-profit child care system and a mandate to form a broad-based national child care advocacy organization.

In 1983, the Canadian Day Care Advocacy Association (later called the Child Care Advocacy Association of Canada—CCAAC) was established by some of the child care activists who attended the 1982 conference. Each province and territory elected representatives to advocate for the development of a universal, publicly funded child care system. A couple of years later, other organizers from the Winnipeg conference established the Canadian Child Care Federation (CCCF) as a professional organization that promotes quality child care. The need for two national organizations reflected the split among child care advocates (including early childhood educators). The CCAAC adopted a strong position on the auspice issue (i.e., non-profit versus for profit) and was (and is) not in favour of directing public dollars to commercial programs. The CCCF does not make a distinction between commercial and non-profit programs (Friendly 2000; Prentice, 2001). Both the CCAAC and the CCCF continue to exist and often collaborate to promote public investment in child care.

The Federal Government and Child Care

Throughout the 1980s and 1990s, an increasingly organized and widespread advocacy for a child care system demanded that the federal government adopt a new policy role. The federal governments of the day attempted to establish a national approach to child care while recognizing the primacy of the provincial role in education and social services (Friendly & Beach, 2005). However, their efforts were not successful.

The 1980s

- In 1983, the federal Liberal government, led by Prime Minister Trudeau, established the Task Force on Child Care to report to the federal government on the development of a system of quality child care in Canada. Its 1985 report called for the development of publicly funded child care and paid parental leave to be implemented over a 15-year period (Cooke et al., 1986).
- In 1986, the new federal Conservative government responded to the Task Force on Child Care report and established the Special Committee on Child Care. The Committee held public hearings across the country in over 30 locations, from Newfoundland to British Columbia. It recommended increased tax credits for families, continuation of subsidies to low-income families through the Canada Assistance Plan, small operating grants for profit and non-profit programs, enhancement of maternity leave to six months, and small capital grants to child care programs. It did not recommend a national child care system (Friendly & Beach, 2005; Prentice, 2001).
- At the end of 1987, the federal government announced a proposal for a National Child Care strategy (including new child care tax deductions and funding for projects and research). In 1988, it introduced the Canada Child Care Act, which would have allowed $3.2 billion to be matched by the provinces over seven years; provinces would make decisions about how the funds would be spent. It was met with widespread, persistent opposition from child care advocates who wanted to ensure public dollars were not allocated to commercial programs.

The 1990s. Public interest in the early years of life exploded in the late 1990s and at the turn of the century. Newspaper headlines, magazine articles, websites, and television newscasts blasted out messages such as "the first years last forever" or "Canada's future prosperity lies in today's cribs." Pamphlets and guidebooks about why the early years are important and what parents and others can do to support healthy child development proliferated. Corporate business leaders joined early childhood educators (Bay Street meets Sesame Street) to raise public awareness about what our youngest children need. Here are some important developments of the 1990s:

- In 1993, the federal government established joint agreements with the provinces and territories for Community Action Programs for Children and Canada Prenatal Nutrition Programs. Federal funding went to community groups and coalitions to offer programs that supported healthy pregnancies and young children's healthy development. Financial support and investments were targeted to families who faced economic and social challenges.

- In 1995, the federal government initiated Aboriginal Head Start to support the early child development of First Nations, Inuit, and Métis children living in urban centres and large northern communities. Aboriginal Head Start program was expanded in 1998 for First Nations children who lived on reserves.

- In 1996, the Canada Assistance Plan (established in 1966), which provided matching federal funding for provincial dollars spent on child care subsidies, was abolished along with ability for the federal government to impose any conditions on child care spending. Federal dollars for provincial health, education, and welfare programs were consolidated into a block fund, the Canada Health and Social Transfer. Provinces and territories can now decide how to allocate funds and are not obligated to spend any of these dollars on child care. Nor can they receive matching new federal dollars if they increase spending on child care.

- In 1997, the National Children's Agenda launched a federal/provincial/territorial dialogue on a comprehensive strategy for children (Social Development Canada, Public Health Agency of Canada, and Indian & Northern Affairs Canada, 2005). The framework for this discussion positioned child care within the broader context of early child development programs. Tensions continued between child care as a distinct program apart from other early child development programs and child care as an integral part of an early child development approach to programs.

- In 1999, the Ontario government published the landmark report *Early Years Study* (McCain & Mustard, 1999). The report brought together research from biology, psychology, sociology, medicine, anthropology, and neuroscience, and it concluded that early brain and child development sets a foundation for lifelong learning, behaviour, and health. Authors McCain and Mustard concluded: "What we envision will be a first 'tier' program for early child development, as important as the elementary and secondary school system and the post secondary education system" (McCain & Mustard, 1999, p. 23). In 2007, *Early Years Study 2* (McCain, Mustard, & Shanker, 2007) recommended that the delivery of early childhood education programs be aligned with the public education system and integrated with family resource programming, early intervention, and family health services.

- In 2000, the federal government established the Early Childhood Development Initiative (ECDI), committing $500 million annually by 2007–8 through the Canada Health and Social Transfer (CHST) to fund programs for children under six targeted at these programs: supports during pregnancy, birth, and infancy; parenting resources; child development programs; and community planning and service integration. Reporting was left to individual provinces and territories, providing little accountability for the funding. Many provinces cut or eliminated their own spending on early childhood programs without penalty (Friendly & Beach, 2005). Only a small percentage of the ECDI dollars were used to increase child care programs (Friendly, Beach, Ferns, & Turiano, 2007). The new money did not leverage integration across early childhood services as recommended in the *Early Years Study*. Instead much of the new investment went to new, lower-cost programs adding to an already uncoordinated mix (McCain, Mustard, & Shanker, 2007).
- The Multilateral Framework Agreement on Early Learning and Child Care was launched by the federal government in 2003. By 2008, the federal government transferred $500 million annually to the provinces and territories primarily for direct services for children under six in settings such as child care centres, family daycare homes, and nursery schools.
- Foundations—**Q**uality, **U**niversality, **A**ccessibility, and **D**evelopmental was a $1 billion annual federal program announced in 2004 to expand child care services based on the principles of quality, universal inclusion, accessibility, and developmentally appropriate programming, or, as it was popularly called, "QUAD." A series of bilateral agreements were signed with each of the provinces. Two years of funding were transferred. The 2005 election resulted in a change of government and the termination of the agreements and all funding by March 2007.

The events of 1990s and the first decade of the 21st century shape today's early childhood education and care policy environment. The commitment to research and projects sustained a number of initiatives, including a regular provincial/territorial reporting of early childhood education and care programs in each province and territory (Beach, Friendly, Ferns, Prabhu, & Forer, 2009), academic research on child care environments (e.g., Doherty, Lero, Goelman, LaGrange, & Tougas, 2000), and the creation of a plethora of resources for professional development and education. Federal–provincial arrangements in Canada shifted. With no federal child care legislation, federal government involvement in shaping a national child care program became more problematic (Beach & Bertrand, 2000; Friendly 2000). Since the collapse of the QUAD agreements, provinces and territories have moved forward designing and expanding early childhood education, often by extending public education to include early childhood education. You will learn more about recent developments in Chapter 9.

Canada does not yet have a cohesive policy of support for the early years, but most Canadians believe that the healthy development of young children is key to our future. The early years agenda is supported by the science of early child development, concern about economic prosperity, and changing demographics and families. Child care has shifted from a private family matter to one of broad public interest and debate. The inability to create a national early childhood education and care system has left developments up to the provinces and territories.

Summary

- The history of the multiple perspectives from education and psychology and social and economic events that have formed today's early childhood education programs explain the diversity of Canadian early childhood programs.
- Early contributors to Canadian beliefs about early education and childrearing include philosophers John Locke and Jean Jacques Rousseau.
- Twentieth-century psychologists including William Blatz, Sigmund Freud, Erik Erikson, Jean Piaget, Len Vygotsky, and Urie Bronfenbrenner have contributed to the practices of early childhood education today in Canada.
- Since the late 1800s, Canadian kindergarten evolved as part of public education while child care evolved as part of the social welfare.
- Hester How, James Hughes, Ada Maream Hughes, William Blatz, and Mary Wright contributed to Canada's early childhood programs.

REVIEW QUESTIONS

1. List several reasons for studying the history of early childhood education.
2. Identify the different occasions when the federal government has taken a role in supporting early childhood education.
3. Explain why early care and education are thought of as two separate entities.
4. Discuss the separate developments of kindergartens and nursery schools in Europe and in North America, identifying key names in each tradition.
5. Order the following names chronologically, stating for each his or her importance in early childhood education and care: William Blatz; Erik Erikson; Sigmund Freud; Howard Gardner; Harriet Johnson; Lawrence Kohlberg; Ada Maream Hughes; Maria Montessori; Jean Piaget; Caroline Pratt; B. F. Skinner; Daniel Keating.

STUDY ACTIVITIES

1. Read one of the articles or books listed in the Suggested Readings to learn more about one of the individuals in this chapter.
2. Write up the history of a nursery school or child care centre in your community.
3. Look for some older early childhood education texts in your college's library. Compare and contrast the early childhood education programs and practices in the older texts to the programs and practices in today's texts.
4. Review the 20th century theories that have shaped early childhood education. For each theory, what do you think is the underlying view about childhood and how children develop and learn?

KEY TERMS

behavioural theory: Also called "learning theory." A psychological theory developed in the United States, according to which behaviour is learned and can be modified by changing the environmental responses of reward and punishment.

child study movement: University-based scientific research on child development that began to be widespread in the 1920s and that facilitated the development of early childhood education.

custodial care: Looking after the basic (primarily physical) needs of children and protecting them from danger.

developmental health: Explains how our earliest social and physical experiences shape the brain's development and set the foundation for learning, behaviour, and health.

kindergarteners: Term used for the first Froebelian-trained kindergarten teachers in the 19th and early 20th centuries.

multiple intelligences: Theory, originated by Howard Gardner, that suggests intelligence may be organized into seven different kinds of abilities.

nursery school: Program modelled after the MacMillan philosophy of physical, emotional, and social development, usually for three- and four-year-olds and usually operated on a part-day basis.

parent co-operative: Nursery schools that involve parents in the classroom and in the administration of the school.

philanthropic organization: Organization established for the provision of social services to better the lives of its clients.

progressive education: Educational philosophy that, based on the tenets of John Dewey, promotes active involvement of the individual in learning.

psychosocial theory: Erik Erikson's theory of personality development, in which the individual has to resolve conflict with the environment, including other persons.

rote learning: Learning by repetition, memory, and habit, rather than from firsthand understanding.

Suggested Readings

Baylor, R. (1965). *Elizabeth Peabody: Kindergarten pioneer.* Philadelphia: University of Pennsylvania Press.

Bradburn, E. (1989). *Margaret MacMillan: Portrait of a pioneer.* London: Routledge.

Froebel, F. (1896). *The education of man.* New York: Appleton.

Gardner, H. (1985). *Frames of mind: The theory of multiple intelligence.* New York: Basic Books.

Gesell, A. (1940). The significance of the nursery school. *Childhood Education, 1*(1), 11–20.

Greenberg, P. (1990, September). Head Start—Part of a multi-pronged anti-poverty effort for children and their families ... before the beginning: A participant's view. *Young Children, 45*(6), 41–52.

Isaacs, S. (1968). *The nursery years.* New York: Schocken Books.

Johnson, H. (1928). *Children in the nursery school.* New York: John Day.

Kohlberg, L, & Lickona, T. (1986). *The stages of ethical development: From childhood through old age.* New York: Harper Books.

MacMillan, M. (1919). *The nursery school.* New York: E. P. Dutton.

Montessori, M. (1967). *The Montessori method.* (A. E. George, Trans.) Cambridge, MA: Harvard University Press.

Paciorek, K., & Munro, J. (Eds.). (1996). *Sources: Notable selections in early childhood education.* Guilford, CT: Dushkin Publishing Group. (Selections from writings by many of the early theorists and practitioners, such as Abigail Eliot, Katherine Read, Elizabeth Peabody, Patty Smith Hill, Friedrich Froebel, Lucy Sprague Mitchell, Maria Montessori, Harriet Johnson, John Dewey, Susan Blow, Margaret MacMillan, Arnold Gesell, Robert Owen, and G. Stanley Hall.)

Prentice, S. (2001). *Changing child care: Five decades of child care advocacy and policy in Canada.* Halifax: Fernwood Publishing.

Prochner, L., & Howe, N. (2000). *Early childhood care and education in Canada.* Vancouver: UBC Press.

Reeves, C., Howard, E., & Grace, C. (1990, Fall). A model preschool: London's Rachel MacMillan Nursery School. *Dimensions, 19*(1), 10–13.

Strong-Boag, V. (1982). "Intruders in the nursery: Childcare professionals reshape the years one to five, 1920–1940." In J. Parr (Ed.), *Childhood and family in Canadian history.* Toronto: McClelland & Stewart.

Weber, E. (1984) *Ideas influencing early childhood education: A theoretical analysis.* New York: Teachers College Press.

Zinsser, C. (1988). The best day care there ever was. In *Early Childhood Education 88/89.* Guilford, CT: Dushkin Publishing Group.

THE MODERN PROFESSION

OBJECTIVES

After studying this chapter, students will be able to

- identify characteristics of a profession
- discuss the professionalization of ECEs in Canada

- identify Canadian professional and advocacy organizations and some of their contributions to the field of early childhood education
- explain pathways to credentialing in Canada's early childhood sector

As we consider the modern emergence of the early childhood workforce, it is both surprising and exciting to realize that you are entering this field only about 50 years into the modern era. As Chapter 7 explained, that era began with the rapid growth of child care centres in Canada and the establishment of Head Start programs and other compensatory programs in both Canada and the United States, which signalled a new period of interest in the importance of early childhood education. These early childhood education programs were also a reflection of the social currents that demanded equality for racial minorities and women and that emphasized the need to expand the early education field.

Early childhood education leaders in Canada began to question how caring for and educating young children and supporting the children's families compared with other professions and how unity could strengthen the efforts of the field. This chapter will describe the discussions that guided some of the developments. In the past four decades, dialogues, position statements, and other pronouncements by professional groups indicate that there are indeed unifying ideas among ECEs, and issues that help the profession continue to evolve.

The concept of a profession suggests that there is already unity and consensus. However, as you have already realized, ECEs have likely come to their work via different entry points and varied training, traditions, and preparation. And the work they do is itself varied. The amount of diversity is atypical of many other professions. This chapter will continue to illustrate this diversity, as it traces the various steps that have been taken to define cohesive knowledge and practices in an evolving profession.

IS EARLY CHILDHOOD EDUCATION A PROFESSION?

Sarah C. works as an assistant in a program for toddlers. She took the job because it was advertised in her local newspaper, and she thought it might be fun for a while. She has no training beyond the orientation given by her director for new staff, and she has no plans to get anything beyond the sixteen hours of workshops she is required to attend each year by child care licensing requirements. Eventually, she'd like to study interior design.

Tom B. is an ECE working in a nursery school. He took the job of assistant several years ago, after volunteering when his daughter attended a nursery school. He liked the daily interactions with young children and decided to stay and to take advantage of the continuing education ECE certificate program training that was offered. He has recently earned the ECE credential and is considering beginning work on a four-year degree, so that he will be qualified to be a teacher in elementary schools. This would offer him a better salary and benefits.

Mary A. is the lead ECE in a mixed-age preschool classroom. She completed an early childhood diploma at her local college, which she attended immediately after graduating from high school.

Martha H. has almost completed a master's degree in early childhood education. After five years in preschool programs, she has just accepted a promotion that includes doing some administration as well as staff training at her centre.

Susanne S. teaches a kindergarten-to-Grade-2 mixed-age grouping in a private school. She has an bachelor of arts in early childhood education and a teaching credential.

Ask yourself: Are these ECEs all early childhood professionals? What criteria did you use to decide? Keep those criteria in mind as we continue our discussion of professionalism.

The individuals listed above demonstrate the complexity of discussing early childhood education as a profession. Working in different strands of the field, with varying educational and training backgrounds and quite separate goals, these individuals illustrate the breadth that must be included in any discussion about early childhood education as a profession. Throughout this book, we have been using the term *profession* to refer to early childhood educators, or ECEs, who are involved in teaching and caring for children in the early years in a variety of environments and who have recognized educational credentials. An ECE is as much a professional as a nurse, a doctor, or a teacher.

The origin of the word *professional* takes us back to "medieval times when an individual took vows in order to be received in a religious community. It was the act of openly declaring or publicly professing a belief or faith" (Giles & Proudfoot, 1994, p. 333). Over time, ***professional*** came to mean belonging to a particular occupation that required specific knowledge and high standards of practice (Giles & Proudfoot, 1994).

Not everyone has agreed that ECEC qualifies as a profession. In 1988, the American early childhood advocate Milly Almy stated flatly that, although the ECE role requires professional attitudes and behaviours, it does not meet the standards for a profession. "With its shaky knowledge base, its ambiguous clientele, and its lack of a code of ethics, early childhood education qualifies only as an occupation or, at best, a semiprofession" (Almy, 1988, p. 50). Almy describes ECEs as double specialists in that their work includes both (1) teaching young children, assessing their development, and working with children and with adults and (2) thinking concretely in practice, and formally, in theory. This certainly sounds like demanding work for something she claims is not a profession.

Ade (1982) agreed that the unique characteristics associated with professional status, including "specialized knowledge, a desirable service, and an assurance of quality, dependability, and effectiveness" (p. 25), were lacking in early childhood education, but that certain changes in the field could help move it closer to professionalization:

- requiring a greater familiarity with the field's knowledge base, thus increasing the specialized knowledge needed to practise and extending the length of the training period;
- identifying and establishing uniform criteria for admitting new members, including entry criteria for training and content of training;
- developing the kind of practitioner licensing system that would ensure meeting of criteria and exclusion of those who do not meet the criteria;
- gaining internal control of the licensing system to allow members to have input for requirements and thus greater self-regulation; and
- obtaining stronger voices by joining with parents and other decision-makers to determine needs and the provision of appropriate services to meet those needs.

Spodek, Saracho, and Peters (1988) suggest that *professional* is used in a variety of ways, sometimes for individuals who are paid to do certain work, without implication of level of skill, and sometimes for those "with a high degree of skill and competence" (p. 7), but more often implying one of the learned professions, which require a high degree of training and usually involve mental rather than physical work. The fields that require less preparation, and therefore, often have lower levels of status, including teaching, social work, and counselling, might be called semiprofessions, having some but not all of the attributes of true professions.

1979

A longitudinal study done by Lazar et al. reports that the Head Start programs create significant, lasting effects.

Action Day Care is established in Toronto. It is an organization of child care activists—parents, caregivers, and other supporters—who are calling for universal child care.

United Nations officially names the "Year of the Child."

1978

The world's first test-tube baby, "Baby Louise," is born in England.

1980

United States has the highest percentage of children living in poverty of all western nations, a figure that continues to rise throughout the 1980s and 1990s.

Toronto Board of Education releases its *Comprehensive Child Care Report.*

1850   1900   1950   2000

Criteria of a Profession

Katz 8つの基準 "プロになるため"

Lilian Katz (1995) suggests that eight criteria must be met before an occupation can be classified as a profession, and that those in the early childhood community must work to gain consensus and take needed steps in the following areas.

①社会性 大事
子どもは8才までとても大事(成長,発達)
社会.財政 ⇒ 子どもの発達に影響

Social necessity. The work of a profession is essential to the well-being of a society, and society would be weakened if the profession did not function. There are few in the early childhood field who do not believe in the absolute importance of the nurturance and development of children in the first eight years of life. Increasingly, public attention and support have been drawn to this truth by the advocacy efforts of practitioners. The longitudinal studies on effects of early childhood education offer empirical evidence about these previously more subjective ideas. But the lack of public respect and fiscal support for early childhood programs suggests that society does not fully understand the absolute necessity of these supports for children and families.

②他利主義 (他人を優先, 思いやり
博愛主義)

Altruism. A profession is said to be altruistic: it is directed toward service rather than profits and is performed unselfishly, with an emphasis on social goals. From the beginning, early childhood education has been grounded in principles of social improvement in the lives of children and families. ECEs certainly rank highly in this characteristic of professionalism, since their salaries could be said to be truly sacrificial, and their concerns are with children and families.

▶ Today's early childhood educators are professionals.

Liquidlibrary/Thinkstock

Autonomy.   Professionals are said to be autonomous in that their clients do not dictate what services are to be delivered, or how they are to be delivered. ECEs are in the somewhat complicated position of defining children, parents, and society as clients, and they are challenged by trying to respond to various opposing ideas about goals and methods for practice. For example, what does the ECE do when parental demands suggest a curriculum that ECEs feel is not in children's developmental interests? What does the ECE do when the community defines family support systems that seem to usurp parental roles? ECEs are often caught in the middle and forced to respond to ideas that limit their autonomy. ECEs are often under the direction of school boards that argue for standards that ECEs feel may not be in children's best interests, and they are controlled by licensing requirements dictated by laypeople in the legislature. ECEs are, therefore, a long way from having the autonomy that would allow them to decide independently on optimal educational directions.

Distance from client.   Since the practice of a profession requires applying specialized knowledge to particular situations, the relationship between professionals and those served is expected to be distinguished by emotional distance that would prevent clouded judgment. In this tradition, for example, doctors are not expected to treat members of their own families. Many practitioners in early education question this aspect of professionalism, noting that it is more important to meet children's needs for closeness and affection than to create professional distance. ECEs struggle with the idea of creating caring relationships with children and families while maintaining some distance that is helpful to all parties. An "optimum distance" allows ECEs to be compassionate and caring and to exercise professional judgment, while protecting themselves from the dangers of emotional overinvolvement and burnout.

Code of ethics.   A profession requires conformity to standards that are defined by a **code of ethics**. All members of a profession adopt this code to ensure that there will be a uniform standard of conduct that reflects a core set of beliefs and values. In addition, there is a professional body that institutes procedures for ensuring that members do not violate this code.

Standards of practice.   Professions adopt standards of practice that apply to the breadth and scope of the practice of early childhood education, to ensure that professionals apply uniform procedures and principles in response to typical situations using their best professional judgment, and to ensure that no professional's behaviour will fall below the standard.

1981

Laurier LaPierre and Ada Scherman write *To Herald a Young Child*.

The Ontario Coalition for Better Day Care (later renamed the Ontario Coalition for Better Child Care) is formed.

1980s

Nobody's Perfect, a parenting program, is developed through public health groups in Atlantic Canada and is widely adopted across Canada.

| 1850 | 1900 | 1950 | 2000 |

④ 長期間のトレーニング
（大学や専門機関での
トレーニング）

＊ 色々なタイプの 施設がある
＊ 免許なくても アリスメでさたり
するし。(保育士不足のため)
＊ 賃金について

Prolonged training.   A major characteristic of a profession is that entrants are required to underggo extensive training, with requirements for entry that screen out individuals. The training is specialized and contains a common core of knowledge. The training is also expected to be difficult. By stretching cognitive abilities, the required training is more extensive than daily practice requires, and it is offered by accredited training institutions. In addition, regular continuing education is systematically required of the profession's practitioners.

As you will recall from earlier chapters, there are enormous variations in the amounts and types of pre-service and in-service training required of early childhood educators, ranging from almost nothing at all to advanced degrees. Further, because of the shortages of caregivers, trained or otherwise, there are virtually no entry requirements for practitioners, other than age and minimal literacy, in many settings. In too many cases, quality of early childhood programs is compromised by the the acceptance of unprepared and unqualified workers. This is a complex dilemma that relates to some of the challenges regarding wages and status of the work that we discussed in Chapter 6. Yet, as we saw in that chapter, the career lattice plan attempts to respond to the varying entry points and training options that currently exist in the field, while facilitating professionalization for those who are employed in programs for young children.

▲ Early childhood educators are guided by standards of practice.

racorn/Shutterstock

Specialized knowledge.   There is fairly universal agreement that a profession is work that involves specialized knowledge and skills that are based on a systematic body of principles. The knowledge is abstract, relevant to practice, and expressed in technical terminology; it is also exclusive, known only to those who have been trained in the profession. Practice based on what we know about early learning and child development offers a body of specialized knowledge to trained early childhood educators. Untrained caregivers, on the other hand, base their actions on goodwill and what comes naturally; they are likely using their best intuitions about childrearing, as parents and laypeople have used for generations.

Saying that you are a professional doesn't make it so; others have to perceive you as professional. Vander Ven (1988) suggests that professionalization refers to the public recognition of, and demand for, a specialized service that can be provided only by people prepared to do it. It will require the joint efforts of us all to make this kind of professionalism a reality. It is this movement toward professionalism that will overcome some of the challenges discussed in Chapter 6 and in Chapter 9.

Spodek, Saracho, & Peters (1988) define seven questions that need to be the focus of efforts toward professionalism:

1. How do we establish standards of quality for practitioners in the field?
2. What standards of early childhood professionalism are reasonable in our field?
3. How should entry to the field be determined?
4. Should the field of early childhood education become more inclusive or more exclusive?

5. How should standards be applied, and by whom?
6. How should gender and economic issues be dealt with?
7. How do we define professional knowledge and values?*

While the discussion of professionalism is ongoing, it is worth noting that even some leaders in the field recognize these kinds of concerns, as well as the benefits inherent in the idea of professionalizing. Specific concerns include

- the possibility that professionals will become separated from contact with children, as happens when increased qualifications and status are associated with positions that remove professionals from the classroom;
- parents' concern that increasing training and professionalism of ECEs will mean increasing institutionalization and uncaring environments for children;
- a wish to avoid the hierarchical systems that result when distinctions are made between non-professionals, paraprofessionals, and more highly trained professionals;
- the increased cost of services that comes with the improved compensation that is necessary for raising the level of professionalism; and
- the possibility of excluding individuals who typically are denied access to higher education because of economic factors, yet who are needed in ECE to represent the cultural diversity of our society.

But the advantages of enhancing professionalism are unmistakable. The benefits include

- better care and education for children, resulting from a shared knowledge base;
- consistency across the settings and developmental continuity between programs;
- ethical behaviour;
- shared meanings and expanded knowledge; and
- improved compensation (Willer and Bredekamp, 1993).

---

*Reprinted by permission of the Publisher. From Bernard Spodek, Olivia N. Saracho, and Donald L. Peters (Editors), *Professionalism and the Early Childhood Practitioner*, New York: Teachers College Press. Copyright © 1988 by Teachers College, Columbia University. All rights reserved.

1982

Mary Ainsworth continues the discussion of attachment in infancy, in *Early Caregiving and Later Patterns of Attachment*.

There are 125 000 daycare spaces in Canada.

The Toronto Board of Education decides to facilitate the development of parent-operated centres in vacant classroom space.

The second National Child Care Conference is held in Winnipeg. Child care activists and early educators pass resolutions calling for a national daycare act, national standards, and support the goal of universally accessible daycare for all Canadians.

1983

The Canadian Day Care Advocacy Association (later the Canadian Child Care Advocacy Association) is established.

Howard Gardner publishes *Frames of Mind*, describing his theory of multiple intelligences.

| 1850 | 1900 | 1950 | 2000 |

It may be more useful to focus on the process of professionalizing and on the concept of professionalism, rather than on the professional. Defining early childhood educators as professional assumes that everyone who works with young children is involved in a process of professional development. Professionalism is the belief in the vision and ideals that guide daily practice. Professionalization describes the kinds of activities and actions that an early childhood educator or the early childhood workforce as a whole can use to achieve the goal of being perceived as a profession.

As a beginning ECE, it is important that you recognize that there is work to be done in the profession as a whole. You should also begin to think of yourself as a member of a profession that has made—and continues to make—major contributions to Canadian families and society. This recognition will allow you to begin your career with a sense of self-respect and will enable you to represent the educated and articulate practitioners who work to gain public recognition of the value of early childhood education. Your program of training will help you see how your own competence and knowledge are developing as you progress through courses and placements. You will see your own movement on the continuum toward increasingly professional behaviour and attitudes. As time goes by, you will work more effectively with children and families, truly representing the best of professional practice, and you will also contribute to this growing profession.

PROFESSIONALIZATION OF THE EARLY CHILDHOOD EDUCATORS IN CANADA

ECEs in Canada share a core knowledge base, codes of ethics, and standards of practice. Credentialing of ECEs is expanding across Canada and the self-governance or self-regulation of ECEs occurs in several jurisdictions. Other issues related to the professionalization of early childhood educators include equivalency, professional development, and unionization.

Core Knowledge

One of the prerequisites to the recognition of early childhood education and care as a profession is identifying the **core knowledge** that defines the early childhood profession. A characteristic of any profession is a specialized body of knowledge and skills shared by all its members. This core of common knowledge is defined by answering these two questions: (Willer, 1994):

1. "Is this knowledge or skill required of every early childhood educator regardless of level or setting or professional role?" (p. 13). That is, does every early childhood educator have to know and be able to do this in order to be effective?
2. "Does the sum of this body of knowledge and competencies uniquely distinguish the early childhood professional from all other professionals?" (p. 13). That is, although other professionals may share some of this knowledge, is most of it different from that required by other professionals?

Core knowledge in early childhood education, or what an ECE needs to be able to do, was described in Chapter 4. This description was compiled from a number of initiatives that have identified the key skills and competencies—or core knowledge—for ECEs working in all early childhood development settings.

The core knowledge of the early childhood workforce combines both theoretical and practical knowledge. Elaine Ferguson from Child Care Connections in Nova Scotia has written extensively on the need to recognize and value both the theory and the practice elements of core knowledge. She recognizes the "importance of a [theoretical] foundation in early childhood education and care and the practice skills necessary to integrate the theory into developmentally appropriate practice" (Ferguson, 1997, p. 2). Ferguson (1995) cautions us to remember this balance and not to devalue or forget the less-visible skills of practical caring as we move forward with more precise definitions of our core knowledge.

Phillips (1991) identifies five themes that address content that every professional in the field should know:

1. Children develop in context.
2. Strategies for working with children are constructed every day.
3. Effective practice requires a comprehensive set of skills.
4. Early childhood professionals know they belong to a profession.
5. Even skilled professionals have limitations.

A shift began in the 1960s which changed the core of knowledge ECEs need, a shift from a focus on centre-based preschool to one that is inclusive of all children from infancy through age twelve in home- and centre-based programs and related early childhood services. More recently, the shift to early childhood education delivered through public education and offering positions to ECES is again changing the core knowledge that ECEs need. ECEs gain core knowledge from professional preparation programs, experiences in early childhood education and care settings, and ongoing professional development.

Everything learned is used, as professionals increasingly refine their skills and broaden their knowledge. This ongoing discussion about what early childhood professionals need to know will enrich and include, rather than stagnate and exclude.

Codes of Ethics

We noted earlier in the chapter that a profession has a code of ethics, which is a statement of principle that governs moral behaviour and ethical decisions.

1985
The report of the government's Task Force on Child Care recommends a national system of child care in Canada.

The National Association for the Education of Young Children (NAEYC) establishes a voluntary accreditation system for centres.

1984
The Royal Commission on Equity in Employment recommends a national child care act to fund and set standards for high-quality child care.

1850   1900   1950   2000

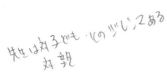

先生は好子でも「このザじ」である
対親

いろいろな問題
ある親が自分の子をなぐった子は誰か?
と聞いてくる
他の先生 abuseしていたのでは?と
うやとさく..

真実が分からない…
すぐに判断していいのか??

In Canada, several professional organizations have developed code of ethics statements for ECEs, to be used as a guide in making day-to-day decisions.

Early childhood educators are frequently faced with ethical dilemmas in their work with young children and their families:

- What would you do when a parent demanded to know who bit her child?
- What would you do when a co-worker complained to you about another co-worker's treatment of a child?
- What would you do if a neighbour told you she heard bad things about the last centre you worked in?
- What would your responsibility be when another teacher told you that symptoms made her suspect child abuse, but that she was afraid to report it?

Often, ECEs have to take action in situations in which all the facts are not known, or when there is no single course of action that is clearly right or wrong. It is sometimes difficult to decide what an ethical response might be. Making ethical decisions and taking ethical actions in early childhood education may require being able to see beyond short-term consequences to consider long-range consequences.

When you work in early childhood education settings, you will be asked to make many decisions about appropriate behaviour. Some of these decisions will require more than your accumulated knowledge of child development or educational practice. Some will pose genuine moral dilemmas, where you have to weigh your actions carefully in considering the parties involved.

The issues raised above, and others like them, are answered only by considering professional ethics, or the system of morals that defines a profession's proper work practices. A code of ethics is "a set of statements that helps us to deal with the temptations inherent in our occupations ... helps us to act in

▶ When facing an ethical decision, it is a good idea to discuss your decision with another ECE.

Jack Hollingsworth/Digitial Vision/Thinkstock

1650　　　　　　1700　　　　　　1750　　　　　　1800

terms of that which we believe to be right rather than what is expedient—
especially when doing what we believe is right carries risks" (Katz, 1991,
p. 3). Such risks could be losing a job or alienating others with whom you must
work. A code expresses the profession's belief about correct, rather than
expedient, behaviour; about good, rather than merely practical, actions;
and about what professionals must never do or condone, for the good and
protection of those they serve.

The value in having an explicit code is that members have a document that
helps them go past their intuition and individual beliefs to focus on core professional values; "it is not so much what I care about but rather what the good
early childhood educator should care about" (Kipnis, 1987, p. 28). The code
can remind ECEs of their priorities and responsibilities, and it can provide solid
guidance and professional support for the decisions and behaviour of an
individual ECE.

In the United States, the NAEYC developed its code of ethical conduct
gradually, after gaining insights from many professionals and practitioners. The
NAEYC board appointed an ethics commission to explore and clarify the early
childhood profession's understanding of its ethics. The commission surveyed
members to learn concerns, held workshops to identify and explore issues,
and followed up with another survey of members to help formulate principles
of ethical action. After further refining a draft code, the NAEYC's governing
board approved the final document in July 1989. (The National Education
Association has had a code of ethics since 1929 for teachers in school systems;
however, there is nothing in the current code about parent–teacher relationships, so the NAEYC code is likely more relevant to your practice in early
education.) The preamble states that the focus of the guidelines is on daily
practice with children and their families in programs and classrooms, although
many of the provisions also apply to specialists who do not work directly
with children.

The Early Childhood Educators of British Columbia (ECEBC) developed a
code of ethics statement in 1992, which guides ECEs in their daily professional
practice. ECEs in that organization adopted the ECEBC Code of Ethics after a
considerable period of discussion and consultation with members, government
representatives, and college and university faculty. It has been a model for the
development of code of ethics statements in other provincial organizations. In

1987

NAEYC publishes its position statement on developmentally
appropriate practice (DAP), revised from a preliminary statement
in 1984.

The Canadian Child Day Care Federation (later the Canadian Child
Care Federation) is established.

1986

The report of the federal government's Special Committee
on Child Care recommends increased tax credits for families,
continuation of child care subsidies to low-income families, and
small operating grants to child care programs.

1850   1900   1950   2000

Code of Ethics, Canadian Child Care Federation

Child care practitioners

- promote the health and well-being of all children;
- enable all children to participate to their full potential in environments that are carefully planned to serve individual needs and to facilitate the child's progress;
- demonstrate caring for children in all aspects of their practice;
- work in partnership with parents, recognizing that parents have primary responsibility for the care of their children, valuing their commitment to their children and supporting them in meeting their responsibilities to their children;
- work in partnership with colleagues and other service providers to support the well-being of children and their families;
- work in ways to enhance human dignity in trusting, caring, and co-operative relationships that respect the worth and uniqueness of the individual;
- pursue, on an ongoing basis, the knowledge, skills, and self-awareness needed to be professionally competent; and
- demonstrate integrity in all of their professional relationships.

Source: Copyright © Canadian Childcare Federation.

2004, the Canadian Child Care Federation adopted a Code of Ethics, adapted from the ECEBC Code of Ethics, as part of its occupational standards for child care practitioners (Doherty, 2003). This is becoming the pan-Canadian early childhood educator code of ethics.

Standards of Practice 実践の基本

Standards of practice indicate the skills and abilities needed to perform tasks effectively. Included are standards of performance; input standards, or the skills and knowledge an individual brings to an occupation; and process standards, or the tasks required by an occupation (Child Care Human Resource Sector Council, 2012).

In child care, supporting and fostering child well-being and development (performance standards) requires the provision of certain experiences (process standards). The extent to which experiences are appropriate and effective depends, in part, on the skills, knowledge, and abilities of the child care provider (input standards) (Doherty, 1998, p. 1).

Standards of practice are useful to a profession in establishing its benchmarks of quality beyond the basics of regulatory requirements. They also contribute to the overall quality of early childhood programs. The professional organizations for teachers and nurses establish and monitor standards of practice for their practitioners (Beach, Bertrand, & Cleveland, 1998). Standards of practice can be used along with the body of core knowledge to guide professional preparation and development, to establish criteria for certifying early childhood educators, and to provide a basis for job descriptions and performance evaluation procedures. A coherent standard of practice statement that has broad support and endorsement can be a useful tool in informational advocacy activities aimed at raising public understanding of value of early childhood educators' work.

The Child Care Human Resources Sector Council prepared and validated occupational standards for ECEs. Occupational standards are written descriptions of the knowledge, skills, and abilities required to do a specific job competently and the behaviours acceptable to recipients of the service and to colleagues. The standards are applicable to early childhood educators working in regulated child care, preschool and nursery school programs, school-based kindergarten, prekindergarten and family literacy programs, family child care, and family support programs. They are designed to identify specific skills and abilities necessary to perform required tasks in a competent manner. More than 900 ECEs developed and validated the standards through interviews, online surveys, regional workshops, and provincial/territorial exercises.

The occupational standards include standards of practice for each of the following categories (Child Care Human Resource Sector Council, 2010):

- child development, learning, and care;
- equipment and facilities;
- family and community relations;
- professional relationships;
- personal and professional development; and
- record-keeping.

Credentialing

Credentials are the evidence that an individual has both the knowledge and skills needed to practise in a specific occupation. **Credentialing** is the process of evaluating knowledge and skills. Doherty (2003) defines three methods of credentialing in the North American early childhood sector: equivalency validation, certification or licensing of early childhood education graduates, and competency-based assessment.

In Canada, some provinces or territories have certification/equivalency/credential recognition practices for ECEs, while others have no formal system or process in place. In some cases, a credential achieved in one province may not be recognized in another, creating a barrier to entry.

1990s

There are 320 288 daycare spaces in Canada.

The average annual salary for an early childhood educator working in a child care centre is $11 639; the average salary of a teacher in a kindergarten program is $32 501.

1989

The Canadian government passes a resolution to eliminate poverty among Canadian children by the year 2000. There are 943 000 poor children in Canada.

1850   1900   1950   2000

What Do I Need to Be Credentialed as an Early Childhood Educator?

The Child Care Human Resources Sector Council (CCHRSC) was a pan-Canadian, non-profit organization that addressed pressing human resources issues in the child care sector. Its projects included research, strategies, and tools to meet the needs of the child care workforce and to achieve related goals. CCHRSC's board included volunteers from national and provincial child care or labour organizations; child care centres, nursery schools, preschools, or private home daycares; post-secondary training institutions; and government. As noted by Jamie Kass in the introduction to this section on p. 190, CCHRSC ceased to exist in 2013, but its resources and reports, which continue to be up to date, are available online.

One document offered by CCHRSC and found online is the *Guide to Early Childhood Education Credentialing in Canada,* which describes the qualifications needed to work in regulated child care and is available online. This guide was developed as part of the project called Pathways to Credentialing in Canada's Early Childhood Education and Care Sector. The *Guide* is intended for anyone who may wish to

- review their province's or territory's requirements to work in regulated child care;
- understand the requirements to work in regulated child care in other parts of Canada;
- learn how their current qualifications would relate to these requirements; and
- understand what is involved in certification, classification, and equivalency in each province and territory.

The *Guide* is also intended as a reference for

- child care licensing officials,
- ECE faculty in post-secondary institutions,
- policymakers and other government officials, and
- others involved or interested in the early childhood sector who may be interested in learning about the requirements and processes in other provinces and territories.

Source: Adapted from "Guide to Early Childhood Education Credentialing in Canada," CCHRSC website, http://www.ccsc-cssge.ca/english/guide/aboutcfm, accessed August 28, 2010.

All provinces and territories have legislation, regulations, and standards that govern the operation of regulated child care programs. They identify requirements for staff, which may include

- Early Childhood Education qualifications or related training;
- ongoing professional development;
- certification or registration with a government or designated body;
- other requirements needed for licensing, such as first-aid training and criminal reference checks; and
- processes to recognize qualifications other than ECE qualifications, or those acquired in a different province or territory.

The requirements and practices vary across provinces and territories. No province or territory requires all staff to have a post-secondary credential in ECE. However, several provinces and territories have minimum "entry level" training requirements for all staff, which vary from 40 to 120 hours of ECE course work, and post-secondary ECE requirements for a percentage of staff. (See Chapter 3, Table 3.1 for details.) In addition to the educational requirements, eight provinces and territories require all or some staff to be officially recognized as Early Childhood Educators. Registration (in Ontario), certification (Alberta, Saskatchewan, Prince Edward Island, Newfoundland and Labrador, and Yukon), licensing (British Columbia), and classification (Manitoba) are all processes that provide official recognition for an ECE.

When an individual requires registration or certification to be employed in an occupation, the regulatory body has the authority to set entry requirements and standards of practice; to assess applicants' qualifications and academic credentials; to certify, register, or license qualified applicants; and to discipline members of the profession, if necessary. For example, in British Columbia, ECEs are required to have a government licence to practise in order to be recognized as qualified staff in a regulated child care centre or preschool. To be eligible for the licence, ECEs must have an early childhood education academic qualification and documented work experience.

Equivalency validation credentials verify that an ECE who does not meet a particular jurisdiction's qualification requirements has comparable or equivalent education and experience. All provinces and territories that have educational qualification requirements for ECEs in early childhood education and related settings have some established procedures for assessing qualifications and credentials from other jurisdictions.

Competency-based assessment "testifies that a person whose formal educational qualifications related to child care are less than those required for entry into the field has the practical competencies required to provide competent child care" (Doherty, 2003, p. 5). The only competency-based assessment process in Canada (outside of prior-learning assessment in colleges and universities) is in Manitoba and is conducted by the provincial government.

Voluntary certification recognizes and endorses the educational qualifications and, sometimes, the performance levels of ECEs, regardless of their work setting. It is a mechanism to monitor standards of practice and to promote both the quality of early childhood education and care services and the professionalism of the early childhood workforce.

In Nova Scotia, the certification process of the Certification Council of Early Childhood Educators of Nova Scotia (CCECENS) stipulates that eligible applicants must have an ECE education qualification and at least two years' experience

1992
Caring for a Living, a national report on child care centre staff working conditions and wages, is released.

The Live-In Caregiver Program is introduced by the federal government.

1991
The first Worthy Wage Day in the United States, organized by the Child Care Employee Project, is held on April 9.

The federal government introduces a ten-week parental leave benefit, in addition to the existing fifteen-week maternity leave benefit, as part of the Unemployment Insurance program.

1993
The Perry Preschool Project publishes its data on the now 27-year-olds who were once in its preschool programs, showing the continued costs and benefits.

The Manitoba Child Care Association initiates the Worthy Wage Campaign.

| 1850 | 1900 | 1950 | 2000 |

working in an early childhood education setting with young children. Applicants are observed at their workplace by a facilitator, who is an early childhood educator with CCECENS certification, to assess their performance against fifteen standards of practice developed by CCECENS. The process can be repeated several times until the applicant meets the criteria. At this point, a validator reviews written evaluations, observes the applicant, and makes a recommendation to CCECENS, where the final decision is made. A certified ECE maintains her certification by paying an annual fee and providing proof of her participation in professional development.

In British Columbia, the government issues a licence to practise to ECEs who have the necessary educational qualifications and hours of work experience.

In Alberta, Prince Edward Island, and Manitoba, ECEs have to submit their education qualifications to the provincial government, which will then assign the appropriate classification for regulated centre-based programs.

In Newfoundland, all qualified ECE staff in regulated child care centres are required (by the provincial child care legislation) to have their certification from the provincial Association of Early Childhood Educators, Newfoundland and Labrador.

The certification processes in Canada aim to improve quality and increase professionalism. However, there are limitations. Because these certification processes are voluntary, only a small proportion of ECEs in each of these provinces is actually certified. In some early childhood education programs, certification is recognized and valued; but there is little overall recognition or motivation to become certified, as certification is not required for employment.

Self-Governance

The self-governance of a profession refers to its authority to establish bodies to regulate its members and their practice through certification, standards of practice, discipline, and requirements for professional education. Self-governance recognizes bodies outside government or organizations that represent the economic or professional development interest of practitioners. That recognition is usually embedded in legislation.

Provincial/territorial professional organizations have taken on tasks—such as voluntary certification, development of codes of ethics, consultation with governments on issues related to equivalency validation, and appropriate course content for professional education programs—which are often associated with self-governance. There are two self-governing bodies in Canada, the Association of Early Childhood Educators of Newfoundland and Labrador, and the Ontario College of Early Childhood Educators. The latter is a legislated, self-regulating professional body. As discussed earlier in this chapter, members are required to meet entry standards and continuing competence in order to be licensed with the College. Certification and licensing with the College is required in regulated early childhood settings (Pascal, 2009a).

The Certification Council of Early Childhood Education, Nova Scotia, and the Early Childhood Educators of British Columbia have proposed legislated or mandated self-regulatory bodies, which would regulate early childhood educators within each of the provincial jurisdictions. To date, the proposals have not been adopted.

College of Early Childhood Educators, Ontario

In 2007, Ontario introduced the *Early Childhood Educators Act* (2007), which defines the practice of early childhood education in this way:

> The practice of early childhood education is the planning and delivery of inclusive play-based learning and care programs for children in order to promote the well-being and holistic development of children, and includes
>
> (a) the delivery of programs to pre-school children and school aged children, including children with special needs;
>
> (b) the assessment of the programs and of the progress of children in the programs;
>
> (c) communication with parents or persons with legal custody of the children in the programs in order to improve the development of the children; and
>
> (d) such other services or activities as may be prescribed by the regulations.

The *Early Childhood Educators Act (2007)* established the College of Early Childhood Educators in Ontario. Membership in the College is required for everyone wishing to use the title of early childhood educator and practise early childhood education in the province. The College of Early Childhood Educators is a professional self-regulatory organization. It regulates the practice of early childhood education, establishes and maintains qualifications for membership, and issues certificates of registration. It also has responsibility to enforce professional and ethical standards, investigate complaints against members, and deal with issues of discipline.

An ECE diploma is required to be eligible for registration. There is one general certificate of registration for the title of Registered Early Childhood Educator (or *Éducateur/Éducatrice de la petite enfance inscrit[e]*). Applicants to the College have to submit the application form, a diploma in ECE, or a transcript from an Ontario College of Applied Arts and Technology (OCAAT) or from a post-secondary institution approved by the College; or they must submit a Letter of Equivalency or Recognition of Equivalency, a guarantor's signature verifying the applicant's educational qualifications, and proof of Canadian citizenship or immigration status. English or French fluency is required for registration.

Sources: Pascal, 2009a; Beach & Flanagan, 2010.

1995

There are 1 472 000 poor children in Canada.

In Canada, approximately three million children under the age of twelve have working parents; there are 474 969 regulated child care spaces.

1994

The Fisher-Price Toy Company sells $800 million worth of toys.

Loris Malaguzzi, founder of the schools in Reggio Emilia, Italy, dies, while the philosophy of his schools continues to influence programs around the world.

1850   1900   1950   2000

Equivalency

The recognition of out-of-province educational qualifications to meet requirements for credentials is another aspect of regulation and certification. Each jurisdiction sets up its own process for determining if educational qualifications from outside that province/territory are comparable or equivalent to those recognized within its boundaries.

It is important for you to be familiar with the requirements in your province or territory. If you think you may wish to move to a different part of Canada, you will want to know how your credentials will apply. You may also want to know how the credits you are now earning could be applied to further education.

Professional Development

Not all early childhood professional education and development is part of post-secondary education programs or part of professional preparation (Beach, 1999). In fact, most of the professional preparation we have considered in this chapter will equip you only with the entry-level skills and knowledge of an early childhood educator. Most ECEs take part in other activities that promote ongoing learning, professional development, and professional practice in working with young children and their families; these learning opportunities are often offered by professional organizations.

The effectiveness of professional development for educators who are working in programs varies. The early childhood sector is a complex and challenging arena for the provision of professional development (Beach & Flanagan, 2007; Cherrington & Wansbrough, 2007). Effective professional development programs are based on research, underpinned by current theoretical perspectives (both content and delivery methods) and are sustained over a period of time (Beach & Flanagan, 2007; Cherrington & Wansbrough, 2007; Flowers, Girolametto, Weistzman, & Greenberg, 2007).

The range of development opportunities that promote skills and knowledge includes workshops, seminars, conferences, publications, and networking. These resources are offered by early childhood education organizations, government departments, community groups, family resource programs, family child care agencies, and child care organizations.

Unionization

Many early childhood educators have been reluctant to form unions to lobby on their own behalf; but unionization is a strategy that could leave to improved compensation and working conditions, as well as to improved quality of the early childhood programs. Unionization has accompanied the professionalization of nurses and teachers in Canada.

The labour movement in Canada has been involved in organizing the early childhood workforce and bargaining for better compensation and working conditions since the 1970s (Beach, Bertrand, Forer, Michal, & Tougas, 2004). To date, approximately 21 percent of ECEs employed in child care centres are members of trade unions in Canada (Beach, Flanagan, & Varmuza, 2014). Employment structures and funding present barriers for the organization of

ECEs. In centre-based child care programs, it is difficult to organize relatively small staff groups into collective bargaining units. ECEs who demand increased compensation are immediately threatened with the inability of parents to afford increased fees—and the parents are people they see and speak with every day, people with whom they have forged relationships. ECEs employed in programs operated within larger institutions (such as municipalities in Ontario or community colleges) are included as a small proportion of a broad bargaining unit, but this solution is less than perfect: it may be difficult within the larger union to address issues that are specific to the child care workforce (Beach, Bertrand, & Cleveland, 1998).

Rates of unionization vary across Canada:

- While the overall level of unionization of full-time staff in regulated child care centres is low, the rate in Quebec is 30 percent (Beach, Flanagan, & Varmuza, 2014).
- Unionization rates across Canada ranged from 30 percent in Quebec to 2 percent in Alberta and 0 percent in New Brunswick (Beach, Flanagan, & Varmuza, 2014).
- ECE and other staff working in unionized child care centres earn higher pay and better benefits than staff in other settings. On average, child care staff earns 25 percent more in unionized centres (Beach, Flanagan, & Varmuza, 2014). They are also more likely to receive benefits such as disability insurance, extended health care, life insurance, employee top-up of maternity benefits, and parental leave benefits and pensions (Beach & Flanagan, 2007).

Unions and Early Childhood Educators

MAKING IT HAPPEN

Unions that represent the early childhood workforce in Canada include the following:

- Canadian Union of Public Employees (CUPE). In Quebec, CUPE is a member of the Quebec Federation of Labour.
- Fédération de la santé et services sociaux (FSSS/CSN), and the Fédération des employées et employés de services publics (FEESP/CSN), two federations which are members of the Confederation des syndicats nationaux (CSN).
- Fédération du personnel de soutien scolaire (FPSS/CSQ) and the Fédération des intervenantes en petite enfance du Québec (FIPEQ/CSQ), members of the Centrale des syndicats du Québec (CSQ).
- Fédération indépendante des syndicates autonomes (FISA).
- B.C. Government and Services Employees Union (BCGEU), Saskatchewan Government and General Employees Union (SGEU), Ontario Public Service Employees Union (OPSEU), and Manitoba General Employees Union (MGEU)—all components of the National Union of Public and General Employees (NUPGE).
- Service Employees International Union (SEIU).
- Health Sciences Association (HSA).
- Public Service Alliance of Canada (PSAC).
- Canadian Auto Workers (CAW).
- Union of Needletrades, Industrial, and Textile Employees (UNITE).
- United Food and Commercial Workers (UFCW).

Professionalization Dilemmas

Within the last couple of generations in Canada, providing child care services for pay has begun to emerge as a legitimate occupation, with recognized standards, training, and improved public recognition. ECEs working in child care now want to define themselves as a respected and reasonably compensated occupation, and they want to get the public acceptance and legislative recognition they deserve.

The number of ECEs who have educational or equivalent qualifications is increasing in early childhood education programs, but many individuals working with young children do not have these qualifications. Another challenge of professionalization of the workforce is that it may exclude many experienced caregivers who are currently working in the field but are unable to go to school to gain the necessary educational qualifications. Professionalism may also limit the participation of caregivers from particular ethnocultural backgrounds.

Another challenge to the process of professionalization of the ECE sector is one that is based in history. For much of the 20th century in Canada, the task of raising children was one that women were expected to do by staying at home when their children were young. As women moved into the labour force, they typically made arrangements through the family and the extended family, or with neighbours, to provide child care, often in exchange for non-monetary types of rewards (as part of intra-family obligations, mutual help arrangements with neighbours, etc.). These providers of child care did not seem to need special training. Early childhood education as a distinct occupation requiring formal education and ongoing professional development, regulations, and standards has, therefore, emerged only slowly.

To consolidate recognition as a profession, ECEs must continue to convince parents, the general public, and governments that there are clear advantages to quality early childhood education programs even though the cost is higher than informal care arrangements. The purpose of child care must be more than allowing parents to participate in the labour force.

EARLY CHILDHOOD EDUCATION ORGANIZATIONS

There are early childhood education organizations and associations at the national, provincial/territorial, and local levels that support the early childhood workforce and advocate for its recognition. In addition to their involvement in advocacy and activities related to professionalism, these groups carry out a range of professional education and development activities.

Organizations face several challenges in their ability to meet the needs of the early childhood workforce (Beach & Flanagan, 2007; Best Start Quality and Human Resources Expert Panel, 2007):

- Most organizations operate with little or no public funding and rely on considerable volunteer labour to carry out their activities.
- The ability of early childhood educators and early childhood programs to sustain organizations through membership fees is limited, reflecting, in part, the low compensation that early childhood educators receive.

- Membership in early childhood organizations is voluntary, and most early childhood educators do not belong to any organization.

Canadian Child Care Federation (CCCF)

The CCCF is a national organization committed to improving the quality of early childhood care and education services across Canada. Its membership includes 18 provincial/territorial organizations, with a total of more than 9000 members across Canada. The CCCF provides leadership to the early childhood workforce on a number of fronts, including the development of national principles for quality early childhood education and care programs and guidelines for professional education programs. It also provides research, publications, conferences and workshops, and information services. The CCCF sponsors projects to develop a national framework for quality assurance and guidelines for family child care training. It is also working with the Association of Canadian Community Colleges to consider an accreditation process for ECE certificate and diploma programs in Canada.

Provincial/Territorial Early Childhood Education Organizations

There is at least one organization in every province and territory (except for the Northwest Territories and Nunavut) that represents the early childhood workforce. These groups have grown out of the needs of early childhood educators and do not have government-defined mandates.

Early Childhood Education Organizations in Canada

MAKING IT HAPPEN

ECEs have access to professional, advocacy, and resource organizations across Canada. The following list is an overview of some organizations and resource groups and their primary purpose. There are also local groups that provide support to early childhood educators.

National

Canadian Child Care Federation (CCCF)
http://www.cccf-fcsge.ca/about/affiliatesmember-council-representatives/
Works to improve quality of child care services across Canada, build an infrastructure for the early childhood education and care community, and provide extensive information and resource services. Includes thirteen provincial and territorial affiliate members. Provides a complete listing of all organizations, professional education and development programs, and related resource groups.

Child Care Advocacy Association of Canada (CCAAC)
On behalf of a coalition of supporters including provincial advocacy associations, provincial advocate representatives, unions, and social action organizations, advocates for
- universal child care as a cornerstone of progressive family policies;
- the right of all children to access a child care system supported by public funds;
- a child care system that is comprehensive, inclusive, accessible, affordable, high-quality, and non-profit; and
- a range of child care services for children from birth to 12 years.

Canadian Association for Young Children (CAYC)
Promotes professional development and communication among early childhood educators in child care programs and school settings.

Canadian Association of Family Resource Programs (FRP Canada)
Provides consultation and support for program development, publications, and professional development to a national network of family resource programs.

Childcare Resource and Research Unit
Provides public education, consultation, and publications; organizes and disseminates information and resources; conducts child care–related research projects; and provides a circulating library and database of resources.

Newfoundland

Association of Early Childhood Educators, Newfoundland and Labrador (AECENL; Affiliate Member of CCCF)
Provides awareness of quality child care and advocates for early childhood educators.

Prince Edward Island

Early Childhood Development Association of P.E.I. (ECDA of PEI; Affiliate Member of CCCF)
Promotes knowledge of early childhood education, promotes professionalism, and provides support to membership.

Nova Scotia

Nova Scotia Child Care Association (NSCCA; Affiliate Member of CCCF)
Represents caregivers in non-profit child care centres and family child care.

Certification Council of Early Childhood Education of Nova Scotia (Affiliate Member of CCCF)
Has offered voluntary certification process for early childhood educators since 1988.

Child Care Connection NS
Connects child care professionals to resources, promotes certification and administration, operates a resource centre library, and sponsors professional development events.

New Brunswick

Early Childhood Care & Education New Brunswick/Soins et éducation à la petite enfance Nouveau-Brunswick (ECCENB/SEPENB; Affiliate Member of CCCF)
Represents child care workers and those who have an interest in quality child care.

Quebec

Quebec Association for Preschool Professional Development (QAPPD)
Represents early childhood educators and promotes professionalism; provides voluntary certification process for early childhood educators.

Ontario

Home Child Care Association of Ontario (Affiliate Member of CCCF)
Promotes and supports quality home child care, with primary focus on regulated home child care.

Ontario Network of Home Child Care Provider Groups
Promotes and advocates for family child care providers.

Ontario Coalition for Better Child Care
Advocates and promotes quality non-profit child care and represents non-profit child care programs.

Ontario Association of Family Resource Programs
Represents and provides support to provincial family resource programs.

Manitoba

Manitoba Child Care Association (MCCA; CCCF Affiliate)
Advocates for a quality child care system; represents non-profit child care programs and regulated family child care; provides services to membership; advances child care as a profession.

Saskatchewan

Saskatchewan Early Childhood Association (SECA; CCCF Affiliate)
Supports caregivers in centre-based care and family child care.

Alberta

Alberta Child Care Association (ACCA; CCCF Affiliate)
A coalition of several recognized child care organizations within Alberta with representation from various stakeholders within government who have a vested interest in child care issues.

Alberta Family Day Care Association (AFCCA; CCCF Affiliate)
Provides support to regulated family child care.

ECE Professional Association of Alberta (CCCF Affiliate)
Supports ECE staff and promotes professional development. Provides voluntary certification process for early childhood educators.

British Columbia

B.C. Aboriginal Child Care Society (Affiliate Member of CCCF)
Supports Aboriginal communities in developing high-quality, integrated child care services within Aboriginal culture and building an Aboriginal child care network in British Columbia.

B.C. Coalition of Child Care Advocates
Promotes and advocates for quality child care.

Western Canadian Family Child Care Association (Affiliate Member of CCCF)
Promotes, supports, and advocates for quality family child care.

School Age Child Care Association of B.C.
Promotes and supports school-age child care and represents school-age child care staff.

Early Childhood Educators of British Columbia (ECEBC; CCCF Affiliate)
Promotes and supports early childhood educators.

Westcoast Child Care Resource Centre
Provides child care resources, information and referral services, and professional development with and through affiliate early childhood education and care organizations.

Yukon

Yukon Child Care Association (Affiliate Member of CCCF)
Promotes centre-based and family child care.

▶ Early childhood educators often seek out opportunities to share experiences and learn from their colleagues.

Rawpixel/Shutterstock

Summary

- A profession shares a core knowledge base, codes of ethics, and standards of practice.
- The Canadian early childhood profession is gaining official recognition through mandatory and voluntary registration and certification requirements.
- The Canadian Child Care Federation represents early childhood educators and their provincial/

territorial professional organizations. The Canadian Child Care Advocacy Association is a coalition of individuals and organizations who advocate for a universal child care system.

- Three methods of credentialing are equivalency validation, certification or licensing of early childhood education graduates, and competency-based assessment.

REVIEW QUESTIONS

1. Describe several of the characteristics of a profession, and discuss how early childhood care and education matches these standards for a profession.

2. Name two major early childhood professional organizations, discussing the services of each.
3. Discuss the ECEBC code of ethics, its component parts, and its uses for ECEs.

STUDY ACTIVITIES

1. Visit your school library to learn what journals from professional early childhood organizations are available. Read several articles from a representative issue, and write brief reports that indicate the kinds of knowledge you obtain. Examine the issues for regular features that would be helpful to early childhood teachers in their practice and in their learning about policy and wider issues of the profession.

2. Using your community resource guide and contacts with early childhood teachers, learn what professional organizations are available and used by teachers in your area. If possible, attend a local meeting. Talk with local teachers who are members of the organization to learn how they have benefited from their membership. If there are no local groups, call or write the nearest affiliate to get a listing of their current activities and to get on their mailing list, if possible.

3. Is there a Week of the Young Child activity held in your community? If there is, find out how you and other students can become involved. If there isn't, what could you do to initiate one?

4. With classmates, use the ECEBC code of ethics to discuss the following issues that could occur in a classroom.

   a. A parent asks an infant caregiver not to feed the baby in the late afternoon, so that she can feed her at home and put her to sleep. The baby cries every day until her mother comes.

   b. A co-worker has discussed a family at your child care centre with her boy friend's family, who ask you about the situation.

   c. A four-year-old is angry when his mother leaves him each morning, and he treats other children aggressively. The assistant teacher is bothered by the lead teacher's response, which is to put him in time-out for long periods.

   d. A supervisor tells an ECE that a child who is absent has contagious diarrhea, so teachers should wash hands carefully. The ECE is surprised that a notice is not posted to inform parents.

   e. An ECE working with three-year-olds is unaware when she is first employed that the number of children in her room exceeds the adult–child ratio standards of the provincial/territorial day care regulations. When the licensing officer comes to inspect, the director tells him that the cook also works regularly in the program.

   f. A mother asks you not to let her four-year-old son nap in the afternoon, since he then wants to stay up late at night and she has to get up early to go to work. The child seems to need his nap to play happily in the afternoon.

5. Go online and look for early childhood organizations in your province or territory. Are there any student membership rates? What services are available?

KEY TERMS

code of ethics: Statements of a profession that govern moral behaviour and ethical decisions. The NAEYC adopted and published its early childhood code of ethics in 1989.

core knowledge: Basic knowledge that a professional group acknowledges to be needed by all its members.

credentialing: Evaluating professional qualifications from recognized educational institutions or professional organizations.

professional: Practitioner who has met the standards of knowledge and performance required by a profession.

Suggested Readings

Ade, W. 1982. "Professionalization and Its Implications for the Field of Early Childhood Education." Young Children, 37 (3), 25–32. Copyright © YEAR NAEYC(R). Reprinted with permission.

Canadian Child Care Federation. (2000). *Partners in quality: Tools for practitioners in child care settings.* Ottawa: Canadian Child Care Federation.

Child Care Human Resources Sector Council. (2010). *Occupational standards for early childhood educators.* Ottawa, ON: CCHRSC. Available at http://www.ccsc-cssge.ca.

Beach, J. & Flanagan, K. (2010) *Examining the human resource implications of emerging issues in ECEC.* Ottawa, ON: CCHRSC.

Cherrington, S. & Wansbrough, D. (2007) *An evaluation of Ministry of Education–funded early childhood education professional development programmes.* Victoria, NZ: Ministry of Education.

ADVOCACY

OBJECTIVES

After studying this chapter, students will be able to
- outline the arguments for investing more in early childhood programs
- review how early childhood education is organized and delivered in Canada and elsewhere
- identify approaches to advocating for early childhood programs and the early childhood workforce
- recognize the role of advocacy groups and other organizations in addressing policy issues related to early childhood education

Advocacy is the act of defending or stating a cause for yourself or someone else. The role of advocacy is played out in early childhood settings and in the world at large. In early childhood programs and the early childhood workforce in Canada, public policy advocacy centres around a collective effort to address three interconnected issues: quality, compensation, and accessibility. Advocates seek to raise public awareness of the rights of young children, the importance of children's early years, and the potential of early childhood education and care programs to contribute to the development of healthy children, strong families, and cohesive communities.

In this expanding early childhood workforce, responses to the needs of children, families, and early childhood educators are propelling changes that affect us all. Some of these trends will strengthen the workforce itself, making it likely that you will see enormous changes during your career. As you enter the early childhood workforce, it is important that you consider the complexity of these issues and decide how you can advocate for yourself and for the children and families with whom you work.

Before you read any further, note in your journal the ideas that you believe might be included in this discussion of advocacy issues. Think about the ideas you have encountered already in your own work experiences and in the course of your early childhood education studies. Reflect on the challenges raised in the first and second sections of this book, where you examined early child development programs and the early childhood workforce, and in Chapter 7, where you considered their historical development.

As you continue your ECE studies and embark on your journey as an early childhood educator, there are guidelines for personal daily practice. The most effective advocate for early childhood education and care programs is a dedicated, reflective practitioner. Your knowledge, skills, and abilities shape the daily lives of young children and families. You also influence the public perceptions, both local and global, about how we should move the early child development agenda forward in the 21st century.

MAKING THE CASE FOR INVESTING IN EARLY CHILDHOOD PROGRAMS

Canada is expanding early childhood education for its youngest citizens. But for many, the current delivery of early childhood education in Canada does not work for parents, early childhood educators, governments, or communities. Most importantly, it often does not work for children. There are not enough programs. Costs are often prohibitive. Quality concerns abound. Poor coordination and a lack of integration at the local level may lead families to be confused about what services they are entitled to and how they can access those services. The typical array of early childhood education and related programs and services available to a young child is a chaotic maze. Many parents do not understand what services are available to everyone, let alone how to access more complex services such as special needs interventions.

The campaign for better early childhood programs spans four decades. Governments of every political stripe have tried to address the "child care issue" but little has changed (White, 2007). The sector itself is often undecided about how to move forward, and it is often marginalized by the visions that emerge from health and education sectors.

▷ All children have the right to participate in quality early childhood programs.

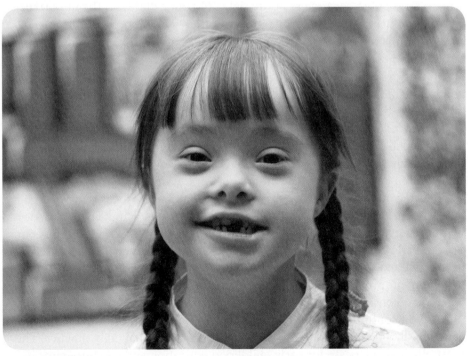

DenKuvaiev/iStock/Thinkstock

Early childhood education programs are not a magic bullet for young children and their families any more than public education has replaced parental guidance, home environments, and safe, inviting community spaces for school-age children. But early childhood programs are a crucial link in the ecology of communities.

Early childhood programs live in neighbourhoods and communities and can offer a comfortable space and meeting place that welcomes all young children and families. Early childhood programs connect families with each other. Children need spaces and places to play with each other. When children play, families from diverse religious, linguistic, and cultural backgrounds can find common ground where everyone belongs.

The arguments for public investment in early childhood programs and a coherent early childhood system are growing. Early childhood educators are advocates who understand these arguments and able to communicate them to colleagues, families, communities, and governments.

Benefits for Children

Early learning and well-being.   All young children have an astounding capacity to learn—astounding both in how much they can learn and in the variety and range of what they can learn. Given the capacity of children to learn, particularly during their early years, it makes sense to keep all avenues, options, and aspirations open. The primary focus becomes one of identifying and introducing the experiences, activities, and challenges that enhance everyone's learning.

Early, regular access to high-quality programs offers young children the kinds of opportunities that benefit language, social competence, emotional maturity, and cognitive development. Research shows that the positive effects of early education carry forward into elementary school to establish a foundation for later success. Disadvantaged children derive more benefit from high-quality early childhood programs, but the advantages apply to all children and they apply whether the mother is in the paid workforce or not. All children show improved educational and social outcomes from regular, sustained participation in early childhood programs (Pascal, 2009b; Shonkoff & Phillips, 2000; Sylva, Melhuish, Sammons, Siraj-Blatchford, & Taggart, 2004; Yoshikawa et al., 2013).

1996

The Canada Health and Social Transfer (CHST) block grant replaces the Canada Assistance Plan.

The National Crime Prevention Council identifies early child care and education programs as essential components of an integrated approach to reduce the long-term incidence of crime.

The National Forum on Health calls for a broad, integrated child and family strategy.

| 1850 | 1900 | 1950 | 2000 |

Large, longitudinal studies report that high-quality early childhood education and care programs that provide sound early learning experiences are more likely to send children into Grade 1 eager to learn and primed to succeed, regardless of their families' socio-economic background (Hodgen, 2007; Osborn & Milbank, 1987; Sylva, Melhuish, Sammons, Siraj-Blatchford, & Taggart, 2004; Sylva et al., 2009; Wylie, 2004).

Participation in high-quality early childhood programs prepares children for school success, higher education, and lifelong learning. But child well-being while in preschool is also a worthy purpose. Early childhood programs play a role in ensuring that children have a good quality of life "here and now" (Friendly, 2008). Childhood is an important phase of life, not just a prelude to adulthood; and the child is an active, competent learner. Early childhood programs become an integral part of children's culture and can amplify children's own interests and aptitudes outside the family.

RESEARCH INTO PRACTICE

Long-Term Impact of Early Childhood Education

The 1970 British Birth Cohort study (Osborn & Milbank, 1987) and New Zealand's Competent Children study (Hodgen, 2007) show that the benefits of early childhood education have a long reach into adolescence and adulthood.

Another important study that examined the effects of preschool education on children's cognitive and social development was the U.K. Effective Preschool and Primary Education (EPPE) (Sylva, Melhuish, Sammons, Siraj-Blatchford, & Taggart, 2004). Three thousand three-year-old children were randomly selected from preschool settings in England and compared with another "home group" with no preschool experience (Sammons, Sylva, Melhuish, Siraj-Blatchford, Taggart, Hunt, & Jelicic, 2008). Researchers performed children's cognitive, language, social, and behavioural assessments at ages 3, 5, 6, 7, 10, 11, 14 and 16 years. Parents were interviewed about the child's history from birth, family characteristics, and learning activities in the home. Researchers also studied the 141 preschool settings attended by the children. The results of the study indicated significant cognitive and social benefits for children who attended preschool compared to those who did not. The quality and length of time in the preschool mattered: every month of preschool after age 2 was linked to better cognitive development, improved independence, ability to attend, and sociability. Higher-quality preschool had enduring effects to age 11 years. The preschools that had the greatest impact were those with an intentional pedagogy that included both guided learning and child-directed play. These programs viewed educational and social development as complementary.

American studies conducted by the National Institute for Child Health and Development Early Child Care Research Network reported similar findings (NICHD Early Child Care Research Network, 2000, 2004). Several empirical research studies in the United States show that children from low-, middle-, and high-income families all benefit from prekindergarten programs for three- and four-year-old children. Higher-quality prekindergarten programs are associated with greater learning benefits (Ackerman & Barnett, 2006; Barnett, 2008; Lynch, 2007; Yoshikawa et al., 2013).

1650   1700   1750   1800

Vulnerable children.   Early childhood education programs can support the development of vulnerable children. As we discussed in Chapter 1, early intervention programs can provide specific services for children who are showing early indications of an identifiable problem or who are significantly at risk of developing a problem. Early intervention is conceptualized as a systematically planned method of taking action based on the child's needs during the first pivotal years of life. It can include programming that compensates for environmental risks and that provides therapeutic interventions that address developmental difficulties. Participation in early children programs benefits all children, but it is has particular importance for children with identified developmental problems.

Early childhood programs are an effective early intervention strategy. Children who have developmental difficulties or who are at risk for less than optimal development benefit from access to early childhood programs. Early childhood programs can reduce the burden of suffering of these children and prevent or reduce later problems.

In addition to development difficulties, family poverty is also linked to poor educational outcomes from birth and early childhood on. Participation in high-quality early childhood programs for infants and toddlers at risk for problems has successfully improved their cognitive performance and social abilities with effects measured years after leaving the programs (Love et al., 2005; Karoly et al., 2005).

Children's rights.   The Convention on the Rights of the Child was adopted by the United Nations in 1989. It includes the idea that children are citizens with rights and are entitled to resources. The child's individual right to resources should be respected, quite apart from the child's value as an asset to society.

Canada supported both drafting the Convention and mobilizing the world's nations to sign it. Its 54 clauses include children's rights that have direct implications for early child development programs (Friendly, 2000). It states that all children have the right to child care services while their parents work, and to educational opportunities that will prepare them to participate in society. Early childhood programs are critical if we value children and respect their rights to their share of our resources.

1998

The federal and provincial/territorial governments introduce the National Child Benefits System.

The child care sector report, *Our Child Care Workforce: From Recognition to Remuneration*, is released.

1997

The federal and provincial/territorial governments agree to develop a National Children's Agenda.

The Quebec government announces major family policy reform, including the expanded provision of early childhood education and care programs.

1850   1900   1950   2000

A child's right to development and education opportunities early in life should be promoted as the priority for all early childhood programs. In the *Early years study*, the authors recognized that children were entitled to a decent childhood and advocated for investing in early childhood as a moral imperative: "Action now will put our children and our future on a firmer foundation for the future. This action is necessary, not only to keep a reasonable standard of living, but also because it is the right thing to do for our young children" (McCain & Mustard, 1999, p. 2).

Children have the right to be accepted and valued as young citizens who belong. Early childhood education can ensure equity and belonging for children and their families. The programs are inclusive of all children, regardless of ethnicity, ability, or socio-economic status. They incorporate diversity and expose children to their own customs and traditions as well as the ideas and experiences of others. Children who are confident in their abilities and comfortable in diverse environments when they are young become engage citizens who value a democratic, pluralistic society.

Benefits for Families

The new extended family.   Early childhood programs support the dual responsibilities of parents to earn a living and raise their children.

We can visualize a more coherent, comprehensive early childhood system as the new extended family. When early childhood programs are organized to provide high-quality early learning experiences, non-parental care and parenting supports, targeted interventions, and community development, benefits accrue to children, their families, communities, and societies. Early childhood education and care programs can offer children what they need: security, relationships, opportunities, and belonging. Just like the best of extended families, early childhood programs can bring more people into the lives of young children, and these people expand what is possible for each child.

Raising children is the shared responsibility of families and society rather than the sole responsibility of parents in isolation. The role of government and public investment in early childhood programs is to support families and young children. The majority of Canadians support public funding for early childhood programs (Environics, 2008).

Parental employment.   Child care programs care for children while their parents are working or studying. Parents who work outside the home, or carry out paid work inside the home, need non-parental care arrangements for their children, particularly for young children who have not entered the formal school system.

About 80 percent of parents of preschool children are in the paid labour force, and about 80 percent of those children (or 64 percent of all preschool children) receive non-parental care regularly (Cleveland, Forer, Hyatt, Japel, & Krashinsky, 2007). About half of the children who are in non-parental care are primarily in regulated child care programs, and if kindergarten and other school-based programs are included, the proportion is closer to two-thirds.

In Canada, outside of Quebec, child care fee subsidies from governments for regulated full-time child care programs are tied to parental labour force participation (Cleveland, Forer, Hyatt, Japel, & Krashinsky, 2007). Parents are eligible for child care fee subsidies if they are working. This funding is explicitly designed to support parental labour force participation among lower income parents.

Early childhood programs will continue to adapt to the practical requirements of families and the community in terms of their proximity, flexible schedules, affordability, accessibility, diversification, and the like.

Parenting resources.   Early childhood programs can support parents in their parenting role through parent involvement, **networking**, modelling, and other parent support resources. When programs can support the role of parents and the home learning environment is enriched, the benefits multiply (Sylva, Melhuish, Sammons, Siraj-Blatchford, & Taggart, 2004).

Early childhood education programs typically offer parents information about child development. Pamphlets, workshops, and YouTube videos may be welcomed by families but are not as effective in changing parenting practices as "learning by doing" opportunities. ECEs who are most effective provide parents with opportunities to observe educators interacting with their children or provide specific opportunities for parents to practise positive interactions with their children (Grindal, Bowne, Yoshikawa, Schindler, Duncan, Magnuson, & Shonkoff, under review).

Benefits for Society

Community development.   Early childhood education programs can make a valuable contribution to community development. They help to transmit social and cultural values. They are places where children are exposed to and influenced by others' values, and where children consolidate their value system, acquire their own vision of the world, and learn to socialize and function as part of a group. Because early childhood programs typically take in all children, regardless of gender, ethnic origin, religion, ability, family composition, or financial situation, they serve an important democratic and civic function—one in which equal opportunity and fairness for all are daily realities, being part of the group is reflected in the activities carried out together and with shared objectives, and the search for the common good takes individual well-being into account.

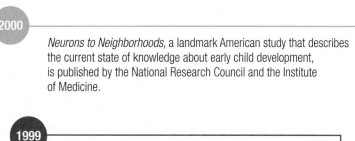

2000

Neurons to Neighborhoods, a landmark American study that describes the current state of knowledge about early child development, is published by the National Research Council and the Institute of Medicine.

1999

The Ontario government releases a landmark report, *The Early Years Study: Reversing the Real Brain Drain*, authored by Dr. J. Fraser Mustard and the Hon. Margaret Norrie McCain.

1850   1900   1950

Early childhood programs can unite families from diverse origins through participation in common activities related to their children—for example, potluck dinners, or weekend picnics. Adults and children find out that co-operation among social classes and ethnic groups is possible and positive. Early childhood education programs can be places that can foster community co-operation. They strengthen appreciation for diversity and promote equity among racial and ethnic groups, enhancing social integration and solidarity.

Early childhood programs are a place of employment for thousands of people in Canada, and they constitute an essential resource that enables parents to participate in the labour market, study, pursue professional development opportunities, and participate in community life—all of which contributes to society's wealth and the community's economic prosperity.

Canadian community economic development studies reveal that early childhood education and care programs generate immediate economic returns (Prentice, 2007). Reports from Manitoba found employment effects from investment in early childhood education and care programs. At the time of the study, every dollar of investment in these programs generated about $1.58 in economic activities. In addition to supporting the labour participation rate of parents, every job in an early childhood program creates or sustains 1.49 jobs (Prentice, 2007).

Economic benefits.   There are many economic benefits to the provision of quality early childhood education. The knowledge and skills that a country's citizens derive from education, training, and experience can be termed human capital. Human capital is a valuable resource to individuals and to the country, particularly in knowledge-based economies. Quality early childhood programs lay a solid foundation for the creation of human capital. High-quality early childhood programs encourage children's knowledge and the skills that they will need to survive, develop, and grow in the present and into the future. They prepare children for public school. Through play and interactions with others, early childhood education lays the foundations for their learning, for integration with the group, for scholastic success, for the ability to live and work with others, and eventually for their full participation in community life. Studies consistently find that that the benefits of early childhood education programs, particularly from age 2 until school entry, are more than the program costs. Investment in early childhood education is a very cost-effective educational intervention and is profitable for society as a whole (Yoshikawa et al., 2013).

Quebec's pioneering early childhood program demonstrates the economic impact of the related increased maternal labour participation. Economists estimate that 40 percent of investments are paid back through increased taxation due to mothers' increased labour force participation. One of the objectives of the Quebec expansion of child care funding was to permit mothers to work full time rather than part time. Mothers' participation in the workforce increased by 21 percent in less than 10 years—more than double the rate of growth in the rest of Canada over the same period (Baker, Gruber, & Milligan, 2006).

Canadian economists who have turned their attention to the returns on investment in early childhood programs are highlighting the monetary benefits. Participation in quality early childhood programs translates into savings in immediate and long-term remedial costs. Canadian economists have estimated the rate of return on investment is 2 to 2.5 dollars for every dollar invested in community-based early childhood programs (Cleveland & Krashinsky, 1998; Fairholme, 2010). Another report suggested, "It is estimated that $1 invested in the early years saves between $3 and $9 in future spending on the health and criminal justice systems, as well as on social assistance" (Chief Public Health Officer's Report on the State of Public Health in Canada, 2008).

Various municipal reports have used economic arguments in recommending expanded services (e.g., Coffey & McCain, 2002; Mahon & Jenson, 2006; Vancouver Board of Trade, 1999). The Toronto Board of Trade (2001), for example, named available child care as part of the social program mix which would stop the flight of capital from the city. Representatives of chambers of commerce have voiced their concerns that a lack of child care spaces is shrinking their employment base and leading to depopulation particularly of rural communities.

On the other hand, Lefebvre and Merrigan (2008) demonstrated that Quebec's investment in $5/day child care (now $7/day) and the expansion to full-day kindergarten programs has had a significant impact on increasing labour participation of Quebec mothers with preschool children. Economists have estimated that for every dollar Quebec invests, it receives $1.05 back in reduced family benefits, increased taxes, and related spending; and the federal government gets back 44 cents (Fortin, Godbout, & St-Cerny, 2012). In the United States, estimates about investment in universal prekindergarten show the same economic benefits (Lynch, 2007).

The economic case for investment in early childhood programs is based on long-term developmental and productivity benefits. These benefits are predicated on regular participation in an early childhood education environment. Early childhood programs that water down either quality or regularity of attendance risk not achieving anything. Studies have found no positive benefits from mediocre-quality or occasional/irregular early childhood programs, and poor-quality programs have a detrimental impact (Pascal, 2009b; Shonkoff & Phillips, 2000).

Canadian studies (see Table 9.1 for a summary of some key studies) point to the economic benefits of public investments in early childhood education:

2003 The Multilateral Framework on Early Learning and Child Care—a provincial/territorial/federal agreement that includes new federal funding specifically for early childhood education and care programs—is adopted.

2002 Maternal and parental benefits for new parents eligible for Employment Insurance is extended from six months to one year in Canada.

2001 The government of Canada announces the Early Child Development Agreement, which includes new federal funding for early childhood and related programs.

1850   1900   1950   2000

Overall, having an efficient, high-quality early childhood program in place, which is accessible for all children and affordable for parents, would be beneficial for children, parents as well as the broader economy. Education is the ultimate tool to address many economic and social challenges (TD Economics, 2012, p. 8).

RESEARCH INTO PRACTICE

Early Childhood Education Cost–Benefit Studies

Three well-known American studies have considered the long-term impact and financial cost-benefits of early childhood programs:

- The *Child–Parent Centres*, located in or near Chicago's public elementary schools, produced positive differences in child development for children three to nine, when compared to children not in the program. The programs included a daily early childhood education and care program for three- and four-year-olds and extended day programming once children entered kindergarten through the primary grades. Parents were encouraged to participate in the program on a regular basis. Key findings of a longitudinal study in Chicago included significantly higher educational attainment and lower rates of juvenile arrest.

- The *Perry Preschool* project examined the lives of 123 African-Americans born in poverty. From 1962 to 1967, at ages three and four, these children were randomly divided into one group that received a high-quality preschool and weekly home visits, and one comparison group that received no interventions. Data has been gathered on the participants over the intervening years. At age 40, those who had attended preschool significantly outperformed the no-program group. They did better on literacy tests; 65 percent as against 45 percent graduated high school; and a higher proportion went on to university. The most substantial savings were from reduced antisocial behaviour in the intervention group, which was measured by fewer arrests for drug, property, or violent crime. The cumulative economic return to society of the program: $258 888 per participant on an initial investment of $15 166 per child or $17.07 for each dollar spent.

- The *Abecedarian* project in North Carolina is a longitudinal experiment that demonstrates the power of comprehensive early childhood programs (Barnett & Masse, 2007). A group of African-American children whose mothers had IQs ranging from 74 to 124 (average 85) were randomly selected for two groups: a control group that received no intervention and another set of infants starting preschool at four months. At school entry, the preschool group was split into two: one received the standard school program and the other an enriched program for the first three years. The no-intervention group was also randomized into a group given three years of special programming when they entered school, and the others were given the standard educational program. The no-preschool group given the special three-year school program showed better reading skills than the group receiving neither preschool nor special education; the effect, however, was much weaker than for the children who attended preschool. The children attending both preschool and special education showed substantially elevated skills in reading and mathematics that continued into early adulthood. In contrast, the preschool children not placed in the special three-year school program had lost a significant portion of their gains by age 21.

Sources: Campbell, Wasik, Pungello, Burchinal, Kainz, & Barbarin, 2008; Reynolds & Temple, 2008; Schweinhart, Montie, Xiang, Barnett, Belfield, & Nores, 2005.

TABLE 9.1 Five Canadian Cost–Benefit Analyses of Early Childhood Programming

Study	Year	Description	Benefits	Ratio
Economic Consequences of Quebec's Educational Child Care Policy Pierre Fortin, Luc Godbout, Suzie St-Cerny	2011	Examined benefits of enhanced maternal employment due to low cost child care	• Quebec gains $1.5B in increased tax revenue • Pays $340M less in tax and social benefits to families • Increased provincial GDP by $5.2B (+1.7%)	• For every $1 spent on ECEC, Quebec receives $1.05 • Federal government receives $0.44
Better Beginnings, Better Futures Ray D. Peters et al.	2010	• $580 000 per site for 5 years to enrich child, parent and neighbourhood programming • 3 sites involving children 4–8 yrs • 5 sites involving children 0–4 yrs • Matched similar neighbourhoods • Children followed to grade 12	• No difference for BBBF sites focused on 0–4 yrs • Reduced use of health, social benefits, special education, child welfare and criminal justice in sites focused on 4–8 yrs cohorts compared to control neighbourhoods	• For every $1 spent, $2 in reduced costs to public and community agencies
Workforce Shortages Socio-Economic Effects Robert Fairholm	2009	• Analysis of potential benefits for every $1M spent on child care	• Child care an effective job creator and economic stimulant	• For every $1 invested $2.42 in increased earnings, improved health, reduced social costs
Child Care as Economic and Social Development Susan Prentice	2007	• Examined economic multipliers from existing child care services in 4 Manitoba communities: Winnipeg, Thompson, Parkland, and St-Pierre-Jolys	• Winnipeg child care sector has gross revenues of over $101M/year • Employs 3200 with annual earnings of $80M	• Every $1 creates $1.38 in the local economy and $1.40 in the Canadian economy • Every 1 child care job creates 2.1 spinoff jobs
The Benefits and Costs of Good Child Care Gordon Cleveland & Michael Krashinsky	1998	• Estimated costs of a universal child care program for every child 2–5 yrs • Assumed educators earn $36K and parents pay 20% of overall costs	• 170 000 jobs created • Increased maternal labour force participation • Lower welfare & related costs	• Every $1 spent creates $2 including: • $0.75 in social savings • $1.25 increased tax revenue from job creation/ working mothers

Sources: Cleveland & Krashinsky, 1998; Fairholm, 2009; Fortin, Godbout, & St-Cerny, 2012; Peters, Nelson, et al., 2010; Prentice & McCracken, 2004. From McCain, Mustard & McCuaig (2011). With permission from Margaret and Wallace McCain Family Foundation.

Stockbyte/Thinkstock

▲ Investing in early childhood programs makes economic sense.

EARLY CHILDHOOD EDUCATION IN CANADA

The Organization for Economic and Co-operative Development (OECD) has conducted extensive reviews of early childhood education systems in its member countries, including Canada (OECD, 2001; OECD, 2006). The review identified policy levers that provide essential infrastructure for early childhood education. *Early years study 3* (McCain, Mustard, & McCuaig, 2011) adapted the policy recommendations of the OECD reports and introduced the Early Childhood Education Report, a policy monitoring tool that tracks progress across Canadian jurisdictions. *Early childhood education report 2014* (Akbari & McCuaig, 2014) provided an update.

Governance

In Canada, as in most jurisdictions in the United States, Australia, United Kingdom, and New Zealand, governance for early childhood programs is a tangle of local, provincial/territorial, and federal public authorities as well as private (commercial and non-for-profit) entities (OECD, 2006; Pascal, 2009a). The myriad problems of this entanglement are explained and aptly termed "chaos" in *Early years study 2* (McCain, Mustard, & Shanker, 2007). This study found that while the number of programs had increased since the first study was released in 1999, these programs were largely uncoordinated and difficult for families to navigate.

The OECD recommends that early childhood education programs have an equal partnership with public education. In recent years, in many OECD countries, the goals of early childhood education services have become more child-centred and focused on early learning and developmental outcomes (OECD, 2013).

Since 2006, Saskatchewan, Ontario, Prince Edward Island, New Brunswick, Nova Scotia, Newfoundland and Labrador, and Northwest Territories have moved regulated child care and related early childhood programs into their respective departments or ministries of education (Akbari & McCuaig, 2014).

Funding

UNICEF recommends that governments spend 1 per cent of their GDP on early childhood education (Unicef, 2008). In 2014, Canada spent .6%, up from .25% in 2006 (Akbari & McCuaig, 2014).

Federal Government. The federal government transfers funds to provinces and territories specifically for early child development programs. In 2014, about $500 000 will be transferred for a range of early child development programs, and additional funds are transferred specifically for early childhood education (approximately $350 million) plus another $250 million for new child care spaces (Akbari & McCuaig, 2014).

| 1650 | 1700 | 1750 | 1800 |

Provincial/Territorial Government. Each province and territory has established fee subsidies to low-income families with specific criteria for eligibility. The target fee subsidies are usually intended for use only in regulated child care settings. In British Columbia and the Northwest Territories, these subsidies may be also used in unregulated family child care settings.

All provinces and territories offer a number of recurring or operating grants to regulated child care programs. Operating grants are public funding paid directly to the child care program to support a portion of its overall operating expenses. Some of these grants are aimed at raising staff salaries or other program expenses, whereas others are applied generally to program budgets.

Public Funding for Early Childhood Education Programs in Canada (2014)		MAKING IT HAPPEN
Child care	$ 6 200 000 000	
Kindergarten (public education system)	4 250 000 000	
Other ECE (public education system)	35 000 000	
Aboriginal Head Start and First Nations/Inuit Child Care	170 000 000	
TOTAL	$10 655 000 000	

Sources: McCain, Mustard, & McCuaig, 2011; McCuaig & Akbari, 2014; CRRU, 2014.

Access

The OECD recommends that 80% of preschool children have access to early childhood education programs. In 2014, 55% of Canadian children ages two- to four- years-old had access to an early childhood education program on a regular basis (Akbari & McCuaig, 2014).

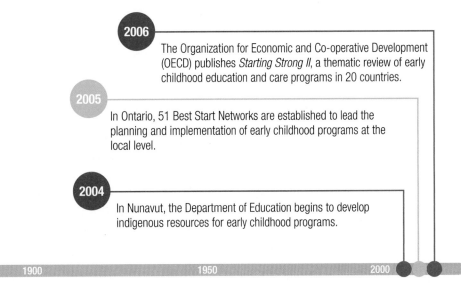

2006
The Organization for Economic and Co-operative Development (OECD) publishes *Starting Strong II*, a thematic review of early childhood education and care programs in 20 countries.

2005
In Ontario, 51 Best Start Networks are established to lead the planning and implementation of early childhood programs at the local level.

2004
In Nunavut, the Department of Education begins to develop indigenous resources for early childhood programs.

1850   1900   1950   2000

Access to early childhood education varies across Canada. Child care and nursery school/preschool programs are in short supply in most regions of the country. Nursery schools, preschools, and kindergarten programs are not organized to support the needs of parents who are working. Regulated child care is too expensive for many families. The subsidy system often does not cover the actual costs, and parent fees to cover the gap are prohibitive for low-income families.

Quality

The OECD recommends policies to support quality through professional preparation, ongoing learning opportunities, and reasonable compensation for educators, and also through curriculum and pedagogical frameworks that are responsive to children's early learning and development.

Over the past decade, most provinces and territories have introduced curriculum frameworks (discussed in Chapter 2) and professional requirements for ECEs (discussed in Chapter 8). Compensation for ECEs remains low compared to other occupations with similar educational requirements (Akbari & McCuaig, 2014; Flanagan, Beach, & Varmuza, 2013). Outside of Quebec, for example, ECEs earn less than 50% of what teachers earn (Akbari & McCuaig, 2014).

Compensation in regulated child care programs is dependent on parent fees and levels of direct government funding. When the majority of the revenue comes from parent fees (including fee subsidies for low income families), it is difficult to offer adequate compensation because raising ECE compensation means raising fees. Compensation is related to quality. Staff with more educational qualifications seek out positions that offer better compensation.

Accountability

The monitoring processes in regulated child care programs set minimum standards and expectations but cannot ensure high-quality environments, as discussed in Chapter 3. The *Early childhood education report 2014* (Akbari & McCuaig, 2014) monitors how Canadian jurisdictions are progressing towards building provincial/territorial early childhood education systems.

EARLY CHILDHOOD EDUCATION OUTSIDE OF CANADA

Many nations outside of Canada have moved toward more comprehensive and integrated approaches to the funding and delivery of early childhood education and care programs. A more systematic approach is the norm with a focus on public funding to support universal access (OECD, 2006). Most European nations, the United Kingdom, Australia, and New Zealand have invested higher levels of public resources in the development, funding, and delivery of early childhood programs (UNICEF, 2008). In these countries, the majority of three- and four-year-olds have access to universal, publicly funded early childhood programs (Friendly, 2010).

| 1650 | 1700 | 1750 | 1800 |

Nine OECD countries now integrate entire early childhood systems for children from birth to age six under one government department. Early childhood programs are seen as an essential part of the preparation of children for public school. These programs are also understood to be an important component of the supports for families, in particular for those with employed parents; and they are a venue for identifying children and families who will need special services.

Internationally, the Nordic countries (Denmark, Finland, Norway, and Sweden) have the most ambitious and comprehensive approaches to the funding and delivery early childhood education and care (UNICEF, 2008; OECD, 2006). The public support available to families with young children begins with extended parental leave, with high levels of income replacement, which is followed by higher-than-average access to licensed child care for children zero to three years of age and significant public expenditures on preschool education for children four and five years of age. In the Nordic countries, the public funding and delivery of early childhood education and care represent sound economic and social expenditures of public resources. Specific attention is paid to the planning of services, the training of staff, and the design of curricula specifically intended to promote child development.

Other European jurisdictions also invest significant public resources in particular early childhood programs, with preschool education and care for children three, four, and five years of age a key area for public investment. The majority of European nations now guarantee four-year-olds some form of preschool program, although the number of hours of service varies considerably.

New Zealand families have access to free, part-time, early learning programs for three- to five-year-olds, with working families able to purchase additional services to provide full-day support. All early childhood education and care programs are part of the education department and have a common curriculum.

In the United States, families' access to early learning programs for four- and five-year-olds varies greatly from state to state (Barnett, 2010). Two states, Georgia and Oklahoma, provide kindergarten programs for all children four

2009
Across Canada, there are approximately 900 000 regulated child care spaces for children from zero to twelve years.

2008
Canada ranks last in its provision of early childhood programs compared to 25 other countries in UNICEF study.

The New Brunswick government announced the initiative Be Ready for Success: A 10-Year Strategy for New Brunswick.

2007
Early Years 2, authored by Dr. J. Fraser Mustard, Hon. Margaret Norrie McCain, and Dr. Stuart Shanker, is released.

In Ontario, the *Early Childhood Educators Act*, 2007, establishes the College of Early Childhood Educators, which regulates the profession of early childhood education.

| 1850 | 1900 | 1950 | 2000 |

and five years of age; and there is both federal and state interest in increasing access to preschool programs and services.

In the United Kingdom, all three- and four-year-old children are entitled to fifteen hours of early education for 38 weeks per year before entering compulsory full-day schooling at age five (OECD, 2006).

POLICY ISSUES

Early childhood education advocates are likely to come across a number of policy issues related to how early childhood education should be designed and implemented. Who should have access? Who should pay? Is it parents' responsibility to make their own arrangements, or does the government have a role in making early childhood education available? What level of government should be responsible—municipal, provincial/territorial, or federal?

Targeted versus Universal

An early intervention approach to funding is reinforced by population estimates of children's learning and development using the Early Development Instrument (Janus & Duku, 2007) and the National Longitudinal Survey of Children and Youth (Willms, 2002). The emphasis is on the numbers and percentages of children who are vulnerable (defined as having a low score in one of the five domains). Across Canada, about one in four children who are five years old is vulnerable. Children from the least affluent families are more likely to be vulnerable, but the total *numbers* of vulnerable children are greatest in moderate-income, two-parent families. Nevertheless, higher vulnerability associated with lower socio-economic status encourages policymakers and practitioners to shore up environments for less affluent children and those who are already experiencing difficulties. In that way, the majority of vulnerable children, who actually live in two-parent, middle-income families, are missed by most targeted early childhood programs (Hertzman & Bertrand, 2007).

The practice of targeting resources to vulnerable and at-risk children is reinforced by what is called the Matthew effect—a biblical reference that the rich get richer and the poor get poorer (Santos, 2009). The idea is that middle-class kids who already have more opportunities will benefit more from programming than their peers who have fewer developmental resources. *Sesame Street* research is often used to support the Matthew effect argument: *Sesame Street* was created in the late 1960s to boost the language, social, and pre-academic skills of disadvantaged preschool children. As it spread across the United States and then the world, researchers studied its impact and found that middle-class children seemed to benefit more than children living in less affluent homes.

Several reports on targeted early childhood programs suggest that these programs often segregate and stigmatize disadvantaged children and families, either discouraging participation or negating benefits (Doherty, 2007). Accurate targeting is difficult. American Head Start programs, North America's largest compensatory early childhood initiative, does not reach most disadvantaged children and serves many children who are not disadvantaged (Barnett, Brown, & Shore, 2004). Vulnerable children may be more prevalent among those living in disadvantaged families, but the majority of vulnerable children actually live in two-parent, middle-income families, and are missed by most targeted early childhood programs (Hertzman & Bertrand, 2007).

University of Toronto economist Dan Treflor (2009) has documented the lost economic opportunities of a targeted approach. Investing in everyone's early learning makes sense because exposing children to optimal learning and development will drive innovation and future prosperity. Moving children from good enough to excellent may not be as dramatic as moving from vulnerable to good enough, but it matters. Also, children who are marginalized and struggling seem to be better served when they take part in programs and experiences that involve everyone. Children identified as at risk, disadvantaged, or vulnerable know who they are from a young age. The stigma sticks. Of course, some kids will need extra efforts to fully participate, and that is where some skillful targeting of resources can be helpful.

Government policies at the federal and the provincial/territorial level often recognize the benefits of early childhood education for all children, but the costs seem prohibitive. When governments move to provide early childhood development opportunities only to the targeted groups of children and families likely to benefit the most, they miss the majority of at risk children using these targets.

Provincial/Territorial and Federal Government Jurisdictions

In Canada, education, social services, and health care are provincial/territorial responsibilities. The federal government transfers funds from tax revenues, and the provinces and territories make decisions about how to allocate their budgets. There are guiding national principles for health care spending, but, with the exception of on-reserve schools, public education is entirely a provincial/territorial responsibility.

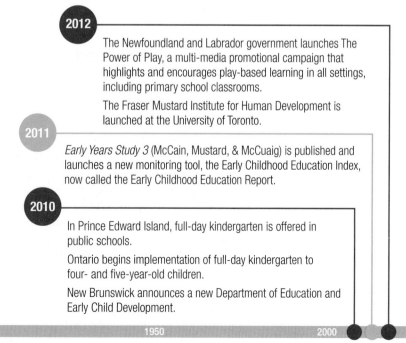

2012

The Newfoundland and Labrador government launches The Power of Play, a multi-media promotional campaign that highlights and encourages play-based learning in all settings, including primary school classrooms.

The Fraser Mustard Institute for Human Development is launched at the University of Toronto.

2011

Early Years Study 3 (McCain, Mustard, & McCuaig) is published and launches a new monitoring tool, the Early Childhood Education Index, now called the Early Childhood Education Report.

2010

In Prince Edward Island, full-day kindergarten is offered in public schools.

Ontario begins implementation of full-day kindergarten to four- and five-year-old children.

New Brunswick announces a new Department of Education and Early Child Development.

1850   1900   1950   2000

Many advocates and campaigns recommend that the federal government should be more involved and establish a national child care plan with principles and criteria that underlie transfer of federal funding (for example, Friendly, 2014). As early childhood education policies are becoming more aligned with provincial and territorial education departments, questions are raised about how the federal government can be involved and transfer funding.

Funding Parents versus Funding Programs

Program funding. Funding for programs may be targeted to specific operating costs, such as salaries or in-service training. Direct grants can also be used for the overall operating costs, reducing, or even eliminating, fees for parents.

Child care tax deductions/benefits. Income tax deductions and benefits channel public funds directly to parents who are paying fees for early childhood education and care programs. The Child Care Tax Deduction now in effect allows parents to deduct up to $7000 for their child care fees for children under seven years. The deduction must be claimed by the parent with the lower income, and a receipt from a family child care provider or an early childhood education and care program must be provided. The resulting reduction in income tax is greater for higher-income earners. An income tax benefit could be targeted to lower-income families.

Public Good versus Private Responsibility

In spite of the available research, Canada continues to be ambivalent about whether early childhood education and care is a public or private responsibility. Ambivalence about women's equality, preferred family structures, and the rights and obligations of parents all come into play. Canadians wonder, Are early childhood education programs a public right for Canada's youngest citizens, or is it the responsibility of their parents to care for and educate children until they reach school age?

Public Education and Early Childhood Education

Across Canada, public education is reaching into the early years. As noted earlier in this chapter, eight jurisdictions have moved or are moving regulated child care and related early childhood education and family programs into education departments or ministries. Kindergarten programs offered as part of the school system are now full-day programs for the majority of five-year-olds. In Ontario, full-day kindergarten is offered to all four-year-olds; and in the Northwest Territories, the implementation of kindergarten for four-year-olds began in fall 2014. Quebec, Manitoba, and Nova Scotia offer programs for four-year-olds in some communities. Saskatchewan has pre-kindergarten programs for three- and four-year-olds in many communities. British Columbia has introduced a province-wide family drop-in program, StrongStart, which offers early childhood education to younger children. See Chapter 1 for more information.

As governments move in this direction, they open up the potential to bring together various early childhood education and care services, such as kindergarten programs in schools, which are part of education ministries; early intervention programs, which are operated by health ministries; and regulated child care services in a common platform linked to schools. Many out-of-school programs, child care centres, nursery schools, and family resource programs are located in school buildings already. Early childhood educators often share information, resources, and expertise with educators in the school system and may receive low-cost or rent-free space.

MAKING IT HAPPEN

Unions Advocate for Child Care

The trade union movement in Canada has a 30-year history of supporting public policies that help ensure the provision of high-quality early childhood programs. Unions have always linked high-quality child care to improved wages, benefits, and working conditions for child care staff. Many unions (both those that represent child care staff and those that do not) have policies stating that child care should be publicly funded, universally accessible, of high quality, and regulated. They are involved in child care advocacy activities and organizations, locally, regionally, and nationally. Often unions who represent early childhood educators in child care centres have child care committees that move issues forward internally and externally. In other cases, unions work on the issue through their equality or women's committees.

A few collective agreements in Canada contain provisions for child care facilities or family support, and those with provisions are concentrated in the public sector, universities, and the automotive industry. The Canadian Auto Workers and the Canadian Union of Postal Workers are examples of unions that have bargained with employers for improved early child development programs.

The Canadian Auto Workers

In 1987, the Canadian Auto Workers (CAW) negotiated a child care fund from the Big Three auto makers—Ford of Canada, DaimlerChrysler Canada, and General Motors of Canada. Extended bargaining won capital funds that helped support child care centres in Windsor, Oshawa, and Port Elgin, Ontario. In order to meet the needs of other members, the Big Three contract negotiated in 1999 included a child care subsidy of $10 per day per child to a maximum of $2000 per year, paid directly to a licensed non-profit child care provider. The contract also included $450 000 to assist existing child care centres to better serve the needs of employees covered under the agreements, including expanding operating hours for shift-working parents. Child care workers at CAW-sponsored centres receive above-average industry wages and benefits. The CAW joined forces with CEOs of General Motors of Canada and DaimlerChrysler to jointly urge the federal government, working with the provinces, to provide a national child care program. The CAW's child care provisions dovetail with the union's social agenda for a national child care program. In 2000, the CAW joined with the City of Toronto and Atkinson Charitable Foundation to support Toronto First Duty, a demonstration project to study the integration of early childhood programs into a new delivery model. The results of this initiative are summarized in Chapter 1.

The Canadian Union of Postal Workers

In 1981, the Canadian Union of Postal Workers (CUPW) bargained for paid maternity leave for its members. After going on strike over the issue, they won a top-up to federal maternity benefits of 93 percent of wages for 17 weeks. Following on the CUPW precedent, many other unions followed suit. CUPW put child care on the bargaining table with Canada Post in the 1980s.

CUPW was successful in achieving a child care fund to help postal worker parents balance work and family. The fund helped members who had the most trouble finding or affording high-quality child care. The fund was used for projects to provide child care and related services to CUPW families, to provide child care information programs, and to undertake needs assessments and child care research. CUPW believes that quality child care should be a right of all children. As part of the union's overall commitment to universal social programs, the union is working along-side advocacy groups to press for a government-funded, universally accessible, high-quality child care system.

The Canadian Union of Public Employees

The Canadian Union of Public Employees (CUPE), Canada's largest union, advocates for universal, high-quality early learning and child care programs, and against for-profit care. In 2009, CUPE included child care as part of its national anti-privatization campaign. CUPE continues to advocator for an early childhood education and care system that is both publicly funded and publicly delivered. It is proposing a system administered and managed by the provinces and territories as part of an overarching pan-Canadian early childhood education and care program supported by federal dollars with a national policy. CUPE has sponsored forums across Canada as part of the campaign.

Rethink Child Care

A group of Canadian unions have joined child care advocates to build a strong campaign to revisit how child care is funded and delivered in Canada. The unions' goal is to mobilize their members to demand better child care policies and programs from all levels of government. The Rethink Child Care campaign, launched in 2013, is on line at www.rethinkchildcare.ca.

Sources: Beach, Bertrand, Forer, Michal, & Tougas, 2004; Cleveland, Corter, Pelletier, Colley, Bertrand, & Jamieson, 2006; Friendly 2010; www.rethinkchildcare.ca.

MAKING IT HAPPEN

Public Policy for an Early Childhood Education System in Quebec

Quebec's child care system is unique in Canada. In 1997, the province revised its family policy away from sizeable payments to parents on the birth of children to a multi-pronged approach: maternity/parental leave for employed and self-employed parents covering up to 75 percent of salary, a progressive child allowance, and low-cost child care.

Maternity and Parental Leave

The changes to maternity and parental benefits are significant, including a change to the eligibility criteria so benefits are more accessible to working parents in non-standard forms of employment (e.g., part-time, self-employment) and an enhanced amount of payable benefits.

Under this legislation, parents who qualify would be eligible for

- up to a maximum of 18 weeks of maternity benefits;
- up to a maximum of 5 weeks of paternity benefits;
- up to a maximum of 32 weeks of parental benefits; or
- up to a maximum of 37 weeks of adoption benefits.

Network of Child Care Programs

Funding for its network of over 900 child care programs is also exclusive to Quebec. Programs receive 87 percent of their funding from government; parents pay a flat fee of $7 per day (originally $5). Children of parents on social assistance are entitled to free enrolment for 22.5 hours a week. The objectives of the policy are to facilitate work–family balance, encourage the labour force participation of parents on social assistance, and provide children, regardless of the financial status of their parents, with high-quality early childhood education and care that fosters their social, emotional, and cognitive development as well as readiness for school.

The system, fuelled by high demand, has gone through a rapid expansion, and now offers over 250 000 regulated child care spaces for children from 0 to age 5 years and another 207 000 for school age children (Akbari & McCuaig, 2014). Ministry jurisdiction is divided by age group. Children aged zero to four are the responsibility of the Ministry of the Family and are served by *centres de la petite enfance*, or CPEs. Each CPE provides both group and family child care for a geographic area in which 300 families reside. The majority of programs (80 percent) are operated by parent boards (at least two-thirds must be parent users). A new government elected in 2003 included for-profit operators in its expansion plans.

At age five, children begin school full time. When twelve or more parents request child care, the education ministry requires school boards to establish before and after programs. The main focus for school age children is to provide recreation and assistance with school assignments.

Staff/child ratios are higher in Quebec than in most other Canadian jurisdictions. For example, infant ratios (0–18 months) are 1:5; preschool 1:8; and school age 1:20.

Quebec has taken steps to improve quality by establishing curriculum expectations and by raising staff qualifications. Previously only one in three staff required a diploma; now two-thirds of staff in non-profit programs have to have a college or university ECE degree. For-profit programs operate under the old guidelines.

A series of labour actions in 2000 led to the establishment of a province-wide wage scale negotiated between the government and the CPE association. The annual salary for an ECE at the top of the provincial wage grid is $48 000, which is 65% of teacher's salary in Quebec (Akbari & McCuaig, 2014). A pension plan has been established.

Challenges to Early Childhood Education System Building

- The original vision for CPEs included plans to forge links with community health and social service centres (CLSCs) in local neighbourhoods. CLSCs provide direct health care, pre- and postnatal supports, family supports, and early identification and intervention programs. However, their funding is now being curtailed, and except for a few isolated situations these links are not happening.
- Programs are refusing children with special needs because funding does not cover costs.
- Quality has been problematic. A study (Japel & Tremblay, 2005) shows only a quarter of programs are meeting objectives. Quality is most problematic in for-profit centres, 27 percent of which were graded inadequate as opposed to 7 percent of non-profit centres.
- Demand has exceeded supply. Children from low-income families are less likely to attend any kind of child care. There is also a significant quality gap: children from poorer families are more likely to be in for-profit child care settings, which are of inferior quality (20 percent versus 9 percent of children from well-off families).

► Work-related child care centres can meet the needs of young children and their families.

mikanaka/iStock/Thinkstock

TAKING ACTION

Advocacy for early childhood education and the early childhood workforce is based on the view that children and families should have access to quality services and that ECEs should be recognized as a critical component of these services. Early childhood educators are powerful advocates who can take action. The first step in being an advocate is to be the best possible early childhood educator you can be. You are just beginning the journey.

There is no simple solution or quick fix for early childhood education and the early childhood workforce. Despite the obstacles, however, the prospects of making the early childhood workforce a well-recognized and well-rewarded profession are promising. The ECE Report 2014 tells us that an increasing number of provinces and territories are requiring professional recognition and on-going professional learning.

Speak up.   Every early childhood educator can be an advocate for herself and for the children and families with whom she works, as well as for other early childhood educators, children, and families. Personal advocacy is based on how you carry out your daily practice and communication with others. It may be as simple as gently correcting a friend or neighbour who suggests that what you do is "just babysitting—something anyone could do."

As we discussed in the previous chapter, ECEs have a specialized knowledge base. You have an understanding of children's early growth and development, and the skills to connect, engage, and interact with young children. ECEs can be powerful communicators about young children, families, and early child development programs. But sometimes we use too much jargon and we are not very effective. Or we use sayings like "Children learn through play" or "Our children are the future" without explaining what they mean.

| 1650 | 1700 | 1750 | 1800 |

To be effective in talking about early child development, follow these guidelines:

- Use everyday language as much as possible, and explain what you mean by terms like "cognitive development" or "gross motor skills." Better yet, try to talk about children learning to think, and use symbols such as pictures or words to represent ideas and objects rather than referring to cognitive development in the abstract.
- Always remember that parents are the experts about their own child. You have much to learn from them. Early childhood educators can contribute their knowledge and expertise about young children in general; parents and other primary caregivers are the experts in how your general knowledge will benefit their specific child.
- Avoid scare tactics, such as using arguments like "Invest in early child development or children will be delayed." Early child development is a foundation of later development, but it does *not* determine later actions.
- Practise speaking and writing about early child development. It will force you to be precise and clarify concepts that are fuzzy. Your communications with parents and other professionals will be informed, and your input will be valued.

▲ New skills, new insights, new growth—the daily life of an ECE!

"Walk the talk." The first step in being an advocate is to be the best possible early childhood educator you can be. This means taking an interest in each child's development and learning, including taking the initiative to ensure a child you are working with has access to needed specialized services. It may mean going out into your community to find out what types of early child development programs are really needed and wanted by families and then trying to match them with local resources.

Be vigilant. Personal advocacy includes being a watchdog and a whistleblower. As you learn about child development and appropriate practices, you are more likely to resist pressure to accept less-than-optimal conditions in early childhood settings. You will advocate for conditions that support the delivery of high-quality care and education. This means being aware of situations in your local communities that may have an adverse effect on children's health, safety, or well-being. For instance, there may be physical dangers in

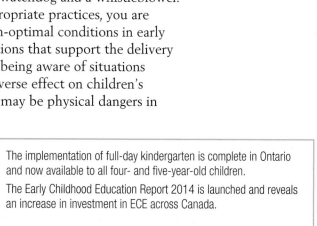

2014

The implementation of full-day kindergarten is complete in Ontario and now available to all four- and five-year-old children.

The Early Childhood Education Report 2014 is launched and reveals an increase in investment in ECE across Canada.

2013

The government of Nova Scotia announces a new Department of Education and Early Child Development.

| 1850 | 1900 | 1950 | 2000 |

playgrounds or schoolyards or a need for safer crossing points on busy streets. Personal advocacy includes keeping yourself informed and being involved in making changes to improve children's environments.

Vote. Children cannot vote on issues that affect them, but you can. You should be registered to vote where you live, and you should exercise your right to vote during elections. You ought to know which politicians represent you and keep an eye on how they vote on issues that affect children and early childhood education and care programs.

Prepare position papers and presentations. Local, provincial/territorial, and federal governments need to hear from early childhood educators. Task force committees, commissions, and public hearings present opportunities to communicate your policy recommendations and to respond to government policy initiatives and budget announcements. This is one way to influence government policy and to draw attention to the challenges facing early childhood education and care programs.

Build coalitions. Coalitions build the base of support for public policy changes at the local, the provincial/territorial, and the national level. They often include child care programs, parents, early childhood educators, community associations, child welfare organizations, trade unions, teachers' federations, child care resource groups, human service agencies, women's groups, and early childhood education students.

Use the media. Television, radio, newspapers, and the Internet are the most effective, powerful tools for maintaining a sustained advocacy campaign. Available daily to a broad cross-section of the population, the media, including social media, provide an opportunity to reach many people outside committed supporters and confirmed opponents. The media must be an important part of any strategy to bring about significant change.

Contact members of the media in person, on the telephone, or through press releases. It is helpful to cultivate contacts with particular media people who seem to have an interest in the issue and will put forward a fair position.

For a major issue or event, a press conference can be assembled. You might organize a press conference when you want to respond to a particularly critical situation or when you are initiating a major campaign.

Tatyana Vyc/Shutterstock

▲ Young children rely on early childhood educators to advocate for their best interests.

<table>
<tr><td>

MAKING IT HAPPEN

</td><td>

Ontario Coalition for Better Child Care

In 1981, the Ontario Coalition for Better Child Care (OCBCC) brought together child care activists, early childhood educators, trade unions, teachers' federations, women's groups, social policy organizations, First Nations, francophones, anti-poverty groups, and parents to form a coalition of interests and organizations at the provincial level.

Since its beginning, the OCBCC has been a powerful force in the campaign for more affordable, accessible, high-quality child care in Ontario. It has also spearheaded a number of

</td></tr>
</table>

initiatives to improve the compensation of early childhood educators, including provincial wage grants and pay equity legislation and grants. The OCBCC continues to play an important role in Ontario's and Canada's struggle for a system of early learning and child care.

The OCBCC advocates for better wages and working conditions for ECEs and for a coherent national and provincial child care system that is funded by the government. It is monitoring changes in Ontario as child care and family resource programs are integrated into the Early Years Division of the Ministry of Education.

Sources: Beach, Bertrand, Forer, Michal, & Tougas, 2004; Friendly & Beach, 2005.

Participate in informational advocacy. Because of their education and experience, early childhood educators can lead the way in advocating for children and families. Those who have knowledge of child development have an obligation to share their expertise with others to help them make informed decisions.

Policies are made that can be harmful to children's development, often in the name of accountability, fiscal economy, and efficiency. Informational advocacy, most often in the form of public education, is a powerful force that early childhood educators can use to counter these policy directions. Early childhood educators can build awareness about what ECEC is and why it is important to young children by

- taking part in information sessions at conventions, shopping malls, or entertainment events;
- building early childhood environments using photographs, videos, multimedia presentations, three-dimensional models, and children's own artwork; and
- seeking out and recognizing individual early childhood educators whose work with young children is an inspiration to others.

Summary

- Investing in early childhood education programs benefits children, families, communities, and societies.
- Early childhood education in Canada varies from province to province to territory in terms of governance, funding, access, quality, and monitoring benchmarks based on the recommendations of the Organization for Economic and Co-operative Development.
- ECEs can be advocates for early childhood education by identifying policy options to meet

the objectives of quality, compensation, and accessibility, then take action and advocate for changes. They can also make advocating for early childhood education as part of their daily communications with colleagues, family, and friends.

- Advocacy organizations, business and labour groups, coalitions for children, and families and other groups can work together to influence policymakers and gain support for specific policy options.

REVIEW QUESTIONS

1. How does your jurisdiction measure up to the suggested benchmarks for governance, funding, access, quality, and monitoring?

2. Identify and discuss individual and group approaches to advocacy in early child development.

STUDY ACTIVITIES

1. Do some informal research on the benchmarks associated with a coherent early childhood system in your community. How are ECE programs governed, or how are decisions made? What are the funding sources? What children are attending? How many qualified ECEs are part of the staff teams? Is there an intentional curriculum? What are the ECE salaries compared to teachers? How are ECE programs monitored?

2. Review the findings of the ECE Report 2014 [http://www.oise.utoronto.ca/atkinson/Main/ index.html]. Consider the changes from 2011 to 2014. Did your province or territory improve? Identify the benchmarks you would like to see improve for the next ECE Report in 2017.

3. Prepare a short presentation about a child development issue that you think would interest and inform parents. Try it out with parents in your next field placement.

4. Find out what kinds of ECE advocacy activities take place in your local community.

KEY TERMS

advocacy: Defending or stating a cause. In early education, supporting the ideas and issues of the profession.

networking: Making connections with others in the profession for mutual support and information, and for professional development and advancement.

Suggested Readings

Akbari, E. & McCuaig, K. (2014) Early childhood education report 2014. Toronto, ON: Atkinson Centre for Society and Child Development, OISE/ University of Toronto.

Jimmy Pratt Foundation. (2013). The early years last a lifetime. St. John's, NL: author. http://jimmyprattfoundation.org/wp-content/uploads/2013/09/ The-Early-Years-Last-a-Lifetime-full-web.pdf

Margaret and Wallace McCain Family Foundation. (2010). *Building for the future.* Toronto: MWMFF.

McCuaig, K., Bertrand, J., & Shanker, S. (2012). Trends in early education and child care. Toronto, ON: Atkinson Centre for Society and Child Development, OISE/University of Toronto.

The Muttart Foundation. (2014). Children and families in the new Saskatchewan: A discussion of early learning and child care. *A Record of Early Childhood Education and Care Stakeholder Discussions–Saskatoon Forum*. Edmonton, AB: author.

The Muttart Foundation. (2013). Toward a provincial framework for early learning and care in Alberta–A draft framework design for discussion. Edmonton, AB: author.

References

Ackerman, D., & Barnett, S. (2006, July). Increasing effectiveness of preschool programs. Preschool Policy Brief, 11. New Brunswick, NJ: NIEER.

Ackerman, D., Barnett, S., & Robin, K. (2005). *Making the most of kindergarten: Present trends and future issues in the provision of full-day programs*. New Brunswick, NJ: National Institute for Early Education Research, Rutgers University, 2005.

Active Healthy Kids Canada (2014). Is Canada in the running? The 2014 Active Healthy Kids Canada Report Card on Physical Activity for Children and Youth. Toronto, ON: Active Healthy Kids Canada.

Ade, W. (1982, March). Professionalization and its implications for the field of early childhood education. *Young Children*, 37(3), 25–32. Copyright © 1982 NAEYC®. Reprinted with permission.

AECEO (The Association of Early Childhood Educators, Ontario). (1997, Spring). Meet the affiliates. *Interaction*, 3.

AECEO. (2005). *Common table for childhood development and care in Canada*. Toronto, ON: AECEO.

Akbari, E., & McCuaig, K. (2014). *Early childhood education report, 2014*. Toronto, ON: Atkinson Centre, University of Toronto.

Alberta Child Care Accreditation. (2004). *Child care accreditation*. Retrieved at http://www.child.gov.ab.ca/whatwedo/childcareaccreditation/page.cfm?pg=index.

Alberta Children and Youth Services. (2009). *2008–2009 annual report*. Edmonton, AB: Alberta CYS.

Ali, M. (2005). Effects of migration on parenting capacity of newcomer parents of young children. *Research Connections Canada: Supporting Children and Families*, 13. Ottawa: Canadian Child Care Federation.

Allen, J. (1991). Caregiver's corner: What is quality child care all about? *Young Children*, 46(6), 18.

Almy, M. (1975). *The early childhood educator at work*. New York: McGraw-Hill.

Almy, M. (1988). The early childhood educator revisited. In B. Spodek, O. Saracho, & D. Peters (Eds.), *Professionalism and the early childhood practitioner* (p. 57). New York, NY: Teachers College Press.

Anderson, C., & Bushman, B. (2001). Effects of violent video games on aggressive behavior, aggressive cognition, aggressive affect, physiological arousal and prosocial behaviour: A meta-analytic review of the scientific literature. *Psychological Science*, 12, 353–359.

Anderson, R. (2005). Do our current practices cater for all children? Discourses and discursive practices that constrain or empower in the early years of schooling. In A. Pandian, M. K. Kabilan, & S. Kaur (Eds.), *Teachers, practices and supportive cultures*. Serdang, Malaysia: Universiti Putra Malaysia Press.

Arnup, K. (1994). *Education for motherhood: Advice for mothers in twentieth-century Canada*. Toronto, ON: University of Toronto Press.

Astington, J. W. (1998). *The child's discovery of the mind*. Cambridge, MA: Harvard University Press.

Ayers, W. (1989). *The good preschool teacher*. New York: Teachers College Press.

Ayers, W. (1993). *To teach: The journey of a teacher*. New York: Teachers College Press.

Baker, Amy C. (1992, July). A puzzle, a picnic, and a vision: Family day care at its best. *Young Children*, 47(5), 36–38.

Baker, M., Gruber, J., & Milligan, K. (2006). *What can we learn from Quebec's universal child care program?* Vancouver: C. D. Howe Institute. Retrieved June 16, 2006, at http://www.cdhowe.org/pdf/ebrief_25_english.pdf.

Balaban, N. (1992, July). The role of the child care professional in caring for infants, toddlers, and their families. *Young Children*, 47(5), 66–71.

Ball, J. (2005). Early childhood care and development programs as hook and hub for inter-sectoral service delivery in First Nations communities. *Journal of Aboriginal Health*, 1(2), 36–50.

Ball, J. (2008, June). Promoting equity and dignity for Aboriginal children in Canada. *IRPP Choices*, 14(7).

Ball, J. (2010). Enhancing learning of children from diverse language backgrounds: Mother tongue-based bilingual or multilingual education in the early years. Paris: UNESCO.

Barnett, S. (2008). *Preschool education and its lasting effects: Research and policy implications*. Boulder and Tempe: Education and the Public Interest Center & Education Policy Research Unit. Available at http://epicpolicy.org/publication/preschool-education.

Barnett, S. (2010). *The state of preschool 2008*. New Brunswick, NJ: NIEER, Rutgers University.

Barnett, S., & Masse, M. (2007). Comparative benefit–cost analysis of the Abecedarian program and its policy implications. *Economics of Education Review*, 26(1), 113–125.

Barnett, S., Brown, K., & Shore, R. (2004). The universal vs. targeted debate: Should the United States have preschool for all? *Preschool Policy Matters*, 6. New Brunswick, NJ: NIEER.

Barnett, S., Yarosz, D., Thomas, J., & Hornbeck, A. (2006). *Educational effectiveness of a Vygotskian approach to preschool education: A randomized trial*. New Brunswick, NJ: National Institute for Early Education Research.

Barnett, W., Epstein, D., Friedman, A., Sansanelli, A., & Hustedt, J. (2010). *The state of preschool 2009*. New Brunswick, NJ: National Institute for Early Education Research.

Baskett, R., Bryant, K., White, W., & Rhoads, K. (2005). Half-day to full-day kindergarten: An analysis of educational change scores and demonstration of an educational research collaboration. *Early Child Development and Care*, 175(5), 419–430.

Beach, J. (1999). Community colleges and the delivery of professional development to the early childhood care and education sector. *Research Connections Canada*, 2, 101–140.

Beach, J. (2010) Environmental scan of ministries of education involvement in early care and learning. Vancouver, BC: ECEBC and Coalition of Child Care Advocates of BC.

Beach, J., & Bertrand, J. (2000). *More than the sum of the parts: An early child development system for Canada.* Occasional Paper No. 12. Toronto, ON: Childcare Resource and Research Unit, University of Toronto.

Beach, J., & Flanagan, K. (2007). *People, programs and practices: A training strategy for the early childhood education and care sector in Canada.* Ottawa: Child Care Human Resources Sector Council.

Beach, J., & Flanagan, K. (2010b). *Pathways to credentialing of Canada's ECEC workforce.* Ottawa: Child Care Human Resource Sector Council.

Beach, J., Bertrand, J., & Cleveland, G. (1998). *Our child care workforce: From recognition to remuneration.* Ottawa: Child Care Human Resources Steering Committee.

Beach, J., Bertrand, J., Forer, B., Michal, D., & Tougas, J. (2004). *Working for change: Canada's child care workforce.* Prepared for the Child Care Human Resources Sector Council. Ottawa: Child Care Human Resources Sector Council.

Beach, J., Flanagan, K., & Varmuza, P. (2013). *You bet we still care!* Ottawa, ON: Child Care Human Resources Sector Council.

Beach, J., Flanagan, K., & Varmuza, P. (2014). *Unionization and human resources in child care: What did we learn from the "You bet we still care" survey?* CUPE & BCGEU.

Beach J., Friendly, M., & Schmidt, L. (1993). *Work-related child care in context: A study of work-related child care in Canada.* Occasional Paper No. 3. Toronto, ON: Childcare Research & Resource Unit, University of Toronto.

Beach, J., Friendly, M., Ferns, C., Prabhu, N., & Forer, B. (2009). *Early childhood education and care in Canada, 2008* (8th ed.). Toronto, ON: Childcare Resource & Research Unit.

Behrmann, M. M., & Lahm, E. A. (1994). Computer applications in early childhood special education. In J. Wright & D. Shade (Eds.), *Young children: Active learners in a technological age.* Washington, DC: NAEYC.

Bellm, D., Gnezda, T., Whitebook, M., & Breunig, G. S. (1994). Policy initiatives to enhance child care staff compensation. In J. Johnson & J. B. McCracken (Eds.), *The early childhood career lattice: Perspectives on professional development.* Washington, DC: NAEYC.

Benner, A. (1999). *Quality child care and community development: What is the connection?* Ottawa: Canadian Child Care Federation.

Bennett, J. (2004). *Starting strong: Curricula and pedagogies in early childhood education and care.* Paris: Directorate for Education, OECD.

Bennett, J. (2005). Curriculum issues in national policy-making. *European Early Childhood Education Research Journal*, 13(2), 5–24.

Bennett, J. (2008). Early childhood education and care systems in the OECD countries: The issue of tradition and governance. In R. E. Tremblay, R. G. Barr, R. DeV. Peters, & M. Boivin (Eds.), *Encyclopedia on Early Childhood Development* (1–5). Montreal: Centre of Excellence for Early Childhood Development. Available at http://www.child-encyclopedia.com/documents/BennettANGxp.pdf

Beretier, C. (1972). An academic preschool for disadvantaged children. In J. S. Stanley (Ed.), *Preschool programs for the disadvantaged: Five experimental approaches to early childhood education.* Baltimore: Johns Hopkins University Press, 1–21.

Bergen, D. (2002, Spring). The role of pretend play in children's cognitive development. *Early Childhood Research and Practice*, 4(1).

Bergmann, B. (1996). *Saving our children from poverty: What the United States can learn from France.* New York: Russell Sage Foundation.

Berk, L., & Winsler, A. (1995). *Scaffolding children's learning: Vygotsky and early childhood education.* Washington, DC: National Association for the Education of Young Children.

Bernhard, J., Freire, M., & Mulligan, V. (2004). *Canadian parenting workshops.* Toronto, ON: Chestnut.

Bernhard, J., Lefebvre, M. L. Kilbride, D., Chud, G., & Lange, R. (1998). Troubled relationships in early childhood education: Parent–teacher Interactions in ethnoculturally diverse child care settings. *Early Education and Development*, 9, 1.

Bernhard, J., Lero, D., & Greenberg, J. (2006). *Diversity, equity, inclusion considerations presented to Best Start Vision and Implementation Joint Work Group.* Toronto, ON: Ministry of Children and Youth Services.

Bernhard, J., Pollard, J., Eggers-Pierola, C., & Morin, A. (2000). Infants and toddlers in Canadian multi-age child care settings: Age, ability and linguistic inclusion. *Research Connections Canada*, 4, 79–154. Ottawa: Canadian Child Care Federation.

Bernhard, J. K. (2003). Toward a 21st century developmental theory: Principles to account for diversity in children's lives. *Race, Gender, and Class*, 9(4), 45–60.

Bernhard, J. K., Cummins, J., Campoy, I., Ada, A., Winsler, A., & Bleiker, C. (2006). Identity texts and literacy development among preschool English language learners: Enhancing learning opportunities for children at risk of learning disabilities. *Teachers College Record*, 108(11), 2006, 2380–2405. Available at http://www.tcrecord.org. Accessed May 15, 2010.

Berton, P. (1991). *The Dionne years.* Toronto, ON: McClelland and Stewart.

Bertrand, J. (2005) *Aboriginal early child development in Canada.* Toronto, ON: George Brown College.

Bertrand, J. (2008). *Understanding, managing and leading early child development programs.* Toronto, ON: ITP Nelson.

Bertrand, J., & Michals, D. (2007). *Literature review and environmental scan.* Prepared for the Training Strategy Project. Ottawa: Child Care Human Resources Sector Council.

Bertrand, J., & Riehl, D. (2009). *Every child, every opportunity.* Compendium report to *With Our Best Future in Mind*. Toronto, ON: Government of Ontario.

Bertrand, J., Beach, J., Michal, D., & Tougas, J. (2004). *Working for a change: Canada's child care workforce. Literature review.* Labour Market Study. Ottawa: Child Care Human Resource Council.

Best Start Early Learning Expert Panel. (2007). *Early learning for every child today.* Toronto, ON: Ministry of Children and Youth Services.

Best Start Quality & Human Resources Expert Panel. (2007). *Investing in quality: Policies, practitioners, programs and parents.* Toronto, ON: Ministry of Children and Youth Services.

Blackstock, C., Bruyere, D., and Moreau, E. (2006). *Many hands, one dream: Principles for a new perspective on the health of First Nations, Inuit and Métis children and youth.* Ottawa: Canadian Paediatric Society.

Blades, C. M. (2002). Full-day kindergarten: "A blessing or a bane for young children?" In *CBE mild and moderate full-day kindergarten project (2001–2002)*. Calgary: Calgary Board of Education.

Blair, C. (2002, February). School readiness: Integrating cognition and emotion in a neurobiological conceptualization of children's functioning at school entry. *American Psychologist, 57*(2), 111–127.

Blair, C., & Diamond, A. (2008). Biological processes in prevention and intervention: The promotion of self-regulation as a means of preventing school failure. *Development and Psychopathology, 20*, 899–911.

Bloom, B. (1964). *Stability and change in human behaviour.* New York: Wiley.

Bornstein, M. (2002) Parenting infants. In M.H. Bornstein (Ed.), *Handbook of parenting* (2nd ed.). Vol. 1. 3–43. Mahwah, NJ: Erlbaum.

Bowman, B., & Beyer, E. (1994). Thoughts on technology and early childhood education. In J. Wright & D. Shade (Eds.), *Young children: Active learners in a technological age.* Washington, DC: NAEYC.

Bradshaw, D. (1997, December). Front line profile, *Ideas, 4*(2), 19.

Bredekamp, S. (Ed.). (1987). *Developmentally appropriate practice in early childhood programs serving children from birth through age 8.* Exp. ed. Washington, DC: NAEYC.

Bredekamp, S. (Ed.). (1990). *Developmentally appropriate practice in early childhood programs serving children from birth through age 8.* Washington, DC: National association for the Education of Young Children.

Bredekamp, S. (1992, January). Composing a profession. *Young Children, 47* (2), 52–54.

Bredekamp, S. (1995, January). What do early childhood professionals need to know and be able to do? *Young Children, 50*(2), 67–69.

Brennerman, K., Stevenson-Boyd, J., & Frede, E. (2009, March). Math and science in preschool: Policies and practice. In E. Frede & S. Barnett (Eds.), *Preschool Policy Brief*, 19.

Broere, A. (1995, December). *Ideas: The Journal of Emotional Well-Being in Child Care, 1*(3), 15–16.

Bronfenbrenner, U. (1979). *The ecology of human development.* Cambridge, MA: Harvard University Press.

Bronson, M. (2000). *Self-regulation in early childhood.* New York: Guilford Press.

Brooks-Gunn, J. (2003). Do you believe in magic: What we can expect from early childhood intervention programs. *Social Policy Report, XVII*(1): 3–7.

Brooks-Gunn, J., & Donahue, E. (2008, Spring). Introducing the issue: Children and electronic media. *Future of Children, 18*(1).

Burts, D. C., Charlesworth, R., & Fleege, P. O. (1992). Observed activities and stress behaviors in developmentally appropriate and inappropriate kindergarten classrooms. *Early Childhood Research Quarterly, 7*, 297–318.

Buysee, V., Wesley, P. W., Bryant, D., & Gardner, D., (1999). Quality of early childhood programs in inclusive and non-inclusive settings. *Exceptional Children, 65*(3), 301–314.

Cameron, C., Moss, P., & Owen, C. (1999). *Men in the nursery: Gender and caring.* London: Paul Chapman Publishing.

Campbell, F. A., Wasik, B. H., Pungello, E., Burchinal, M., Barbarin, O., Kainz, K., Sparling, J. J., & Ramey, C. T. (2008). Young adult outcomes from the Abecedarian and CARE early childhood educational interventions. *Early Childhood Research Quarterly, 23*, 452–466.

Canadian Child Care Federation. (1991). *National statement on quality child care.* Ottawa.

Canadian Child Care Federation. (2000). *Tools for practitioners in child care settings.* Ottawa: CCCF.

Canadian Council on Learning. (2007) *Redefining how success is measured in First Nations, Inuit and Métis learning.* Ottawa, ON: Canadian Council on Learning.

Canadian Council on Social Development. (2006). *Growing up in North America.* Ottawa: CCSD.

Canadian Day Care Advocacy Association & Canadian Child Day Care Federation. (1992). *Caring for a living: Final report: A study on wages and working conditions in Canadian child care.* Ottawa: Author.

Canadian Education Association. (1993). *Admission to faculties of education in Canada: What you need to know. A report from the Canadian Education Association.* Toronto, ON: Author.

Canadian Education Association. (1999). *Education in Canada.* Toronto, ON: CEA.

Canadian Institute for Health Information (CIHI) and Canadian Population Health Initiative. (2004). Aboriginal Peoples' health. In *Improving the Health of Canadians*. Ottawa, ON: CIHI. Available at https://secure.cihi.ca/estore/product-Series.htm?locale=en&pc=PCC180

Canadian Paediatric Society. (2012). *A guide for physicians: Physical activity and sedentary behaviour in children and youth.* Ottawa, ON: author.

Carew, D. (1980). Observation study of caregiver and children in day care homes. Paper presented at the Society for Research in Child Development meeting. San Francisco.

Carnegie Commission on Educational Television. (1967). *Public television: A program for action.* New York: Carnegie Corporation.

Carson, L. (1978). Notes from a municipal day care worker. In K. G. Ross (Ed.), *Good day care: Fighting for it, getting it, keeping it.* Toronto, ON: The Women's Press.

Carter, M., & Curtis, D. (1994). *Training teachers: A harvest of theory and practice.* St. Paul, MN: Redleaf Press.

Caruso, J. (1977, November). Phases in student teaching. *Young Children, 32*(1), 57–63.

Center for the Study of Child Care Employment. (2008). *Early childhood educator competencies: A literature review of current best practices, and a public input process on next steps for California.* Berkeley, CA: Centre for the Study of Child Care Employment, Institute for Research on Labor and Employment, University of California at Berkeley.

Centre for Community Child Health. (2007). *Parenting young children.* Melbourne, VIC: Centre for Community Child Health. Available at http://www.rch.org.au.cch/policy-briefs.cfm.

Centre for Community Child Health. (2008). *Policy Brief No. 12: Towards an early years learning framework.* Melbourne, VIC: Centre for Community Child Health. Available at http://www.rch.org.au.cch/policybriefs.cfm.

Centre for Community Child Health. (2009). *Policy Brief No 14: The impact of poverty on early childhood development.* Melbourne, VIC: Centre for Community Child Health. Available at www.rch.org.au.cch/policybriefs.cfm.

Chandler, P. A. (1994). *A place for me: Including children with special needs in early care and education settings.* Washington, DC: NAEYC.

Chera, P., & Wood, C. (2003). Animated multimedia "talking books" can promote phonological awareness in children beginning to read. *Learning and Instruction, 13,* 33–52.

Cherrington, S., & Wansbrough, D. (2007). *An evaluation of Ministry of Education funded early childhood education professional development programmes.* Victoria, NZ: Ministry of Education.

Child and Youth Officer for British Columbia. (2005). *Special report: Healthy early childhood development in British Columbia.* Victoria: Government of British Columbia.

Child Care Human Resource Sector Council. (2009). *Portrait of Canada's ECEC workforce.* Ottawa: CCHRSC.

Child Care Human Resource Sector Council. (2010). *Occupational standards for early childhood educators.* Ottawa: CCHRSC.

Child Care Human Resource Sector Council. (2012). *Human resource toolkit for the early childhood education and care sector.* Ottawa, On: CCHRSC. Accessed Oct. 10, 2014 at http://www.ccsc-cssge.ca/hr-resource-centre/hr-toolkit.

Childcare Resource and Research Unit (CRRU). (2014).

Christie, J. F., & Enz, B. (1992). The effects of literacy play interventions on preschoolers' play patterns and literacy development. *Early Education and Development, 3*(3), 205–220.

Chumak-Horbatsch, R. (2004). Linguistic diversity in early childhood education: Working with linguistically and culturally diverse children. *Canadian Children, 2* (2), 20–24.

Chumak-Horbatsch, R. (2012) *Linguistically appropriate practice: A guide for working with young immigrant children.* Toronto, ON: University of Toronto Press, Higher Education Division.

City of Toronto. (2004). *Toronto Report Card on Children, 5,* update 2003. Toronto, ON: Children's Services Division, Children and Youth Advocate, City of Toronto.

City of Toronto, (2007). *Inclusion: Policy development guidelines for early learning and care programs.* Toronto, ON: Children's Services Division, City of Toronto.

Clarke-Stewart, K. (1987). In search of consistencies in child care research. In D. Phillips (Ed.), *Quality in child care: What does the research tell us?* (105–120). Washington, DC: National Association for the Education of Young Children.

Clements, D. (1994). The uniqueness of the computer as a learning tool: Insights from research and practice. In J. Wright & D. Shade (Eds.), *Young children: Active learners in a technological age.* Washington, DC: NAEYC.

Cleveland, G., & Krashinsky, M. (1998). *The benefits and costs of good child care: The economic rationale for public investment in young children.* Toronto, ON: Childcare Resource & Research Unit.

Cleveland, G., Corter, C., Pelletier, J., Colley, S., Bertrand, J., & Jamieson, J. (2006). *Early childhood learning and development in child care, kindergarten and family support programs.* Toronto, ON: Atkinson Centre at OISE/UT.

Cleveland, G., Forer, B., Hyatt, D., Japel, C., & Krashinsky, M. (2007). *An economic perspective on the current and future role of non-profit provision of early learning and child care services in Canada.* Available at http://www.childcare-policy.net/ documents/final-report-FINAL-print.pdf.

Cleveland, G., Forer, B., Hyatt, D., Japel, C., & Krashinsky, M. (2008, October). New evidence about child care in Canada: Use patterns, affordability and quality. *IRPP Choices, 14*(12).

Cleverley, J., & Phillips, D. (1986). *Visions of childhood: Influential models from Locke to Spock.* New York: Teachers College Press.

Coffey, C., & McCain, M. (2002). *Commission on early learning and child care for the city of Toronto.* Final report 2002. Toronto, ON: City of Toronto.

Colley, S. (2005). *Integration for a change: How can integration of services for kindergarten aged children be achieved?* Toronto, ON: Institute for Child Study at OISE/UT.

Combs, A. W., Blume, R. A., Newman, A. J., & Wass, H. L. (1974). *The professional education of teachers: A humanistic approach to teacher education.* (2nd ed.). Boston: Allyn and Bacon, Inc.

Cooke, K., et al. (1986). *Report of the task force on child care.* Ottawa: Government of Canada.

Cooke, M., Keating, D., and McColm, M. (2005). *Early learning and care in the city: Update, June 2005.* Toronto, ON: Atkinson Centre at the Ontario Institute for Studies in Education of the University of Toronto and Centre of Early Childhood Development at George Brown College.

Corbett, B. (1989). *A century of kindergarten education in Ontario.* Mississauga: The Froebel Foundation.

Corson, P. (2005). Multi-age grouping in early childhood education: An alternative discourse. *Research Connections Canada, 13,* 93–108.

Corter, C., & Fleming, A. (2002). Psychobiology of maternal behaviour in human beings. In M. Bornstein (Ed.), *Handbook of parenting Volume 5: Practical issues in parenting* (141–182). Mahwah, NJ: Lawrence Erlbaum Ass. Publishing.

Corter, C., & Pelletier, J. (2005). Parent and community involvement in schools: Policy panacea or pandemic? In N. Bascia, A. Cumming, A. Datnow, K. Leithwood, & D. Livingstone (Eds.), *International handbook of educational policy,* 295–327. Dordrecht, The Netherlands: Kluwer Publishers.

Corter, C., Bertrand, J., Pelletier, J., Griffen, T., McKay, D., Patel, S., & Ioannone, P. (2006). *Toronto First Duty phase 1 summary: Evidence-based understanding of integrated foundations for early childhood.* Toronto, ON: Atkinson Centre at OISE/UT. Retrieved at http://www.toronto.ca/firstduty.

Corter, C., Janmohamed, Z., & Pelletier, J. (Eds.). (2012). *Toronto First Duty phase 3 report.* Toronto, ON: Atkinson Centre for Society and Child Development, OISE/University of Toronto.

Corter, C., Pelletier, J., Janmohamed, Z., Bertrand, J., Arimura, T., Patel, S., Mir, S., Wilton, A., & Brown, D. (2008) *Toronto First Duty Phase 2 final research report: December 2008.* Toronto, ON: Atkinson Centre for Society and Child Development: Institute of Child Study, Department of HDAP, Ontario Institute for Studies in Education, University of Toronto.

Côté, S. M., Geoffroy, M.-C., and Pingault, J.-B. (2013). Early child care experiences and school readiness. In M. Boivin & K. L. Bierman (Eds.), *Promoting school readiness and early learning: Implications of developmental research for practice* (pp. 133-164). New York: Guilford Press.

Cruickshank, D. R. (1987). *Reflective teaching: The preparation of students of teaching.* Reston, VA: Association of Teacher Educators.

Cryan, J. R., Sheehan, R., Wiechel, J., & Bandy-Hedden, I. G. (1992). Success outcomes of full-day kindergarten: More positive behavior and increased achievement in the years after. *Early Childhood Research Quarterly. Special Issue: Research on Kindergarten, 7*(2), 187–203.

Da Costa, J. L., & Bell, S. (2003). *Full-day vs. half-day kindergarten: Narrowing the SES gap.* Paper presented at the annual meeting of the Canadian Society for Studies in Education, Halifax.

Daycare Trust. (2007). *Childcare nation? Progress on the childcare strategy and priorities for the future.*

DeCesare, D. (2004). Full-day kindergarten programs improve chances of academic success. *The Progress of Education Reform, 5*(4). Denver, CO: Education Commission of the States.

deJong, M., & Bus, A. (2002). Quality of book-reading matters for emergent readers. *Journal of Educational Psychology, 94,* 144–155.

Deloitte & Touche. (2000). *États Généraux sur la Petite Enfance.* Report to the Ontario Ministry of Education, Toronto.

Derman-Sparks, L. (1989). *Anti-bias curriculum: Tools for empowering young children.* Washington, DC: NAEYC.

Diamond, A., Barnett, W. S., Thomas, J., & Munro, S. (2007, November 30). Preschool program improves cognitive control. *Science, 318,* 1387–1388.

Diamond, A., Barnett, W.S., Thomas, J., & Munro, S. (2008). Preschool program improves cognitive control. *Science.*

Diamond, K. E., Hestenes, L. L., & O'Connor, C. E. (1994, January). Integrating young children with disabilities in preschool: Problems and promise. *Young Children, 49*(2), 68–73.

Dickinson, D., & Tabors, P. (2001). *Beginning literacy with language.* Baltimore, MD: Brookes.

Doherty, G. (1997). Zero to six: The basis for school readiness. Research paper, Applied Resources Branch. Ottawa: Human Resources Development, Canada.

Doherty, G. (1998). Elements of quality. *Research Connections Canada, 1,* 1–20.

Doherty, G. (2000). Issues in Canadian child care: What does the research tell us? *Research Connections Canada, 5,* 5–106. Copyright © Canadian Childcare Federation.

Doherty, G. (2003). *Occupational standards.* Ottawa: Canadian Child Care Federation. Retrieved at http://www.cccf-fcsge.ca/subsites/training/pdf/occupational-final-e.pdf.

Doherty, G. (2007). Ensuring the best start in life: Targeting versus universality in early childhood development. *IRPP Choices, 13*(8).

Doherty, G. (2011, May). *The mentoring pairs for child care project: Final outcome report.* Thorold, ON: Early Childhood Community Development Centre.

Doherty, G., & Stuart, B. (1996). *A profile of quality in Canadian child care centres.* Guelph: University of Guelph.

Doherty, G., Friendly, M., & Beach, J. (2003). OECD thematic review of early childhood education and care: Canadian Background Report, Canada.

Doherty, G., Lero, D., Goelman, H., LaGrange, A., & Tougas, J. (2000). *You bet I care! A Canada-wide study on: Wages, working conditions and practices in child care centres.* Guelph: Centre for Families, Work and Well-Being, University of Guelph, Ontario.

Doherty, G., Lero, D., Goelman, H., Tougas, J., & LaGrange, A. (2000). *You bet I care! Caring and learning environments: Quality in regulated family child care across Canada.* Guelph: Centre for Families, Work and Well-Being, University of Guelph, Ontario.

Doherty-Derkowski, G. (1995). *Quality matters: Excellence in early childhood programs.* Reading, MA: Addison-Wesley Publishers Ltd.

Doxey, I. (Ed.). (1990). *Child care and education: Canadian dimensions.* Toronto, ON: Nelson Canada.

Duff, E., Mac, H., & Van Scoy, I. J. (1995). Reflection and self-evaluation keys to professional development. *Young Children, 50*(4), 81–88.

Edwards, C. (1994). Partner, nurturer, and guide: The roles of the Reggio teacher in action. In C. Edwards, L. Gandini, & G. Forman (Eds.), *The hundred languages of children: The Reggio Emilia approach to early childhood education.* Norwood, NJ: Ablex Publishing Corporation.

Eggleton, A., & Keon, A. (2009). *Early childhood education and care: Next steps.* Ottawa: Standing Senate Committee on Social Affairs.

Einarsdottir, J. (2000). Incorporating literacy resources into the play curriculum of two Icelandic preschools. In K. A. Roskos & J. F. Christie (Eds.), *Play and literacy in early childhood: Research from multiple perspectives* (77–90). New York: Erlbaum.

Elicker, J., & Mathur, S. (1997). What do they do all day? Comprehensive evaluation of a full-day kindergarten. *Early Childhood Research Quarterly, 12*, pt. index issue (4), 459–480.

Elkind, D. (1983, January). Montessori education: Abiding contributions and contemporary challenges. *Young Children, 38*(2), 3–10.

Elkind, D. (1988). *Miseducation: Preschoolers at risk.* New York: Alfred A. Knopf.

Epstein, A. (1993). *Training for quality: Improving early childhood programs through systematic inservice training.* Ypsilanti, MI: High/Scope Educational Research Foundation.

Epstein, J., & Sanders, M. (2002). Family, school, and community partnerships. In M. H. Bornstein (Ed.), *Handbook of parenting, 2nd edition (Vol. 5: Practical issues in parenting).* Mahwah, NJ: Lawrence Erlbaum Associates.

Espinosa, L. M. (2007). English-language learners as they enter school. In R. C. Pianta, M. J. Cox, & K. L. Snow (Eds.), *School readiness and the transition to kindergarten in the era of accountability.* Baltimore: Paul H. Brookes.

Espinosa, L. M. (2008, January). Challenging common myths about young English language learners. *Foundation for Child Development Policy Brief, Advancing PK-3*, No. 8. New York, NY: Foundation for Child Development.

Fairholm, R. (2009). *Literature review of socioeconomic effects and net benefits—Understanding and addressing workforce shortages in Early Childhood Education and Care (ECEC) Project.* Ottawa: Child Care Human Resource Sector Council.

Fairholm, R. (2010). *Economic and social payoffs of full-day early learning.* Toronto, ON: Centre for Spatial Economics.

Fearn, T. (2006). *A sense of belonging: Supporting healthy child development in Aboriginal families.* Toronto, ON: Best Start: Ontario's Maternal, Newborn and Early Childhood Development Research Centre.

Ferguson, E. (1995). *Child care … Becoming visible.* Halifax: Child Care Connection-NS.

Ferguson, E. (1997). *Child care administrator credentialing: A work in progress.* Halifax: Child Care Connection-NS.

Ferguson, E. (1998). *Caring in practice: Child care substitute youth internship program. A synopsis.* Halifax: Child Care Connection-NS.

Ferns, C., & Friendly, M. (2014). *The state of early childhood education and care in Canada, 2012.* Toronto, ON: Childcare Research and Resource Unit.

Ferrao, V. (2010). *Paid work.* Women in Canada: A gender-based statistical reportcomponent of Statistics Canada Catalogue no. 89-503-X. Ottawa, ON: Statistics Canada.

Flanagan, K. (2010). *The early years report—early learning in PEI: An investment in the island's future.* Charlottetown: Government of PEI. Retrieved at http://www.gov.pe.ca/photos/original/edu_earlyyrsRpt.pdf.

Flanagan, K., & Beach, J. (2010). *Examining the human resource implications of emerging issues in ECEC.* Ottawa: Child Care Human Resource Sector Council.

Flanagan, K., Beach, J., & Varmuza, P. (2013) You bet we still care! Ottawa, ON: Child Care Human Resources Sector Council

Flowers, H., Girolametto, L., Weitzman, E., & Greenberg, J. (2007). Promoting early literacy skills: Effects of inservice education for early childhood educators. *Canadian Journal of Speech-Language Pathology and Audiology, 31*, 6–18.

Fortin, P., Godbout, L., & St-Cerny, S. (2012). Impact of Quebec's universal low-fee childcare program on female labour force participation, domestic income, and government budgets. Working paper 2012/02. Université de Sherbrooke.

Frede, E., & Ackerman, D. (2002). *Curriculum decision-making NIEER.* Retrieved April 2, 2006, at http://nieer.org/resources/research/CurriculumDecision Making.pdf.

Freire, P. (1970). *Pedagogy of the oppressed.* New York: Continuum.

Friendly, M. (2000). *Child care and Canadian federalism in the 1990s: Canary in a coal mine.* Toronto, ON: Childcare Resource and Research Unit, University of Toronto.

Friendly, M. (2008). Building a strong and equal partnership between childcare and early childhood education in Canada. *International Journal of Child Care and Education Policy, 2*(1), 39–52.

Friendly, M. (2009). *Joining-up and scaling-up: A vision for early childhood education and care.* Canadian Education Association.

Friendly, M. (2010) *From vision to action: Early childhood education and care in 2020.* Toronto, ON: Childcare Research and Resource Unit.

Friendly, M., & Beach, J. (2005, May). *Early childhood education and care in Canada 2004.* (6th ed.). Toronto, ON: Childcare Resource and Research Unit.

Friendly, M., Beach, J., Ferns, C., & Turiano, M. (2007). *Early childhood education and care in Canada 2006.* Toronto, ON: Childcare Research and Resource Unit.

Friendly, M., Doherty, G., & Beach, J. (2006). *Quality by design … What do we know about quality in early learning and child care and what do we think? A literature review.* Toronto, ON: Childcare Resource & Research Unit, University of Toronto. Available at http://www.child-carequality.ca. Accessed 15 May 2006.

Friendly, M., Halfon, S., Beach, J., & Forer, B. (2013). Early childhood education and care in Canada 2012. Toronto, ON: Childcare Resource and Research Unit.

Frontline Profile. (1997, December). *Ideas: The Journal of Emotional Well-Being in Child Care, 4*(3), 19.

Fullan, M. (2001). *Leading in a culture of change.* San Francisco: Jossey-Bass.

Gaffield, C. (1991, June). Children, schooling, and family reproduction in nineteenth-century Ontario. *Canadian Historical Review, LXXII*(2), 157–191.

Galinsky, E. (2006, February). *Economic benefits of high-quality early childhood programs: What makes the difference?* The Committee for Economic Development, February 2006.

Galinsky, E., Howes, C., Kontos, S., & Shinn, M. (1994). The study of children in family child care and relative care—Key findings and recommendations. *Young Children, 50*(1), 58–61.

Gandini, L. (1993, November). Fundamentals of the Reggio Emilia approach to early childhood education. *Young Children, 49*(1), 4–8.

Gersten, R., & Keating, T. (1990). Long-term benefits from direct instruction. In M. Jensen & Z. Chevalier (Eds.), *Issues and advocacy in early education.* Boston: Allyn and Bacon.

Gestwicki, C. (1996). *Home, school, community relations.* (3rd ed.). Albany, NY: Delmar Publishers.

Gestwicki, C. (2011). *Developmentally appropriate practice: Curriculum and development in early education.* (4th ed.) Albany, NY: Delmar Publishers Inc.

Giles, T. E., & Proudfoot, A. J. (1994). *Educational administration in Canada.* (5th ed.) Calgary: Detselig Enterprises Ltd.

Ginsburg, H., Lee, J. S., Boyd, J. (2008). Mathematics education for young children: What it is and how to promote it. *Social Policy Report, XXII*(I). Society for Research in Child Development.

Gladwell, M. (2002). *The tipping point.* Boston: Little, Brown & Co.

Goelman, H., & Pence, A. (1987). Effects of child care, family and individual characteristics on children's language development: The Victoria day care research project. In D. Phillips (Ed.), *Quality child care: What does research tell us?* Research monograph, Vol. 1. Washington, DC: National Association for the Education of Young Children.

Goelman, H., Doherty, G., Lero, D., LaGrange, A., & Tougas, J. (2000). *You bet I care! Caring and learning environments: Quality in child care centres across Canada.* Guelph: Centre for Families, Work and Well-Being, University of Guelph, Ontario.

Gonzalez-Mena, J. (2005). *Diversity in early care and education: Honoring differences.* Toronto, ON: McGraw-Hill.

Goodson, B. D. (2005). Parent support programs and outcomes for children. In R. Tremblay, R. Barr, & R. Peters (Eds.), *Encyclopedia on early child development* (online). Montreal, QUE: Centre of Excellence for Early Childhood Development. Available at: http://www.excellence-early-childhood.ca/documents/GoodsonANGxp.pdf

Gopnik, A. (2009). *The philosophical baby: What children's minds tell us about truth, love and the meaning of life.* New York: Farrar, Straus & Giroux.

Gopnik, A., Meltzoff, A. N., & Kuhl, P. K. (1999). *The scientist in the crib: Minds, brains, and how children learn.* New York: William Morrow.

Goss Gilroy Inc. (1998). *The family child care provider survey.* Ottawa: Canadian Child Care Federation.

Goulet, M. (1995). Building responsive relationships in infant care. *Ideas, 2*(1), 9–13.

Goulet, M. (2001). *Handout #5: Curriculum development.* Toronto, ON: George Brown College.

Government of Ontario. (2014). How does learning happen? Ontario's pedagogy for the early years. Available at Ministry of Education website: http://www.edu.gov.on.ca/childcare/pedagogy.html.

Graue, E., Clements, M. A., Reynolds, A. J., & Niles, M. D. (2004, December 24). More than teacher directed or child initiated: Preschool curriculum type, parent involvement, and children's outcomes in the child-parent centers. *Education Policy Analysis Archives, 12*(72). Retrieved July 15, 2007, at http:// epaa.asu.edu/epaa/v12n72.

Greenberg, P. (1990, January). Why not academic preschool? (Part 1). *Young Children, 45*(2), 70–80.

Greenspan, S., & Shanker, S. (2004). *The first idea: How symbols, language and intelligence evolved from our primate ancestors to modern humans.* Cambridge, MA: Da Capo Press.

Greenwood, M. (2001). Aboriginal perspectives on child care. In G. Cleveland & M. Krashinsky (Eds.), *Our children's future: Child care policy in Canada.* Toronto, ON: University of Toronto Press. 234–249.

Greenwood, M. (2006). Children are a gift to us: Aboriginal-specific early childhood programs and services in Canada. *Canadian Journal of Native Education, 29*(1): 12–28.

Griffin, S. (1994). *Professionalism: The link to quality care.* Ottawa: Canadian Child Care Federation.

Griffin, S., & Case, R. (1998). Re-thinking the primary school math curriculum: An approach based on cognitive science. *Issues in Education, 4*(1), 1–51.

Grindal, T., Bowne, J. B., Yoshikawa, H., Schindler, H., Duncan, G. J., Magnuson, K., & Shonkoff, J. (2013, under review). *The added impact of parenting education in early childhood education programs: A meta-analysis.* Manuscript.

Guy, K. (1997). *Our promise to children.* Ottawa: Canadian Institute of Child Health.

Harms, T., & Clifford, R. (1980). *Early childhood rating scale.* New York: Teacher's College Press.

Harms, T., Clifford, R., & Cryer, D. (1998). *Early childhood environment rating scale.* Rev. ed. New York: Teachers College Press.

Hart, B., & Risley, T. (1995). *Meaningful differences in the everyday experiences of American children.* Baltimore, MD: Paul H. Brookes Publishing Co.

Hart, B., & Risley, T. (1999). *The social world of children learning to talk.* Baltimore, MD: Paul H. Brookes Publishing Co.

Hebrew University of Jerusalem (Israel), National Council of Jewish Women Research Inst. for Innovation in Education. (1993). *HIPPY: Home instruction program for preschool youngsters.* Proceedings of the HIPPY International Research Seminar (1st, Jerusalem, Israel, December 16–19, 1991), 48.

Helburn, S., Culkin, M., Morris, J., Morcan, N., Howes, C., Phillipsen, L., … Rusticic, J. (1995). *Cost, quality & child outcomes in child care centres.* Bloomington, IN: Phi Delta Kappa Educational Foundation.

Herman, B. E. (1984). *The case for the all-day kindergarten*: *Fastback 205.* Bloomington, IN: Phi Delta Kappa Educational Foundation.

Hernandez, D., Denton, N. & Macartney, S. (2008) Children in immigrant families: Looking to America's future. *Social Policy Report,* Vol XX11 No. III.

Herry, Y., Maltais, C., & Thompson, K. (2007). Effects of a full-day preschool program on 4-year-old children. *Early Childhood Research and Practice*, 9(2). Available at http://ecrp.uiuc.edu/v9n2/herry.html.

Hertzman, C., & Bertrand, J. (2007). Children in poverty and the use of the Early Development Instrument mapping to improve their worlds. *Paediatrics & Child Health*, 12, 687–692.

Hill, P. S. (1987, July). The function of the kindergarten. *Young Children, 42*(5), 12–19.

Hillman, C. (1988). *Teaching four-year-olds: A personal journey.* Bloomington, IN: Phi Delta Kappa Educational Foundation.

Hodgen, E. (2007). *Early childhood education and young adult competencies at age 16. Technical report 2 from the age-16 phase of the Longitudinal Competent Children, Competent Learners Study.* Wellington, NZ: New Zealand for Educational Research.

Houston, A. (2004). In the new media as in old, context matters most. *Social Policy Report, XVIII*(IV).

Howe, N., Jacobs, E., & Fiorentino, L. (2000). The curriculum. In L. Prochner & N. Howe (Eds.), *Early childhood care and education in Canada.* Vancouver: UBC Press.

Human Resources Development Canada. (1994). *Child care and development: A supplementary paper.* Ottawa: Government of Canada.

Human Resources Development Canada, and Indian & Northern Affairs, Canada. (2001). *Federal/provincial/territorial early childhood development agreement: Report on government of Canada activities and expenditures 2000–2001.* Ottawa: Minister of Public Works and Government Services Canada.

Hunt, J. McV. (1961). *Intelligence and experience.* New York: Ronald.

Hyson, M. C. (1982, January). Playing with kids all day: Job stress in early childhood education. *Young Children, 37*(2), 25–31.

Irwin, S. (1995). *Charting new waters.* Wreck Cove, NS: Breton Books.

Irwin, S., Lero, D., & Brophy, K. (2004). *Inclusion: The next generation in child care in Canada.* Wreck Cove, NS: Breton Books.

Isenberg, J., & Quisenberry, N. (1988). Play: A necessity for all children. *Childhood Education*, 64(3), 138–145.

Jacobs, E., Mill, D., & Jennings, M. (2002). *Quality assurance and school age care.* Final report for the National School-Age Care Research Project 1997–1999. Montreal: Concordia University.

Janmohamed, Z. (2006). *Building bridges: Lesbian, gay, bisexual, transsexual/transgender and queer families in early childhood education.* Toronto, ON: Ontario Coalition for Better Child Care.

Janus, M., & Duku, E. (2007). The school entry gap: Socioeconomic, family, and health factors associated with children's school readiness to learn. *Early Education and Development, 18*(3), 375–403.

Janus, M., & Offord, D. (2000). Readiness to learn at school. *Isuma, 1*(2), 71–75.

Japel, C., & Tremblay, R. (2005). *Quality counts.* Montreal: Institute for Research on Public Policy.

Joffe, C. (1977). *Friendly intruders.* Berkeley, CA: University of California Press.

Johnson, D. L., & Walker, T. (1991). A follow-up evaluation of the Houston parent-child development center: School performance. *Journal of Early Intervention*, 15(3), 226–236.

Johnson, J. & McCracken, J. (1994). *The early childhood career lattice.* Washington DC: NAEYC.

Johnson, J., Christie, J., & Wardle, F. (2005). *Play, development and early education.* Boston: Pearson/Allyn and Bacon.

Johnson, K., Lero, D., & Rooney, J. (2001). *Work-life compendium 2001: 150 Canadian statistics on work, family & well-being.* Guelph: Centre for Families, Work and Well-Being, University of Guelph.

Johnson, L., & Mathien, J. (1998). *Early childhood services for kindergarten-age children in four Canadian provinces: Scope, nature and models for the future.* Ottawa: The Caledon Institute of Social Policy.

Jones, E. (Ed.). (1993). *Growing teachers: Partnerships in staff development.* Washington, DC: NAEYC.

Jones, E., & Nimmo, J. (1994). *Emergent curriculum.* Washington, DC: NAEYC.

Johnson, J., & McCracken, J. (Eds.). (1994). *The early childhood career lattice: Perspectives on professional development.* Washington, DC: NAEYC.

Kaga, Y., Bennett, J., & Moss, P. (2010). *Caring and learning together: A cross-national study on the integration of early childhood care and education within education.* Paris: UNESCO.

Kaiser, J., & Rasminsky, S. (1991). *The good day care book.* Toronto, ON: Little, Brown.

Kamii, C. (Ed.). (1990). *Achievement testing in the early grades: Games grown-ups play.* Washington, DC: NAEYC.

Karoly, L., Kilburn, R., & Cannon, J. (2005). *Early childhood interventions proven results, future promise.* Santa Monica, CA: RAND Corporation.

Katz, L. (1984, July). The professional early childhood teacher. *Young Children*, *39*(5), 3–10.

Katz, L. (1991). Ethical issues in working with young children. In L. Katz & E. Ward (Eds.), *Ethical behaviour in early childhood education*. Exp. ed. Washington, DC: NAEYC.

Katz, L. (1993). *Five perspectives on quality in early childhood programs*. Perspectives from ERIC/EECE. Monograph series, 1. Urbana, IL: ERIC Clearing House on Elementary and Early Childhood Education.

Katz, L. (1995). *Talks with teachers: A collection.* Norwood, NJ: Ablex Publishing Corp.

Katz, L., Evangelou, D., & Hartman, J. (1991). *The case for mixed-age grouping in early education.* Washington, DC: NAEYC.

Keating, D. (1998). Enhancing learning readiness: The family and the preschool child. *Transition*, 13–14.

Keating, D., & Hertzman, C. (1999). *Developmental health and the wealth of nations*. New York: Guilford Press.

Kellerman, M. (1995). *The 1995 report on family resource programs across Canada.* Ottawa: Canadian Association of Family Resource Programs.

Kershaw, P., Irwin, L., Trafford, K., & Hertzman, C. (2006). *The British Columbia atlas of child development.* 1st ed. Vancouver: Human Early Learning Partnership.

Kilbride, K. (1997). *Include me too! Human diversity in early childhood education*. Toronto, ON: Harcourt Brace.

King, A., & Peart, M. J. (1990). *The good school*. Toronto, ON: Ontario Teacher's Federation.

Kipnis, K. (1987, May). How to discuss professional ethics. *Young Children*, *42*(40), 26–30.

Kirp, D. (2007). The kids-first agenda. In *Big ideas for children: Investing in our nation's future.* Washington, DC: First Focus.

Kochendorfer, L. (1994). *Becoming a reflective teacher.* Washington, DC: National Education Association.

Kraft, K. C., & Berk, L. (1998). Private speech in two preschools: Significance of open-ended activities and make-believe play for verbal self-regulation. *Early Childhood Research Quarterly*, *13*, 637–658.

Kyle, I., & Kellerman, M. (1998). *Case studies of Canadian family resource programs: Supporting families, children and communities.* Ottawa: Canadian Association of Family Resource Programs.

Lafreniere-Davis, N. (2005). *Early childhood in Canada's francophone minority communities: A transformative analysis.* Ottawa: Commission nationale des parents francophones.

Langford, R. (2010). Innovations in provincial early learning curriculum frameworks. Occasional Paper 24. Toronto, ON: Childcare Resource and Research Unit.

Lazer, I., & Darlington, R. (1982). Lasting effects of early education: A report from the consortium for longitudinal studies. *Monographs of the Society for Research in Child Development*, *47*, 2–3.

Le, V., Kirby, N., Barney, H., Setodji, C., & Gershwin, D. (2006). *School readiness, full-day kindergarten and student achievement.* Santa Monica, CA: RAND Corporation.

Lee, W., & Carr, M. (2002). Documentation of learning stories: A powerful assessment tool for early childhood. Conference paper.

Lefebvre, P., & Merrigan, P. (2008). Childcare policy and the labor supply of mothers: A natural experiment for Canada. *Journal of Labor Economics*, *26*(3), 519–548.

LeFevre, J., Skwarchuk, S., Smith-Chant, B., Fast, L, Kamawar, D. & Bisanz, J. (2009). Home numeracy experiences and children's math performance in the early school years. *Canadian Journal of Behavioural Science* © 2009 Canadian Psychological Association 2009, Vol. 41, No. 2, 55–66.

Leitch, K. (2008). *Reach for the top: A report from the advisor on healthy children and youth*. Ottawa, ON. Department of Health

Lero, D., & Irwin, S. (2008). *Improving quality, enhancing inclusion: Partnerships for inclusion—Nova Scotia*. Guelph, ON: Centre for Families, Work and Well-Being, University of Guelph.

Lero, D., Irwin, S., & Darisi, T. (2006). *Partnerships for inclusion—Nova Scotia: An evaluation based on the first cohort of child care centres.* Guelph: Centre for Families, Work and Well-being, University of Guelph.

Liebert, R., & Sprafkin, J. (1988). *The early window: Effects of television on children and youth*. New York: Allyn and Bacon.

Love, J. M., Kisker, E. E., Ross, C., Raikes, H., Constantine, J., Boller, K., Brooks-Gunn, J. ... & Vogel, C. (2005). The effectiveness of Early Head Start for 3-year-old children and their parents: Lessons for policy and programs. *Developmental Psychology, 41*(6), 885–901.

Love, J. M., Kisker, E. E., Ross, C. M., Schochet, P. Z., Brooks-Gunn, J., Paulsell, D., ... Brady-Smith, C. (2002). *Making a difference in the lives of infants and toddlers and their families: The impacts of early head start*, Volume 1: Final technical report. Princeton, NJ: Mathematica Policy Research, Inc.

Lynch, R. (2007). *Enriching children enriching the nation: Public investment in high-quality pre-kindergarten*. Washington, DC: Economic Policy Institute.

Lyon, P., & Canning, M. (1995). *The Atlantic day care study*. St. John's: Memorial University of Newfoundland.

MacNaughton, G. (2006). Respect for diversity: An international review. Working Paper 40. The Hague, The Netherlands: Bernard van Leer Foundation. Available at http://www.bernardvanleer.org/Respect_for_diversity_An_international_ overview.

MacNaughton, G., & Davis, K. (2001). Beyond "othering": Rethinking approaches to teaching young Anglo-Australian children about indigenous Australians. *Contemporary Issues in Early Childhood*, *2*(1), 153–169.

Magnuson, K., Meyers, M., Ruhm, C., & Waldfogel, J. (2006). Inequality in preschool education and school readiness. *American Education Research Journal*, *41*, 115–157.

Mahon, R., & Jenson, J. (2006). *ELCC report 2006—Learning from each other: Early learning and child care experiences in Canadian cities.* Toronto, ON: Social Development

Canada, City of Toronto, Vancouver Joint Council on Child Care. Retrieved at http://www.toronto.ca/children/pdf/elcc_report.pdf. Accessed May 12, 2008.

Malaguzzi, L. (1993). History, ideas, and basic philosophy. In C. Edwards, L. Gandini, & G. Forman (Eds.), *The hundred languages of children: The Reggio Emilia approach to early childhood education*, 41–89. Norwood, NJ: Ablex.

Malaguzzi, L. (1993, November). For an education based on relationships. *Young Children*, *49*(1), 9–12.

Malcomson, J. (2002). *Putting the pieces together: A conceptual framework of family support practice.* Ottawa: FRP Canada.

Margaret and Wallace McCain Family Foundation. (2010). *Building for the future.* Toronto, ON: Author.

Mathien, J. (1990). School programs for young children in Ontario and Toronto. Unpublished manuscript.

Mathien, J. (2001). Children, families and institutions in late 18th century and 20th century Ontario. Unpublished master's thesis, Ontario Institute for Studies in Education, University of Toronto.

McCain, M., & Mustard, J. F. (1999). *Early years study.* Toronto: Ontario Children's Secretariat.

McCain, M., Mustard, J. F., & McCuaig, K. (2011). *Early years study 3.* Toronto, ON: Margaret and Wallace McCain Family Foundation.

McCain, M., Mustard, J. F., & Shanker, S. (2007). *Early years study 2: Putting science into action.* Toronto, ON: Council for Early Child Development.

McCuaig, K. (2014). *Review of early learning frameworks in Canada.* Toronto, ON: Atkinson Centre, OISE, University of Toronto. http://www.oise.utoronto.ca/atkinson/UserFiles/File/Resources_Topics/Resources_Topics_CurriculumPedagogy/Review_of_Early_Learning_Frameworks_in_Canada-all.pdf.

McCuaig, K., Bertrand, J., & Shanker, S. (2012) *Trends in early education and child care.* Toronto, ON: Atkinson Centre for Society and Child Development, OISE/University of Toronto.

McElgunn, J. (2006, Fall). Opening our doors … for the children. *The CAP Journal*, *14*(3), 28–30.

McIvor, O. (2005). The contribution of Indigenous heritage language immersion programs to healthy early childhood development. *Research Connections Canada: Supporting Childdren and Families, 12* (5–12). Ottawa, ON: Canadian Child Care Federation.

Mehta, S., Janmohamed, Z., & Corter, C. (2011). *An investigation of the career paths of internationally trained early childhood educators transitioning into early learning programs*. Toronto, ON: Atkinson Centre for Society and Child Development, OISE/University of Toronto.

Meisels, S., & Shonkoff, J. (1990). Preface. In S. Meisels and J. Shonkoff (Eds.), *Handbook of early interventions*. New York: Cambridge University Press.

Melaville, A., & Blank, M. (1999). *Together we can: A guide for crafting a pro-family system of education and human services.* Washington: US Dept of Education, Office of Educational Research and Improvement and US Dept of Health and Human Services, Office of the Assistant Secretary for Planning and Evaluation.

Miller, E., & Almon, J. (2009). *Crisis in the kindergarten: Why children need to play in school.* College Park, MD: Alliance for Children.

Millichamp, D. (1944). *Toronto day nurseries.* Toronto, ON: Institute of Child Study.

Millichamp, D. (1974). *Epilogue to* The adult and the nursery school child, *by Margaret Fletcher.* Toronto, ON: University of Toronto Press.

Mitchell, L., Wylie, C., & Carr, M. (2008). *Outcomes of early childhood education: Literature review.* Wellington, NZ: New Zealand Council for Educational Research.

Modigliani, K. (1988, March). Twelve reasons for the low wages in child care. *Young Children*, *43*(3), 14–15.

Moran, P., Ghate, D., & van der Merwe, A. (2004). *What works in parenting support: A review of the international evidence.* Research Report RR 574. London, UK: Department for Education and Skills.

Mort, J. (2004). *The EDI impact study: BC schools embracing young children.* Vancouver: Human Early Learning Partnership, UBC.

Mort, J. (2007). *Documentation: Strong Start pilot sites, stage 1.* Vancouver: Human Early Learning Partnership, UBC.

Mort, J. (2008). *Evaluation of Strong Start British Columbia— School-based (preschool) family drop-in centres.* Vancouver, BC: Human Early Learning Partnership, University of British Columbia.

Moss, P. (2000). *Workforce issues in early childhood education and care*. Prepared for consultative meeting on International Developments in Early Childhood Education and Care, May 11–12, 2000. New York: Columbia University.

Moss, P. (2004). *Setting the scene: A vision of universal children's spaces.* London: Daycare Trust.

Moss, P. (2007). *Bringing politics into the nursery: Early childhood education as a democratic practice*. Working Papers 43. The Hague, Netherlands: Bernard Leer Foundation.

Mustard, F. (2008). *Investing in the early years—closing the gap between what we know and what we do*. Adelaide, South Australia: Government of South Australia

National Association for the Education of Young Children (NAEYC). (1995). *Guidelines for preparation for early childhood professionals associate baccalaureate, and advanced levels. Position statement.* Washington, DC: NAEYC.

National Association of Elementary School Principals and Collaborative Communications Group. (2005). *Leading early childhood learning communities: What principals know and should be able to do.* Alexandria, VA: NAESP.

National Center for Education Statistics. (2004). *Full-day and half-day kindergarten in the United States: Findings from the early childhood longitudinal study, kindergarten class of 1998–99.* Washington, DC: N.CES.

National Research Council. (2000). *Eager to learn.* Washington, DC: National Academy Press.

National Research Council. (2001). *Eager to learn: Educating our preschoolers* (Committee on Early Childhood

Pedagogy of the Commission on Behavioral and Social Sciences and Education). Washington, DC: The National Academies Press.

National Scientific Council on the Developing Child. (2004). *Young children develop in an environment of relationships.* Working Paper No. 1. Available at http://www.developing-child.harvard.edu.

Native Council of Canada. (2001). *Native child care: The circle of care.* Ottawa: Native Council of Canada.

Neuman, S. B., & Roskos, K. (1992). Literacy objects as cultural tools: Effects on children's literacy behaviors in play. *Reading Research Quarterly, 27*(3), 202–225.

NICHD Early Child Care Research Network. (2000). Characteristics and quality of child care for toddlers and preschoolers. *Journal of Applied Developmental Science, 4*, 116–135.

NICHD Early Child Care Research Network. (2004). *Early child care and children's development in the primary grades: Follow-up results from the NICHD study of early child care.* Washington, DC: NICHD-ECCRN.

Nicholson, Simon. (1974). How not to cheat children: The theory of loose parts. In G. Coates (Ed.), *Alternate learning environments.* Stroudsberg, PA: Dowden, Hutchinson and Ross.

Office of Head Start. (2008). *Dual language learners: What does it take?* Washington, DC: Administration of Children and Families, U.S. Department of Health and Human Services.

Oldershaw, L. (2002). *National survey of parents of young children.* Toronto, ON: Invest in Kids.

Olds, D., Henderson, C. R., Chamberlin, R., & Tatelbaum, R. (1986). Preventing child abuse and neglect: A randomized trial of nurse home visitation. *Pediatrics, 78*(1), 65–78.

Ontario Best Start Panel on Early Learning. (2007). *Early learning for every child today.* Toronto, ON: Ministry of Children and Youth Services.

Organisation for Economic Co-operation and Development. (2001). *Starting strong: Early childhood education and care.* Paris: OECD.

Organisation for Economic Co-operation and Development. (2004). *Early childhood education and care policy: Canada: Country note.* OECD Directorate for Education, 2004.

Organisation for Economic Co-operation and Development. (2006). *Starting strong II.* Paris: OECD.

Organisation for Economic Co-operation and Development. (2013, February). *Educator indicators in focus.*

Osborn, A., & Milbank, J. (1987). *The effects of early education.* Report from the Child Health and Education Study. Oxford: Clarendon Press.

Osborn, D. (1991). *Early childhood education in historical perspective.* (3rd ed.). Athens, GA: Education Associates, Div. of The Daye Press, Inc.

Pagani, L., Fitzpatrick, C., Barnett, T., Dubow, E. (2010). Prospective associations between early childhood television exposure and academic, psychosocial, and physical well-being by middle childhood. *Archives of Pediatrics and Adolescent Medicine, 164*(5), 425.

Pagani, L. S., Jalbert, J., Lapointe, P., and Hebert, M. (2006). Effects of junior kindergarten on emerging literacy in children from low-income and linguistic-minority families. *Early Childhood Education Journal, 33*, 209–215.

Paley, V. G. (1990). *The boy who would be a helicopter.* Cambridge, MA: Harvard University Press.

Pascal, C. (2009a.) *With our best future in mind: Implementing early learning in Ontario* Report to the Premier by the Special Advisor on Early Learning.

Pascal, C. (2009b.) *With our best future in mind: Summary of evidence.* Compendium report to the Premier by the Special Advisor on Early Learning.

Pelletier, J. (2006). *Parent involvement.* Best Start Expert Panel on Early Learning Working Paper. Toronto, ON: Ministry of Children and Youth Services.

Pelletier, J. (2011). *What works? Research into practice.* Toronto, ON: Literacy and Numeracy Secretariat, Minister of Education.

Pelletier, J. (2014). Ontario's full day kindergarten: A bold public policy initiative. *Public Sector Digest,* May 15–June 13.

Pelletier, J., & Brent, J. (2002). Parent participation in children's school readiness: The effects of parental self-efficacy, cultural diversity and teacher strategies. *International Journal of Childhood Education*, 45–60.

Pence, A. (1990). The child care profession in Canada. In I. Doxey (Ed.), *Child care and Canada.* Toronto, ON: Nelson Canada.

Pence, A. (2005). Horton and the worlds of ECD: Hearing and supporting other voices. *Research Directions Canada*, 13. Ottawa: Canadian Child Care Federation.

Penn, H. (1999). *Values and beliefs in caring for babies and toddlers.* Toronto, ON: Childcare Resource and Research Unit, University of Toronto.

Perlman, M., & Fletcher, B. (2008, Winter). Literacy instruction in Canadian child care centers. *Journal of Research in Childhood Education*. Available at http://findarticles.com/p/articles/mi_hb1439/is_2_23/ai_n31442380/?tag=content;col1.

Perrone, V. (1991). *A letter to teachers: Reflections of schooling and the art of teaching.* San Francisco: Jossey-Bass Publishers.

Perry, B. (1996). Neurodevelopmental adaptations to violence: How children survive the intragenerational vortex of violence. In *Violence and childhood trauma: Understanding and responding to the effects of violence on young children.* Cleveland, OH: Gund Foundation.

Peters, R. (2001). *Developing capacity and competence in the Better Beginnings, Better Futures communities: Report summary.* Kingston, ON: Research Coordination Unit, Queen's University.

Peters, R. D., Nelson, G., Petrunka, K., Pancer, S. M., Loomis, C., Hasford, J., Janzen, R., Armstrong, L., & Van Andel, A. (2010). *Investing in our future: Highlights of Better Beginnings, Better Futures research findings at Grade 12.* Kingston, ON: Better Beginnings, Better Futures Research Coordination Unit.

Phillips, C. (1991). At the core: What every early childhood professional should know. In J. Johnson & J. B. McCracken (Eds.), *The early childhood career lattice: Perspectives on professional development.* Washington, DC: NAEYC.

Phillips, J. C. (2003). Powerful learning: Creating learning communities in urban school reform. *Journal of Curriculum and Supervision 18*(2), 240–258.

Physical and Health Education. (2014). http://www.phecanada.ca/programs/physical-literacy/what-physical-literacy.

Pianta, R., La Paro, K., & Hamre, B. (2008). *Classroom assessment scoring system (CLASS) manual, K–3.* Baltimore, MD: Brookes Publishing.

Plucker, J. A., Eaton, J. J., Rapp, K. E., et al. (2004). *The effects of full day versus half day kindergarten: Review and analysis of national and Indiana data.* Indianapolis: Indiana Association of Public School Superintendents.

Pollard, J. (1996). Student and sponsor-educator relationships during early childhood education practicum. Unpublished master's thesis, School of Child and Youth Care, University of Victoria.

Prentice, S. (2001). *Changing child care: Five decades of child care advocacy and policy in Canada.* Halifax: Fernwood Publishing.

Prentice, S. (2007). *Rural childcare: Childcare as economic and social development in parkland.* Winnipeg: Child Care Coalition of Manitoba.

Prentice, S., & McCracken, M. (2004). *Time for action: An economic and social analysis of childcare in Winnipeg.* Winnipeg, MB: Child Care Coalition of Manitoba.

Prochner, L. (1996). Quality in care in historical perspective. *Early Childhood Research Quarterly, 11*, 5–17.

Prochner, L. (2000). A history of early education and child care in Canada, 1820–1966. In L. Prochner & N. Howe (Eds.), *Early childhood care and education in Canada.* Vancouver: UBC Press.

Public Health Agency of Canada. (2007). *Aboriginal Head Start in urban and northern communities: National impact evaluation.* Paper presented to the International Union for Health Promotion and Education, June 11, Vancouver. Ottawa, ON: PHAC.

Ramani, G. B., Siegler, R. S. (2011). Reducing the gap in numerical knowledge between low- and middle-income preschoolers. *Journal of Applied Developmental Psychology, 32*, 146–159.

Ramani, G. B., Siegler, R. S., & Hitti, A. (2012). Taking it to the classroom: Number board games as a small group learning activity. *Journal of Educational Psychology, 104*, 661–672.

Raymond, J. (1991). *The nursery years.* Toronto, ON: University of Toronto Press.

Reynolds, A., & Temple, J. (2008). Cost-effective early childhood development programs from preschool to third grade. *Annual Review of Clinical Psychology*, *4*, 109–30.

Reynolds, A. J., Temple, J. A., Robertson, D. L., & Mann, E. A. (2002). Age 21 cost-benefit analysis of the Title I Chicago child-parent centers. *Educational Evaluation and Policy Analysis, 24*, 267–303.

Reynolds, A. J., Wang, M. C., & Walberg, H. J. (Eds.). (2003). *Early childhood programs for a new century.* Washington, DC: CWLA Press.

Rideout, V., Vandewater, E., & Wartella, E. (2003). *Zero to six: Electronic media in the lives of infants, toddlers and preschoolers.* Menlo Park, CA: Kaiser Family Foundation.

Robin, K., Frede, E., Barnett, S. (2006). *Is more better?* NIEER Working Paper. New Brunswick, NJ: NIEER.

Robinson, K., & Diaz, C. (2006). *Diversity and difference in early childhood education: Issues for theory and practice.* Berkshire, England: Open University Press.

Roskos, K., & Christie, J. (2004). Examining the play-literacy interface: A critical review and future directions. In E. Ziegler, D. Singer, & S. Bishop-Josef (Eds.), *Child's play: The roots of reading* (95–124). Washington, DC: Zero to Three.

Rubenstein, J., & Howes, C. (1979). Social-emotional peers and individual differences. In S. Kilmer (Ed.), *Advances in early education and day care* (Vol. 3, 13–45). Greenwich, CT: JAI.

Rubenstein, J., & Howes, C. (1983). Caregiving and infant behaviour in day care and in homes. *Developmental Psychology, 15*(1), 1–24.

Sammons, P., Sylva, K., Melhuish, E., Siraj-Blatchford, I., Taggart, B., & Elliot, K. (2004). *The Effective Provision of Pre-school Education (EPPE) project: Technical paper 11—The continuing effects of pre-school education at age 7 years.* London, UK: DfES/Institute of Education, University of London.

Sammons, P., Sylva, K., Melhuish, E., Siraj-Blatchford, I., Taggart, B., Hunt, S. & Jelicic, H. (2008). *Effective Pre-school and Primary Education 3–11 (EPPE 3–11), Influences on children's cognitive and social development in year 6.* Nottingham, UK: Department for Children, Schools and Families Publications.

Santayana, G. (1905). *Life of reason, reason in common sense.* Scribner's.

Schorr, L. (1998). *Common purpose: Strengthening families and neighbourhoods to rebuild America.* New York: Doubleday.

Schulz, P. (1978). Day care in Canada: 1850–1962. In *The good day care book.* Toronto, ON: The Women's Press.

Schweinhart, L., & Weikart, D. (1993, Summer). Changed lives, significant benefits: The High/Scope Perry Preschool project to date. *High/Scope Resource*, 10–14.

Schweinhart, L. J., Montie, J., Xiang, Z., Barnett, W. S., Belfield, C. R., & Nores, M. (2005). Lifetime effects: The High/Scope Perry Preschool through age 40. *Monographs of the High/Scope Educational Research Foundation, 14.* Ypsilanti, MI: High/Scope Press.

Schweinhart, L., Weikart, D., & Larner, M. (1986). Consequences of three preschool curriculum models through age 15. *Early Childhood Research Quarterly, 1*, 15–45.

Searls, D. T., Mead, N. A., & Ward, B. (1985). The relationship of students' reading skills to TV watching, leisure time reading, and homework. *Journal of Reading, 29*, 158–162.

Segal, M. (2004). The roots and fruits of pretending. In E. Ziegler, D. Singer, & S. Bishop-Josef (Eds.), *Child's play: The roots of reading* (33–48). Washington, DC: Zero to Three.

Seifert, K. (1988). Men in early childhood education. In B. Spodek, O. N. Saracho & D. L. Peters (Eds.), *Professionalism and the early childhood practitioner.* New York: Teachers College Press.

Sénéchal, M. (2006). Testing the home literacy model: Parent involvement in kindergarten is differentially related to Grade 4 reading comprehension, fluency, spelling, and reading for pleasure. *Journal for the Scientific Study of Reading, 10,* 59–87.

Service Canada. (2014). Employment insurance special benefits for self-employed people. Available at http://www.servicecanada.gc.ca/eng/ei/publications/sew_publication.pdf.

Shanker, S. (2010). Self-regulation: Calm, alert and learning. *Education Canada, 50,* 3.

Sherry, J. (2001). The effects of violent video games on aggression: A meta-analysis. *Human Communication Research, 27,* 409–431.

Shonkoff, J., & Meisels, S. (Eds.). (2000). *Handbook of early childhood intervention* (2nd ed.). Cambridge: Cambridge University Press.

Shonkoff, J., & Phillips, D. (2000). *Neurons to neighborhoods: The science of early childhood development.* Washington, DC: National Science Council.

Siddiqi, A., Irwin, L., & Hertzman, C. (2007). *Total environment assessment model for early child development evidence report.* Vancouver: Human Early Learning Partnership.

Siegler, R. (1994). Cognitive variability: A key to understanding cognitive development. *Current Directions in Psychological Science, 3,* 1–5.

Silin, Jonathan G. (1985, March). Authority as knowledge: A problem of professionalization. *Young Children, 40*(3), 41–46.

Singer, J., & Lythcott, M. (2004). Fostering social achievement and creativity through sociodramatic play in the classroom. In E. Ziegler, D. Singer, & S. Bishop-Josef (Eds.), *Child's play: The roots of reading* (77–94). Washington, DC: Zero to Three.

Singleton, C. (1997). The development and implementation of a reflective mentoring program for early childhood educators. Unpublished master's thesis, Memorial University of Newfoundland.

Siraj-Blatchford, I. (2006). Diversity, inclusion and learning in the early years. In. G. Pugh and B. Duffey (Eds.), *Contemporary Issues in the Early Years* (4th Ed.). London, UK: Paul Chapman.

Siraj-Blatchford, I., & Manni, L. (2007). *Effective leadership in the early years sector: The ELEYS study.* London: Institute of Education, University of London. Available at http://www.ioe.ac.uk/publications.

Siraj-Blatchford, I., & McCallum, B. (2005). *An evaluation of SHARE at the foundation stage: Final evaluation report.* Coventry, England: ContinYou.

Siraj-Blatchford, I., & Sylva, K. (2004). Researching pedagogy in English pre-schools. *British Education Research Journal, 30,* 5, 713–730.

Siraj-Blatchford, I., & Taggart, B. (2009). Conceptualising progression in the pedagogy of play and sustained shared thinking in early childhood education: A Vygotskian perspective. *Educational & Child Psychology 26*(2), 77–89.

Siraj-Blatchford, I., Sylva, K., Taggart, B., Melhuish, E., Sammons, P., & Elliot, K. (2003). *Technical paper 10 intensive case studies of practice across the foundation stage.* The Effective Provision of Pre-school Education (EPPE) project. London, UK: Institute of Education, University of London.

Smart Start Evaluation Team. (2003). *Smart Start and pre-school child care quality in North Carolina: Change over time and relationships to children's readiness.* Chapel Hill, NC: FPG Child Development Institute, University of North Carolina at Chapel Hill.

Snow, C. (2007). Preparing teachers to teach reading: Knowledge to support professional development of pre-school teachers. In Jia Qiong (Ed.), *International perspectives on early education,* 211–230.

Social Development Canada, Public Health Agency of Canada and Indian & Northern Affairs Canada. (2005). *Early childhood development and early learning and child care activities and expenditures 2003–2004.* Ottawa: Government of Canada. Retrieved at http://www.socialunion.ca.

Spodek, B. (1994). The knowledge base for baccalaureate early childhood teacher education programs. In J. Johnson & J. B. McCracken (Eds.), *The early childhood career lattice: Perspectives on professional development.* Washington, DC: NAEYC.

Spodek, B., & Saracho, O. N. (1991) In D. Osborn (Ed.), *Early childhood education in historical perspective.* 3rd ed. Athens, GA: Education Associates, Div. of The Daye Press, Inc.

Spodek, B., Saracho, O., & Peters, D. (Eds.). (1988). *Professionalism and the early childhood practitioner.* New York: Teachers College Press.

Statistics Canada. (2001). *A portrait of Aboriginal children living in non-reserve areas: Results from the 2001 Aboriginal peoples survey,* cat. no. 89–597–XIE. Ottawa, ON: Statistics Canada. Available at: http://www.statcan.ca/bsolc/english/bsolc?catno= 89-597-X&CHROPG=1.

Statistics Canada. (2006). *Aboriginal peoples in Canada in 2006: Inuit, Métis and First Nations, 2006 Census,* cat. no. 97-558- XIE. Ottawa, ON: Statistics Canada. Available at http://www12.statcan.ca/english/census06/ analysis/aboriginal/pdf/97-558-XIE2006001.pdf

Statistics Canada. (2008). *Aboriginal children's survey, 2006.* Ottawa, ON: Statistics Canada.

Stanton, J. (1990). The ideal nursery school teacher. Reprinted in *Young Children, 45*(4), 19. Used with permission of New York State AEYC. Originally published in *New York Nursery Education News,* Winter 1954.

Stevenson, J. (1990). The cooperative preschool model in Canada. In I. Doxey (Ed.), *Child care and education: Canadian dimensions*, 221–239. Toronto, ON: Nelson.

Stone, S., & Christie, J. (1996). Collaborative literacy learning during socio-dramatic play in a multiage (K–2) primary classroom. *Journal of Research in Childhood Education*, 10(2), 123–133.

Strong-Boag, V. (1985). Intruders in the nursery: Childcare professionals. In J. Parr (Ed.), *Childhood and family in Canadian history*. Toronto, ON: McLelland & Stewart.

Surbeck, E. (1994, Summer). Journal writing with preservice teachers. *Childhood Education*, 70(4), 232–35.

Sure Start Research Team. (2005). *National evaluation report: Early impacts of sure start local programmes on children and families*. London: Queen's Printer.

Sutherland, N. (1976). *Children in English-Canadian society: Framing the 20th century consensus*. Toronto, ON: University of Toronto Press.

Sylva, K. (1994). School influences on children's development. *Journal of Child Psychology and Psychiatry*, 35(1), 135–70.

Sylva, K. (2009). *Effective Pre-school and Primary Education 3–11 (EPPE 3–11). Final report from the primary phase: Pre-school, school, and family influences on children's development during key stage 2 (Age 7–11)*. London, UK: Institute of Education, University of London.

Sylva, K., Melhuish, E., Sammons, P., Siraj-Blatchford, I., & Taggart, B. (2004). *The final report: Effective pre-school education*. Technical paper 12. London, UK: Institute of Education, University of London.

Sylva, K., Melhuish, E., Sammons, P., Siraj-Blatchford, I., & Taggart, B. (2009). *Effective pre-school and primary education 3–11 (EPPE 3–11). Final report from the primary phase: Pre-school, school, and family influences on children's development during key stage 2 (Age 7–11)*. London, UK: Institute of Education, University of London.

Tabors, P., & Snow, C. (2001). Young bilingual children and early literacy development. In S. Neuman & D. Dickenson (Eds.), *Handbook of early literacy research*. New York: Guilford Press.

TD Economics. (2012, November 27). Early childhood education has widespread and longlasting benefits. *TD Special Report*. Toronto, ON: TD.

Thomas, B. (1998). *Family literacy in Canada*. Welland, ON: Soleil Publishing.

Thomas, B. (2000). In N. Howe & L. W. Prochner (Eds.), *Early childhood care and education in Canada*. Vancouver BC: UBC Press.

Toronto Board of Trade. (2001). *Investing in cities: An urban competitiveness agenda for Ontario; 2001 pre-budget submission to the Province of Ontario*. Toronto, ON: Toronto Board of Trade.

Treflor, D. (2009, June 30). Why invest in early childhood development? *Globe and Mail*.

Tremblay, R., & Craig, W. (1995). Developmental crime prevention. In M. Tonry & D. P. Farrington (Eds.), *Building a safer society: Strategic approaches to crime prevention*. Chicago: University of Chicago Press, 151–239.

Tremblay, R. E., Barr, R. G., Peters, R. De V., & Boivin, M. (Eds.). (2009). Synthesis on child care (0–5 years). How important is it? *Encyclopedia on early childhood development*. Montreal: Centre of Excellence for Early Childhood Development. Available at http://www.child-encyclopedia.com/en-ca/child-care/what-do-we-know.html, accessed June 10, 2010.

Tzelepis, A., Giblin, P. T., & Agronow, S. J. (1983). Effects of adult caregiver's behaviours on the activities, social interactions, and investments of nascent preschool day care groups. *Journal of Applied Developmental Psychology*, 4, 201–216.

United Nations. (1989). *Convention on the rights of the child*. Ottawa: Human Rights Program Department of Canadian Heritage.

United Nations Children's Fund (UNICEF). (2008). *The childcare transition*. Innocenti Report Card 7. Florence: UNICEF Innocenti Research Centre. Available at http://www.unicef-irc.org/publications/pdf/rc7eng.pdf.

United States Department of Commerce. (2002). *A nation online: How Americans are expanding their use of the Internet*. Washington, DC: U.S. Department of Commerce.

U.S. Census Bureau. (2001). *Table 4. Preprimary school enrollment of people 3 to 6 years old, by control of school, mother's family income, race, and Hispanic origin: October 2000. In school enrollment—Social and economic characteristics of students: October 2000* (PPL-148). Washington, DC: Author. Retrieved May 31, 2006, at http:// www.census.gov/population/socdemo/school/ppl-148/tab04.txt.

Van Arsdell, M. (1994). Preparing early childhood teachers for careers in learning. In S. G. Goffin & D. E. Day (Eds.), *New perspectives in early childhood education: Bringing practitioners into the debate*. New York: Teachers College Press.

Vancouver Board of Trade. (1999). *Task force on early child development and child care*. Vancouver: Vancouver Board of Trade.

Vander Ven, K. (1988). Pathways to professional effectiveness for early childhood educators. In B. Spodek, O. N. Saracho & D. L. Peters (Eds.), *Professionalism and the early childhood practitioner*. New York: Teachers College Press.

Vander Ven, K. (1994). Professional development: A contextual model. In J. Johnson & J. McCracken (Eds.), *The early childhood career lattice*. Washington, DC: National Association for the Education of Young Children and National Institute for Early Childhood Professional Development.

Van Stanton, J. (1954, Winter). The ideal nursery school teacher. Reprinted in *Young Children*, 45(4), 19. Used with permission of New York State AEYC. Originally published in *New York Nursery Education News*, Winter 1954.

Watson, J. (1928). *Psychological care of infant and child*. London: Allen and Unwin.

Weiss, A. D. G., & Offenberg, R. M. (2002, April). *Enhancing urban children's early success in school: The power of full-day kindergarten*. Paper presented at the annual meeting of the American Educational Research Association, New Orleans, LA.

Weiss, H., Caspe, M., & Lopez, M. (2006). Family involvement in early childhood education. *Family involvement makes a difference*. Harvard Research Project No. 1. Boston, MA: Harvard University.

Welsh, J. (2002). *Full-day kindergarten a plus*. Pioneer Press. Minneapolis Public Schools.

West, J., Denton, K., & Germino-Hausken, E. (2000). *America's kindergartners: Early childhood longitudinal study—Kindergarten class of 1998–99, fall 1998* [Statistical analysis report]. Washington, DC: U.S. Department of Education, National Center for Education Statistics.

Western Arctic Aboriginal Head Start Council. (2006). *Ten years of Aboriginal Head Start in the NWT: Northwest Territories Aboriginal Head Start program 1996–2006*. Yellowknife: Western Arctic Aboriginal Head Start Council.

White, L. (2002). Partisanship or politics of austerity? Child care policy development in Ontario and Alberta, 1980–1995. *Journal of Family Issues*, 18(1), 7–29

White, L. (2007, March 19). Fragmentation and continuity in liberal early childhood education and care (ECEC) regimes. Paper presented at the Lunchbox Speakers Series, Social Economy Centre, Ontario Institute for Studies in Education, University of Toronto.

Whitebook, M. (1995, May). What's good for child care teachers is good for our country's children. *Young Children*, 50(4), 49–50.

Whitebook, M., & Granger, R. (1989, May). Mommy, who's going to be my teacher today? Assessing teacher turnover. *Young Children*, 44(4), 11–14.

Whitebook, M., & Sakai, L. (2004). *By a thread: How child care centers hold on to teachers, how teachers build lasting careers*. Kalamazoo, Mich: W.E. Upjohn Institute for Employment Research.

Whitebook, M., Hnatiuk, P., & Bellm, D. (1994). *Mentoring in early care and education: Refining an emerging career path*. Washington, DC: National Center for the Early Childhood Work Force.

Whitebook, M., Phillips, D., & Howes, C. (1990). *Who cares? Child care teachers and the quality of care in America*. Final report of the National Child Care Staffing Study. Oakland, CA: Child Care Employee Group.

Whitebook, M., Phillips, D., & Howes, C. (1993). *The national child care staffing study revisited: Four years in the life of center-based child care*. Oakland, CA: Child Care Employee Project.

Whitebook, M., Sakai, L., & Howes, C. (1997). *NAEYC accreditation as a strategy for improving child care quality*. Washington, DC: National Center for the Early Childhood Work Force.

Whiteland, T. (2006, Fall). Early childhood development: Introduction to the fall edition of the CAP journal. *The CAP Journal, 14*(3), 4–5.

Willer, B. (1994). A conceptual framework for early childhood professional development. NAEYC position statement. In J. Johnson & J. B. McCracken (Eds.), *The early childhood career lattice: Perspectives on professional development*. Washington, DC: NAEYC.

Willer, B., & Bredekamp, S. (1990, July). Redefining readiness: An essential requisite for educational reform. *Young Children, 45*(5), 22–24.

Willer, B., & Bredekamp, S. (1993, May). A new paradigm of early childhood professional development. *Young Children*, 48(4), 63–66.

Willms, D. (2002). *Vulnerable children*. Edmonton: University of Alberta Press.

Willms, J. D. (2000). *Three hypotheses about community effects relevant to the contribution of human and social capital to sustaining economic growth and well-being*. Report prepared for the Organization for Economic Cooperation and Development and Human Resources Development Canada. Fredericton, NB: Canadian Research Institute for Social Policy, University of New Brunswick.

Wilson, L. (2010). *Partnerships: Families and communities in early childhood development*. (4th ed.). Toronto, ON: Nelson Thomson.

Wolanski, A. (2008). *Peel early years hubs and readiness centres implementation and outcome evaluation*. Mississauga, ON: Peel District School Board.

Wooldridge, M. (2014). *The magic touch: Interactive screen technology for infants, toddlers and preschoolers*. Presentation at Early Years Conference 2014: Shaping childhood: Factors that matter. January 31 to February 1, 2013. Vancouver, BC: Continuing Professional Learning, University of British Columbia

Wright, J., & Shade, D. (Eds.). (1994). *Young children: Active learners in a technological age*. Washington, DC: NAEYC.

Wright, J. C., & Huston, A. C. (1995). Effects of educational TV viewing of lower income preschoolers on academic skills, school readiness, and school adjustment one to three years later: A report to Children's Television Workshop.

Wright, J., Huston, A., Vandewater, E., Bickham, D., Scantlin, R., … Finkelstein, J. (2001). American children's use of electronic media in 1997: A national survey. *Journal of Developmental Psychology, 22,* 31–47.

Wright, M. (2000). Toronto's Institute of Child Study and the teachings of W. E. Blatz. In L. Prochner & N. Howe (Eds), *Early childhood care and education in Canada* (96–114). Vancouver: University of British Columbia Press.

Wylie, C. (2004). *Competent children at 12*. Wellington, NZ: New Zealand Council for Educational Research.

Yau, M. (2005). Do parenting and family literacy centres make a difference? *Research Today, 1*(1), 1–4.

Yonemura, M. V. (1986). *A teacher at work: Professional development and the early childhood educator.* New York: Teachers College Press.

Yoshikawa, H., Weiland, C., Brooks-Gunn, J., Burchinal, M., Espinosa, L., Gormley, W., Ludwig, J., Magnuson, K., Phillips, D., & Saslow, M. (2013, October). *Investing in our future: The evidence base on preschool education.* Society for Research in Child Development and New America Foundation.

Youcha, G. (1995). *Minding the children: Child care in America from colonial times to the present.* New York: Scribner.

Young, N. (1994). *Caring for play: The school and child care connection.* Toronto, ON: Exploring Environments.

Zellman, G., & Perlman, M. (2006). Parent involvement in child care settings: Conceptual and measurement issues. *Early Child Development and Care*, Preview Article, 1–18.

Ziegler, E., Singer, D., & Bishop-Josef, S. (2004). *Child's play: The roots of reading.* Washington, DC: Zero to Three.

Index